Oxford Readings in
The Roman Novel

Oxford Readings in

The Roman Novel

Edited by

S. J. HARRISON

OXFORD
UNIVERSITY PRESS

OXFORD
UNIVERSITY PRESS

Great Clarendon Street, Oxford OX2 6DP

Oxford University Press is a department of the University of Oxford.
It furthers the University's objective of excellence in research, scholarship,
and education by publishing worldwide in

Oxford New York

Athens Auckland Bangkok Bogotá Buenos Aires Calcutta
Cape Town Chennai Dar es Salaam Delhi Florence Hong Kong Istanbul
Karachi Kuala Lumpur Madrid Melbourne Mexico City Mumbai
Nairobi Paris São Paulo Singapore Taipei Tokyo Toronto Warsaw
with associated companies in Berlin Ibadan

Oxford is a registered trade mark of Oxford University Press
in the UK and in certain other countries

Published in the United States
by Oxford University Press Inc., New York

British Library Cataloguing in Publication Data
Data available

Library of Congress Cataloging in Publication Data
Marshall, Geoffrey
Oxford readings in the Roman novel / edited by S. J. Harrison.
Includes bibliographical references
1. Latin fiction—History and criticism. 2. Petronius Arbiter.
Satyricon. 3. Literature and history—Rome. 4. Apuleius.
Metamorphoses. 5. Rhetoric, Ancient. I. Harrison, S. J.
II. Title: Roman novel.
PA6091.094 1998 873'.0109—dc21 98–40793
ISBN 0–19–872173–0 (hbk)
ISBN 0–19–872174–9 (pbk)

1 3 5 7 9 10 8 6 4 2

Typeset in Photina
by Graphicraft Limited, Hong Kong
Printed in Great Britain
on acid-free paper by
Biddles Ltd., Guildford and King's Lynn

PREFACE

This volume aims to make more widely available some significant scholarly articles on the Roman novels of Petronius and Apuleius published over the last thirty years. This has been a period of rapid expansion of scholarly interest and of university courses in the area of the ancient novel. Though I hope that specialist scholars will profit from it, this book is also intended to be of particular help to university teachers and their students: a few classic pieces are translated from German and Italian, and the introduction attempts to put the contents of the volume into context through a survey of scholarly work on Petronius and Apuleius since 1900.

I have various obligations to record. First, to Hilary O'Shea and her staff and advisers at the Oxford University Press, who encouraged the project and brought it to fruition. Second, to three Corpus classicists who were equally indispensable to the project's completion: Gideon Nisbet, who compiled the bibliography and did the cross-referencing for the footnotes, and Barbara Graziosi and Martin Revermann, who translated the Italian and German articles respectively. It is a privilege to work in a community which can supply such expert assistance. Last, but not least, I should like to thank all the contributors to this volume for kindly agreeing to the reprinting of their pieces, for (in appropriate cases) checking and revising the English translations of their originals, and (in appropriate cases) providing addenda and corrections to their original articles.

Though it was not the main project for my tenure of the award, the last stages of this book have been facilitated by a Leverhulme–British Academy Senior Research Fellowship for 1997–8, which has given me precious time for research activity, and for which I am extremely grateful.

S.J.H.

Corpus Christi College, Oxford
March 1998

CONTENTS

LIST OF CONTRIBUTORS

Dr S. J. Harrison *(Corpus Christi College, Oxford, UK)*

Prof. Froma Zeitlin *(Princeton University, Princeton, NJ, USA)*

Prof. Roger Beck *(University of Toronto in Mississauga, Mississauga, Ontario, Canada)*

Dr Raymond Astbury *(University College, Dublin, Ireland)*

Prof. Gianpiero Rosati *(Università degli Studi di Udine, Udine, Italy)*

Prof. Dr Hubert Petersmann *(Universität Heidelberg, Germany)*

Prof. Alessandro Barchiesi *(Università di Verona/Università di Siena[Arezzo], Italy)*

Prof. Dr Antonie Wlosok *(Johannes-Gutenberg-Universität, Mainz, Germany)*

Prof. James Tatum *(Dartmouth College, Hanover, NH, USA)*

Prof. Warren S. Smith *(University of New Mexico, Albuquerque, N. Mex., USA)*

Prof. H. J. Mason *(University of Toronto, Toronto, Canada)*

Dr R. Th. van der Paardt *(Rijksuniversiteit Leiden, Leiden, The Netherlands)*

Prof. F. G. B. Millar *(Brasenose College, Oxford, UK)*

Prof. J. G. DeFilippo *(University of North Dakota, Grand Forks, N. Dak., USA)*

Prof. Ellen Finkelpearl *(Scripps College, Claremont, Calif., USA)*

NOTE ON ABBREVIATIONS

Ancient texts are usually cited using the abbreviations of Liddell and Scott and the *Oxford Latin Dictionary*, periodicals using the abbreviations of *L'Année Philologique*.

INTRODUCTION
Twentieth-Century Scholarship on the Roman Novel

S. J. HARRISON

Neither the designation of Petronius' *Satyrica* (hereafter *Sat.*) and Apuleius' *Metamorphoses* (hereafter *Met.*) as 'novels' nor the notion that these two texts jointly represent something called 'the Roman novel' is without complication and controversy. This volume and this bibliographical survey set the two side by side, partly for practical convenience, but also in the belief (shared in antiquity—cf. Macrobius, *Somn. Scip.* 1. 2. 8) that these two texts have enough features in common to be treated as belonging to the same literary kind, for which the anachronistic 'novel' is as good a label as any other (cf. Callebat 1992). As for the label 'Roman novel', it is again a convenience: these are the only two texts of prose fiction in pre-Christian Latin which are in some sense Roman originals rather than direct translations of Greek texts, though some might wish to include with them the *Historia Apollonii regis Tyrii* (see the recent discussion of Schmeling 1996b: 528–38). Both the *Sat.* and the *Met.* are long Latin fictional narratives in settings of low-life realism of Roman imperial date, and show similar narrative techniques, combining first-person main narration (homodiegesis) with extensive inserted tales, and similar literary textures, including extensive irreverent allusion to other genres, in particular parody of the essential scenario of the Greek romantic novel with its heterosexual lovers, their separation, perils, reunion, and eventual marriage. Apuleius clearly imitates Petronius' work to some extent, though here as always the radical incompleteness of the *Sat.* renders investigation problematic. No extant Greek novel shows the combination of low-life realism, first-person narrative, and frequent inserted tales common to Apuleius and Petronius; and though it can no longer be claimed (since the discovery of the fragments of the Iolaus papyrus and Lollianus) that sexually explicit low-life realism was a distinctive feature of Roman as opposed to Greek fiction, such sexual interest is not a fundamental element in any of the Greek novels which have been preserved in their entirety. Likewise with first-person narrative and inserted tales: a first-person main narrative is found in Achilles Tatius but in no other extant Greek novel, and though there are a number of notable inserted tales in the Greek novels (for example, in Heliodorus and *Daphnis and Chloe*), frequent use of this device for apparently casual subordinate narratives is peculiar to Petronius and Apuleius within ancient prose fiction. This particular feature may have followed the narrative technique of the Milesian tales of Aristides and their translation by Sisenna, which may have considerably influenced both the content and the form of the two extant Roman novels much more than those of their Greek counterparts (cf. Harrison 1998*a*).

Of course, there are elements of variation between the two Roman texts. The prosimetric form of Petronius' *Sat.*, its consequent possible links with Varronian–Menippean prosimetric satire, and its evident relation to the themes of Roman hexameter satire are elements which differentiate it from Apuleius' *Met.* But none of these elements demands that Petronius' work be separated from the literary tradition of the novel. Prosimetric form can now be shown through the Iolaus papyrus to have belonged to the tradition of Greek prose fiction and not to have been unique to Menippean satire, and texts commonly classed together as Greek novels can differ as much as the *Sat.* and the *Met.* owing to the influence of other literary genres, for example, the evident contrast between the pastorally coloured *Daphnis and Chloe* and Achilles Tatius or Heliodorus. Such literary colouring by use of other genres seems indeed to be a key feature of the developed ancient novel as a whole. Thus, elements of similarity (by both contrast with and analogy to Greek fiction) outweigh factors of divergence: the *Sat.* and *Met.* can be coherently and plausibly classed together as Roman novels. In this survey, necessarily selective and partial, an attempt is made to trace the chief lines of scholarly discussion for each of them since 1900.

I. PETRONIUS, *SATYRICA*

I.1. *Complete Texts*

Bücheler (1862) was the first reliable text of Petronius and provided the first effective apparatus criticus; its quality is shown by the fact

that in its various revisions (especially that of Heraeus in the sixth
edition of 1922) it remained authoritative for almost a century until
the appearance of Müller's first edition (Müller 1961), which provides
a solid and accurate basis for the modern study of Petronius, both
in its reporting of the manuscript evidence and in its approach to the
complex textual tradition. The fragmentary text of the *Sat.* outside the
Cena has survived through the activities of Carolingian excerptors,
represented for us by one ninth-century manuscript (B, Bernensis 357)
and a number of twelfth-century and later manuscripts, while
most of our text of the *Cena* derives from a single fifteenth-century
manuscript (H, the *codex Traguriensis*, Parisinus lat. 7989). The resulting lines of transmission are too complex to be summarized briefly here,
but for an excellent account, see Reeve (1983), importantly amending
Müller.

Müller's text has now reached a fourth edition (Müller 1995).
There have also been two texts produced in Italy: that of Pellegrino
(1975), which has little additional to offer apart from adjustments to
Müller's view of the transmission, and Giardina–Cuccioli Melloni
(1995), which adds a few more conjectures to Müller's apparatus while
retaining his general view of the tradition. Much work has been done
on the textual tradition and the intricacies of its transmission,
notably by van Thiel (1971*a*) and Richardson (1993); for further and
more recent details, see the preface to Müller (1995). One issue of dispute has been that of the degree of interpolation: in 1961 Müller, partly
under the influence of Eduard Fraenkel, argued for a considerable
amount of later interpolation (Müller 1961: pp. xxxix–xlvii), though
in his later editions many of the passages bracketed in 1961 were re-
instated (cf. Müller and Ehlers 1965: 425–30, 1978: 486–95; Müller
1995: pp. xxvii–viii), and the question of the degree of interpolation
in the transmitted text has been much debated (Richardson 1972; Coccia
1973; Sullivan 1976; and now Coccia 1996). Müller's editions have
also influenced the accepted title of Petronius' work (for a pre-Müller
discussion, cf. Henriksson 1956: 74–7). Most scholars now follow him
in viewing the transmitted *Satyricon* as a misunderstood Greek genitive plural (σατυρικῶν *libri*, cf. the Vergilian *Georgicon libri*), suggesting an original title *Satyrica* (σατυρικά). This is persuasive, since, as
Perry pointed out (Perry 1967: 191–2), *Satyrica* offers clear and significant parallels with other novelistic titles such as *Aethiopica* and
Ephesiaka, as well as etymological links with *satyrus* and *satura* (cf. Walsh
1970: 72).

I.2. Commentaries and English Translations

There is still no modern commentary on the complete text of Petronius; the running commentary of Paratore (1933) contains critical paraphrase rather than detailed exegesis. Three are currently promised: the first volume of one has appeared (Pellegrino 1986, which I have as yet been unable to see), and two are still in progress, one by the late J. P. Sullivan and Gareth Schmeling and one by Gian Biagio Conte and Mario Labate. The *Cena Trimalchionis* has always been popular in separate commented editions: the most useful and recent of these is that of M. S. Smith (1975), making good use of Müller's textual work. Of other editions Friedländer (1891, 1906), building on the textual work of Bücheler, still has much historical and cultural material of interest, and Maiuri (1945) is still worth consulting for its author's expertise in Campanian topography and *Realien*. Much used in their countries of origin were Sedgwick (1925, 1950), Perrochat (1939, 1952, 1962), and Marmorale (1947, 1961). Separate commentaries and detailed studies of the poetic passages of the *Sat.* have also been popular since the initial and important work of Stubbe (1933); cf. in particular Zeitlin (1971*b*). Guido (1976) and Grimal (1977) have concentrated at length on the so-called *Bellum civile* (*Sat.* 119–24), while Courtney (1991) has briefly but usefully commented on all the poems except the longer *Bellum civile* and the *Troiae halosis* (*Sat.* 89). The work of Connors (1998) now provides a detailed, nuanced, and sophisticated treatment of all the poems and of poetic parody within the *Sat.* The inserted tales have also been popular in separate editions—notable here are Pecere's splendid running commentary on the Widow of Ephesus (*Sat.* 111–12; Pecere 1975; cf. since then Müller 1980 and Huber 1990*a*), Pacchieni's commentary on the two Milesian tales of the Boy of Pergamum (*Sat.* 85–7) and the Widow of Ephesus (Pacchieni 1978), and the brief account of all the inserted tales by Fedeli and Dimundo (1988). There is also a commentary on the episode of Quartilla (Aragosti *et al.* 1988).

Of English translations before 1945, it is worth mentioning the first (Burnaby 1694) and the one intriguingly attributed to Oscar Wilde (Lewis 1927). Since 1945 the most important have been that of the poet and critic William Arrowsmith (1959), and the Petronian scholar J. P. Sullivan (1965, 1977*a*), both witty and fluent, which between them made Petronius accessible to a whole generation, and in Sullivan's case incorporated Müller's work on the text (unlike the Loeb translation of Heseltine (1969), revised by Warmington, which was nevertheless much used). Two very recent translations of different characters look set to dominate the end of the century: Walsh (1996), a solid and reliable translation by a respected Petronian scholar, and Branham and Kinney (1996), a collaboration between a classicist and a translator which by using lively American idiom has restored to Petronius his racy and colloquial element (see 1.4.3 below).

I.3. Concordances and Bibliographies

Apart from the electronic text of Petronius (apparently Müller 1978) on the Packard Humanities Index (PHI) CD-ROM containing all pre-AD 200 Latin literary texts, best searched with software such as TLG Workplace, there is a conventional computerized concordance in print using the third edition of Müller (von Korn and Reitzer 1986). There are two extensive Petronius bibliographies, one from the Renaissance to 1975 (Schmeling and Stuckey 1977), the other covering 1945–82 (Smith 1985); both provide purely alphabetical lists without subdivision or comment, though Smith has a final category index. Schmeling (1996a) has a massive undivided final bibliography on the ancient novel in general, which includes many recent items on Petronius. Amongst annotated bibliographies and surveys on Petronius Gaselee (1910) provides material to 1908, Lommatzsch (1919, 1925, 1932, 1938) items for the years 1908–36, Helm (1943) for the years 1936–40, Muth (1956) for the years 1941–55, Schnur (1957) for the years 1940–56, Schmeling (1969) for the years 1957–68, Bowie and Harrison (1993) for the years 1967–92; particular bibliography on the Troiae halosis and Bellum civile is provided by Helm (1956). Sullivan (1971, 1977b) provides accounts of scholarly controversies in the 1960s and 1970s. Apart from the annual listings in L'Année Philologique and Gnomon, full yearly bibliographical updates on all aspects of the ancient novel are provided by the Petronian Society Newsletter, compiled and published since 1970 by Gareth Schmeling of the University of Florida, Gainesville. This journal has been available on-line since volume 26 (1996) at http://www.chss.montclair.edu/classics/petron/PSNNOVEL.html.

I.4. Scholarly and Interpretative Issues

I.4.1. Date, Authorship, and Historical and Cultural Setting. After some
controversy, almost all scholars now support a Neronian date for
the *Sat.*, and most would regard it as probable that T. Petronius,
Nero's *arbiter elegantiarum* (cf. Tacitus, *Ann.* 16. 17–20), was its
author (an identification apparently already made by the fifth century
AD: Macrobius, *Somn. Scip.* 1. 2. 8). In 1892 Collignon could already
list a wide range of datings from the first century BC to late antiquity
(Collignon 1892: 341–5), but the general consensus of the nineteenth
century was for a Neronian date (so Collignon himself and Kroll:
RE 19. 1201 ff.). Battle was hotly joined on the issue in Italy in the
twentieth century: in 1933 Paratore favoured a date under Claudius,
while in 1937 Paoli argued for an Antonine dating (Paoli 1937), a
thesis immediately refuted by Marmorale (1937), which returned to
the traditional Neronian date. But in 1948 Marmorale changed his
view, and argued at length for an even later date than Paoli's, the third
century AD. This introduced a lively international controversy on the
'Petronian question' (for accounts of this, cf. Schnur 1957; Sullivan
1977b). But the case for the Neronian dating and for the ascription
to Tacitus' Petronius has now been convincingly made in a number
of publications by Sullivan (1968a, 1985a,b), and especially in a careful monograph by Rose (1971). Another controversy has surrounded
the identity of the *Graeca urbs* (*Sat.* 81. 3) which forms the setting for
the pre-Croton section of the narrative (*Sat.* 1–99): the modern consensus suggests Puteoli; for a summary of the question and the basic
arguments, see conveniently Paratore (1933) and Rose (1962). The
main characters are plainly Greek in origin, as their names suggest;
this and other Greek elements in the *Cena* are discussed in detail by
Salonius (1927).

Subsequently, the *Sat.* has been effectively related to the social and
intellectual history of the Neronian period. Material of this kind is to
be found especially in the works already mentioned which defend
a Neronian date, but amongst those particularly interested in history and culture Veyne (1961) and D'Arms (1981) have looked at
Trimalchio as typifying the class of successful freedmen under the Julio-
Claudians, Kennedy (1978) has related the presentation of the rhetors
Agamemnon and Menelaus to other evidence for imperial declam-
atory schools, Horsfall (1989) has examined the cultural horizons
revealed in the *Cena Trimalchionis*, and Elsner (1993) has persuasively

viewed the episode in the art gallery as satirizing the pretensions of contemporary art criticism. The high profile of *literary* criticism in the *Sat.*, owed partly to the literary pretensions of its characters, also clearly reflects a highly literary court under Nero; here the writings of Sullivan (1968a, 1985a,b) gives the broadest cultural context. One particular issue has been whether the long hexameter poem on the civil war of Caesar and Pompey delivered by Eumolpus at *Sat.* 119–24, conventionally called the *Bellum civile*, relates to the contemporary poem on the same subject by Lucan. Three positions have been taken: Petronius is responding to Lucan (the most common and in my view the most persuasive position; e.g. Rose 1971: 87–94; Sullivan 1985a: 162–72); Lucan is responding to Petronius (Grimal 1977); and there is no relation between the two, with Petronius simply indulging in Vergilian pastiche (George 1974). Similar arguments can be made about the iambic so-called *Troiae halosis* (*Sat.* 89): the subject-matter is that of *Aeneid* 2, but there are good grounds for supposing engagement with the similar contemporary tragedies of Seneca (cf. esp. Cervellera 1975). A more general survey of the literary-theoretical ideas expressed within the text is provided by Soverini (1985).

I.4.2. Reconstructions. The highly fragmentary nature of the transmitted text of the *Sat.* has naturally led to much speculation about its original form. The testimony of the transmission is contradictory, and assigns to the extant parts of the *Sat.* book numbers between 14 and 16 (for the best discussion, cf. van Thiel 1971a: 21–4). Müller (1961: pp. xxx–i) argued that the fifty-six Teubner pages of the *Cena Trimalchionis* (*Sat.* 26. 7–78) constituted a single book of the original *Sat.*, probably book 15, and that *Sat.* 1–26. 6 are excerpts from book 14, with *Sat.* 79–141 being excerpted from book 16 and possibly later books as well. This would make the *Cena* a very long book compared to the longest book of Apuleius (book 9, thirty-four Teubner pages) and even the longest book of Heliodorus (book 10, thirty-nine Teubner pages), and Müller's later view (1995) that the *Cena* probably contains two books (following van Thiel 1971a: 23, who suggests as many as three) seems most plausible. A related question is that of the total number of books in the original *Sat.* Paratore (1933), usefully summarizing previous views, examines the arguments for sixteen or eighteen, with the concomitant assumption that the text as we have it runs out close to its original end; Sullivan (1968a), in the most extensive reconstruction, guesses twenty (as did Heinze 1899), but estimates them all at the length of the *Cena* plus 1–11 and 79–99, which he improbably regards as one book (see above); his consequent final length of some 400,000 words (eight times as long as Apuleius) thus comes out as greatly excessive. Van Thiel (1971*a*) tentatively suggests twenty-four, but shorter; at say twenty Teubner pages each (about 5,000 words), this would come out at about 100,000 words for the whole, less than twice as long as Apuleius and a more realistic figure. A length of twenty-four books is perhaps attractive given that it is a Homeric number and that the *Sat.* is partly concerned with the parody of the *Odyssey* (see 1.4.5*b* below); but the present exiguous state of the evidence means that all must be speculation here. Otherwise, in terms of the missing sections of the plot and the general shape of the work, Sullivan's reconstruction is perhaps the most helpful and suggestive in imagining what the whole *Sat.* was actually like, though van Thiel uses the evidence of transmission most closely.

I.4.3. Language and Style. Petronius' Latin was much discussed in the nineteenth century, usually from the point of view of its uniformly 'decadent' character and relation to colloquial Latin, a comparison partly stimulated by the publication of 'vulgar' inscriptions from Pompeii and other sites (cf. especially Ludwig 1869 and von Guericke 1875). More recently, scholars have questioned this monolithic view of Petronian Latin, and realized its sophistication and mixture of different levels, especially in the distinction between the main narrative style and the speech of different types of characters (Süss 1926; Marbach 1931; Nelson 1947; and especially Petersmann 1977; a subsequent survey by Petersmann 1985 is translated later in this volume—see also Petersmann 1995*b* and Gerschner 1997). There has been particular interest in the evidently 'incorrect' Latin of the freedmen's stories at the *Cena*: do they present comically exaggerated solecisms, or do they present valuable evidence for colloquial Latin in the Neronian period? A recent contribution on this topic, including a full survey of other views, is that of Boyce (1991), who suggests that Petronius is fundamentally concerned in the language of the freedmen with the realistic depiction of lower-class Latin speech.

I.4.4. The Relation to Greek Novels. Two works at the end of the nineteenth century dealt with this important topic. Collignon (1892) had cautiously suggested that there might have existed a tradition of Greek comic fiction which Petronius followed (322–4), while Heinze (1899) had argued in a celebrated article that the *Sat.* was a parody of the ideal Greek novel, inverting its faithful heterosexual couple by presenting a promiscuous homosexual couple, and representing on the low-life level its themes of travel and adventure. Heinze's view swiftly became established doctrine, and is fundamental for many modern discussions of the *Sat.* (though it is partly assailed by Sullivan 1968a: 93–8; for a more positive view, cf. Walsh 1970: 8–9, 78–80). The publication of important papyri of Greek fiction in the second half of the twentieth century suggests that Collignon's supposition (shared also by Perry 1925, who relevantly brought in the evidence of the *Onos*) was correct. We not only now have a few fragments of the *Phoinikika* of Lollianus, plainly a low-life comic narrative which shows interesting parallels with Apuleius (cf. Henrichs 1972; Jones 1980; Winkler 1980; Stephens and Winkler 1995: 314–57); we also possess in the Iolaus papyrus a prosimetric low-life narrative which has been called a 'Greek *Satyricon*' (Parsons 1971; cf. also Parsons 1974; Stephens and Winkler 1995: 345–74). The impact of these discoveries on our view of Greek fiction generally, and their particular consequences for the Greek prehistory of Petronius and Apuleius, have been well assessed by Astbury (1977) and Barchiesi (1986), both reprinted later in this volume (Chapters 3 and 6 respectively). That there was a low-life species of Greek narrative fiction is now well established; that it existed before Petronius is very likely. Thus the *Sat.* is fundamentally influenced by the Greek novel tradition, both as a parody of the 'ideal' romantic novel and as a text which is close kin to the low-life Greek fictions which have recently been rediscovered (for another possibility in this direction, cf. Alpers 1996).

I.4.5. Literary Interpretation

(a) *General Accounts.* Collignon (1892) provides an interesting perspective on Petronius at the end of the nineteenth century. Its main concerns are with the literary character of the *Sat.* and its use and parody of other literary genres (already noted in 1.4.4 above is its prescient suggestion of Greek comic novels as underlying models); it regards the dating and authorship of the work as ultimately mysterious (340), and views the work as amoral and without an ideological message other than an 'Epicurean' self-indulgent hedonism (329). It provides an interesting comparison (47–8) between Petronius and Apuleius, seeing the *Sat.* as much more interested in literary criticism and the *Met.* as much more interested in magic and religion; both share

low-life realism and sexual interests. I have been unable to consult
Cahen (1925), but its title suggests the same kind of interests as
Collignon. Perry's final view of Petronius accepted Heinze's notion that
the *Sat.* burlesqued the Greek ideal novel, but stressed its wide range
of other literary sources, seeing its uniquely mixed character as 'an
accident of time, place and individual personality' (Perry 1967: 206).

Petronian scholarship in the period 1920–60 was chiefly occupied
with the hotly debated question of the date and authorship of the *Sat.*
(see 1.4.1 above) and with the issue of Petronian style and language
(see 1.4.3); for a wider view, including a reconstruction of the original *Sat.* (see 1.4.2 above) and a discussion of its literary character,
essentially agreeing with Heinze, the introductory volume of Paratore
(1933) is of interest. With the more literary interests of the 1960s came
two important works of general literary interpretation: Sullivan
(1968a) and Walsh (1970). Sullivan, apart from his over-extensive
reconstruction of the original (see 1.4.2 above), argued that the *Sat.*
chose the literary tradition of Menippean satire and a framework of
epic parody, playing down Heinze's theory of parody of the Greek novel.
He firmly placed the work in a Neronian context of literary criticism
and literary parody, and characteristically provided useful discussions of its treatment of humour and sex, topics which had not been
directly approached before in quite the same way: for subsequent discussions, cf. Gagliardi (1980) and Gill (1973). The book remains of great
use thirty years on, even if some of its interests (such as the psychological discussion of scopophilia; 238–53) seem very much of its time.
The continuing value of Walsh (1970) has also been marked by a recent
reprint (1995). Like Sullivan, Walsh decides firmly for a Neronian date
(244–7), but in his discussion of the genres lying behind the work he
allows more than Sullivan to the parody of the Greek romance, and
also to two important strands much stressed in recent years—the Greek
and Roman epic as a structural model for the work and many of its
episodes, and the Greek and Roman mime as a model for the comic
and slapstick scenes (see further below). In general, his book provides
a solid guide to most aspects of the *Sat.*, more cautious, balanced, and
reliable than the adventurous Sullivan, and equally valuable to the
modern student.

Perhaps understandably, the 1970s saw no general book on
Petronius of note (that of Rankin 1971 is really a collection of relatively unconnected studies), though mention should be made of the
influential article by Zeitlin (1971a) (reprinted in this volume as

Chapter 1), presenting the *Sat.* as a subversive and anarchic text, representing a view of a world falling apart (this has plain links with moralizing views; cf. 1.4.5*d* below). Since then, there have been two overviews, which reflect the increasing influence of literary-theoretical ideas on the study of classical literature in the 1980s and 1990s. Slater (1989) uses a reader-response approach, appropriate for a text like the *Sat.* which appeals to a specific repertory of literary knowledge; his reading of the work, though perhaps too abstract towards the end, singles out important themes such as role-playing and improvisation, or the link between reading texts and reading pictures. Most notably, he brings into the criticism of Petronius the view of Bakhtin (1981) that the novel is essentially a parodic non-genre incorporating other literary kinds; this leads him to the view that the generic character of the *Sat.* is essentially indeterminate. Here Slater seems to allow too little for the discovery of low-life Greek comic novels, even prosimetric ones (cf. 1.4.4 above), which surely allow Petronius to be located in a firm tradition of Greek narrative. Most recently, Conte (1996) has concentrated with excellent effect on narrative technique and on the contrast between the author and narrator (see 1.4.5*c* below), but shows a clear sympathy with the general view of the *Sat.* taken by Zeitlin (1971*a*): though we are presented with the literary pretensions of the narrator and their deflation by the author, the text as a whole reveals nostalgia for an irrecoverable literary and moral greatness, and its deflating irony at least sometimes engenders 'a paradoxical suspicion of a profound seriousness' (Conte 1996: 169).

(*b*) *Genre and Literary Character.* The literary affinities of the *Sat.* have been a key aspect of its interpretation (see already 1.4.4 and 1.4.5*a* above). Until the publication of the Iolaus papyrus in 1971 most scholars were happy to acknowledge that the prosimetric form of the *Sat.* was owed to the Roman prosimetric tradition of Varro's Menippean satire. But the existence of a low-life prosimetric narrative in Greek which has no apparent Menippean connections has caused some rethinking, and it is now possible to argue that the Menippean tradition is less significant for Petronius (cf. now Conte 1996: 140–70, an important discussion). Indeed Astbury (1977), reprinted in this volume as Chapter 3, has argued that prosimetric form is the only feature shared by the *Sat.* and the Menippean tradition, though the Menippean character of Petronius' work has also been recently reasserted (Adamietz 1987, 1995; for a balanced view of the controversy, cf. Horsfall 1991–2). The remains of Varronian Menippean satire suggest a surreal whimsicality and a strong moralizing content which Petronius conspicuously lacks; and though the *Apocolocynctosis* of Seneca, the only fully surviving Latin Menippean satire, suggests that this literary form was revived in Petronius' own Neronian period, its explicit function as a topical pamphlet sets it apart from the *Sat.*, which contains observations on contemporary culture but not specific attacks on individual contemporaries. I would agree with Petersmann (1986), Schmeling (1994, 1996c), and Conte (1996) that the narrative aspect of the *Sat.* and the existence of prosimetric non-Menippean comic narratives in Greek suggest for it a fundamentally novelistic, and a Menippean, affinity. And it should not be forgotten that the *Cena* and other satiric themes derive not from Menippean satire but from Roman hexameter satire, an important element for Petronius (cf. Conte 1996: 124 n. 25).

Apart from the low-life tradition of Greek narrative as evidenced in the Iolaus papyrus and Lollianus' *Phoinikika*, and parody of the Greek ideal novel (for both of which, see 1.4.4 above), there is a third stream of Greek narrative of importance for the *Sat.* Petronian scholars generally agree that Eumolpus' inserted tale of the Boy of Pergamum (*Sat.* 85–9) and the Widow of Ephesus (*Sat.* 111–12) derive from the tradition of obscene and witty short stories known as the Milesian tales, written in Greek by Aristides in the second century BC and rendered into Latin by Sisenna in the first, which may have been connected in some kind of narrative framework. Though the evidence for the Milesian tales is scanty and controversial (for the best collection and discussion, see Schissel von Fleschenberg 1913a), this tradition is implicitly mentioned as a model by Apuleius (*Met.* 1. 1, 4. 32), it may be that it influenced both the low-life content and the narrative framework of both the Roman novels. The colourful tales of the *Sat.* have also been related to Roman popular storytelling (Sc...1930, 1931), though folk tale has been generally played down in the interpretation of Petronius as compared to that of Apuleius 11.4.4(b) below). There have also been those who have argued the *Sat.* is fundamentally influenced by the fantastic Greek adventure stories to which Lucian's *True History* related, especially Veyne (1964), though the element is equally easily ascribed to the tradition of the Greek novel.

Literary parody (as already mentioned) has been recognized as a crucial element in the *Sat.*, and much

Collignon (1892); useful articles are Courtney (1962) and Cameron (1969), the latter neatly suggesting that the speeches of the freedmen in the *Cena* parody those in Plato's *Symposium* (cf. more recently Bessone 1993), and Sullivan (1968a) and Walsh (1970) both treat the subject at length (see 1.4.5(a) above), with proper emphasis on the parody of epic texts such as the *Odyssey* and *Aeneid*, and poetic parody (especially that of epic) is treated with particular sophistication in Connors (1998). The fact that such a wide range of texts is drawn on through parody and other forms of allusion has commonly led to the view that the *Sat.* is simply a unique work which is unclassifiable; but the central importance of a wide range of literary parody to both Petronius and Apuleius (see II.4.4(b) below) suggests that this is a characteristic element in the Roman novel, especially as it is considerably less important for the Greek novels as a whole. This idea intersects neatly with Bakhtin's influential theory of the novel as an 'open' literary form, a generic and polyphonic mixture, which he himself applied with success to Petronius and Apuleius (Bakhtin 1981: III–29; cf. Gagliardi 1993; Fusillo 1996: 279–80).

A further literary and indeed sub-literary generic strand in the *Sat.* which has rightly become more prominent is that of drama and the mime. This interest began as early as Moering (1915), but has been especially prominent in Walsh (1970), Sandy (1974), and most recently Panayotakis (1995), a book which is now the prime resource for any investigation of this topic. The importance of popular drama in Petronius not only stresses its low-life and contemporary realism, but also allows the interpretation of particular episodes in theatrical mode: this has been done excellently for the *Cena* by Rosati (1983), reprinted in this volume as Chapter 4, and for the *Cena* and a large number of other episodes by Panayotakis (1995).

(c) *Narrative Technique and Structure.* Modern study of Petronius, with its increased interest in narrative analysis and narratology, has naturally become more interested in narrative technique and structure, though this is an area where the incompleteness of the text of the *Sat.* is especially problematic. The main issue has been recently well stated by Fusillo (1996: 286), arguing that the *Sat.* 'shows a very complex dialectic among author, I-narrator and I-character; in every part of the work we perceive the destructive irony of the first and the constant tension between the second and the third, that is the various attempts of Encolpius to interpret his experience as the main actor of adventures'. This tension in the first-person narrator was first discussed by Veyne (1964), who suggested that in the *Cena* Encolpius was Petronius' mouthpiece, conveying authorial judgements as well as voicing the narrative, but that he functioned elsewhere as a more objective voice without authorial views. This does not do full justice to the complex double role of Encolpius in the *Cena*; more illuminating is the account of Beck (1973), reprinted in this volume as Chapter 2, which argues that the *Sat.* (and particularly the *Cena*: cf. also Beck 1975) is narrated by an older and wiser Encolpius looking back on his youthful errors, producing the double perspective of young Encolpius *actor* and older Encolpius *auctor*, to use the terms popularized by Winkler (1985). Beck has also examined the characterization of Eumolpus as sub-narrator and poet (1979), while Fedeli and Dimundo (1988) have usefully examined narrative technique in the inserted tales, and Perutelli (1990) has stressed the difference of the discreet main narrator Encolpius from the other more exhibitionist sub-narrators of the *Sat.* Most recently Conte (1996) sees Encolpius as a 'mythomaniac narrator', a naive young intellectual reading the low-life events of a sordid story in terms of elevated literary models such as epic and tragedy, while placed by the 'hidden author' (the Petronius of the text) in low-life melodramatic situations from novelistic and pantomimic contexts, with irony resulting from the evident gap between the two. This seems a very fruitful model for negotiating the gap which the narrative technique of the novel plainly opens up, and a view which adds a narrative aspect to the importance of parody in the *Sat.* (see 1.4.5(*b*) above). We may again observe a connection with Apuleius, where the question of the identity of the first-person narrator is similarly problematized (see II.4.4(*c*) below); deliberate complication of the I-narrator is a feature of both Roman novels.

The structure of the narrative in the *Sat.* is clearly a difficult topic, outside the unified episode of the *Cena*, and is plainly linked with the issue of reconstructing the work's original form (see 1.4.2 above). Ciaffi (1955) approached the issue for the whole *Sat.* from the angle of internal structural rhythms, and contains much useful material without developing an overarching scheme. This is certainly provided by Hubbard (1986), which seems at times over-schematic, though it argues interestingly from the micro-narrative level of the Quartilla episode to the macro-narrative level of the whole work. Jones (1987) links narrative structure with a modified version of Beck's view of Encolpius, and contains much useful detailed analysis, even if its approach seems sometimes over-subtle. Finally, patterns of closure, a popular topic in classical criticism since Fowler (1989), have been invest-igated for the *Sat.* by Schmeling (1992).

(d) *Ideology.* Interpreters have sometimes wanted to make the *Sat.* a moralizing text. In its least convincing form, this drive for serious-ness has viewed the work as a satire with reforming purpose (Highet 1941, unwarrantedly assuming a moral function for all ancient satire). A little more attractive are arguments that its nihilistic and amoral character suggests a genuine world-weariness and an indictment of failing Roman society (so Zeitlin 1971*a*, reprinted in this volume as Chapter 1) and that it provides an Epicurean cautionary tale (so Arrowsmith 1966; for a more sustained but wholly unrealistic case that Petronius' novel is a concealed Epicurean tract, cf. Raith 1963). Though the positing of a serious ideological purpose for Petronius' work is in no sense absurd (Conte 1996: 169 momentarily inclines this way), most modern scholars tend to support the view of Collignon (1892) that there is no real 'message' in the *Sat.*, a view shared by both Sullivan (1968*a*) and Walsh (1970); for specific (and in my view convincing) arguments against the moralistic interpretation, see Sullivan (1971), Walsh (1974*a*), and Anderson (1982: 65–73). No religious inter-pretation has yet been advanced of Petronius, not even by Merkelbach; Grondona (1980), whose title promises something of the sort, has much material of interest on the presentation of death and superstition in the *Cena*, but exaggerates Trimalchio's morbidity and the general seri-ousness of the work, while Petersmann (1995*a*) also collects and analyses examples of superstition.

(e) *Reception.* The *Nachleben* of Petronius has been a strong interest throughout twentieth-century scholarship. Collignon (1905) looked at the influence of Petronius in France, Rini (1937) investigated Italy, while de Smet (1996) has studied the impact of Petronius on Latin Menippean satire in early modern Europe. There is as yet no com-prehensive treatment of the influence of Petronius in English liter-ature; for a brief taster, cf. Stuckey (1972). Useful general overviews of Petronian *Nachleben* have been provided briefly in the last chapter of Walsh (1970), and at greater length in Gagliardi (1993), now the best place to start investigating the influence of the *Sat.* on the modern novel since the Renaissance; for the general reception of the *Sat.* in neo-Latin humanist fiction a good starting-point is de Smet (1997). For use of individual episodes, many articles are listed for the period 1945–82 in Smith (1985: 1665); the episode of the Widow of Ephesus has attracted particular recent attention (Carleton 1988; Boldrini 1989; Galand 1989; and (most substantially) Huber 1990a,b).

II. Apuleius, *Metamorphoses*

II.1. Complete Texts

The Budé edition of Robertson and Vallette (1940–5; text by Robertson) still provides the best-constituted text of the *Met.*; for the background, see Robertson (1924), Robertson and Vallette (1940–5: vol. i, pp. xxxviii–lv) and the recent summary in Marshall (1983). The texts of Helm (1931a), Giarratano (1929), and Giarratano and Frassinetti (1960) provide a fuller range of conjectures than Robertson, and must still be consulted. The manuscript tradition of Apuleius is somewhat more easily untangled than that of Petronius. All extant manuscripts of the *Met.*, usually preserved in a group with the *Apologia* and *Florida* in the order *Apol. Met. Flor.*, are generally agreed to be descended from the eleventh-century F (Laur. 68. 2), which goes back ultimately to a double revision made in AD 395 and 397, as the subscription to *Met.* 9 usefully records; it may be, as argued by Pecere (1984), that some of the later manuscripts close to F are copied from an immediate ancestor of F rather than F itself, but the further supposition that the text of the *Met.* given in F is incomplete and that there was originally a twelfth book (van Mal-Maeder 1997), though a fascinating hypothesis, must remain a daring speculation. F is thus the most valuable witness for any constitution of the text, but is in parts illegible and can be usefully supplemented from two further sources: φ (Laur. 29. 2), copied from F in s.xii–xiii after damage to fragment 160 of F, and a group of four manuscripts of s.xiv–xv, descended from another copy of F made before the damage (A, U, E, and S).

All the manuscripts named so far agree in naming the work *Metamorphoseon libri*, which as the *subscriptio* to book 2 in F confirms, was its title in AD 395–7; Augustine in the early fifth century (*Civ. Dei* 18. 18. 1) refers to 'Apuleius in libris quos Asini aurei titulo inscripsit', which has led to the alternative title *Golden Ass (Asinus aureus)*. Winkler (1985: 292–320) has recently argued for an original double title *Asinus aureus* περὶ μεταμορφωσέων. I would prefer to keep the nominative *Metamorphoses* both because Winkler is too much influenced by the model of Varro's Menippean double titles which often have περὶ-alternatives, and in order to match more exactly the *Metamorphoses* of both Lucius of Patrae and Ovid, both of which are plainly key models for Apuleius. The general notion of a double title is an attractive explanation of Augustine's statement, and also matches the way in which a number of the Greek novels seem to possess double titles, not least in the pseudo-Lucianic *Lucius; or, the Ass*: cf. Xenophon's *Ephesiaka; or, Anthia and Habrocomes*, Heliodorus' *Aethiopika; or, Anthia and Habrocomes*, and Longus' *Poemenika; or, Daphnis and Chloe*. I would ultimately favour *Asinus aureus/Metamorphoses* (along with Münstermann 1995: 46–56, though I would not agree with his Isiac arguments for it).

II.2. Commentaries and English Translations

There is no commentary on the whole work since Hildebrand (1842), still occasionally useful, but the twentieth century looks set to complete a set of extensive commentaries on the *Met*. Two phases of activity at Groningen in the Netherlands have been crucial here (chronicled by Hofmann 1992). The first phase produced book 1 by M. Molt (1938), book 2 by B. J. de Jonge (1941), and book 5 by J. M. H. Fernhout (1949); the second phase, of which book 3 by R. T. van der Paardt (1971) was in a sense a foretaste, has led to book 4. 1–27, book 6. 25–32, and books 7, 8, and 9, all by the Groningen collective led at various times by B. L. Hijmans, Jr., Heinz Hofmann, and Maaike Zimmerman (Hijmans *et al.* 1977, 1981, 1985, 1995); another product of this activity has been the *Groningen Colloquia on the Novel*, of which there have been twenty so far with nine volumes of proceedings (Hofmann 1988, 1989, 1990, 1991, 1992, 1993, 1995; Hofmann and Zimmerman, 1996, 1997, 1998). Maaike Zimmerman's own book 10 is imminent, and the collective commentary on the Cupid and Psyche section (*Met*. 4. 28–6. 24) and new commentaries on book 1 and book 2 are due to be completed by the time the Groningen project winds up in 2000. The Groningen commentaries are on a large scale, with Helm's text and an English translation, and discuss a wide range of philological and theoretical issues, especially in the more recent volumes.

Outside Groningen the episode of Cupid and Psyche, which like Petronius' *Cena* received a number of separate editions in the nineteenth century, has been particularly popular, being edited by Purser (1910), Grimal (1963), Kenney (1990*a*; a particularly useful book), and Moreschini (1994), amongst others, as has book 11, the Isis book, edited by Fredouille (1975) and Griffiths (1975), the last being an extraordinarily rich treasure-house of material on the Isis cult. There has also been a useful edition of book 1 by Scobie (1975) and a brief but serviceable commentary on book 9 by Mattiacci (1996). Amongst English translations Gaselee's old Loeb edition (1915), a revised version of Adlington's classic translation of 1566, the two-volume translation by H. E. Butler (1910), and the lively version by Lindsay (1932) held the field before Robert Graves's racy but impressionistic rendering (1950, 1990). Most recently, three translations have appeared which take full account of the progress of Apuleian scholarship, and are readable as well as reliable: Hanson's splendid new Loeb (1989) in two volumes (with an unremarkable text), and the excellent renderings by Walsh (1994) and Kenney (1998), both seasoned Apuleian scholars.

II. 3. Concordances and Bibliographies

There is no computerized concordance of the *Met.*, but the availability of Robertson's text on the easily searchable PHI CD-ROM (see 1.3 above) more than compensates for this. For the non-computerized the *Index Apuleianus* (Oldfather *et al.* 1934) is still useful, but (like the Groningen commentaries) refers to the text by Helm's page and line numbers rather than Robertson's subsections of chapters. Amongst unannotated bibliographies the full list in Molt (1938) offers effective coverage of important items up to 1937, and the period since 1971 is accounted for both in the ever-useful annual listings of ancient novel publications in the *Petronian Society Newsletter* (see 1.3 above) and in the splendid on-line searchable Apuleius bibliography maintained by Luca Graverini (http://www.unisi.it/ateneo/ist/anc_hist/online/apuleio/bibintro.htm), which also has some pre-1971 items; the bibliographical lists at the beginning of the Groningen commentaries on the *Met.* (see ii.2 above) are also very useful. Amongst annotated bibliographies a good account of work in the period 1897–1914 (299 items!) is offered by the Bursian surveys of Lehnert (1915, 1919), while an excellent survey by Schlam (1971) deals with the years 1938–70, and Bowie and Harrison (1993) selectively covers the years 1967–92.

II.4. Scholarly and Interpretative Issues

II.4.1. Date, Authorship, and Historical and Cultural Setting. There is
no doubt that the *Met.* were written by Apuleius and that he was
born in Madauros (not Madaura) in Roman North Africa in the mid-
120s AD: the works of Apuleius other than the *Met.*, and some other
ancient sources such as Augustine, give us a fair amount of information
about his life (for recent accounts, cf. Flamand 1989; Zimmerman 1996;
Harrison 1996; Sandy 1997). However, scholars since the nineteenth
century (stimulated by Rohde 1885) have argued whether the *Met.*
is a work of Apuleius' exuberant youth or a sophisticated product
of mature age; for the pre-1937 debate, cf. Molt (1938: 6–8), and for
recent arguments, cf. Dowden (1994), for an early date, and Harrison
(1996) for a late one. There is much debate about possible dating
evidence within the text, where attempts to use *Realien* for this purpose have usually concluded indeterminately, owing to the vague
nature of the evidence (cf. Summers 1973; Summers has also investigated the legal elements in the *Met.* from the *Realien* angle (1967,
1970, 1972) but concludes that they are largely vague and unhelpful,
a view upheld by Elster 1991). One key point lies outside the *Met.*: those
who wish to regard it as an early work need to explain why it is
not mentioned in Apuleius' other writings, and especially in the
Apologia, where it would surely have been used by the prosecution in
their attempts to blacken Apuleius by reference to his immoral literary works. This would suggest a date after AD 158–9, the agreed date
of the *Apologia*.

The status of Apuleius as a second-century Latin sophist and of his
novel as a reflection in Latin of the contemporary Greek Second
Sophistic has been the topic of some discussion (briefly in Tatum
1979 and especially in Sandy 1997, but more remains to be said); the
intellectual colouring of the novel with Platonism (see II.4.4(*d*)
below) is clearly part of this aspect, as is its dense texture of literary
allusion, designed amongst other things to display epideictically the
learning of its author. In terms of contemporary history and society,
attempts to extract from the *Met.* hard information about provincial
life in the second century AD (for one of the best treatments, see
Millar 1981, reprinted in this volume as Chapter 12) usually come up
against its vagueness and literary character: for example, the robbers
in *Met.* 4 are surely primarily a literary topic from the Greek novel
rather than an index of the breakdown of order in the empire.

II.4.2. Greek Novelistic Sources. Scholars have now largely agreed in interpreting the evidence of Photius, *Bibl.* cod. 129 (for the passage's difficulties, cf. Kussl 1990) as suggesting that the extant pseudo-Lucianic *Onos* and the *Met.* of Apuleius are separately derived from a lost Greek *Met.* attributed by Photius to Lucius of Patrae, of which the extant *Onos* is an epitome; Apuleius' fundamental change to the plot of the two Greek ass tales was the introduction of the Isiac conclusion in book 11 (replacing a comic ending in the Greek tradition). The relation between these three texts was perhaps the chief issue of Apuleian studies in the early twentieth century, following Rohde (1885) and Burger (1887), the latter arguing essentially the modern consensus. For useful surveys of the controversy, see Lehnert (1915), Walsh (1974*b*), and Mason (1978), the last reprinted in this volume as Chapter 10 (cf. also Mason 1994, a larger treatment). Cocchia (1915) argues for the Apuleian authorship of the lost Greek *Met.* as well as the Latin text! The decisive contribution was van Thiel (1971*b*), which supports the *communis opinio*, though it was still possible to argue at the same date for the *Onos* as the sole source (so Bianco 1971, unconvincingly).

Another related issue was the sources of the inserted tales in Apuleius: were they derived in some degree from the longer lost Greek *Met.*, or were they all Apuleian additions? Here almost all scholars have held that the long tale of Cupid and Psyche (4. 28–6. 24) is an Apuleian addition. Of the many other inserted tales, Lesky (1941) reasonably argued that some of the tales in the lost Greek *Met.* (though not Cupid and Psyche, universally regarded as Apuleian) were reproduced in the extant Apuleian *Met.*, since the *Onos* as an epitome would naturally remove the original's tales, and there are plainly contexts in the extant *Onos* where tales appear to have been cut out; Junghanns (1932) and Paratore (1924, 1942) argued that all the tales were Apuleian additions, the former because he believed that the Greek *Met.* was only five pages longer than the *Onos*, but Lesky's moderate position has largely carried the day amongst modern scholars (cf. e.g. Mazzarino 1950; Effe 1976; Holzberg 1984). Contact with other extant Greek novels is otherwise vague and unclear, but there is no doubt that (for example) the Greek novel tradition is drawn upon in the presentation of the heroines Psyche and Charite (cf. Sandy 1994, a useful survey).

Another issue has been the connection of Apuleius' *Met.* with the Milesian tales, whether in the Greek version of Aristides or the

Roman version by Sisenna (for the evidence for both, see still Schissel von Fleschenberg 1913*a*), since its text makes specific and programmatic allusions to that literary tradition (*Met.* I. 1, 4. 32). Is it simply that some of the many obscene, sensational, and witty tales in the novel are taken from that tradition as well as from the Greek *Met.* (not improbable, since according to Photius the part of that text used by Apuleius was only two books long, and Apuleius needed to get bulk from somewhere)? Or does the overall form of the *Met.* as a racy narrative interspersed with *risqué* stories reflect the structure of the lost Milesian tales? Paratore (1942) and Mazzarino (1950) made some useful suggestions here, though the latter thought that the so-called *spurcum additamentum* in *Met.* 10. 21 was a genuine survival from Sisenna, a view suitably exploded by Fraenkel (1953) and Mariotti (1956), who both point to its late antique provenance. More recently, Moreschini (1990, 1994) has expanded the label 'Milesian' to refer to the whole broad tradition of the ancient novel before Apuleius as we now know it, arguing that Apuleius follows this by mixing together low-life material and religious or philosophical elements for the enjoyment of the reader, but the serious element implied here seems entirely foreign to all we know of the Milesian tradition. Harrison (1998*a*) suggests that the connections of the *Met.* with the Milesian tales may extend to a narrative frame encompassing both a story of travel and the telling of tales in and about an exotic location.

II.4.3. Language and Style. The language and style of Apuleius has always been of interest to Latinists; for an early treatment which still has useful material, cf. Koziol (1872). Like the Latin of Petronius, the language of Apuleius was at first investigated for its decadent and non-classical qualities; in the nineteenth century it was often seen as representing 'African Latin' (for a useful summary, see Brock 1911: 161–261, and for a modified revival, cf. Lancel 1987), but that notion was thoroughly discredited by Norden (1899), in an influential discussion which marginalized Apuleius in a different way in seeing him as a 'juggler of words' and the apogee of the 'Asianist' tradition in Latin. More recently, however, scholars have concentrated on the diversity of linguistic levels in Apuleius and particularly on his use of poeticisms and colloquial archaisms; the two contemporary studies by Médan (1925) and Bernhard (1927) have been followed by Callebat (1968), the most significant treatment—for a later outline of his views, cf. Callebat (1978). While vocabulary has been thoroughly explored,

the most remarkable features of Apuleian syntax, the repeated para-
taxis, isocolon, rhythm, and rhyme, which make his style instantly
recognizable and which Norden discussed so memorably, still need further investigation (a good brief account is to be found in Kenney 1990a),
as does Apuleius' use of *clausulae*, following the old treatments by
Schober (1902) and Kirchoff (1904) and the modern but necessarily
partial analyses by Hijmans (1978) and Nisbet (forthcoming).

II.4.4. *Literary Interpretation*

(a) *General Accounts.* In the first half of this century the view of Perry
(1926, essentially his view of 1967) was widespread, considering
Apuleius as a poor literary artist and regarding the *Met.* as a work
with little unity or artistic polish. The question of the work's unity and
the function of book 11, so notoriously treated by Perry (1967:
244–5), has been dealt with by Wlosok (1969, reprinted in this volume as Chapter 7) and others. For a summary of the issue (how can
an apparently religious book be the conclusion to a collection of low-
life tales and adventures?), see Sandy (1978), and for another good
unitarian treatment, Alpers (1980). The rehabilitation of Apuleius which
has taken place has had two essential thrusts: a stress on his religious
and philosophical content and symbolism, and a growing recognition
of his sophisticated narrative and literary techniques. These two topics are dealt with in more specific detail below (xxxvii–viii and
xxxiv–vii). It was Riefstahl (1938) who specifically set out to rebuild
Apuleius' literary standing in a treatment which combined an appreciation of the unity and narrative texture of the *Met.* with a perhaps
over-enthusiastic stress on the existentialist aspect of Lucius (though
this aspect was laudably linked in a general way with Apuleius'
Platonism); Junghanns (1932) and Paratore (1942) were both similarly concerned to raise the estimate of Apuleius' literary standing.
   By the time of Walsh (1970) the status of Apuleius as a major
literary artist was a fundamental notion; his treatment remains a
sound guide to the basic texture of the *Met.*, with the same virtues
as in his account of the *Sat.* (see xx above). Also useful guides to the
novel are Tatum (1979), an elegant treatment which begins to set
the novel in its contemporary cultural context, and Schlam (1992),
summarizing the author's views of the previous twenty years and a
short but densely informative account of the novel and its major
issues. James (1987) and Krabbe (1989) are also useful on many

points of interpretation and literary technique. But the outstanding modern treatment of the *Met.* is clearly that of Winkler (1985), a book which has justly had more impact on modern Apuleian studies than any other. In a work of delightful wit and intellectual brio, Winkler suggests that the *Met.* resembles a detective story in that its whole plot turns out to need reinterpretation when the final twist of Isiac conversion is revealed in book 11, and that even then the solution to the mystery is not determinate: we are not sure whether the religious climax of the novel is to be taken seriously, whether at the end Lucius is a true shaven devotee or a clownishly bald dupe. The general divided narrative structure of the novel in books 1–10, with the omniscient *auctor*, the retrospective first-person narrator commenting with hindsight on the actions of the naive *actor*, the first-person character in the story, breaks down in book 11, and the reader is given no retrospective analysis by the narrator with which to judge the events of that book: hence the remaining indeterminacy at the end.

This ultimate indeterminacy owes something to deconstruction, but it is also according to Winkler a key authorial strategy (124):

My ultimate assessment of the Golden Ass is that it is a philosophical comedy about religious knowledge. The effect of its hermeneutic playfulness, including the final book, is to raise the question whether there is a higher order that can integrate conflicting judgements. I further argue that the effect of the novel and the intent of Apuleius is to put that question but not to suggest an answer.

But Winkler's indeterminacy is not a necessary response to his careful exposure of the satirical and undermining elements in book 11. This evidence can be made to argue strongly for a non-serious interpretation of that book and its coherence with the playful tone of the rest of the novel, and thus constitutes an important corrective (partly anticipated by Anderson 1982: 82–5) to a critical tradition which had generally either emphasized the work's lack of unity (e.g. Perry 1967: 244–5) or argued for its unity on the basis of a serious religious interpretation (e.g. Wlosok 1969, reprinted in this volume as Chapter 7; for religious interpretations see xxxvii–viii below). But Winkler's rich indeterminacy has allowed subsequent critics to jump either way while recognizing the value of his work; one can jettison all serious notion of a genuine religious purpose, regarding the religious material as authorial manipulation and learning (Harrison 1996) or argue that the gaps and slippages identified by Winkler represent the disintegrating

world-view of a narrator in a conversion crisis of religious experience
(Shumate 1997).

(b) *Genre and Literary Affinities.* Few have doubted that the *Met.* is to
be included amongst ancient prose fictions, with the convenient label
'novel' (for a good discussion, cf. Callebat 1992). Apart from the issue
of its direct Greek model (see II.4.2 above), scholarly debate has
centred on its literary texture: strong assertions have been made of
folk-tale origins, even for the whole novel (so Scobie 1983), and particularly for the long episode of Cupid and Psyche (see especially
Mantero 1973 and Hoevels 1979, and for the earlier contributions
to the argument, Binder and Merkelbach 1968, along with the useful
survey by Moreschini 1994). In these earlier interpretations of Cupid
and Psyche, Reitzenstein at first (1912) rejected all connection with
allegory, Plato, or folklore in favour of an ancient oriental religious
myth of a goddess, but then (1930) admitted the idea of a *Kunst-
märchen*, an elaborated folk tale, which may have had a Greek origin,
but still a religious one. Kerényi (1927) saw an Isiac–Egyptian origin,
later famously taken up by Merkelbach (1958, 1962). Reitzenstein's
modifications were partly due to Helm's important article (1914),
which followed Reitzenstein in rejecting allegory and folk tale, but
rejected any mythico-religious origins and stressed the importance of
literary sources, especially erotic poetry (here under the influence of
Rohde). This opposition to any folkloric–religious origins of Cupid and
Psyche has been pursued by modern scholars, most notably Fehling
(1977), justly admired by Kenney (1990a); Schlam (1976) argued
for influence from artistic representations, but later adopted a more
literary view (1993), while Wright (1971) adopted a moderate position, stressing the combination of folkloric and literary sources.
Zimmerman (1998), essays from a Groningen conference on Cupid and
Psyche, presents a wide range of views, but perhaps the most important aspect agreed by modern scholarship is that the tale reflects the
main narrative of the novel, a general Apuleian technique (cf. Tatum
1969a, reprinted in this volume as Chapter 8), with the figure of
Psyche matching Lucius in her foolish *curiositas*, consequent sufferings, and final divine rescue (cf. Wlosok 1969, reprinted in this volume as Chapter 7; Kenney 1990a, introd.).

   Modern scholarship has in general tended to stress the wide range
of literary sources of the *Met.* (see now especially Finkelpearl 1998),
partly under the influence of Bakhtin's theory of the novel (see

1.4.5(a) above). Here links with epic have been much explored, a natural line of enquiry given that in antiquity epic provided the only major predecessor of the novel as a long fictional narrative, and had many episodes and structures that could be suitably reworked, usually parodically; this idea is prominent in Walsh (1970), and intertexts recently studied have included the *Odyssey* (Harrison 1990*b*; Frangoulidis 1992*a,b,c*), the *Aeneid* (La Penna 1985; Lazzarini 1985; Finkelpearl 1990, reprinted in this volume as Chapter 14; Frangoulidis 1991*b*; Graverini 1998; Harrison 1998*b*; Münstermann 1995), and Ovid's homonymous *Met.* (Scotti 1982; Bandini 1986; Krabbe 1989; Müller 1998). Greek tragedy has also been seen as a source (Schiesaro 1988; Mattiacci 1993), and historiography (Loporcaro 1992; Graverini 1997).

(*c*) *Narrative Technique and Structure.* The serious study of Apuleius' narrative technique, deemed inferior and negligent by scholars such as Helm (1910) and Perry (1923, 1926), began with two articles by Hammer (1923, 1925), which stressed the careful construction of the *Met.* from literary sources, and the relevance of some of the inserted tales to their contexts. Junghanns (1932), in a book largely devoted to the relation of the *Met.* to the Greek ass tales, also argued for the relevance of the tales to their context and for sophisticated patterns of narrative, and Riefstahl (1938) included an appreciation of Apuleian narrative technique (64–9) as 'well-pondered, playful, and ironic' (64) in his general rehabilitation of the *Met.* Narrative technique has been a favourite topic of modern Apuleian scholarship: apart from the *tour de force* of Winkler (1985) (see II.4.4*a* above), particularly useful contributions have been made by Tatum (1969*a*), the first treatment systematically to link all the inserted tales to their narrative contexts and reprinted in this volume as Chapter 8, Smith (1972), a good account of the difficulties, also reprinted in this volume as Chapter 9, Sandy (1972–3) on suspense, Pennacini (1979) on the pre-transformation narrative style of Lucius, Dowden (1982) and Laird (1990) on the use of the first person, and Laird (1993) on claims to truth. Implicit or explicit in much recent work is the application of narratological theory, especially in Winkler (1985) and the work of the Groningen group (cf. esp. Hijmans *et al.* 1995: 7–14; van der Paardt 1978; see further Fusillo 1996). Other stimulating approaches include that of Slater (1998), who analyses the use of visual art in the *Met.* and applies this to a darker interpretation of the story of Lucius.

Two passages of the *Met.* crucial for its narrative technique have
been particularly debated. The first is the prologue (*Met.* 1. 1), where
the unnamed speaker has been variously interpreted as Apuleius the
author, Lucius the narrator, a combination of the two, an anonymous
prologus in the manner of Roman comedy (so Smith 1972, followed
by e.g. Winkler 1985), or even the book itself (Harrison 1990a, which
gives the extensive previous bibliography on the issue); further discussion is promised by Kahane and Laird (forthcoming), a book
which contains a large number of short treatments of the prologue
from many angles. The second is the celebrated passage near the end
of the last book (11. 27), where the priest Asinius Marcellus reports
to the narrator Lucius that he (Asinius) has been told in a dream that
a man from Madauros (*Madaurensem*) would come to him for initiation and achieve great glory in literature, implicitly identifying
Lucius with the man from Madauros, the birthplace of Apuleius himself, an identification which Lucius fails to deny. Several earlier
scholars have attempted to remove the problem by emendation (see
Griffiths 1975: 334), but most have seen *Madaurensem* as a signal
of Apuleian autobiography in some sense, and thus of the seriousness of the last book as a religious testimony (see 11.4.4(*d*) below).
Narratological considerations, however, offer a third solution which
says nothing about the book's 'sincerity', and suggest that this is a
playful gesture akin to the determinedly anonymous speaker of the
prologue, providing a deliberately balanced complication of the first-
person voice at the beginning and the end of the text: thus narrative
considerations can add a further approach to the old problem of
unity in the *Met.*, of coherence between books 1–10 and 11.

In more detail on 11. 27 van der Paardt (1981), in an important
short article reprinted in this volume as Chapter 11, pointed out
that this is not the only moment when Apuleius the author or extradiegetic narrator seems to replace the nominal intradiegetic narrator
within the story, a 'metalepsis' in the terms of Genette (1980: 234–7)
(the other is at *Met.* 4. 32), while Penwill (1990) attractively suggested
that the occurrence of *Madaurensem* within a message from a god
relayed to Lucius by a third party constitutes a severe case of Chinese
whispers: the priest has got it wrong, and what the omniscient god
actually predicted was not the intradiegetic meeting with Lucius
but the extradiegetic fact that Apuleius would in the future achieve
literary glory by writing about the events of the story. Whatever
explanation is applied, the switch of identity in the narrator seems

momentary (the post-11. 27 narrator still appears to be Lucius, not Apuleius), and to balance the switch of identity at the beginning from someone else to Lucius at 1. 2. The successful application of narrative theory to the *Met.* is largely owed to the work's plain interest in narratological complication, an interest shared not only with Petronius (see 1.4.5(*c*) above) but also with Greek novels such as *Daphnis and Chloe* and Heliodorus' *Aethiopica*.

(*d*) *Ideology.* Apuleius' probable introduction to the story of Lucius of an Isiac conclusion instead of a comic ending (see 11.4.2 above) has suggested to many scholars that the *Met.* had some kind of religious or moral intention—if not to convert readers to the cult of Isis, then to give them a moral warning about the consequences of reckless self-indulgence; the tale of Lucius has often been considered one of fall and redemption (for a sophisticated modern version of this thesis, cf. Penwill 1975). Book 11 has been constantly studied both as a detailed repository of information about the Isiac religion (so de Jong 1900; Berreth 1931; Wittmann 1938; a tradition culminating in Griffiths 1975) and as an important document of religious experience in the Roman empire (so Nock 1933; Festugière 1954; and (with less historical emphasis) Shumate 1997). The fact that Isiac–Egyptian material is plainly not restricted to book 11 but can be traced throughout the work (Grimal 1971; Griffiths 1978) means that it can be related to the issue of unity: there is a clear thread of continuity between the Egyptian hints to be found as early as the prologue and the extended Isiac narrative of the last book (see esp. Wlosok 1969, reprinted in this volume as Chapter 7).

This Isiac thematic continuity has been famously used by some to argue that the whole work, and especially the tale of Cupid and Psyche, is a symbolic exposition of the rites of initiation into the cult of Isis (Kerényi 1927; Merkelbach 1962, 1995). Most modern scholars consider this approach somewhat extreme (see the important critique of Turcan 1963, a partial resuscitation in Münstermann 1995, and a recent balanced view in Beck 1996), and the recent tendency to destabilize and undermine the content of book 11 through narrative analysis (cf. 11.4.4(*c*) above) has perhaps made it more difficult to accept. Though the Isiac detail of book 11 is plainly both extensive and accurate (Griffiths 1975; Turcan 1996: 110–16), and though this detail may well derive from Apuleius' own status as an Isiac initiate (he says at *Apologia* 55 that he was initiated into several

mystery cults), it now seems too problematic to label the *Met.* as a proselytizing text for the cult of Isis, or to see book 11 as the personal credo
of the author, marked by the famous *Madaurensem* at 11. 27 (see 11.4.4(c)
above). One way forward (Harrison 1996) is to view the Isiac material of book 11 as a matter of epideictic display, showing off recon-
dite and prestigious religious knowledge in sophistic manner, and to
view the Isiac thread in the novel as simply one of a number of unifying factors structuring the whole work. The use of Isiac material need
not imply an Isiac ideology for the *Met.*

   The other ideological character often suggested for the *Met.* is that
of Platonic philosophy (for recent versions, cf. Gianotti 1986, a useful
book, and Fick-Michel 1991, extensive if a little diffuse). Here there
is again evidence from Apuleius' own career, since he openly proclaimed a Platonic allegiance (*Apologia* 10), and from the *Met.* itself:
a connection with known Middle Platonist philosophers is proclaimed at the work's beginning (1. 2), the Cupid and Psyche story
shows clear knowledge of the Platonic account of the soul in the
Phaedrus (*Met.* 5. 24 ~ *Phaedrus* 248c), and the centrality of *curiositas*
(Lucius' main vice) has been persuasively argued to be Platonic in
character (so DeFilippo 1990, reprinted in this volume as Chapter
13, which provides an extensive bibliography on *curiositas*, perhaps
the most discussed concept in the *Met.*). For the direct use of Plato
in the *Met.*, cf. further Thibau (1965), Schlam (1970), Moreschini (1978),
Kenney (1990b), and Münstermann (1995); in particular, it can be
argued that the work shows an interest in epistemological dualism of
a strongly Platonic kind (so Gianotti 1986; Harrison 1996). The link
between Isiac and Platonic thought, most evident in Plutarch's
Platonizing *De Iside et Osiride*, importantly discussed in connection with
Apuleius by Walsh (1981), has also been studied, and linked interestingly with Hermetic interests by Münstermann (1995). But again,
as with Isiac religion, this undeniable Platonic texture need not
determine the ideological character of the work; it could simply take
its place alongside Isiac material as a means of structuring the narrative and as a suitably learned and prestigious subject of epideictic
display, since a literary Platonism was the common intellectual currency of the second century AD (cf. Whittaker 1987).

   (e) *Reception*. There is no modern general account of the *Nachleben* of
the *Met.*: we await a successor to Haight (1927), which is useful but
now outdated, and the last chapter of Walsh (1970), which is neces-

sarily brief, though there is much of interest on Apuleian influence in European literature to be found in Doody (1996). The medieval reception of Apuleius, earlier considered by Costanza (1937) is surveyed briefly by Schlam (1990) and a connection with French romance traced by Rollo (1994), while the influence of the *Met.* on Shakespeare has been discussed by Tobin (1984), extensive but often speculative; a good larger account of the influence of the *Met.* in Renaissance England is promised in a published version of Carver (1991). Recent years have seen a number of individual studies on aspects of Apuleian reception: Scobie (1978a), de Jong (1989), and Wilson (1994) have looked at the influence of the *Met.* in Renaissance France and Italy; the reception of Cupid and Psyche in Italy has been treated by Moreschini (1994); Apuleius and Boccaccio by Mass (1989); Apuleius and Renaissance Latin by Prete (1988); Apuleius in Holland by van der Paardt (1989); and 'Apuleius and the Movies' by Elsom (1989).

I

Petronius as Paradox: Anarchy and Artistic Integrity

FROMA I. ZEITLIN

The recent renewal of interest in the *Satyricon* has produced many new and valuable insights into this strange work.[1] But enigmatic it still remains—both in respect of its form or genre and of the purpose or stance of the author—while contradictory theories continue to be vigorously propounded, attacked, and defended.[2]

Perhaps this enigmatic quality of the *Satyricon*, aggravated by the fragmentary condition of the text, will inevitably defeat the possibility of any consensus among its readers, but the present lack of consensus may also be a clear indication that a new approach to the *Satyricon* is needed. It might be argued that any ambiguous work of literature which fundamentally defies the ready classifications and explications that are offered by conventional criticism ought to be re-examined in unconventional terms. For its resistance to definition by rigorous classical canons may well be a clue to its purpose, and the uneasiness its ambiguity may create in the reader by baffling his expectations may well be a key to its meaning.[3]

---

[1] This paper came into being largely as a result of an undergraduate seminar on Petronius given at Rutgers University in the spring of 1971. Special acknowledgement is made to Myron Jaworsky, Ronald Kopnicki, and Kathleen Miller for their contributions. I am indebted to Professors Gilbert Highet and S. Palmer Bovie and to Craig Knobles who offered many valuable suggestions.

[2] Textual references to the *Satyricon* will be cited from the Budé edition, ed. A. Ernout (1967).

[3] Such is the case, for example, with Laurence Sterne's *Tristam Shandy*. 'Is it simply a scrambled comic novel . . . ? Is it a collection of playful speculative essays like Montaigne's, but with a more fictional sugar coating than Montaigne felt necessary? Or is it a satire in the tradition of Swift's *A Tale of the Tub*, taking in, as Sterne himself put it, "everything which I find laugh-at-able in my way"?' (Booth 1961: 222). See further Booth's analysis of the work—the problem of formal coherence and the unity of *Tristram Shandy* (221–40).

There are some criteria even in the controversial field of aesthetic theory by which we try to evaluate literature.[4] The first posits in a work of art an organic connection between form and content, where artistic form imposes itself upon and disciplines its 'formless' subject matter to create a 'symbolic integrity of a work of art.'[5] The second requires that fusion of form and content should result in some significant statement, implicit or explicit, about the human condition as perceived by the artist, who may legitimately select his material from the entire range of human experience. But we often ask more than this by adding a third criterion—an expectation that art achieve a formal intelligible ordering of experience to satisfy a deeply felt human need of apprehending an intelligible world order. Aesthetics, in this sense, can independently play the same role as religion or political ‖ ideology by guaranteeing a viable concept of a world-order rather than just a world-view.

As soon as the third expectation is applied to Petronius, the reader is apt to shake his head in disbelief, for Petronius seems not to order experience but to disorder it, by irony and ambiguity of tone, by disorganized plot, by shifting characterizations, and by bewildering incongruities, to name only a few of his more prominent 'failings.' But when it is examined in terms of the first two criteria, we should expect to find in the *Satyricon* an inner coherence and an interrelation of form, style, literary devices, plot, mode of characterization, themes, images, and symbols which create a world-view that is intelligible when seen within the framework of its own inner logic. If Petronius sees the world as irrational, confused, and illusory, this *Weltanschauung* should be accepted as his legitimate right. Although it need not be adopted or even admired by the reader, the *existence* of this view can be acknowledged and understood.

The purpose of this paper, then, is to take an approach to the *Satyricon* that accepts its paradoxes, its inconsistencies, its ambiguities, its absurdities, and its incongruities as integral emblems of a world-view that expresses a consistent vision of disintegration through the

---

[4] If the following exposition of some basic principles of literary theory seems too rudimentary to be mentioned, I ask the reader's indulgence. Such an exposition, oversimplified as it is, seems to me to be necessary in view of much of the recent evaluations of Petronius which tend to ignore these principles.

[5] Kiremidjian (1970: 236). By form I mean 'the aesthetic structure of a literary work—that which makes it literature.' By content (or materials) I mean 'human behavior experience . . . and human ideas and attitudes.' Wellek and Warren (1956: 241). See their entire chapter. 'Evaluation,' 238–51, and the bibliography cited therein.

interrelationship of form and content. What has been called 'literary opportunism'[6] will then prove to be conscious artistic choice.

This approach first asks for a genuine acceptance of the radical originality of the *Satyricon*, so that it may be judged in terms of its own premises, although assistance can and should be sought in comparisons with literary works of later ages which display similar characteristics. Although the special originality of the *Satyricon* has been acknowledged by many, the deeper implications of this recognition have not been explored.[7] ||

Secondly, this approach requires a relinquishing of the canons of classical or neo-classical aesthetic theory as our standard for judging Petronius, while, at the same time, allowing Petronius his own close acquaintance with those canons. For, as I hope to prove, the *Satyricon* is a radically anti-classical work, which, by its subversion and rejection of classical aesthetic theory with its attendant expectations, sets out to project a radically anti-classical world-view.

I. GENRE AND CLASSICAL GENRE THEORY

The classical theory of genres, which reigned supreme in antiquity and still continues to exercise a strong influence today, especially on critics of classical literature, must judge Petronius a hopeless misfit. This theory, as has been observed, is

---

[6] Sullivan (1968a: 266–7).

[7] Sullivan (1968b: 81–3) calls the *Satyricon* 'a highly original work unparalleled in ancient literature,' but lays his emphasis on the debts Petronius owes to tradition (especially to Menippean satire) which, in his opinion, predetermined Petronius' choice of material. Courtney (1962: 100), too, concludes that Petronius' 'exuberant genius . . . embarked on a "Kreuzung der Gattungen" which for breadth and audacity has no parallel in ancient literature and which completely overrides the extremely formal canons of ancient literary theory,' but he too relates this feature mainly to the tradition of Menippean satire. Walsh (1970: 7) asserts that 'nothing remotely comparable to its plot survives in Greek literature, and the Roman atmosphere of many of its episodes encourages the belief that he has brought to birth a new type of fiction,' but in his analysis he too stresses the importance of the formative genres. Perry (1967: 186–90, 202–10) offers the most illuminating discussion of the originality of the *Satyricon*. But, while he rejects the usual emphasis on *Quellenforschungen*, he attributes the adoption of this radically unusual form to Petronius' desire for 'a safe place in which to experiment artistically with various types of poetry, rhetorical declamation, and criticism' (209). Cameron (1970) comes closer to an appreciation of the wider implications of Petronius' originality as expressed through the interrelationship of form and content; see especially 423–4, and cf. Arrowsmith (1966: 304–25).

the . . . doctrine of purity of genre. . . . Though it was never worked out with sharp consistency, there was a real aesthetic principle . . . involved: it was the appeal to a rigid unity of tone, a stylized purity and 'simplicity,' a concentration on a single emotion . . . as on a single plot or theme. There was an appeal also to specialization and pluralism: each kind of art has its own capacities and its own pleasure. . . . Classical theory had too its social differentiation of genres. . . . And that sharp distinction in the *dramatis personae* proper to each kind has its concomitants in the doctrine of 'decorum' (class 'mores') and the separation of styles and dictions into high, middle, low. It had, too, its hierarchy of kinds, in which not merely the rank of the characters and the style counted as elements but also the length or size (the capacity for sustaining power) and the seriousness of tone.[8]

But the *Satyricon* violates many of these prescriptions. For instance, ‖ it exhibits no rigid unity of tone, no stylistic purity and simplicity, no concentration on a single emotion, and probably not on a single plot or theme (certainly if the Aristotelian doctrine of the causal plot is taken as the only acceptable norm).

In descriptive terms, the *Satyricon* belongs to no traditional classical genre; it contains elements from many and varied genres in prose and poetry. It has affinities with epic, with the *Reiseroman*, with romance, with formal satire (both Lucilian and Menippean), with the Milesian tale, and with the mime, among others.[9] It may use or abuse elements from all these genres, but it has metamorphosed this blend of genres into something singular, a 'unique hybrid,' as it has been called.[10] The absence of any one traditional category into which

---

[8] Wellek and Warren (1956: 234). See D'Alton (1931: 398–482) for a full discussion of the classical theory of kinds and for enumeration of the ancient sources. See also Perry (1967: 18–27).

[9] For a discussion of the various influences on the *Satyricon* with relevant bibliography, see especially Perry (1967: 186–9); Walsh (1970: 7–31); Sullivan (1968a: 89–98, 115–57); and Veyne (1964: 310–12).

[10] Cameron (1970: 404). See also Kroll (1924: 223–4). 'Petronius makes use of various types of subject matter that were topical or prominent in . . . antecedent literary forms . . . ; but these for him were simply building materials. Like so many bricks, they tell us nothing about the architectural scheme of the *Satyricon* as a whole and the purpose that guided the author in the construction of it.' Perry (1967: 206).

Courtney (1962: 90) and Sullivan (1968a: 81–114) insist that Menippean satire is to be classified in this category. But I concur in Cameron's judgment that 'there is no sign that there existed in the shadowy satires of Varro anything of the rich invention of the *Satyricon*' (404). See also Schmeling (1971: 49–50). Despite the presence in Menippean satire of genre mixture, literary allusions, parody, and prosimetric form, the scale of the *Satyricon* (even in its mutilated state), its characterizations, its complicated plot, and its whole conception militate against such a narrow viewpoint.

the *Satyricon* can comfortably fit might then be taken, paradoxically, as a salient descriptive quality of the work. Its guiding principle seems to be an incongruous, unexpected juxtaposition or fusion of genres, undertaken with the deliberate intention of defeating the expectations of an audience accustomed, far more than we, to an organizing literary form.

The theory of genres not only implies the principle of order in defining the nature of the form and content with a given genre, but its procedure of classification and differentiation of separate genres is also a principle of ordering aesthetic experience. Therefore, Petronius, both by his rejection of a single form and by his mixture of established forms, introduces a fundamental disorder into his work. ‖

There are further implications involved in Petronius' rejection of traditional genre theory. Although genres may be universal categories, which transcend time and place, each culture, each tradition 'will have disqualified certain forms and means of expressions as invalid and impossible; by the same process, it will suggest others as now possible and valid.'[11] Although, in one sense, as we shall see, the *Satyricon* is a product consonant with its time, in another sense, Petronius, on his own initiative, overturns this principle too. For in addition to the mixture of genres, he raises to the literary level sub-literary prose fiction and the still more sub-standard mime, thus enlarging the range and focus of subject matter and its treatment which are permissible for literature. On the other hand, in contrast to the upgrading of some genres, a reverse process is going on at the same time—the debasement of legitimate genres, especially epic, by parodistic and ironic techniques. In his treatment of the different genres within the work, he often reverses the doctrine of decorum in reference both to style and to *dramatis personae*, which creates still another kind of disorder.[12]

---

[11] Kiremidjian (1970: 236).

[12] 'Parody, in effect, violates the doctrine of decorum, by making a relationship between a genre and its style which is not proper or decorous at all,' but, in fact, is 'a reverse relationship.' Watson (1969: 94). This technique of sundering the union of form and content was, of course, an accepted technique in antiquity. See Lelièvre (1954), Cèbe (1966), and Courtney (1962: 86–100). Yet nowhere else in antiquity is parody used so pervasively and with such a wide range of targets. The effect of Petronius' extravagant engagement with parodistic expression deserves an examination of the deeper implications which parody may bear over and beyond its humorous appeal and its value as a mode of literary criticism. But since parody in Petronius extends beyond the main genre categories to general stylistic considerations, this examination will be deferred for the moment.

For viable literature, however, there must be a tension between the inherent limitations imposed by the form and all it represents and the necessary freedom allowed to the individual artist to exercise creative invention within these limits (leading often, in the case of the great artist, even to the expansion of a given form) to affect the audience with a sense of both recognition and novelty. 'The genre represents, so to speak, a sum of aesthetic devices at hand, available to the artist and ‖ already intelligible to the reader. . . . The totally familiar and repetitive pattern is boring; the totally novel form will be unintelligible . . .'.[13]

The separation of form from creative invention signals the exhaustion of form; the literature of each successive age must revitalize the current forms, expanding them by cross-fertilization from other forms, drawn both from literary and non-literary sources. It should be free also to develop forms appropriate to the ethos of the age. But the classical theory of genres, by its 'regulatory and prescriptive' rules established for existing forms and by its unwillingness to tolerate other aesthetic systems,[14] became a still more rigid and confining system in the hands of the Romans. For they did not address themselves, for the most part, to the creation and development of their own organic forms but adapted (often successfully) to their own special needs the organic forms of another and, in many ways, alien culture. But once those special needs had been defined, they did not encourage the free development of new or changing standards. On the contrary, they canonized existing standards with eventually stultifying effects. Even satire (the one genre which the Romans claimed for their own, and which, according to one derivation, signified 'medley' or 'potpourri'), a form that inherently should have been able to tolerate a wider range of experimentation, rapidly standardized satirical material and treatment into recognizable *topoi*.

It is well-known that Nero's literary tastes encouraged experimentation and discussion of styles and practices. Silver Latin literature did mark an attempt to revitalize old forms, although it was hampered in its task by a lack of political freedom.[15] But it should be noted that, with the exception of Petronius, the experimentation was confined to work within the existing genres such as satire, epic, and tragedy, and here rhetoric played far too great a role. But rhetoric, which has been accused as the cause of the decline in Roman literature, was, at least,

---

[13] Wellek and Warren (1956: 235).   [14] Wellek and Warren (1956: 233–4).
[15] On the literary interests of the Neronian court, see Sullivan (1968a: 81–6, 1968b).

one of the ways in which the traditional forms might be given a new and different touch. Yet since rhetoric puts the emphasis on stylistic brilliance and superficial effects, it is ultimately an empty || substitute for the aesthetic freedom denied to literature by current political conditions and by too early and too rigid definitions of genres.

The choice, however, by a specific culture of its acceptable genres is dictated to a large extent by the needs of the society which range beyond the limits of pure aesthetic enjoyment, based on inherited tradition and values and yet capable of alteration and expansion to suit the demands of the living age. In this sense, the literary form can be viewed as an 'institution of society—as church, university or state is an institution.'[16] An acceptance of the traditional literary norms is, in some sense, a conformity, perhaps even a commitment, to the larger social norms.

This is an especially valid observation for Roman society, which was highly institutionalized in many ways, which required for its psychic needs a high degree of organization, and which, in general, clung tenaciously to tradition. Literature, too, had been institutionalized to some extent; Roman prose and poetry, particularly in the preceding Augustan age, had often been closely allied to the programs of the state, and its practice had been encouraged and subsidized by the formal system of literary patronage offered to the artists by the upper classes and later by the court.

The theory of genres, viewed as an institution of society, upholds the orderly status quo through its formal ordered structure. By its contents, it also lends support to the ideals of that society. It may then be legitimate to regard Petronius' rejection of its tenets as an implicit rejection of other larger institutions and their ideologies. This suggestion seems to be verified by the content of the *Satyricon*, which, as we shall see, hits out in varied and oblique ways at the other institutions of Roman society.

In one sense, Petronius' rejection of the theory of genres can be seen as a genuine aesthetic experiment in the revitalization of literature and also as a rejection of the traditional values of his society and its institutions. In another sense, his technique of mixing genres can be viewed as a device used to create an impression of disorder, which he felt to be an appropriate representation of reality for his particular age. ||

[16] Wellek and Warren (1956: 226) and see their chapter 'Literature and Society' (94–109). See also Levin (1946).

Such a theory, based on observation of the text, is complicated, however, by the tenets of traditional literary criticism offered by Agamemnon, Encolpius, and Eumolpus in the *Satyricon*, which have often been taken as expressions of the 'real' opinions of Petronius and have been extracted from the text for insertion into histories of literary criticism. Petronius, thereby, has been marked as a literary conservative, who looks back to the classical norms of the past for his models.[17]

But, taken in context, the formal expositions of clichés in praise of the past in the arts and sciences (88), in the rules set down for formal educational training based on immersion in the classics of the past (5), and in the prescriptions for writing poetry in the epic genre, also based on the models of the past (118), are undercut in a complex way by those who make the formal expositions. For example, Agamemnon does not follow his own regimen for educational training. Eumolpus, in his *Bellum civile*, is not consistent in the principles he propounds on the technique of writing epic poetry, which makes his role as an arbiter of literary standards appear incongruous.[18] The resulting epic effort, a pastiche of Lucan and Vergil, faithful to neither and yet not a creative new fusion, seems to me to question the very notion that epic poetry or any other literary genre can be reduced to a single set formula which will guarantee its success. I would go still further and see, by extension, an oblique attack on a society which lives by a faith in such established technical rules and rejects freer experimentation in favor of conscious archaization and legislation of norms. Vergil and Horace were, after all, standards of achievement for *their* age, and no amount of wishful thinking can assimilate the product of a 'cupientis exire beluae gemitus' (115. 1) to that of a 'furentis animi vaticinatio' (118. 6). ‖

Eumolpus is always ready with a set piece to match a specific occasion. Shorn tresses on shipboard suggest a vapid *elegidarion* on hair (109. 9–10); a corpse washed up on the beach evokes a verse epitaph

[17] See Sage (1915) and Sullivan (1968a: 158–70), who sees the two characteristics of Petronius' criticism as 'propriety and classicism' (165).

[18] I am in agreement here with Walsh (1970: 49–50), who remarks that 'in keeping with the characterization of the conservative theorist of mediocre talent, the poem handles the theme of the civil war in a traditionalist manner, but in style [often] echoes the stridency and monotonous versification of the poet whom Eumolpus is condemning. The irony is characteristic of Petronius.' Although Vergil's influence on the versification is also apparent (see Duckworth 1967: n. 83), mannerisms of Lucan are also prominent. For the theory that this poem is a serious critique of Lucan, see Sullivan (1968a: 165–86) and for the ideological implications of the poem beyond the confines of literary method, see Zeitlin (1971: 67–82).

(115. 20); a painting in an art gallery calls for an *ekphrasis* (89), and Eumolpus' poem on the capture of Troy is no more successful as poetry than his *Bellum civile*.

Most significant of all, of course, is the undermining of the value of rigid classical prescriptions by Petronius' own violations of the tradition in the *Satyricon*. For while Eumolpus' mixture of Seneca and Vergil in the *Troiae halosis* (the crossing of genres) and of Lucan and Vergil in the *Bellum civile* (the crossing of generations) may be viewed as further evidence of Petronius' technique of deliberate confusion, nevertheless, the woeful sterility of Eumolpus' derivative creations, containing the lesser of both the new and the old, provides a strong contrast to Petronius' own fertile and imaginative use of a similar technique in the body of the text.

Moreover, the moralizing statements, representative of an even more traditional Roman attitude, characterized by a nostalgia for the idealized past, have generally been recognized as undercut and partially invalidated by the behavior of those who voice them. If the objects of satire become the satirists themselves, as do the moralist philosophers, by the same reasoning the practitioners of literary criticism are equally subject to satire, especially since the teachers of both types of dogma are the same men. Especially too since art and morals are joined together in the traditional Roman unity (88).

This is not to say that the moralizing statements aimed at the excesses of the present are not objectively true, given the evidence of Seneca and of the *Satyricon* itself, or that the statements on art, which castigate the literary vices of the present and recognize the great achievements of the past, have no external validity. One ambiguity lies in the relationship established between the external validity of the complaints and their *traditional* presentation (which includes the *traditional* prescription for their amelioration by a return to the conditions of the past). The personal characters of the individual speakers create a second ambiguity. The behavior of those who theorize, but who do not, and probably cannot, put their theories into practice, demonstrates the insufficiency of the theories as a valid guide to life or to art. The suspicion thus ‖ grows that the traditional rules for the diagnosis and cure of the present ills, which were formulated in the past and maintained in a closed and stagnant system, may be, after all, pure cant.

Satire often takes as its theme the 'setting of ideas and generalizations and theories and dogmas over against the life they are supposed

to explain,' ... so that 'satire may often represent the collision
between a selection of standards from experience and the feeling that
experience is bigger than any set of beliefs about it.'[19] This skeptical
attitude towards dogmatic pronouncements seems to me, in fact,
precisely what Petronius aims to project in these scenes. He surely
satirizes Stoicism and he even satirizes Epicureanism, too.[20] His statements on art seem not so much to advocate a fixed position in the
literary controversies of his day, but to demonstrate the futility of
explaining art by intellectual theories.[21] Thus, his mixture of genres
can be || seen also as another expression of his rejection of fixed the-
oretical criteria for aesthetic theory.

Mode and Form

To project his sense of the unintelligibility of the world, Petronius
had to make his view intelligible to the audience. There is a balance

---

[19] Frye (1957: 229, 230).

[20] On the satirical treatment of Stoicism and Seneca, its leading exponent, see
Sullivan (1968a: 193–211, 1968b: 461–2). Although it has been claimed recently that
Petronius espouses a popular brand of Epicureanism (see Raith 1963; Walsh (1970:
50, 82, 109–10; and, to some extent, Sullivan 1968a: 33, 88, 108, 212; 1968b: 465),
the text does not seem to support any consistent adherence to a single philosophy. In
fact, on shipboard, Epicurus earns a satirical reference of his own. Eumolpus cites Epicurus'
disdain for the vatic properties of dreams in order to dissuade Lichas and Tryphena from
investigating the meaning of their dreams (104. 3), but these dreams, in fact, turn out
to convey accurate information .

[21] See the exposition of this theory in Sullivan (1968a: 85–9) and its sequel in
Sullivan (1968b: 453–67), where the evidence and the arguments seem to me to be
less convincing. In any case, Sullivan (1968a: 268) recognizes that 'it must be confessed
that Petronius' literary theories and artistic practice finally impress the reader, despite
their successes, as not quite fully thought out. His complaints about the unreality
of contemporary rhetoric are not consonant with his traditionalist's admiration of
Vergilian epic; his defence of the realism of the *Satyricon* . . . conflicts with the differ-
ently conceived fantasy of much of the Crotonian episode, as well as with many of the
irrelevant insertions, prose and verse, which serve merely to display his stylistic invention and skills.' Frye's (1957) remarks on the use of satire and irony provide a useful
explanation of this apparent 'gap' between theory and practice. 'The romantic fixation
which revolves around the beauty of perfect form, in art or elsewhere, is also a logical
target for satire. The word satire is said to come from *satura*, or hash, and a kind of
parody of form seems to run all through its tradition, from the mixture of prose and
verse in early satire to the jerky cinematic changes of scene in Rabelais. . . . *Tristram Shandy*
and *Don Juan* illustrate very clearly the constant tendency to self-parody in satiric rhetoric
which prevents even the process of writing itself from becoming an over-simplified
convention or ideal. . . . An extraordinary number of great satires are fragmentary,
unfinished, or anonymous. In ironic fiction a good many devices turning on the
difficulty of communication . . . serve the same purpose' (233–4).

necessary between the recognition of a given literary form by the audience and the expectation of novelty, a requirement which normally leads to a slow development within or even outside a genre form. Petronius cannot deny the expectations of the audience altogether. To do so would be to produce a totally private and uncommunicable work.

The comic mode is traditionally the mode most open to free invention of plot, to fantasy, to absurdities, to reversals of roles and to other confusions.[22] It is therefore an effective literary means for obtaining from the audience an acceptance of novelty in plot, and perhaps, to a lesser degree, in form. It is also, to some extent, a protective device, for it can legitimately allow the members of the 'outer' audience to respond to a comic work on the level of amiable nonsense. Yet the comic mode, too, preserves the underlying, shifting relationship between humor and gravity which is essential in great comedy and to which the members of the 'inner,' more perceptive audience can respond, if they wish.

In addition, intrinsic to the use of a fictional narrative or novelistic form are the paucity of rigid conventions and a concomitant need for wide invention so as to create an impression of the complex sprawl of life.[23] In truth, this basic 'formlessness' is an indigenous and legitimate trait of the novel, the art form which Henry James called 'that || loose and baggy monster.'[24] This fact has not always been recognized in its full implications, for adherents of neo-classical theory have applied to the European novel the classical Aristotelian standard of the causal plot and hence made the standard of the genre the 'realistic' novel.[25] But if we grant that the *Satyricon*, despite its mixture of classical genres, nevertheless belongs to a species of narrative fiction

[22] On the recurrent features of the comic mode, see Frye (1957: 163–86). On the freedom of invention allowed to comedy, see Perry (1967: 89), although I cannot agree with his notion that no rules whatsoever apply to the writing of comedy. Perry's definition of a comic novel is also useful to this discussion—'anything that one would call burlesque, picaresque, satirical, realistic, disillusioning, unmoral or unideal' (87). Satire should be subsumed under the larger rubric of the comic mode insofar as it exhibits 'wit or humor founded on fantasy or a sense of the grotesque or absurd' (Frye 1957: 224), but it should be remembered that satire is not the only source of the comic in the *Satyricon*. The mime, as well as comic drama, exercises an important influence.

[23] See Watt (1957: 13).

[24] Henry James, preface to the revised version of *The Tragic Muse*, in James (1934: 84).

[25] See Miller (1967: 9–10); see also Booth (1961: 23–60). On the *Satyricon*'s failure as a 'realistic' novel, see Sullivan (1968a: 96–8).

and is entitled to be called a novel, then we can judge Petronius according to the norms of fiction.

By the criteria of modern theory, we need not judge Petronius against the classical standard of the causal plot, to his detriment; nor need we judge him by the neo-classical norm of the 'realistic' novel. We can also understand that the use of satire in a novel is different from satire encompassed within the limits of its own more slender form.[26] Moreover, we are free to compare his fictional mode with other types of fiction that have appeared since his time—notably, the picaresque novel of Renaissance Spain (which his work seems to anticipate) and some of our modern novels.[27] It is significant that the evaluations of both have suffered when the 'realistic' novel is held to be the norm. ∥

Yet, at the same time, in our approach to Petronius, first, we can recognize his own unconventional use of the novel form as an acceptable literary form along with its implications. Secondly, we can refer back to the stylized prose romance in antiquity and to the epic, that other long fictional form, both of which Petronius recalls in his work for his own particular purposes. Thirdly, we can keep in mind the Aristotelian requirement of causality for all fictional plots, which he rejects, as he did the formal theory of genres.

In other words, we have a distinct advantage in that we can estimate the shock value of the *Satyricon* for an audience of Petronius' time, but we are not limited by the constrictions of classical theory in our own assessment of the meaning and value of Petronius' work.

Modern theory asks only that 'this world or *kosmos* of a novelist—this pattern or structure or organism, which includes plot, characters, setting, world-view, "tone"—is what we must scrutinize when we

---

[26] 'Whereas the novelist aims at understanding the complexities of life, satire aims at simplification, at a pretence of misunderstanding, and at denunciation. The sheer size of the open-ended form of the novel has also much to do with the difficulty that satirists have in using it: Satire seems to require a light and closed form which helps to make a simple point effectively—the form is itself a component of wit without which satire is unbearable. It follows that no full-length novel is likely to be satirical throughout, and indeed not one example among the classics comes to mind.' Hodgart (1969: 214). See his entire chapter 'Satire in the Novel' (214–40).

[27] Walsh (1970: 224–43) has pointed out the relationship of Petronius (and Apuleius) with the picaresque novel, but he has confined himself to speculations as to the influence of the Roman writers on later literature. (See further below, n. 48.) There have been several studies on similarities between Petronius and more modern writers—Cameron (1970) on Petronius and Joyce, Pound, and Eliot; Rankin (1970a: 197–213) (Proust, Joyce, and Fitzgerald); MacKendrick (1950) and Arrowsmith (1960: p. viii), who suggests a comparison with Vladimir Nabokov's *Lolita*.

attempt to compare a novel with life or to judge ethically or socially a novelist's work.'[28] The word *kosmos* here may seem ironical, if *kosmos* is felt to bear its root meaning, since the salient feature of the world of Petronius is its lack of *kosmos* or order. But when *kosmos* is interpreted as 'world,' then Petronius should be judged in terms of his own 'creative and humorous presentation of an imaginatively realized world.'[29]

If a novel is, as Stendhal says, 'a mirror carried along the road,'[30] then who is to say that that mirror may not be crazed and even cracked and so produce its own highly individual refractions? But to understand the particular nature of these refractions in Petronius, we must first examine his style and then the plot and other components of his world-view.

II. STYLE

Sullivan remarks with some justice that Petronius exhibits 'several distinguishable styles' in the *Satyricon*; the first, an 'elaborate style . . . used for literary criticism, parody, and various rhetorical purposes;' ‖ the second, a 'plain but careful rhythmical style which is the chief narrative medium, a kind of artistic *sermo urbanus*,' differentiated for 'leisurely elaboration . . . and rapid descriptions of action;' and the third, a 'vulgar style (*sermo plebeius*)' used primarily in the *Cena* to imitate proletarian daily speech. The conclusion drawn is that 'in each case, Petronius would see a particular style as suitable to a particular subject matter and this would be part of his and the Roman idea of literary decorum.'[31]

This analysis of the several styles of the *Satyricon*, valid as it may be, does not, however, convey a sense of the style of the book, taken as a whole. That style might be described as eclectic, varied, or even multitudinous. The *sermo urbanus*, often taken as the preferred style of Petronius himself, is one voice in a dissonant chorus of voices, albeit an important stabilizer in the continuity of the first-person narrative. One could better describe the style of the *Satyricon* as a synthesis of incongruous juxtapositions of styles and varying planes of literary

---

28 Wellek and Warren (1956: 214).
29 Sullivan (1968*a*: 264), but he never makes clear what he means by this phrase.
30 'Un roman: c'est un miroir qu'on promène le long d'un chemin' (Stendhal 1953: 76). 31 Sullivan (1968*a*: 164).

suggestiveness which yield to and crowd in upon each other with a general effect of confusion. The high level of verbal wit also contributes to the stylistic complexity.

In addition, there is the shift between poetry and prose that makes an irregular alternation between two fundamentally different modes of discourse. But the general principle of variation applies to both modes, for the styles of poetry in the text are also varied in tone, genre, and length. The distinction might be better subsumed under the general rubric of rapid stylistic variety. This trait has been attributed to a brilliant 'literary opportunism' which capriciously moves from style to style as a display of technical virtuosity and wit.[32] I would attribute it rather to another fundamental statement made by the work —namely, that the insistence on a fluidity and plasticity and changeability of styles in a rapid series of incongruities is an intentional device designed to represent stylistically those same qualities of confusion in the world. In other words, stylistic disorder mirrors world disorder.

Moreover, the frequent use of puns, verbal wit, literary allusions, and, above all, parody, appeals to the reader's education and intellectual skills as well as to his sense of humor. Thus an inherent antithesis is || created between the flow of the plot and the demands of recognition in these verbal techniques which slow down and usually break the narrative of action and episode. There is a

rhythm created . . . by interplay between the narrative . . . and the verbal surface. The verbal play constantly interrupts our attention to the narrative— we are constantly torn from the story to consider, ponder, and admire the intense activity of the verbal level. Our attention is constantly alternation between style and action in a way that gives birth to an instantaneous and irregular rhythm in reading the book.

And this 'jagged reading rhythm suggests a correspondence with the jagged episodic plot, the rush of events, and the internal chaos of the characters'[33] which I will explore in a later section. In addition, the rhythm of the narrative is also broken by other formal devices such as the digressions on literature, art, philosophy, and morals, and even, to some extent, by the inserted Milesian tales.

---

[32] Sullivan (1968a: 267) is the leading proponent of this view.

[33] Miller (1967: 112). This statement describes the style of Francisco de Quevedo's *El Buscón*, a picaresque novel of the Spanish Renaissance (1616), but it is even more applicable to the *Satyricon*.

The stylistic incongruities have been observed and well analyzed by Sullivan, but these matters are treated under the heading of 'Humor,' an appropriate rubric but one that effectively removes from consideration an approach to these incongruities that might see them as expressive of more than a comic versatility.

On the one hand, he describes Petronius' distribution of styles as consonant with the Roman doctrine of decorum. For example, when Encolpius speaks of literature or of art, he employs a polished rhetorical style. But, on the other hand, Sullivan sees the 'basic humor' of the work as 'an application of a refined literary and stylistically sophisticated narrative medium to disreputable low-life adventures and sexual escapades of a number of unprincipled . . . characters.'[34] This technique is clearly a violation of the doctrine of decorum where the relationship between form and content is disrupted, and that relationship is thereby held up to scrutiny.

Moreover, Sullivan continues by noting that there is 'sometimes an incongruity . . . between the high moral sentiments, the sensible, sometimes serious literary criticism and the persons that voice them . . . || sometimes an incongruity . . . between the style of the prose or verse and the lowliness or absurdity of the incidents, or alternatively, between the high-flown declamatory style of some of the characters and the actual station or attainments in life.'[35] But this last incongruity, while again a violation of the doctrine of decorum, is, in another sense, the fulfillment of a second stylistic dictum, namely, consonance of style with character—*qualis vir, talis oratio*.[36]

The freedmen in the *Cena*, regardless of their accomplishments, speak with a style that betrays their origins. But Eumolpus, who shifts his style to suit the appropriate subject, although all his styles are appropriate to an educated man, expresses his shifting and opportunistic nature through the instability of his style.[37] Encolpius, another even more unstable character, is a better case in point. In the digressions he responds to the rhetorical nature of the subjects with rhetorical prose. Events he generally narrates in the *sermo urbanus*, but as soon as he is confronted with positive action on his own, or more precisely, when his emotions are directly involved, he generally lapses into a mock-heroic or sentimental romantic style. This lapse reveals his bookish pretensions and his corresponding naiveté about real life. This

---

[34] Sullivan (1968a: 215).   [35] Sullivan (1968a: 215–16).
[36] See George (1966: 337 and 357 n. 2).
[37] See George (1966) on Eumolpus (347–48).

stylistic habit also reflects the disparity between the actual events and his own inflated view of them. He must constantly draw his emotional responses, not from inner conviction, but from stock responses to stock situations. This perverse habit ironically calls into question the theory behind the doctrine of decorum. It calls into question the 'handbook' approach to life, much as Eumolpus' poetry calls into question the 'handbook' approach to literature. Thus Petronius uses stylistic incongruities also for genuine characterizations of his incongruous personages,[38] who, by their instability and unreality, reflect the culture which produced them.

The dense literary texture, which I noted earlier in connection with the jagged and disorderly reading rhythm, serves another even more important function. The *Satyricon*, both in style and in the themes of || some episodes, is permeated with reminiscences of other genres and other styles, ranging, in effect, through the whole of the classical tradition. The enumeration of the categories of oratory, historiography, legal and diplomatic formulae, epic, epistolography, erotic elegy, philosophical essay, satire, romance, tragedy, and comedy probably does not exhaust the list.[39] In the process, the text also touches on most of the major figures in Latin literature, with a special preference for the Augustans of the preceding age.[40] But the chief mode of literary allusion is parody in all of its different forms, a technique which distorts the primary references.

Parodistic technique has generally been considered a secondary literary activity, effective on the level of humor or of literary criticism. For in the mimetic theory put forth by Aristotle, art should imitate life, while parody 'does not imitate an action in nature; it imitates another work of art.'[41] But recently it has been shown to possess an important aesthetic of its own by its imitation of art. Parody expresses what is often inexpressible in other ways when it is practiced on its highest level by those of marked artistic merit. Cervantes, Shakespeare, Proust, Joyce, and Mann, for instance, use parody in important and primary ways.[42]

---

[38] For a discussion of Petronius' subtle discrimination in the speaking styles of his personages to reveal character, see George (1966: 336–58).

[39] For an exhaustive and sometimes overzealous list of literary allusions in the *Satyricon*, see Colligon (1892). See too Courtney (1962: 86–99) and Walsh (1970: 32–52).

[40] See Walsh (1970: 35–6). For a more detailed study of Petronius' use of Vergil and Ovid, see Zeitlin (1971: 58–82).   [41] Kiremidjian (1970: 233).

[42] See Kiremidjian's discussion (1970: 232, 234–5). On the modern writers, see, for example, Kenner (1956: 7–18) and Heller (1961: 253–90).

Parody works backwards; it dislocates the union of form and content and thus raises the larger question of the gap between 'art and life, between artifact and nature, between real and irreal,' which art has tried to solve.[43] It lays open to examination the validity of the marriage between certain art forms and certain modes of thought and action which have become legitimate for them. In the process, parodistic technique will seek to push art beyond the restrictions laid upon it by formal requirements. But parody, especially where art is closely bound up with social and cultural ideas as it was in Rome, asks || too for a scrutiny of the ideas and actions inherent in the forms. Eumolpus, as the poet, is determined to play the classical role of poet as ethical teacher. By the failure of his academic poetry, and by the gap exposed between his preachings and practice, he is the most persuasive argument for the impotence of the old forms to validate existence in a new and different age.

In Petronius the secondary form of parody is embedded in the primary form of the novel, and can make no claim to stand on its own; it must serve to make some contribution to the whole. To some critics its only contribution may be that of humor or of limited literary criticism of individuals, but it is important to note that it is 'generally at the end of a tradition when established forms are exhausted, that this kind of original [use of] parody will appear.'[44] Otherwise, when the canonical forms are still felt to be viable, then 'parody is in fact the province of poets of lesser range', used more as 'forms of homage.'[45] What parody does in this later stage is to 'dramatize the pathos of dissonance' between form and content.

It revokes in effect those relationships which would usually occur in art during periods of relative cultural health when primary forms supply the mode of expression. . . . In a culture where usurpation of function and confusion of polarities are the rule, the very instability of parody becomes the means of stabilizing the subject matter which is itself unstable and fluid, and parody becomes a major mode of expression for civilization in a state of transition and flux.[46]

For Petronius parody seems less of a stabilizer and more of a continuing statement about the cultural and spiritual crisis of his time. The past is invoked through literary allusions only to be distorted and made comic, while the literary and moral digressions, which lay claim to a 'serious' consideration, cast doubt on the validity of their

---

[43] Kiremidjian (1970: 237).   [44] Kiremidjian (1970: 240).
[45] Kiremidjian (1970: 241).   [46] Kiremidjian (1970: 242).

traditional precepts by their cliché-ridden presentations. In effect, parody in Petronius, by embracing an entire literary tradition, expresses the incongruity and absurdity of an entire culture.

The individual incongruities of Petronius' style evoke laughter from the audience. Collectively, they seem to evoke a certain sense of loss || for what was once taken for granted in a more secure and ordered world where form and content attained a stable fusion. As one critic has remarked, 'what most distinguishes the *Satyricon* is its extraordinary style, a style that is a conglomeration of every Greek and Roman style reduced to mockery and held together by that special quality' which 'is a melancholy like no other in literature . . . As a living body is sustained and nourished by its bloodstream, the style of Petronius is suffused by a sense of indefinable sorrow which haunts and corrupts all possible achievement. The nostalgia of the gutter and the melancholy of grandeur flow together and wash away the very idea of accomplishment.'[47]

Behind the anti-hero stands always the hero who once existed. Petronius' technique exposes the basic incongruity between the sordidness of reality and the literary texture which recalls a reality that no longer exists, while his disorderly conglomeration of styles reflects the confusions of the present reality as expressed in the clearest fashion by the plot and its characters.

III. CONTENT: PLOT AND CHARACTER

'Picaresque novel,' a term often used to describe the *Satyricon*, is a reference to a genre of fiction 'created' during the Renaissance in Spain and later taken up by other European writers.[48] The genre is || distinguished by an episodic plot using a first-person narrative in

---

[47] Rexroth (1969: 101).

[48] The earliest example of the picaresque novel (but considered by some critics to be proto-picaresque or a precursor of the picaresque) is the anonymous *Lazarillo de Tormes* (1554). Other notable Spanish representatives include Mateo Alemán, *Guzmán de Alfarache* (pt. I 1599, pt. II 1604), and Francisco de Quevedo, *El Buscón* (1616). A lone Elizabethan entry is Thomas Nashe, *The Unfortunate Traveller* (1594). Alain René Lesage heralds the French tradition with *Gil Blas* (1715, 1724, 1735), although most recent criticism detects many important deviations from the norm. The main German contender is Hans Jacob Christoffels von Grimmelshausen, *Der abenteuerliche Simplicissimus* (1668), which uses the historical background of the Thirty Years' War as the setting for the hero's picaresque adventures. The English tradition includes, again with reservations, Tobias Smollett, *Roderick Random* (1748) and Daniel Defoe, *Moll Flanders*

which an itinerant rogue or picaro undergoes a series of sensational low-life adventures. Strong social satire and a cynical realism are also important elements of this form, but critics, when they apply the epithet 'picaresque' to the *Satyricon*, rarely seem to consider these corollaries, nor have they investigated the larger implications of the genre.

But this is not surprising, since, in general, studies of the novel have tended to denigrate the worth of the picaresque type on the premise that, in a neo-classical evaluation based on Aristotelian doctrine, the episodic plot is not as satisfying as the causal plot of the 'realistic' novel. Recently, however, critics have adopted new attitudes towards the picaresque in which the techniques of that form are seen as expressive of a world-view which is different from that posed in the 'realistic' novel, but one that is not inferior.[49] The picaresque need not be deemed a primitive type of fiction which preceded a more mature development of prose fiction. This point is borne out by the renewal of the picaresque mode in modern fiction.[50] Picaresque form, then, like that of the *Satyricon*, represents conscious artistic choice rather than technical failure.

Although many of the observations I shall make on the *Satyricon* proceeded originally from my study of the text itself, the recent work on the picaresque novel parallels my own conclusions closely enough to warrant application of the special features belonging to the later picaresque form to the *Satyricon*. Viewing Petronius within the picaresque frame has the advantage of identifying his work as a recurrent literary phenomenon which arises in response to similar social conditions in history, which gives us a wider perspective. But, at the same time, it allows us to assess the originality of the work when placed

(1722). Henry Fielding, *Tom Jones* (1749), which owes much to the genre, is not in fact a picaresque novel.

On the history of the picaresque novel and for a more complete list of representatives of the form, see del Monte (1957) and Parker (1967). For other more detailed studies of the characteristics of the genre, see especially Alter (1964) and Miller (1967).

[49] Miller (1967: 9, 132). This contention informs his entire study of the picaresque genre in which he takes a structural and not a historical approach.

[50] More modern 'revivals' of the picaresque might include Stendhal, *Le Rouge et le noir* (1830), Mark Twain, *Huckleberry Finn* (1884), Saul Bellow, *The Adventures of Augie March* (1953), Thomas Mann, *The Confessions of Felix Krull* (1955), Joyce Cary, *The Horse's Mouth* (1944), and Ralph Ellison, *Invisible Man* (1947). One or more of the novels of Céline, Henry Miller, Thomas Pynchon, William Burroughs, Jean Genet, and Günther Grass have also been mentioned as possible contenders. But there is no general consensus on any of these later works.

in its own Roman context and within the frame of the ancient || classical tradition. Moreover, the use of the picaresque as a point of reference will enable us to see the significant variations from the type in the *Satyricon* and to gauge their import.

Plot

Picaresque form and its devices aim at projecting a view of a chaotic and disordered world. The picaresque novel sees experience as fragmented, disjointed, and unstable. It is unlike the 'realistic' novel, which, by its causal plot, projects an underlying rational principle which guides the world in which cause and effect assert a basic cosmic order in human events. It is unlike comedy in which the world is first turned topsy-turvy and made chaotic, but order is reaffirmed at the end in the re-establishment of social norms. It is unlike romance which seems to set forth a chaotic unpatterned world like that of the picaresque, for 'in romance cause and effect do operate,' although 'the probability of their operation is more remote than in the realistic novel. There is an ordering of events, but it is not a probable ordering: the wonderful romance plot unravels a complicated pattern of chance and coincidence that works mysteriously towards some end.'[51] That end is the perfect union of love which has overcome the random blows of Fortune and triumphs at the last.

The picaresque, by contrast, never really resolves the chaotic appearance of the world. Although our text of the *Satyricon* is fragmentary, ancient testimonia which presumably refer to the work as a whole, do not give the impression that a radically unpicaresque ending made any restoration of harmony or an assertion of classical values. Scurrilous and scabrous it probably remained until the end.[52]

The picaresque plot asserts that experience is ultimately devoid of order and intelligibility. Episode follows upon episode without true causal connection. The result is a kind of jagged fragmentation. Anything can and does happen, including 'the fantastic, the improbable, and the weird.'[53]

The *Satyricon* displays these same features in its variety of episodes. Think, for example, of the *Cena* which ranges back and forth between || the realistic and the grotesque, of the bizarre scenes on board the

[51] Miller (1967: 10).
[52] See Sullivan (1968a: 77), and see his collection of ancient testimonia (111–14).
[53] Miller (1967: 10).

ship, and of the surrealistic quality of the Croton adventure. As in the picaresque, 'nothing strictly *happens*. The . . . plot merely records fragmented happening after fragmented happening.'[54] This impression of fragmentation in the *Satyricon* is magnified by the mutilated state of the text, but transitions, when they occur (as after the *Cena* 79), only reinforce the impression of haphazard adventure.[55]

Generally, characters appear and disappear in the *Satyricon*, as in the picaresque, with no lasting effects. Once the trio has given Agamemnon the slip at the end of the *Cena* (78. 8), we hear no further allusion to him. Quartilla fades from view just as effortlessly. When characters make a brief reappearance, they do so purely by coincidence, and there is no guarantee of an orderly pattern to the hero's experience which might give it some coherence. What emerges instead is a 'dance pattern' which teases us with the possibility of a meaningful pattern but which is then denied.[56] The unwelcome reunion with Lichas and Tryphaena is an example of this device. After the furor and the commotion die down, the corpse of Lichas is washed up on the shore to provide a starting point for mock philosophical remarks on the human condition (115. 7–20), but then it is cremated and forgotten. The characters assume new roles and turn resolutely towards the new adventure in Croton.

In the *Satyricon* a variation of the 'dance pattern' occurs among the main characters themselves which lends a frenetic pace to the proceedings. Encolpius and his companions rapidly come and go, now finding each other, now losing each other. They shift alliances and sexual liaisons. Ascyltos steals away from Encolpius at the rhetorical discussion (6. 1) and meets him again coincidentally at the brothel (7. 4). The two quarrel over Giton and plan to break up the threesome. This solution is postponed (10. 4–7), but later Giton goes with Ascyltos leaving the astounded Encolpius alone (80. 5–8). Giton then returns to Encolpius at the inn (91. 1–7); soon Ascyltos comes to look for Giton (97. 1–3). Giton and Encolpius make their escape with Eumolpus, the new third man and the new rival for Giton (99. 4–6). Ascyltos ‖ now disappears never to reappear in the extant text. Many other more temporary combinations are possible too—in the orgy scene with Quartilla, on board the ship, and in Croton. Circe is exchanged

---

[54] Miller (1967: 12).

[55] Perhaps this is why the frequent lacunae in the text do not, for the most part, seriously diminish the reader's enjoyment or even comprehension.

[56] On the 'dance pattern,' see Miller (1967: 13–20).

for Chrysis, and so on. This type of complicated but ultimately meaningless 'dance pattern' points to the inability of the hero and his companions to form lasting emotional ties and will be examined further
in a later discussion of character.

Not only is the plot disjointed and episodic; it is frequently punc-
tuated by digressions of varying sorts, which, as I mentioned in the
analysis of style, contributes to a jagged reading rhythm and which
makes the action appear still more episodic.

Another device often used to enhance the chaos of the episodic
plot is the rapid pace of action. Events pile upon events within a given
episode and have 'the effect of dazzling both reader and picaro with
the accumulated chaos of life's action.'[57] This happens frequently in
the *Satyricon*. For example, in the Quartilla episode (16–26. 6) Quartilla
enters unexpectedly with a maid and a small serving girl and tricks
the three male characters into an orgy. Catamites enter and add
to the confusion. More attendants enter, a banquet begins, and after
further sexual antics, they all fall asleep—but only for a short while.
Two thieves burst in, wreak havoc, and wake everyone up, but they
avoid detection by another trick. Festivities are renewed; more entertainers come in, another catamite follows, and Giton is finally paired
off with the young serving girl, while Quartilla continues her amat-
ory games. The scene breaks off here and further chaos probably followed to put an end to the episode.

The element of slapstick in the orgy is tempered by the rapid succession of unpleasant tricks and the unwelcome assaults upon the characters.[58] Tricks and random violence are commonplace events of the
picaresque world. The world is shown to be chaotic and illusory, and
the hero can and must adapt to it by playing his own tricks. The scene
at the inn after the pinacotheca episode shows an elaborate pattern
of tricks and countertricks (92–9). Characters are locked in and out,
a mock suicide is enacted, violence erupts. The confusion ‖ grows apace
as more and more characters become involved, until finally, after a
temporary reconciliation, escape is made to a new chaotic experience
on board the ship, which itself follows a variation of the same pattern.

Episodes are not resolved; they disintegrate. Often events get out of
hand, and the hasty exit of the hero and his confrères concludes the

---

[57] Miller (1967: 21), and see his discussion of the rhythm in picaresque novels
(21–7).
[58] See especially *Sat.* 20, 21. 1–3, 26. 7. On the prevalence of physical violence in
the picaresque novel as a reflection of social disorder, see Alter (1964: 66).

scene. Something like this must have happened in the brothel scene
(8. 4). It happens at the end of the *Cena* (78. 5–8), and in the pinacotheca (90. 1). The sea storm, that universal image of turbulence,
puts an end to the entanglements on board the ship (114–115. 5). It
happens again at the end of the Oenothea scene (138. 3–4).

Typically, unpredictable and often unpleasant accidents occur
which further emphasize the chaotic and even malevolent aspect
of reality. Violence, assault, or punishment far out of proportion to
the so-called 'crime' is a familiar pattern in the picaresque as in the
Satyricon. For instance, Oenothea, the witch, tumbles off a rotten stool
and crashes down on the hearth. The neck of the pot breaks and puts
out the fire. Oenothea is singed by a burning coal and rushes off to
get some live embers for the fire. Meanwhile, Encolpius is attacked by
some angry geese and he batters the leader of the flock to death,
unaware that it is a sacred bird (136. 1–5).

Violence inflicted upon the hero most often takes place within the
sexual milieu. These sexual scenes are usually regarded as pornographic,
but the patterning of unpredictable sexual tricks or accidents assault
the hero rather than arouse him. The whole sadistic tenor of the
Quartilla scene is an obvious example (especially 21. 1, 26. 7).
Encolpius' brief rendezvous with Giton is interrupted by Ascyltos
who suddenly bursts into the room and threatens Encolpius with a
lashing (11). Encolpius' impotence earns him a flogging ordered by
Circe (132. 2–4), and the treatments prescribed for his ailment by both
Proselenos and Oenothea involve unpleasant violence (131. 4–6,
134. 3–6, 138. 1–2).[59] Verbal assaults are common too throughout
(9. 6–9, 57. 1–3, 58, 81. 4–5). ‖

---

[59] Sullivan's treatment of the pornographic elements of the *Satyricon* isolates
voyeurism and exhibitionism as the chief perversions, which he interprets as peculiarit-
ies of Petronius himself (238–53). Since he stands virtually alone among Petronian
scholars in his willingness to discuss this hitherto taboo subject, other critics have
accepted his conclusions without any further qualifications (e.g., Walsh and Cameron).
His theory can be questioned on several grounds. First of all, voyeurism and exhibitionism are only minor motifs in the range of pornographic situations which Petronius
sets before us. Second of all, these two acts are integral ingredients of any pornographic
work which typically includes orgies and other scenes of group sex. (See Kronhausen
(1964: 228–84, 314–15.) The extant portions of the *Satyricon* present rather the
multiplicity and variety of sexual possibilities with the attendant breaking of taboos
which are the major distinguishing marks of pornographic literature in any age.
Homosexual and heterosexual encounters, brothels, composite sexual scenes, incest motifs
(Philomela's offspring), seduction of children (the defloration of Pannychis, the
Pergamene boy), the permissive mother figure (Philomela), sadism, flagellation, inversion of religious ritual, even mild necrophilia (the Widow of Ephesus) and so on are all

A particular device used in the *Satyricon* to heighten the senseless drift of experience might be seen in the recurrent pattern of Encolpius losing his way. The first time he ends up in a brothel (6. 3–7. 4), the second time in a fishpond (72. 7–73. 2). The third time he is rescued by Giton's forethought in marking out the way with chalk, but not until he and his companions have dragged their bleeding feet for nearly a whole hour over the flints and broken pots which lie out in the road (79. 1–5).

The last pattern which contributes to the general impression of chaos in the world is the rapid change in the hero's own fortunes. Events constantly assault the hero, but he cannot ultimately claim control over them. 'His fortune goes up or down as it pleases. His fate is in the lap of the gods, but the gods are continually dropping it' which leads to a 'senseless and unstoppable whirling.'[60]

Fortuna is often invoked in the *Satyricon*. 'O lusum Fortunae mirabilem,' exclaims Encolpius at the discovery of the long-lost tunic (13. 1). After the loss of Giton, he observes: 'non multum oportet consilio credere, ‖ quia suam habet Fortuna rationem' (82. 6). He reacts in a similar way to the recognition of Lichas' voice (100. 3, 101. 1). When the storm begins, he laments that Fortune will not even allow Giton and himself to die in a lovers' embrace (114. 8). His speech over the corpse of Lichas rhetorically elevates the theme of the mutability of men's fortunes (115. 8–17). But his genuine awareness of his precarious position is revealed in the skeptical attitude he takes towards his present good fortune in Croton (125):

Eumolpus, drunk with his success, had so far forgotten the past that he began to boast to his intimates that no one in Croton dared to cross him and that, for any crimes we might commit, he could easily get us off through the

---

found in Petronius in addition to the incidents of voyeurism and exhibitionism. The most striking characteristics of almost all these encounters in Petronius, however, are the high level of sadism involved and the generally low level of satisfaction obtained. The pornographic imagination projects fantasies of super-sexual prowess (size and performance), not random assault and impotence. It also projects its characters as willing or at least acquiescent participants in almost every type of sexual activity. The two Milesian tales with their successful consummations which both partners eventually enjoy are representative of the usual pornographic scheme. The Circe episode, on the other hand, is an excellent example of Petronian adaptation (or perhaps parody?) of pornographic material. What should be a typical pornographic experience turns instead into failure, humiliation, and rejection. Most often, sex in the *Satyricon* is either a source of frustration or an assault upon an unwilling victim. See below in the discussion of character for further implications of Encolpius' impotence.

[60] Miller (1967: 28).

influence of his new friends. For my part, thanks to the excellent food and the other gifts which Fortune showered on us in prodigious profusion, I had begun to put on weight again and had almost convinced myself that luck was no longer my enemy. Still, I couldn't help reflecting now and then on our present life and how it had come about. 'What would happen,' I used to wonder, 'if one of these legacy-chasers had the wit to send off to Africa for information and then exposed us? Or suppose Eumolpus' hired servant got bored with his present luck and dropped a hint to his friends, or gave the whole show away out of spite? No mistake about it: we'd have to run for it, right back to our old life of poverty. Why, we'd have to start begging again. And, gods in heaven, an outlaw's life is a miserable business. Always waiting to be punished . . .' (tr. Arrowsmith).

This concept of a cruel and random fortune contradicts the view that the *Satyricon* is patterned on a comic wrath of Priapus which would make some sense of Encolpius' adventures.[61] But if one takes the wrath of Priapus as a single motif, rather than as a controlling frame,[62] an incongruous analogy to the *Odyssey* rather than an accepted fact, the Fortuna theme retains its primary force as an expression of the perilous chaos of the world.

The objective devices of a picaresque plot—the rush of events, the jagged reading rhythm, the accidents and sudden violence, and references to a malevolent Fortuna—all interact to project a chaotic ‖ sense of reality. Furthermore, the picaresque world is illusory and unreal. It is a world of appearances, tricks, deceptions, and counter-deceptions. Nothing and no one turns out to be what it or he seems. Hence arises the prominent element of satire in the picaresque genre which strips off the mask and reveals the hypocrisy of society and its members. All the conventional values and conventions of respectability are exposed. The insistent theme in the picaresque and in the *Satyricon* is that the world is roguish.

The respectable *matrona* tricks Encolpius and brings him to a brothel (6. 4–7. 2). An equally unassuming *paterfamilias* deceives Ascyltos in the same way (8. 2–3). Philomela, another *matrona*, acts as procuress for her daughter, after age has withered her charms (140. 1–4). The Widow of Ephesus deceives her neighbors and relatives, thereby proving the inconstancy of womankind (111–12). The earnest tutor wins the family's confidence only to corrupt the Pergamene boy by his tricks (85–7). The idealized goddess-figure Circe has a taste

---

[61] This is the theory first proposed by Klebs (1889).
[62] See Sullivan (1968a: 93).

for vulgarity (126. 1–7). The innocence of youth too is unmasked in the person of the Pergamene boy who proves an apt pupil, while Giton's modest demeanor and coy naiveté hide his unscrupulous manipulations.

Institutions are similarly treated both in the picaresque and in the *Satyricon*. Justice guaranteed by due process of law is rightly suspected by Ascyltos and the others (14. 1–2; cf. 15. 2–5). Religion is exposed as a fraud by its lecherous priestess Quartilla. She bemoans sacrilege but prescribes an orgy as mock expiation and as remedy for her ague (16. 2–18. 5). Oenothea's wrath at the killing of the goose is immediately assuaged by the offer of money (137. 5–9). Philosophical dogmas are held up to ridicule as are the philosophers, and moralists receive the same unmasking. Traditional education is attacked, and the rhetorician is shown unequal to his preaching. Likewise, the traditional theories of art, as I have pointed out earlier, are shown to be clusters of clichés and the poet who follows those precepts turns out jejune verses. Eumolpus is no ethical guide of men; he is a corrupt teacher.[63] In addition to the exposure of the favorite Roman traditions of prescriptive ethical and aesthetic theory, Roman political ‖ ideology, centering about the fall of Troy and the Civil War, is slyly emptied of its meaning and subverted.[64]

In its revelation of social and intellectual hypocrisy, the *Satyricon* serves to 'break up the lumber of stereotypes, fossilized beliefs, superstitious terrors, crank theories, pedantic dogmatism [and] oppressive fashions,'[65] thus performing an important function of satire and irony. But when the *Satyricon*, by its accidents, tricks, and chaotic events, shows the world in general to be a chaos of appearances, it takes up the function of a still more radical irony. The 'technique of disintegration' is used to cast doubt 'even on ordinary common sense as the standard. For common sense too has certain implied dogmas, notably that the data of sense experience are reliable and consistent, and that our customary associations with things form a solid basis for interpreting the present and predicting the future. . . .'[66] 'In the riotous chaos of . . . Petronius [and others],' Frye finds that 'satire plunges through to its final victory over common sense. When we have finished with their weirdly logical fantasies of debauch, dream, and

---

[63] On the roguishness of society and its institutions in the picaresque vision, see Alter (1964: 94–5).   [64] For this thesis, see Zeitlin (1971: 56–82).

[65] Frye (1957: 233). In his scheme, this type of activity is termed 'second-phase irony.'

[66] Frye (1957: 234). This technique of disintegration characterizes 'third-phase irony.'

delirium we wake up wondering if Paracelsus' suggestion is right
that the things seen in delirium are really there, like stars in the day-
time and invisible for the same reasons.'[67] Petronius, by his various
picaresque devices, uses satire and irony in his novel to show that 'heroism and effective action are absent, disorganized or foredoomed to defeat,
and that confusion and anarchy reign over the world.'[68]

The Cena *as Microcosm*

The *Cena* has often been treated separately from the rest of the
work both because it is a digression in the adventures of Encolpius
and because of its realistic language and portraiture. But I have
deliberately deferred consideration of the *Cena* until the picaresque
world-view || in the *Satyricon* was outlined. For the *Cena* provides a
microcosm of the larger world confronting Encolpius, and it does so
on several different ironic levels. Seen as a whole, the *Cena* represents
a shifting, unreliable, and unpredictable reality.

The host, Trimalchio, is himself a shifting character, unstable and
arbitrary, who now blows hot, now cold. He is capricious, for
instance, in his treatment of his wife. He is even more capricious in
his treatment of his slaves, playing now the tyrant, now the benefactor.[69]
But even his harsh actions towards his slaves are suspect, since the
anger is more than often feigned or, at least, assuaged with ease. He
vacillates between vulgarity and attempts at erudition. Above all, he
alternates between pretensions to greater status than he actually has
and his pride in his humble beginnings.

Trimalchio is a master impresario of tricks, deceits, and disguises.
The *trompe l'œil* painting of the dog which terrifies Encolpius (29. 1)
is an emblem of this theme of deception and illusion which continues
throughout the *Cena*. The dishes are never what they seem; they invariably conceal something else within. As has been pointed out, the
archetypal artist Daedalus is reduced to the cook who metamorphoses pork into a myriad of other forms.[70] Moreover, the presentation of the dishes and of the other events at the *Cena* is usually

---

[67] Frye (1957: 235). The Croton episode fits into his category of 'sixth-phase
irony'—demonic epiphany with its image of the 'femme fatale' and its setting of 'the
city of dreadful night in the desert' (238–9).

[68] Frye (1957: 192). He sees this as the archetypal theme of satire and irony.

[69] 'Interdiu severa, nunc hilaria' (64. 13). See Walsh's (1970) analysis of
Trimalchio (129–30), and see Rankin (1970: 135–6).

[70] Cameron (1970: 406–7) on *Sat.* 70. 1–2.

carefully staged, but designed to simulate spontaneity, which reinforces the resemblance to real life.

Deceit and disguise are expressed on still another level in the digressive stories of the werewolf and the changeling boy (61. 6–62, 63. 3–10). No one is what he seems; human forms are unstable, and beneath the humorous veneer lies the uneasy sensation that the world is not rational or coherent.[71] When Trimalchio philosophizes that, ‖ after literature, the hardest professions are those of the doctor and of the moneychanger, because the doctor must know the insides of men and a moneychanger must see the copper beneath the silver (56. 1–3), he is only reacting to a world whose reality proves to be illusory and counterfeit, and, therefore, ultimately unintelligible.

This chaotic reality is mirrored in the *Cena* by the constant series of planned and occasionally unplanned surprises. Ceilings yawn to discharge their contents; acrobats and other entertainers perform their tricks; riddles and puns are visually enacted. Dogs burst in; thrushes fly out. The steward of the estate intrudes unexpectedly into the banquet milieu with his reading of the daily gazette (53. 1–10). Each new presentation promises a new derangement of sensibilities.

Accidents, too, both planned and unplanned, add to the chaotic atmosphere. Violence and assault are often feigned but sometimes real. Proposed punishments are too extravagant for offenses both real and imaginary, or the slave is punished ultimately for a different and more trivial offense. A cook is threatened with a flogging for his stupidity in having forgotten to gut the pig, when, in truth, he has substituted sausages and blood puddings for entrails (49–50. 1). But dishes are dropped (34. 2–3, 52. 3–4), and a clumsy acrobat injures Trimalchio (54. 1–2). Dogs first enter on cue in a hunting tableau to introduce a dish of game (40. 1–4). But later, Scylax, Trimalchio's huge dog, is brought in. A real dog-fight ensues, which ends in the upsetting of a lamp and the breaking of glassware, while some of the guests are unpleasantly spattered with oil (64. 6–10). Two boys simulate a quarrel and smash each other's water pots only to release

---

[71] On the theme of metamorphosis, see especially Arrowsmith (1966: 311–12 and 315). See also Zeitlin (1971: 63).

In Ovid, metamorphosis is a change to a permanent new state of being. In Petronius, change is only temporary and hence unreliable. (I am indebted to Ronald Kopnicki for this observation.) Cf. too the metamorphosis of Lucius at the end of Apuleius' novel. On the general meaning of metamorphosis in antiquity, see Rüdiger, 'Nachwort', in Rode (1960: 517–59).

a cascade of oysters and cockles for the guests (70. 4–6). But later Trimalchio quarrels with Fortunata in earnest and hurls a cup in her face (74. 8–11). This type of real violence is concentrated towards the end of the *Cena* as the outside world begins to intrude more and more, and Trimalchio, the stage director, begins to lose control over the proceedings.

The rhythm of the picaresque world is maintained in the hectic 'rush of events.' Slaves move with lightning speed; dishes are whisked in and out; foods are prepared and cooked in an instant. Conversations interrupt the flow of events at irregular intervals, and the whole episodic effect is one of frenetic assault on the guests. One || event of staged chaos follows on the heels of another until the fire brigade, deceived as to the meaning of the trumpet blast, rushes in and hacks down the doors, making a grand finale of unstaged chaos (78. 5–8). The real world finally destroys the artificial world staged at the banquet, but, on closer inspection, the two are found to be the same. Thus artifice and nature both support and reinforce each other, while each casts doubt on the reality of the other with an ironic ambiguity. The *Cena* shows life to be a *theatrum mundi*, a theme that runs through the *Satyricon* in the frequent references to the mime and the stage.[72]

Another aspect of the *Satyricon*'s world-view is also stressed in the *Cena*. Incongruities and confusions appear on many levels. Like the *trompe l'œil* painting of the dog which is paradigmatic of the theme of illusion, the motif of incongruity is signalled at the very beginning of the episode by the paintings of the *Iliad* and the *Odyssey* grouped with one that depicts the gladiatorial games (29. 9). Colors are juxtaposed in jarring combinations. Slaves recline with guests at the table.

The verbal level is often confused. Here too vulgarity alternates with feigned refinement. Greek and Latin are intermixed. The freedmen ramble on at will on a variety of topics. The long speech of Echion, for instance, has an effect that is close to a stream-of-consciousness (45–6). Jokes and poor puns proliferate, confusing the primary meaning of words. Trimalchio leaps from subject to subject as the fancy strikes him. Aetiologies are distorted; chronologies and characters of myth and history are confounded. The colloquial speech in the *Cena* has been praised for its faithful reproduction of vulgar diction, but this trait too supports the confused and disorganized impression of the outside world which invades the formal literary symposium.

---

[72] See Walsh (1970: 24–5) and *Sat.* 19. 1, 80. 9, 94. 15, 106. 1, 117. 4.

Moreover, there is a confusion of modalities. The basic one involves a confusion between life and death which frames the *Cena* and which is thematically developed throughout, and this confusion reaches its climax in the great scene at the end of the banquet in which the feast turns into a mock funeral for Trimalchio (77. 7–78. 1–7).[73]

Encolpius reacts to the staged microcosm of chaos and illusion with || amazement, terror, consternation, anxiety, apprehension, bewilderment, disgust, and only rarely with laughter, not unlike his reactions to events in the outside world.[74] It is only the enlarged scale and the concentrated focus of the *Cena* that make it different from the other episodes in this respect.

But there is still another level on which the *Cena* operates which makes the microcosmic analogy even more cogent. Encolpius is an outsider to the milieu of the freedmen at the banquet. Even if his role of *scholasticus* is an assumed one, his educational training and his outlook put him into a different category. The picaro's position is inevitably that of a misfit in society who wanders through life freed from the normal restraints and obligations imposed on respectable people. It is this position as a marginal man which allows the picaro his delicious satiric view of a hierarchical system. Encolpius, in this role, can observe the antics at the banquet and can present a detached view of the proceedings.

But the particular society into which Encolpius is thrust in the *Cena*, while a discernible and defined stratum of the social heap, is itself a marginal and precarious one, which can thus mirror, to some extent, the position of the picaro. Freedmen are torn between two worlds —that of slavery and that of freedom and respectability. The guests at the *Cena* constantly reveal their anxiety at their ambiguous status. The frequent definitions of what a man really is, the insistence on the theme of *libertas* in jest and in earnest,[75] and the proud statement of one freedman that he was a slave for forty years, but no one could tell whether he was a slave or a free man (57. 9) are expressions of this deep preoccupation.

The key to status, in their eyes, is the acquisition of wealth, but wealth itself is a shifting and variable commodity, subject finally to the

---

[73] See Arrowsmith (1966: 306–12), for a fuller exposition of this point.

[74] Veyne (1964: 301–6) contends that Encolpius' reactions to the *Cena* as narrator display a false naiveté in contrast to his behavior in the rest of the text. See Sullivan (1968a: 215) for a more accurate description.

[75] See especially 40. 3–41. 4, 41. 6–8, and 71. 1–2.

whims of Fortune. Capricious Fortuna, here more than elsewhere in the extant text, is felt to be the determining factor in man's fate. A man may be a millionaire one day and a pauper the next. Speculation may succeed, but failure is possible too. The memory of poverty || and slavery haunts them. One can try to stave off the effects of Fortuna by learning a trade, by asserting the value of initiative and hard work, but luck is always needed.

Auerbach has commented upon this concept of changing fortunes, no longer viewed against the classical stable social order, but now seen as historical change against a background of social disorder. 'For him [the freedman], the world is in ceaseless motion, nothing is certain, and wealth and social position are highly unstable.'[76] He further notes that prior to Petronius 'in the mimetic literary art of antiquity, the instability of fortune almost always appears as a fate which strikes from without and affects only a limited area [and a few special individuals], not as a fate which results from the inner processes of the real, historical world.'[77] In the narrative which Auerbach cites (37–8. 1–12)

four persons are mentioned who are all in the same boat, all engaged in the same turbulent pursuit of unstable Fortune. Though each of them individually has his private destiny, their destinies are all similar; their lot, for all its turbulence, is the common lot, common and vulgar. And behind the four persons who are described, we see the entire company, every member of which, we surmise, has a similar destiny which can be described in similar terms. Behind them again, we see in imagination a whole world of similar lives, and finally find ourselves contemplating an extremely animated historico-economic picture of the perpetual ups and downs of a mob of fortune-hunters scrambling after wealth and stupid pleasures. . . . Such a society most clearly reflects the ups and downs of existence, because there is nothing to hold the balance for it; its members have neither inward tradition nor outer stability; they are nothing without money.[78]

Thus, the *Cena*, as microcosm of an unstable and illusory reality, moves up to still another plane—that of a reflection of the general society itself in which Encolpius, another reflection of that society, moves. The values of the freedmen are not very different from those of the *ingenui* or those of the society as a whole. Money is everywhere the standard by which men are judged in the *Satyricon*. Even the gods || are not immune (88. 10). All dream of hidden treasure (38. 8,

---

[76] Auerbach (1953: 28).   [77] Auerbach (1953: 29).
[78] Auerbach (1953: 29–30).

88. 8, 128. 6), and the imposture of Eumolpus in that grotesque
world of legacy hunters, where all pretense to any other interest in
life is abandoned (116. 3–9), only confirms the social norm. The
freedmen aim for status and respectability, and while their distortions
of elegance and taste demonstrate the gulf that yawns between them
and the stable upper classes, their preoccupations are the same, and,
at least, admitted with greater honesty. The satire of the *Cena* can move
in the other direction to expose the foibles of the dominant group.
For if the freedmen must ape the mores of established society, generally, in their values and aspirations, and specifically, in the staging of
a banquet extravagant in its excesses and ostentation, the society itself,
which they are so desperate to join, becomes the primary target of the
satiric barb.

Encolpius, as picaro, is freed from the rat race for wealth and status. He is well aware of the degradations and dangers of poverty, but
he never seeks to acquire wealth for its own sake. He travels light, as
picaros do, but he has his own non-picaresque illusions and pretensions which weigh him down with invisible baggage and prevent him
from forming any realistic view of the inconstant world.

In the *Cena*, the pretensions to literature and to philosophy satirize
the gaucherie of the freedmen, but the inadequacy of these standards
as a sign of aristocracy and *humanitas* is also mocked. There are
important flashes of this ironic insight in the *Cena*, when *rhetores* and
obsonatores end up under the same zodiacal sign (39. 12; cf. 39. 5),
where practical education is praised, with some truth, over aspirations
to higher culture (46. 3–8, 58. 7–14), and above all, when the freedmen, in turn, expose the hollow pretensions of the *scholastici* guests
(48. 4–6, 57. 8–11).

Thus, the *Cena*, on several levels, serves as a microcosm of the world
of the *Satyricon*. The external techniques of Petronius—the mixture
of styles and genres,[79] the episodic, irregular 'rush of events,' and the
succession of tricks, deceits, and illusions—convey a sense of disordered chaos. The *Cena* reveals the world of the freedmen and the world
of society at large as a chaos of appearances. But it also exposes the
picaresque hero as another chaos of appearances. To assess the ‖ importance of his unmasking, we must now turn to an examination of the
character of the picaresque hero.

---

[79] This is seen in the new use of the symposium form, the variety of intellectual topics
covered by Trimalchio and his guests, and by the different kinds of verse insertions.

Character

An examination of the characterization of Encolpius and his friends might best be conducted by viewing their personalities against the typical traits of the picaresque hero. Then it can be shown how, in many instances, Encolpius never learns to be a true picaro, and therein lies the special quality of the *Satyricon*, and perhaps the meaning of its message.

The picaro, as mentioned earlier, is inherently an outsider to his society—an outsider who lives on its fringes, exploits its hierarchical structure, but is not enslaved by it. He 'is an inveterate displaced person. He has no home, no calling, no sure set of values.'[80] He is mobile, burdened with few material possessions (10. 4), and is always ready to move on with the episodic flow of life. He has no fixed destination or purpose which would give coherence to his trials and adventures.

In order to survive in the disordered and chaotic world, the protagonist must be able to divine the roguishness of the world and to guarantee his own existence by joining it as a rogue. The world provides his education as a picaro, and this 'pattern of education by the world reflects on the world more than on the picaro. . . . In affirming the world's outer chaos by becoming a picaro, the hero gives up hope of personality and order. Having become a manipulator of appearances, the picaresque character settles into the non-reality of becoming an appearance itself.'[81]

The picaro or rogue is a scoundrel, a delinquent, but not a criminal who does harm for its own sake.[82] The pressure of outward events often engenders the roguish pattern. Hunger, for instance, is an effective goad in the picaresque novel,[83] and Encolpius, in his prayer to ‖ Priapus, pleads straitened circumstances as justification for his transgressions (133, lines 6–9).[84]

The world is full of illusions in which the picaro is assailed by tricks of all kinds, as Encolpius is tricked by the old lady at the beginning, by Quartilla, by the events in the *Cena*, by Ascyltos, by Giton, and later by Eumolpus. In retaliation, the picaro learns to play tricks too.

---

[80] Alter (1964: 123).   [81] Miller (1967: 56–7).

[82] See Parker (1967: 3–6).

[83] Hunger is a dominant element in the Spanish picaresque novels. On this theme in *Lazarillo de Tormes*, see Alter (1964: 1–10). Cf. too *El Buscón*, esp. chs. 3 and 4.

[84] See Sullivan (1968: 40–2) on speculations as to Encolpius' earlier role at Massilia as ritual scapegoat. The victim is fed at public expense for a year before being driven from the city.

Encolpius, however, shows only a limited aptitude for trickery, and one that is also not initiatory but collaborative. In the marketplace (12–15), in the plans for disguise on board the ship (101. 6–103. 5), and in the preparations for the mime at Croton (117. 1–10), he follows along with the schemes of others. In this respect, he never completes his picaresque education, but retains a fundamental naiveté. He is an intermittent rogue, who never masters the art of gratuitous trickery, and yet neither does he remain virtuous and incorruptible.

In order to meet the shifting picaresque world, the picaro must and does assume 'protean forms.' He should be adept at role-playing and disguise. 'Typically, he can turn his hand to anything, assume the disguise of every profession and vocation.'[85] The picaro often takes on the slave or servant role under a succession of masters. For

the servant's position offers him the opportunity both to observe and to take advantage of society without being concerned with many of the demands that society makes on the individuals belonging to it. Servitude implies, among other things, irresponsibility. The picaro takes what he can from others because he never collects the various kinds of baggage of his 'own' which would encumber him. Servitude allows him in this way to be his own master, in fact, though not in form, as he could not be were he to take a 'respectable' place in society. . . . By voluntarily becoming a serving man he retires from the general scramble for status and respect and puts himself in a position to survey that scramble with great clarity.[86]

Encolpius is only a partial picaro, for, at least, in the extant portions of the text, he poses mainly as a *scholasticus* and only twice briefly as a || slave. Here his intellectual pretensions preclude him from assuming a lowly role for long or in earnest. The picaro is most often a member of the lower classes, generally a young man with too high a degree of intelligence or education for his station.[87] Encolpius and his friends, on the other hand, can be characterized as 'bohemians— the unemployable, overeducated, miseducated members of the *lumpen* intelligentsia.'[88] Thus when Encolpius adopts the role of slave, he does so not so much as a change in form, but as the playing of a trick.

[85] Miller (1967: 70).   [86] Alter (1964: 16–17).

[87] See Miller (1967) on the origins of the typical picaresque hero (47–55). Unless Encolpius were a thoroughgoing impostor (and the organization of his personality seems to preclude this), his educational training and his outlook would seem to indicate at least an upper middle-class background.

[88] Rexroth (1969: 101), who remarks that Encolpius and his friends are the first of their kind in literature, but they are not, as he states, to become 'the common characters of all picaresque romances.'

On board the ship Encolpius and Giton pose temporarily as branded fugitive slaves to avoid detection. Ironically, the disguise closely approximates reality, for, in the eyes of Lichas and Tryphaena, they are fugitives from justice, but their disgrace is short-lived. In the second instance, Encolpius' role as a slave in Croton is part of a more commodious trick in which the master is also fictitious. This type of role playing seems to be more of a comic adjustment to society without a real sacrifice of integrity of personality.[89] Encolpius remains a figure who looks at society *de haut en bas*, although it will be shown that it is this view which is ultimately illusionary.

The true picaro becomes radically 'other-directed,' and as 'the infinitely adaptable man . . . he sits on the pole furthest from integrity. He speaks of the thousand daily compromises we make with reality, of our lack of true inner stability, our lack of self, our lack of heroism.'[90] In later literature, the hero, no longer a true picaresque figure, may vacillate between 'protean disguiser or adjuster to circumstances, and the adamant inner directed romance hero' as is the case, for instance, || with Smollett's *Roderick Random*.[91] But Roderick Random finds himself in a true romance situation with his beloved Narcissa, while Encolpius' romantic view of his sordid and unromantic liaisons is only an illusion on his part. Giton, Ascyltos, and Circe may speak in the same terms as Encolpius, but they are not fundamentally deceived by their illusions. Consequently, their behavior approaches role-playing of romantic parodies, while Encolpius genuinely suffers.[92] This is the single most radical difference between

[89] Miller (1967: 75) on the character of Gil Blas. Encolpius is never called upon to perform the duties required of a slave, or to remain for long in a servile imposture. He plays only a temporary game. On the other hand, Lucius in *The Golden Ass*, by his transformation into an ass, a beast of burden, is compelled to endure the real hardships engendered by his situation.

[90] Miller (1967: 72). 'The picaresque character is not merely a rogue, and his chaos of personality is greater than any purely moral chaos. It reflects a total lack of structure in the world, not merely a lack of ethical or social structure' (Miller 1967: 131).

[91] See Miller's (1967) analysis of the shift in Roderick Random's character (93–4), and Alter (1964: 77–9).

[92] Giton expresses himself in the same type of literary language that Encolpius uses (George 1966: 338–42) but he does so as an adaptation to his situation, not as an indication of his outlook on life. He has rather a 'cynical self-centeredness and a bland insolence which might ensure his survival and perhaps even make his fortune' (Rankin 1970: 133). Love for him is a pose, an attitude by which he ingratiates himself with others and gratifies his own narcissistic desires. Encolpius, on the other hand, despite the extravagant hollowness of his language, is genuinely infatuated with the boy, and his jealousy is not feigned.

Encolpius and the picaro. Picaros harbor no illusions, and are willing 'to deal with the world on its own corrupt terms.'[93] But Encolpius, when events touch him personally, relinquishes the picaresque view in favor of self delusion. Yet the chaotic reality of his circumstances divined beneath his romantic outlook remains recognizably picaresque. In the *Satyricon* it is only the picaro who does not acquiesce in the full acceptance of this world, but, at the same time, he does not possess the internal stability with which to resist the circumstances of that world.

One of the prominent traits of the picaro is his loneliness and fundamental lack of real love. Real attachment to others provides a meaningful haven of security in the chaotic rush of life. For a picaro, the lack of attachment is 'a practical reaction to the disorder [in the world]. If things are chaotic outside, one cannot practically attach oneself to any person or thing; Fortune will blast all attachments, or other men will be revealed as unable to reciprocate love. . . . The unanchored self (or non-self) is the only possible self in such a world.'[94] Feeling for others exists, even compassion, or 'a gesture in the direction of human solidarity, but it is scarcely an emotional attachment ‖ that organizes the picaro's psyche or behavior in any deeper or lasting way.'[95]

Encolpius forms no lasting relationships despite his illusions, nor do any of his friends. The 'dance pattern' of these shifting alliances, as I have pointed out earlier, is symptomatic of this instability of personality. Giton plays off Ascyltos and later Eumolpus against Encolpius. Ascyltos steals Giton away but is later seen in the baths going home with the highest bidder for his prodigious equipment (92. 7–10). Encolpius, who might have us believe otherwise, was involved in some relationship with Tryphaena, Lichas, and Lichas' wife, and later with Ascyltos before taking up the liaison in earnest with Giton.[96] In Croton he shifts back and forth between Giton and Circe. In fact, his ambivalence as a bisexual is indicative of his basic instability. Although, by his reactions and by his language, he distinguishes between the random sexual escapades (which we have seen as further evidence of a chaotic world), and those attachments in which he is emotionally involved, he cannot remain for long with those passions which he persists in viewing as genuine romantic loves. Thus the loneliness that he experiences after the loss of Giton (81. 1–3), in

---

[93] Alter (1964: 110).   [94] Miller (1967: 78).
[95] Miller (1967: 79), and see Alter (1964: 10).
[96] *Sat.* 105. 9, 106. 2, 108. 11, 113. 3 and see Sullivan (1968*a*: 43–4).

ACCOUNT SALE   001 001   0352808
CASHIER: TAMARA   01/21/02 15:21

01 PALM V KEYBOARD
      530 10417751   1 N   99.00
02 GREAT JONES/REMAINDER
      290 10341513   1 N   5.95
03 POWELLS CHI/REMAINDER
      290 10364697   1 N   9.95
Tax Exempt: 930386908

                  Subtotal   114.90

     Items   3   Total   114.90

A/R CHARGE   114.90
  Cust: JUDAIC STUDIES RESEARCH
  Acct: DEPARTMENTAL
  Bal: -114.90

                  Change Due   0.00

        THANK YOU FOR SHOPPING AT
          REED COLLEGE BOOKSTORE

one sense, is another reflection of a romantic reaction to the separation from his beloved, but, on the other hand, is an externally valid expression of the true loneliness that falls to the lot of the picaro.

The organizing principle of the world of romance is one of true love which withstands all vicissitudes and provides stability in an unstable world. The romance hero, after his suffering and after his loneliness, eventually finds a final and permanent union with his beloved. The constancy of his love enables him to persevere. Encolpius fluctuates, changes his resolves, and changes his partners. His reunion with Giton proves to be a shallow and absurd echo of the romance world, for the constancy of chastity gives way to random promiscuity.

In short, Encolpius displays a strange kind of internal instability of character. On the one hand, he possesses traits that are typical of the picaro. He is willing to assume different roles, willing to participate in roguish trickery. He shows inconstancy in his resolutions; he || alternately flees and rejoins the world, alternately threatens suicide and embraces life. The picaro is unlike those

characters in whose inner stability, whether throughout the work (comic, romance) or at the end (tragic), we feel joy and exaltation . . . The picaro is neither a round nor a flat character. A flat character is defined by one trait [the miser, the cuckold], a round character, by the organic interrelation or organization of his traits. The picaro differs from the flat in having many traits, from the round in having shifting traits that present no order, that seem random in their appearances and disappearances and connections. While most literary characters speak for the ordered side of our personalities, he speaks for the disordered side.[97]

Sullivan's description of Encolpius' character as 'disorganized and fragmentary,' . . . as 'alternately romantic and cynical, brave and timorous, malevolent and cringing, jealous and rational, sophisticated and naive'[98] might seem to label Encolpius as a pure picaro. But the instability of the picaro is supported by the picaro's clear view of the roguish world to which he belongs.

---

[97] Miller (1967: 45–6) and on the distinction between the round and flat character, see further in Wimsatt (1949: 77–9).

[98] Sullivan (1968a: 119). In his view, however, Encolpius' character is 'disorganized and fragmentary, not because he is at odds with himself or suffering from a spiritual instability . . . but because he is the structural and narrative link for the different themes the Petronius has chosen as well as the victim of certain comic and satiric situation.' See also Veyne (1964: 308 n. 1), who holds similar views, but cf. Rankin's (1970) evaluation of Encolpius' instability (128–30), which he interprets as a reflection of the conditions of the age rather than as an expedient for the author's different purposes.

However, when Encolpius tries to organize his emotional life in terms of the diametrically opposed world of romance, he only succeeds in disorganizing his personality still further, this time in a non-picaresque way. Because of these romantic and heroic illusions, he is rarely able to maintain even a temporary mastery over events or to preserve his own picaresque independence. More often than the true picaro, he becomes a victim.

The successful picaro alternates between mastery of and subjection to life's chaotic events, and these alternations of fortune, although not organized in any coherent way, reflect his attunement to the chaotic world. Encolpius never fully joins that world, although the world ‖ in the *Satyricon* is shown to be truly picaresque. Thus he obtains few of the benefits of his position.

The theme of freedom has been proposed as an important theme of the picaresque form, supplying a counterbalance to the uneasiness aroused by the external chaos. The picaro is seen as a genuine affirmation of the individual man, and of his 'longing for a free nat-ural existence . . . unhampered by conventions of a complex social order.'[99] The picaro,

by remaining apart from the stability of the fixed social order, takes upon him-self both more freedom and more vulnerability than the ordinary, socially 'adjusted' man. Rugged individualist that he must be, the picaro has to assume direct and personal responsibility for shaping the course of his exist-ence, and in this regard he is freer than other men. . . . The picaro as master of his fate is the jack-of-all-trades, skilled manipulator, adept deceiver, artist of disguises, adaptable to all situations and all men. The picaro as the butt of fortune is the man of many adversities, continually tossed on the breakers of a sea of vicissitudes, never allowed rest or security.[100]

Encolpius more frequently falls into the second category.

If one searches the *Satyricon* for a character who plays this picaresque role more fully, Eumolpus emerges as the most likely can-didate, although his pretensions to art, providing that he seriously believes them, may somewhat disqualify him. Life has its ups and downs for him; he is stoned in the gallery (90. 1); he receives similar treat-ment in the bath and has difficulty in retrieving his clothes, unlike the more fortunate Ascyltos (92. 6–11). The mutilated end of our extant text suggests that time is running out on his imposture in Croton (141. 1). In the story of the Pergamene boy he first shows his roguish

---

[99] Parker (1967: 16, 17).   [100] Alter (1964: 71–2).

abilities and then is tricked in turn by his apt pupil (85–7). He displays a real flair for gratuitous trickery; he masterminds the disguise on board the ship, while the others flounder in more impractical plans. He dreams up the scheme in Croton. He can play many roles; he appears now as a serious poet and teacher, now as a bawdy raconteur, now as a practiced diplomat, now as a wealthy old man who is grief stricken over the loss of his only son. He adapts to situations with ease, and when fisticuffs are called for in the inn, he is equal to the ‖ occasion and accepts his injuries with equanimity (95. 4–9, 98. 7). Relationships for him are sexually oriented. He has no other interest in Giton than his physical beauty, and when Philomela offers him her daughter, he works out a plan whereby he can maintain the illusion of his impotence and enjoy the girl at the same time (140. 1–11).

For Eumolpus impotence is part of his disguise of debility. For Encolpius it becomes an unpleasant fact of his existence. Picaros are lusty, healthy fellows with a strong appeal to women. Encolpius' appetites may be broader, but he most often falls short of fulfillment. The theme of impotence which is associated with the recurrent motif of death is unusual for a well-adjusted picaro, but it is an excellent image for the picaro manqué.

Encolpius' physical impotence parallels his inability to meet the modern world on its own terms. When it is objected that the *Satyricon* presents no 'unified point of view,' the burden of this 'failure' falls on the narrator who should be able to supply that 'missing' outlook.[101] To strip off the mask from others he ought to have some sense of honesty, if only a uniform cynicism. Encolpius does not, for while he prepares a face to meet the faces that he meets, he is unable to peer behind his own mask with any consistency. A narrator who can see the pack on another's back but not on his own provides shifting planes of irony and ambiguity which are often difficult to fathom. His failure to present a stable ordered personality, *qua* picaro, is due to the conditions a picaresque world imposes on him. But his impotence, emotional illusions, and false rhetoric are due to the defects of his formal traditional education which do not allow him to complete the picaresque education which the world demands of him. Encolpius, the anti-hero in a world in which heroism is dead, persists in the fantasy of viewing his life in heroic terms and gauging his responses

---

[101] See Sullivan (1968*a*: 267) for this widely held view, but on the host of complex problems raised by the techniques of the unreliable narrator and of impersonal narration, see Booth's (1961) brilliant discussion (149–65, 271–391).

accordingly. He is an outsider, like all picaros, because of his loss of place in the social hierarchy. But he is even more a psychic outsider, who by persisting in living in a vanished mode, can never come to terms with the world.

He is an odd combination of the picaresque and quixotic types. To ‖ a roguish world he often responds with the appropriate roguishness. But, as a quixotic type, he projects himself as a kind of noble simpleton who sees the world through the lens of myth, epic, and romance. Yet nobility is precisely the trait he is lacking, for he has not the virtue and the strength that lies behind the idealistic faith of Cervantes' hero. Don Quixote

rejects society as it is—and brings himself to see the world as it is not . . . because he has culled from literature an ideal image of what the society should be. . . . The picaro's imagination is pragmatic, the Don's idealistic. . . . The picaro improvises his manner of acting as he goes; he preserves a strong sense of spontaneity in the way he lives. Don Quixote, on the other hand, tries to follow a pattern that he has learned from the printed page: life for him amounts to the fulfillment of a duty—both to himself and to the world. In sum, the picaro lives by ear; Don Quixote lives by the book.[102]

Encolpius, too, lives by the book, although in a shallow and hedonistic way, for he feels no sense of duty either to himself or to the world. What is even more important, he does not continually live in this fashion, a situation which deranges his character still further. A violent clash results between the picaresque mold and the quixotic mutant which renders Encolpius even more unstable than the world around him, and produces another level of chaos that approaches the schizophrenic.

But by this technique, the nature of the chaos in Petronius' world is more closely defined. For the present world which is revealed as chaotic and illusionary is held up against a background of the established literary tradition. This tradition, in turn, points to a heroic and romantically idealized view of the Roman world which was perpetuated through literature but was finally trivialized through the emptiness of rhetoric. Rhetoric is a symptom of this vacuum that exists between the facts of the present and the values of the past. It is also a cause of the disparity. Hence the images of death and of impotence and of losing one's way are important metaphors of the failure of culture. The *vitrea fracta*, the phrase which describes the *sententiae* of

[102] Alter (1964: 108–9).

rhetoric (10. 1), are also strewn over the ground outside Trimalchio's house on whose fragments the characters, unable to find their way, ‖ cut and bloody their feet (79. 1–3). The broken glass fragments of rhetoric supply a mirror of life that is inevitably distorted, deranged, and ultimately fragmentary.[103] Serious intellectual activities are also ironically refracted, for no character is capable of speaking about them without resort to rhetoric. The ideas and their rhetorical presentation are indissolubly bound up with each other.

Encolpius, in two instances, makes his plight clear to the reader. In the opening attack against the traditional education of his day, he exposes its irrelevancies and unrealities (1–2); it fails to prepare students to cope actively with life; it is intoxicated with the sheer flow of empty verbiage; it constricts free development of the intellect by the use of the set speech. In short, its effect is one of enervation and paralysis. In his diagnosis, Encolpius unwittingly exposes the reasons for his own vulnerability to circumstances and his own failure to adapt successfully to the outside world. When he accuses the rhetoricians of fostering absurdities of language, 'ut corpus orationis enervaretur' (2. 2), his later impotence takes on an added meaning.[104] But Encolpius, nevertheless, commits the same faults he castigates. He 'is naive enough and suggestible enough to parrot his teacher, hypocrisy and all.'[105] His speech against declamation is revealed as still another declamation, and this is the term that Agamemnon uses to cut off the verbal flood (3. 1).[106] His language and his presentation betray his lack of real understanding of the stultifying limitations of Roman education. In addition, the remedies of a return to the literature of the past which he and Agamemnon propose, will, if carried out, perhaps sharpen his literary tastes but will not help him solve his real-life problems. He will only increase his bookish pretensions without any palpable growth in emotional maturity.

In the second instance, Encolpius has another important inkling of the gap that lies between his private reality of epic and romance and the objective reality of life. The placement of these remarks is significant, for Encolpius, distraught by his physical impotence, determines to lop ‖ off his offending member, a plan, which, in his typical inconstancy, he fails to carry out. He grasps the need for language

---

[103] I owe this observation to Myron Jaworsky.

[104] On the theme of impotence and its relationship to language, see Arrowsmith (1966: 309, 318–20).   [105] George (1966: 351).

[106] George (1966: 351); Walsh (1970: 84–5).

and behavior which are both honest and realistic, but this insight can be no permanent truth for him. He lapses immediately into parodistic verse which recalls literary approaches to the same problem, and thus his statement is given the same air of unreality (132. 6–15).

It is, in my opinion, an egregious error to isolate this passage as the personal view of Petronius who is said to be advocating a return to an earlier classical tradition of simplicity.[107] The very terms of Encolpius' presentation deny this, and, moreover, he has not had difficulty before in speaking of these matters in a refined way. Frankness is surely one of the refreshing attributes he has exhibited on occasion, but only when he plays the role of picaro. Perhaps Encolpius here is trying to bridge the gap between the picaresque vision he occasionally shares and the romantic vision he too often entertains, but the mode of his observation shows that he fails to grasp its essential import. The burden of the past becomes too great and overwhelms him; he has only composed another *declamatio*, as he himself calls it, and words are again substituted for action (133. 1). When Encolpius scolds Eumolpus for his 'disease' of spouting literature, he remarks that he has spent two hours with him, 'et saepius poetice quam humane locutus es' (90. 3). Unfortunately, Encolpius suffers from a variation of the same malady, but he cannot make that diagnosis; hence the irony of his situation.

IV. WORLD-VIEW

It is therefore idle to look in the *Satyricon* for a conventional moralist who takes up the terms of a moribund set of dogmas offered in fossilized form. Petronius surely is no neo-Epicurean, no neo-satirist in the old tradition, no neo-classicist who looks back to established time-hallowed forms for a revitalization of the present.

All his techniques point instead to a radically anti-classical stance. He thumbs his nose at the doctrine of the purity of genres, at stylistic uniformity, and at the doctrine of decorum. Literature of the past is reduced to parody and absurdity. Traditional philosophical and ‖ moralistic views are undermined and even annulled. What is more, his entire tale is anti-classical in viewpoint.

One has only to compare the *Odyssey* or its later definition in the *Aeneid* to gauge the difference. Odysseus is a rogue, it is true—the

---

[107] This is Sullivan's (1968*a*) contention (33, 109–10, 259).

archetypal rogue of Western literature—but he never becomes a true picaro. He exults in gratuitous trickery, but he has an integrated ordered personality and the fixed destination of a stable ordered society about which he organizes his existence. He normally maintains his mastery over circumstances. The external chaos of the world resides permanently in the fabulous and mysterious regions of the remote world. Chaos at home in the social frame gives way to the order which is reestablished by Odysseus himself and validated by the gods' assurance of justice.

The *Aeneid* has its own set of referents for creating a coherent world in which the framework of history embraces the past, the present, and the future of Rome. In plot, in the patterning and interrelationship of books, in its poetic exposition of themes, the Roman epic represents a point at which the *furor* of passion and irrationality yields, at least for a time, to the stable order achieved by the application of high ideals and reason and sanctioned by Fate.

The *Satyricon* sees only a disorderly world unsupported by the rational guidance of the gods or their substitutes. The balance, the symmetry, the perfection of pure form that resides in the classical mode finds a radical antithesis in the hectic rush of irrational episodes narrated in a mixture of styles and genres. 'The *Satyricon* is all uproar, guffaws, rumpus, commotion, but behind its noise there is always present a long recurrent note—the ebb and flow of human irrelevance.'[108] This is a world where 'things fall apart; the center cannot hold; / Mere anarchy is loosed upon the world.'[109] Where the center is lost, purpose and direction are also lost.

Classicism feels secure in the proven models of the past which have demonstrated their validity as artistic representations of human existence, while the *Satyricon* rejects the forms of the past and confounds the organizing principles of classical theory. Yet there is also a poignant regret for what is past and gone, and the ghosts of the past || which hover over the *Satyricon* only increase the uneasiness engendered by the new picaresque world. But there is no turning back to the old models in these changed circumstances. Petronius is a revolutionary who articulates in art his sense of a transitional society in the throes of a cultural and social crisis.

There is one other example of a classical author who approaches Petronius in his concept of the world, and he does so by techniques

---

[108] Rexroth (1969: 101–2).
[109] W. B. Yeats, 'The Second Coming', in Yeats (1959: 184–5).

that are also meant to express the turbulence of another cultural crisis. That author is Euripides writing in the declining days of the Athenian democracy, 'haunted by the disappearance of the old integrated culture and the heroic image of man that had incarnated that culture.'[110] Allowing for the fundamental difference in mode between tragedy and comedy, in form between drama and novel, in temperament between Greek and Roman, Euripides and Petronius show many startling similarities.

Like Petronius, the drama of Euripides assumes 'a universe devoid of rational order or of an order incomprehensible to men . . .', a feeling which he 'reports with great clarity and honesty . . . [as] the widening gulf between reality and tradition; between the operative and professed values of his culture; between fact and myth . . . between life and art.'[111]

Euripides mixes genres and tones so that tragedy slides towards comedy, romance, and melodrama. A late play, like the *Helen*, defies satisfactory classical genre description. The *Helen* is an excellent example since its philosophical premise rests on the confusion between reality and illusion.[112] 'At any point in a tragedy, the comic, or more accurately, the pathetic or ludicrous, can erupt with poignant effect, intensifying the tragic or toughening it with parody.'[113] Aeschylus, for instance, is held before the audience in a parodistic way, notably in the recognition scene in the *Electra* and in the outburst of the Phrygian slave in the *Orestes*, which is an absurd imitation of the mad scene of Cassandra in the *Agamemnon*.

Euripides, like Petronius, is an antitraditional artist who experiments ‖ with various forms, with innovations in language and music, with new plots and with old ones given new complications in a sharp contrast to the austere economy of the traditional drama (e.g., *Ion*). His plays are crowded with characters and with rapid series of actions, rendering a more complex view of life. Coincidences and improbabilities abound.

Realism is another feature of Euripidean theater, which creates a dissonance in the drama. Incongruities are everywhere. Myth conflicts with the more sordid reality of experience, and the harshness of their juxtaposition is not softened (e.g., *Heracles*). The heroic figure is domesticated, debased, and deheroized, like Jason or Orestes. In

---

[110] Arrowsmith (1968: 15). [111] Arrowsmith (1968: 16, 18).
[112] See Burnett (1960). [113] Arrowsmith (1968: 22).

Euripides, realism invades the mythological sphere with disquieting effects;[114] in Petronius, the situation is reversed.

In Euripides, characters assume elaborate disguises and plot intricate deceptions (e.g., *Helen, Iphigenia in Tauris, Electra*). The passions and irrationalities of human behavior are thrust into prominence. Derangement and abnormality of personality are explored (e.g., *Orestes, Electra*). Emphasis is laid on the plight of the individual who is adrift and isolated in a chaotic world, whether in actual exile (*Iphigenia in Tauris, Helen*) or in a state of psychological alienation (*Electra, Orestes*).[115] Heroes are often weak and inconstant. They waver in resolution and change their minds, reflecting the epistemological problem of the world's coherence (*Hippolytus, Iphigenia in Aulis*).[116] *Tyche*, blind and senseless Fortune, gains in importance, and the restoration of the order demanded by the myth is often effected artificially by the *deus ex machina*, sometimes a mechanical contrivance in the fuller sense of the word (*Orestes, Electra*). 'His theater everywhere insists upon a scrupulous and detailed recreation of the complexity of reality and the difficulty of moral judgment.'[117] In his chaotic contemporary world, Euripides, like Petronius, responded to the loss of the coherent social system and its attendant values with revolutionary ideas and techniques. ‖

But Euripides is not as nihilistic or ironic as Petronius. He questions old values in the search for new ones. In vaunting the individual and his solitary experience as the ultimate touchstone of action, he sees redemption in the loyalty of personal relationships, in the assumption of inner moral convictions, in the power of the young, the old, the weak, and the innocent to redeem their society and to recreate its values.[118]

Petronius is more difficult to read. He has not suggested any unambiguous solutions to the problem of establishing a new order or even of effecting a means for revitalization. Parody is ultimately an unstable and temporary mode of expression appropriate to the experience of an unstable world. The colloquial speech of the freedmen may reflect an aesthetic experiment, a 'rebarbarization' of literature,[119] but

---

[114] Arrowsmith (1968: 17–20).   [115] See Wolff (1963).
[116] See Knox (1966) on the indecisiveness of Euripidean characters.
[117] Arrowsmith (1968: 24).   [118] See Wolff (1963) and Förs (1964).
[119] 'Rebarbarization' is used in the sense of a return or resort to subliterary modes of expression (such as those found in folk or oral literature (e.g., ballad, mime) and to subliterary interests such as a 'preoccupation with the physical sexual experience.').

the contents of their conversations, while they are to be commended for their more realistic view of the world, also display an enslavement to the general values of the society which the freedmen yearn to enter. Nor can the old tradition that once validated social norms serve to reestablish order, for Petronius has diagnosed one important symptom of the cultural failure in Encolpius' enslavement to the past.

He has not offered an aesthetic and ideological alternative in his world, but he has used new form, new technique, and new content to diagram the predicament of his age. The ironic approach he adopts, like that of the picaresque, 'need not have any positive moral purpose; it is critical without necessarily assuming a clear standard of desired behavior. Ultimately, picaresque irony is an individualist, asocial exercise of the intellect, and as such it reflects the condition of rootlessness which is the heart of the picaresque situation.'[120] It is an 'irony || of disintegration.' but it is not a bitter denunciation. Instead there is laughter, exuberance, and vitality.

The one important positive aspect of his vision is finally that exuberance, that vitality, that rich sense of the comic tempered with compassion and with understanding.[121] This sense of the comic sees the absurdity of man, his society, and his world, but it makes that vision endurable through the medium of wit and irony which expresses not hatred and disgust but a sense of partnership in and commitment to the human condition. Habinnas sums up this insight that informs the *Satyricon*: 'Nemo nostrum . . . non peccat. Homines sumus, non dei' (75. 1). It is an insight that renounces the classical hero, both comic and tragic, and his aspirations to moments of superhuman achievement, but one that is consonant with the changed condition of the world.

Historical Perspective

The *Satyricon*, in its ambiguities, ironies, parodies, and incongruities, is essentially related to those forms of literature which unsettle the reader

The effect of this 'rebarbarization' can be a renewal of cultural vigor. See the valuable article Lerner and Mums (1933, esp. 526–7). See also the discussion of this concept in Wellek and Warren (1956: 235–6).

[120] Alter (1964: 102). By contrast to this type of irony, one might point to Fielding's use of responsible social irony. 'His [Fielding's] irony, far from being radically disturbing like that of Swift, is, in intention, corrective and orthodox; it undermines deviations from a healthy, sensible, social morality; it prunes society of perversions. Unlike the irony of Gibbon or Samuel Butler II, it does not unsettle traditional ethics and Christian orthodoxy—it is the irony of integration rather than disintegration.' Humphreys (1942: 183). See also Alter (1964: 102–3).   [121] See Arrowsmith (1966: 326).

by their anarchic view of life, and which generally appear in times of cultural and social stress of varying kinds. The picaresque novel, for instance, arises in Spain in the wake of the breakup of the feudal order and in Germany during the chaos of the Thirty Years' War.[122] Uncertainty, dislocation, and anxiety are the impulses which produce a cynical realism, a satire of society, and a distrust of dogma and tradition.

In the Rome of Petronius' time several sets of conditions encourage the genesis of a work like the *Satyricon*. First, there are the special conditions at the court of Nero. A literary salon existed dedicated to experimentation, and the courtiers were imbued by their emperor with sophisticated tastes, a strong iconoclastic sense, a contempt for the || conventions of Roman aristocratic life, and a *nostalgie de la boue*.[123] The *Satyricon* could easily find acceptance and even inspiration from such an audience.

On another level, however, the shifting and capricious temper of a deranged ruler must also be taken into consideration. Nero, who may have encouraged an unconventional and frank acknowledgement of men's secret desires and vices (Suet. 29), invited hypocrisy and flattery too by destroying those who asserted or seemed to assert any independence of thought or action. His paranoid fears, which often prompted arbitrary and irrational behavior, would tend to create an atmosphere in which the world of the courtiers must have appeared chaotic and illusionary. The echoes of court practices in the *Cena* and the reminiscences of the traits of Nero and other emperors in the figure of Trimalchio support this assumption still further.[124]

Secondly, the political climate of the Neronian age, owing to the repressive imperial policies, had demoralized the senatorial class, whose major function and source of prestige had been active public service; it also demoralized the lower classes who felt still less of a share in controlling their own destinies. This group, energized by spectacles which channelled off their aggressive instincts and de-energized or pacified by the hydrotherapeutic influences of the baths, had, to a large degree, also lost any real sense of national purpose. The intellectuals perhaps suffered a larger degree of alienation. Augustan ideals of the lofty goals of Roman destiny became for many of them another rigid convention, like the moral conventions, openly subscribed to and

[122] See Alter (1964, *passim*), del Monte (1975), and Borgers (1960–1).
[123] On the theory that the *Satyricon* was composed for an audience of Nero's courtiers, see Rose (1966).	[124] See Walsh (1970: 137–9) and Crum (1952).

privately denied. The sense of communal values was thereby seriously diminished.

The third factor, the larger socio-economic situation, is still more important. This was 'an age of great economic growth in the shadow of a principate which had struck root, and it produced patches of prosperity from which a number of individuals benefited to a vast degree.'[125] It was the beginning of a time of physical and social || mobility. The *Cena*, in its presentation of the freedmen's milieu, reflects the disruption of that hierarchical society in which each man knew his place and his prospects. The urban sprawl of a polyglot, cosmopolitan population in a technologically complex society leads always, even as in our own time, to a dehumanization of man. The individual loses a sense of participation in a coherent group, and turns inward to personal and private means of the validation of life. This movement towards individual standards is evident already in Euripides' response to the more limited social crisis of his age. It is still more evident in the social developments of the Hellenistic age which gave rise to the prose romance.[126] It also becomes a factor in Roman literature of the late Republic; the writers of that period responded to the complexities of urban life with an emphasis on the worth of personal experience.[127]

That Petronius should create a character who is a delinquent, an outsider, a marginal man, who belongs in no social milieu, who has no past or future, no destination or purpose beyond passing pleasures and the will to survive, whose personality is unstable, whose relationships are insecure, and who should have learned by experience that the world is roguish, unpredictable, and ultimately without any coherent design, marks the first step taken in literature towards the vision of our modern desacralized world and the image of the radically alienated man who is familiar to us from the pages of modern fiction.

But, in another more positive sense, the *Satyricon*, like the picaresque form but on a diminished scale,

affirms the primacy of individual experience—to begin with, the most basic aspects of individual experience—in a kind of existence where any larger order must be very much in question. It is a literary form characteristic of a period of disintegration, both social disintegration and disintegration of belief. Like

---

[125] Rankin (1970: 126).   [126] See Perry (1967: 44–95).
[127] On this subjective element in Latin literature, see Otis (1967).

Descartes, the picaresque writer finds any existing systems to be of the shakiest kind, and he too, tries to effect a basic reconstruction by beginning again with the one self-evident fact of the experiencing 'I'.[128] ||

This condition accounts for the fact that in cultural history the novel itself receives late acceptance as a serious and important literary genre.

The novel is the form of literature which most fully reflects this individualist and innovating reorientation. Previous literary forms had reflected the general tendency of their culture to make conformity to traditional practice the major test of truth; the plots of classical and Renaissance epic, for example, are based on past history or fable, and the merits of the author's treatment are judged largely according to a view of literary models in the genre. This literary traditionalism is first and most fully challenged by the novel, whose primary criterion was truth to individual experience—the individual experience which is always unique and therefore new.[129]

Here, in this perspective, lies the basis for an evaluation of Petronius and the radical originality of his work seen within its classical context. The use of a long fictional narrative as his form becomes a significant and important choice. Within the loose confines of that form, Petronius has succeeded in creating an inner coherence and logic which is proper to its purpose of commentary upon and elucidation of the human condition. Form, style, and content are all integrated into a unitary world-view, which may dismay us by its vision of anarchy, but which we may admire paradoxically for the integrity of its presentation in Petronius' art. ||

[128] Alter (1964: 84).   [129] Watt (1957: 13).

2

Some Observations on the Narrative Technique of Petronius

ROGER BECK

One of the most problematic questions in the *Satyricon* is the character of the hero and narrator of the story, Encolpius himself. Critics rightly point out the fluctuations and seeming inconsistencies in Petronius' portrayal of him, as the following pen sketches from two recent studies show: 'alternatively romantic and cynical, brave and timorous, malevolent and cringing, jealous and rational, sophisticated and naive';[1] 'simple soul and man of the world, sadist and soft-hearted sentimentalist, parasitic flatterer and ingenuous guest'.[2] Explanations of these seeming inconsistencies, however, differ widely. Some find the self-contradictory character convincing in itself, in an Aristotelian sense consistently inconsistent. H. D. Rankin sees him in a rather modern light as a decayed intelligence, registering and aware of the experiences that flow over him but unable to confront and master them, a victim of random emotions and anxieties.[3] For Walsh the inconsistencies are primarily a matter of Encolpius' position as narrator: 'He is the chameleon of the I-narrator who see the complexities within himself but only the consistent traits in others.'[4] Others explain the discrepancies in terms of the economy of the *Satyricon* as a whole. Sullivan insists that 'Encolpius' character is disorganized and fragmentary, not because he is at odds with himself and suffering from a spiritual instability that the author is interested in exploring, but because he is the structural and narrative link for the different themes that Petronius has chosen, as well as the victim of certain comic and satiric

---

[1] Sullivan (1968a: 119). [2] Walsh (1970: 81).
[3] Rankin (1971: 11–31, 19).
[4] Walsh (1970: 81). Walsh adds that the contradictions are also 'explicable in part by the comic pose of the anti-hero as simpleton' (ibid.); cf. Veyne (1964), who sees a consistent pose of *fausse naïveté* in Encolpius' conduct at the *cena*.

situations. The character of Encolpius . . . is composed *of those traits, even if contradictory, which are appropriate responses to the demands of the particular episode.*'[5] On a somewhat different tack, P. George accounts for the discrepancy between the quality and sophistication of the narrative and the naivety, stupidity, and poor taste of the narrator in terms of the author's wish to retain the vividness and the comic and satiric possibilities of first person narrative without ‖ stunting himself with the limitations of a style appropriate to the narrator.[6]

It will be noted that both of the last two explanations (George and Sullivan) imply a certain failure on Petronius' part, despite the brilliance of individual episodes (or, perhaps, because of it), to sustain an over-all plausibility and consistency in the writing of narrative fiction; or at least they suggest a willingness to sacrifice plausibility and consistency of narration for other effects. This, to some extent, is typical of the mainstream of Petronian criticism which tends to treat the *Satyricon* primarily in terms of parody, satire, and a medley of literary entertainment (the heaviest arguments being concerned with the genres that go to make the mixture and with Petronius' attitude towards them), and only secondarily as an extended novel.[7] In the study that follows I propose to take an opposite approach and to suggest a means of reconciling the discrepancies in Encolpius' character that at the same time sees in the *Satyricon* a well-wrought, sophisticated, and self-consistent work of narrative fiction.

The key to the solution is, I believe, a realization that in dealing with Encolpius one is concerned not with a single person but with two: Encolpius the narrator and Encolpius the subject of the narration. Not only are they two distinct persons separated by what is presumably a considerable span of time (the narrator is looking back on his own *past* adventures) but they are also two very *different* characters. The narrator, as we shall see, is sophisticated and competent, while his former self is chaotic and naïve. Strictly speaking, one should say only that *that version* of his former self *which the narrator chooses to present* is chaotic and naïve. For we should be aware that the Encolpius who is the protagonist in the adventures related is as much the creation of the Encolpius who tells the story as are the other characters who

    5 Sullivan (1968*a*).   6 George (1966: 349 ff.).

    7 This observation is perhaps somewhat unfair to George who, in the earlier part of his article (1966), demonstrates brilliantly the care which Petronius takes to make the rhetoric of different persons (in particular Giton) match and define their characters in the context of the narrative.

make their appearance in the novel. And as we shall also see, there is excellent reason to suppose that the very last thing that interests Encolpius the narrator is an accurate, factual reconstruction of his own past life and character. In the *Satyricon* we have in fact two levels of creation: the author creates the narrator and the narrator creates the narrative together with the various characters (himself included), using as a basis—but as no more than that—his own past experiences. In a sense, of course, the author creates the totality of the work, but to be aware of this alone is to rest on a generality which ignores the particular approach here taken by Petronius. ‖ The genius of the *Satyricon*, considered as a work of narrative fiction, lies in the subtlety with which Petronius has delineated a highly sophisticated and complex narrator who defines himself brilliantly and consistently in the telling of his story.

That there is a real difference between the narrator and his former self and that an awareness of this difference might help in appreciating the structure and economy of the *Satyricon* is a consideration that has so far played virtually no part in the criticism of the work.[8] This unfortunate state of affairs is due to a number of factors. First, the mutilation of the text has deprived us of the beginning and end of the novel, points at which we might reasonably expect that the author would have shown us the narrator introducing and concluding his narration. At the most elementary level, then, we are never made aware of the narrator as an individual existing in his own right outside the context of the narrative, as we are, for example, by Clitophon's meeting with the author in Achilles Tatius' *Leucippe and Clitophon* or by Apuleius' introduction of himself to his audience in the *Metamorphoses*. Secondly, Petronius' narrator does not draw attention to himself by frequent use of a first person clearly referring to his present rather than his former self (a rare example occurs in 65. 1 where the narrator comments on the *matteae* served at the banquet: 'quarum etiam recordatio me, si qua est dicenti fides, offendit'). Thirdly, as we shall see, the narrator takes considerable pains to avoid the sort of aloof, superior, and judicious tone that would reveal beyond question his separate identity as a distinct person distanced from the action and looking back at past events from the vantage point of hindsight and experience. Finally, though, the main reason why the

---

[8] The possibility of a distinction is intimated by Veyne (1964) but is not further explored: 'L'auto-ironie du *Satiricon* se justifait-elle par la conversion finale d'un Encolpe parvenu, après tous see voyages, au port de la sagesse?' (307).

distinction between the narrator and his former self is generally ignored may well be a matter of the marginal status of prose fiction as a genre in ancient literature. Classical antiquity simply does not possess a large corpus of sophisticated prose fiction, and as a result the necessary critical approaches, such as 'point of view' analysis, evolved in the study of other literatures are not by and large known to classicists or applied to such novels as fall within their sphere. Fortunately, with T. Hägg's recently published *Narrative Technique in Ancient Greek Romances* an excellent start has been made at remedying this deficiency.[9]

The starting point for an assessment of Encolpius as narrator must surely be Encolpius' own attitude towards the telling of his tale, since it || is that which determines the whole character of the narration and thus of the novel itself. Why does he tell his story, what purpose is the narrative intended to serve? Lacking any explicit statement of aims, one must work backwards from the evidence of the structure and tone of the narrative itself. The answer is not difficult to find. It is abundantly clear that Encolpius' main—one is even tempted to say exclusive—aim in recounting his adventures is to *entertain*. One receives throughout the novel the consistent impression of a narrator *shaping* the adventures and encounters of his past life into episodes which will delight and amuse. The clearest proof of this is the narrator's use of realism. Where realism serves the end of effective story-telling realism is maintained. Thus, in the *cena*, where the main thrust of the narration is to build up a picture of a freedman magnate and his circle, realism dominates both the narrative and the reported speeches, since realism will clearly produce the effect desired. Yet even here unrealistic elements intrude when they contribute to the building of the narrator's portrait of Trimalchio and his world, for example the fantastic exaggerations of the bulletin read out by the *actuarius* (53. 2): on a single day on a single estate 30 boys and 40 girls born, 500,000 *modii* of grain processed, 500 oxen broken in! When, however, different effects are aimed at in the story-telling, realism is sometimes jettisoned entirely. Take, for example, the introduction to the adventures with the legacy hunters at Croton. Here the narrator intends to entertain us with satire of sorts, and to set the scene

[9] Hägg (1971). See in particular (*a*) Hägg's chapter on 'Points of View' (112–37) and especially the section on Achilles Tatius (124 ff.) whose novel, like Petronius', takes the form of a first person narration, and (*b*) his bibliography with its coverage of writers, especially American, on the novel in general.

he has the adventurers meet a certain *vilicus* who obligingly gives them a thumb-nail sketch of the predators and their prey (116. 6–9):

In hac . . . urbe non litterarum studia celebrantur, non eloquentia locum habet, non frugalitas sanctique mores laudibus ad fructum perveniunt, sed quoscumque homines videritis, scitote in duas partes esse divisos. nam aut captantur aut captant. in hac urbe nemo liberos tollit, quia quisquis suos heredes habet, non ad cenas, non ad spectacula admittitur, sed omnibus prohibetur commodis, inter ignominiosos latitat. qui vero nec uxorem umquam duxerunt nec proximas necessitudines habent, ad summos honores perveniunt, soli fortissimi atque etiam innocentes habentur. adibitis . . . oppidum tamquam in pestilentia campos, in quibus nihil aliud est nisi cadavera quae lacerantur aut corvi qui lacerant.[10]

In that town literature and the arts go utterly unhonored; eloquence there has no prestige; and those who lead the good and simple life find no admirers. Any man you meet in that town you may be certain belongs to one of two classes: the makers of wills and those who pursue the makers of wills. You will find no fathers there, for those with natural heirs of their own are regarded as pariahs. A father is someone who is never invited to dinner, never entertained, who, in short, is compelled to spend his life, outcast and excluded, among the poor and obscure. Those, however, who remain bachelors in perpetuity and have no close relatives are held in the highest honor and esteem: they and they alone are men of honor and courage, brave as lions, paragons without spot or flaw. In short, sirs, you are going to a place which is like a countryside ravaged by the plague, a place in which you will see only two things: the bodies of those who are eaten, and the carrion crows who eat them. (tr. Arrowsmith) ‖

Now the point here is not that such a tirade is unrealistic in content: people frequently castigate cities in an exaggerated way as moral cesspools where only rogues thrive. Rather, the point is that such a speech with its neat summary of the state of affairs, its brisk style and clever antitheses is utterly implausible in the mouth of a farm bailiff encountered by chance by a party that has lost its way on a country road. Since the narrator, as we know from the *cena*, is more than capable of reporting realistically the talk of the uneducated, we must assume that he has other motives for presenting the conversation with the *vilicus* as he does. Here, as in other situations, the principle at work appears to be the effective presentation of the episode as an entertaining tale shaped to a certain pattern. The pattern here is a satiric farce in which legacy hunters prey on the rich, the rich on legacy hunters,

[10] Müller (1961).

and Eumolpus and company on all comers. The speech of the *vilicus* provides with considerable neatness, but also with total lack of plausibility if verisimilitude is taken into account, an alluring introduction to the episode.

The narrator gives us, then, not a precise and factual account of his past life and adventures but a version of them shaped imaginatively for the entertainment of an audience. In effect, he offers implicitly what Apuleius offers explicitly ('varias fabulas conseram auresque tuas benivolas lepido susurro permulceam,' I. I), and he offers it perhaps more wholeheartedly, since in Apuleius' case a good part of the author-narrator's purpose—though unstated—is the glorification of Isis and the redeemed life. In the *Satyricon* there is no such ulterior motive at work. Petronius portrays a narrator spinning tales to amuse an audience, tales which we may suppose to be *based* on the narrator's experiences, but not an accurate *reconstruction* of them. Realism can at any point be sacrificed for effect, and we can never know just how close we come to the 'facts' of the narrator's past life, though we can be quite sure that most of the time there is a high proportion of fantasy, imagination, and artistic editing to the mixture. Continuity and consistency in the *Satyricon* lie not in the *content* of the narration but in the *persona* of the narrator as an artist shaping a highly selective and fanciful autobiography.

It is the *persona* of the narrator that above all justifies the frequent appearance of verse in his story-telling. The verse is an organic part of the narrative because the narrator himself is firmly characterized throughout as a self-conscious practitioner of the art of words, as one who moulds the experiences of life into literary forms, and as a fascinated student of the poetic imagination—and its delusions. Moreover, the subjects of his narrative are often themselves the devotees—and victims—of rhetoric, of poetry, and of literary culture in general. They include not only such obvious figures as Eumolpus and Agamemnon, but also the hero's sexual associates (Giton and Ascyltus), and above all his own past self. The ‖ difference between the narrator's approach to literary culture and that of the subjects of his narration is a topic I hope to explore more fully on a later occasion. At present the point I wish to emphasize is simply that it is the ubiquitous literary concerns of the narrator and his subjects that permit the frequent resort to verse without any loss of the novel's unity. This, indeed, is one of Petronius' subtlest achievements: the transformation of his chosen genre, the mixed prose and verse medium of

Menippean satire, into coherent narrative fiction. The means that won him this triumph is the creation of his cultured and imaginative narrator. To realize the nature of Petronius' achievement one has only to compare the near contemporary *Apocolocyntosis* in which the movement from prose to verse is inexplicable in terms of any logic of narrative or character, and which therefore remains more or less at the level of a satiric medley.

The verse in the *Satyricon* may be divided into two categories: that which the narrator attributes to characters other than himself and that which he either attributes to his own past self or else presents in his own person as narrator. The first category is obviously the more straightforward, in that in each instance the verse must be presented as the spoken words of the character to whom it is attributed. More often than not the verse in this category is realistic enough, in the sense that it fits the character and the occasion. The best example of this sort is perhaps Eumolpus' 'little elegy on hair' (*capillorum elegidarion*) and the hendecasyllables that follow (109. 9–10). What could be more natural than that in the merry-making following the reconciliation on Lichas' ship the irrepressible old aesthete should deliver himself of a humorous medley of prose and verse, taking as an obvious starting point the ludicrously shorn and painted appearance of Giton and Encolpius?

... cum Eumolpus et ipse vino solutus dicta voluit in calvos stigmososque iaculari, donec consumpta frigidissima urbanitate rediit ad carmina sua coepitque capillorum elegidarion dicere. (109. 8)

... when Eumolpus, being well in his cups, got the idea of throwing out some quips about bald heads and brandmarks, until exhausting his weak witticisms he went back to his poetry and began reciting a little elegy on hair. (tr. Sullivan)

Just as realistic (if we grant the convention of the narrator's total recall of lengthy poetry) is Eumolpus' *Sack of Troy* (89) with its genesis in the conversation between the two newly met *littérateurs* and the picture that confronts them in the gallery; even his *Civil War* (119 ff.), despite its huge length, is reasonable enough, given his addiction to verse-making and recitation and the established tastes and interests of the narrator which lead him to report it. Other examples of verse that fits both character and situation without any violation of realism are the lines of Agamemnon on training for the arts (5) and the execrable pieces of ‖ Trimalchio on mortality (34. 10 and 55. 3). Of

verse that is unrealistic in this sense the best example is probably
Tryphaena's appeal to the combatants on board Lichas' ship (108. 14).
In 'real' life such murderous conflicts springing from the passions of
desperate men (*rabies libidine perditorum collecta*, 108. 8) are seldom
settled by the measured rhetoric of Vergilian hexameters. But realism
is, of course, the last thing that interests the narrator in his description of the fight. Rather, his aim is to turn the fracas into an entertaining farce. Hence Giton's histrionics with the dummy razor (108.
10–11), and hence too the narrator's ironic elevation of the brawl into
'no commonplace war' (*non tralaticium bellum*, 108. 12) which can only
be settled by due ritual (*data . . . acceptaque ex more patrio fide*, 108. 13)
and the formulas of solemn treaty (109. 2–3). Into this presentation
Tryphaena's verse with its pretentious allusions to the sea flights
of Paris and Medea fits admirably. The heroic and tragic overtones
render the actual mêlée by contrast only the more ludicrous.

A further example of verse which is unrealistic and implausible in
its given context is the poem of Oenothea on her powers as a witch
(134. 12). The poem merits some close attention since it leads us directly
to certain highly significant features of the narrator's over-all design.
The content of the poem is commonplace enough. Oenothea simply
attributes to herself the standard accomplishments of witchcraft that
one meets throughout ancient literature:[11] control of crop growth,
the raising and stilling of tempests, power over animals, and—the
supreme accomplishment—the ability to change the motions of
the heavenly bodies. If one accepts lines 11–16,[12] Oenothea then cites
the great mythical practitioners of her art: Medea, Circe, Proteus. In
both language and content the poem is utterly trite. What gives it point
is nothing in the poem itself but rather the contrast between, on the
one side, the claims that it makes and the images that it conjures up,
and on the other, the reality of Oenothea's person and abilities. For
as the narrative proceeds, it becomes abundantly clear that Oenothea
is a drunken, incompetent, libidinous, and venal hag whose 'magic'
cannot fool even the credulous Encolpius. This counter-picture the
narrator paints in vivid detail: the dilapidated state of her cottage with
its loose pegs (135. 4) and rotten stool collapsing under her weight
and scattering the fire needed for the ritual (136. 1–2), the snack of
decaying pig's head (135. 4 and 136. 1) and the spitting out of the

[11] Cf. Ap. Rhod. 3. 531–3; Virg. *Ecl.* 8. 69–71, 95–9; *Aen.* 4. 487–91; Tib. 1. 2. 43–52;
Ovid, *Ars am.* 2. 1. 23–8.   [12] See Müller (1961).

bean shells 'veluti muscarum imagines' (135. 6), the quick change of
attitude over the slaughtered goose once payment is offered (137. 7–8),
the pretense of divination by the nuts which even Encolpius realizes
sink or swim in the wine depending on whether or not their kernels
are properly formed (137. 10), and finally the drunken and ‖ lecherous pursuit as Encolpius makes his escape (138. 3). So glaring, then,
is the contrast between the pretensions of the verse and the sordidness of the actual situation that one is lead to suppose that it is an
intended element in the narrator's design. The verse is included not
for its own sake (and certainly not for its artistic merits), but deliberately to set up this contrast between illusion and reality—though here,
of course, one must bear in mind the fact that the 'real' world is as
much the narrator's creation as is the never-never land of poetic delusion (the farcical element built into the world of the everyday should
keep us aware that this side of things is also shaped artistically, not
merely recorded). What, though, is the purpose of this contrast? To
suppose that it is intended to make a point about Oenothea herself,
that her performances do not measure up to her pretensions, is to run
into an immediate difficulty. For the narrator draws the contrast in
so extreme a manner that it becomes scarcely credible that so squalid
and uncultured a person could possibly entertain and express in correct—though hackneyed—form the literate and imaginative sentiments
attributed to her in the verse. In other words, if we suppose that the
contrast is purely a matter of opposite traits in Oenothea *alone*, we must
also admit that the narrator's over-all portrait of her fails to achieve
either unity or plausibility. There is, however, another possibility.
Might we not suppose that the verse represents not the narrator's
reconstruction of Oenothea's own pretensions to magical powers,
but rather the reconstruction of what he himself in the past, with the
fervid literary imagination that he carried into all his adventures, would
expect a witch to claim on first encounter? The verse, on this supposition, would not really be Oenothea's at all, but rather the
imaginings of Encolpius himself *projected* on to Oenothea in his later
re-shaping of his adventures for narration. The interpretation is
admittedly a complicated one. It depends for its plausibility on the realization that this would merely be a variation on a game which the
narrator is constantly playing in his story-telling: the drawing of
contrasts between the delusions engendered on his own past thinking by literary stereotypes and the often squalid truth about the
people whom he met and the adventures which befell him. Most
often this contrast is effected by means of the verse which the narrator

either presents in his own person or attributes specifically to his own past self. It is to the verse of this type that we must now turn.

The verse of Encolpius falls naturally into two groups. The first, which is much the smaller, consists of those poems which are presented as the words and thoughts of the protagonist *in situ*. Encolpius' supplication of Priapus (133. 3) is one such poem; it is set out unambiguously as his spoken words on the particular occasion: 'positoque in limine genu *sic deprecatus sum* numen aversum' (133. 2). Another is the poem in which he attributes his misfortunes to the wrath of Priapus and assimilates his || sufferings to the pattern of the divine persecution of the great heroes (139. 2). The present tenses (*persequitur, sequitur*) guarantee it as his own words, or at least his thoughts (the absence of its prose framework from the text prevents us from knowing which), *in situ*. The same is true of the flamboyant challenge to Jupiter to sample Circe's charms (126. 18). Again, the text is mutilated in its surroundings, but we could well construe it as a conceit spoken aloud to compliment and impress Circe herself (such an interpretation would fit well with the sentence that appears next in the text: 'delectata illa risit . . . ,' 127. 1). Finally, I would also classify as Encolpius' words *in situ* the verse deprecating the censoriousness of would-be *Catones* (132. 15), which I shall argue is actually a continuation of his soliloquy in defense of the rhetorical onslaught which he has just delivered against his recalcitrant member.

I am well aware that such a reading of the verse at 132. 15 runs counter to the generally accepted interpretation. Most critics have understood the piece not as the words of Encolpius at all, but as a direct appeal by Petronius himself justifying, in his own person, the approach and subject matter of the *Satyricon*. Such, for example, was Collignon's opinion: 'Il semble même qu'à un moment donné, Pétrone s'applique ouvertement à mettre son récit sous le patronage d'Épicure. Au chapitre 132 se lit une pièce de quatre distiques, où l'on croit entendre *l'auteur lui-même s'adressant à ses lecteurs et non plus cette fois par la bouche d'un de ses personnages*' (my italics).[13] The same view is adopted, as an unargued assumption, by both Arrowsmith ('a rare aside, that defends [Petronius'] work from the attacks of prudery')[14] and Sullivan ('an aside of the author to his audience, explaining part of his intentions and principles in a defense of the subjects of the *Satyricon* and his literary treatment of them').[15]

---

[13] Collignon (1892: 53).
[14] In the introduction to his translation (1959: p. xvi).
[15] Sullivan (1968a: 98).

The view is a difficult one to refute. For it depends not on any evidence in the text that can be challenged as a matter of fact, but on an unexamined and fixed determination to discover at all costs the presence—and opinions, whether aesthetic or moral—of the author himself in his work. It is this preconception of the nature of the *Satyricon* as necessarily a vehicle for the tastes and opinions of its author (if only we could agree what they are!) that leads critics to seize on the verse at 132. 15 as Petronius' direct address to us in his own proper person. But, in fact, we are not dealing with an author such as Fielding, part of whose technique—and a highly successful part—consists in regularly and explicitly entering his own work to explain, to justify and to point the moral. The verse to the *Catones* would be the *only* such intrusion to be found in the very sub- ‖ stantial portions of the *Satyricon* that have survived. We would have to assume, then, that for the sake of a meagre few lines of personal apologetics the author has chosen to sabotage his whole carefully contrived effect of a story communicated throughout not by himself but by a narrator with his own distinct and subtly drawn *persona* recreating his own adventures.

But, in fact, the generally accepted view of the poem, with its disastrous implications for Petronius' narrative technique, is quite unnecessary. The poem may be read—and read more naturally—as a continuation, without any break, of the rhetorical soliloquy that immediately precedes it. Shortly beforehand Encolpius had delivered his tirade. He had then, however, experienced feelings of shame at having 'bandied words with that part of the body which men of the stricter sort (*severioris notae homines*) usually do not admit even to their thoughts' (132. 12). But his mood now veers again, and he reflects that his imprecations are only natural. His words are given in direct speech (132. 13–14):

Quid autem ego . . . mali feci, si dolorem meum naturali convicio exoneravi? aut quid est quod in corpore humano ventri male dicere solemus aut gulae capitique etiam, cum saepius dolet? quid? non et Ulixes cum corde litigat suo, et quidam tragici oculos suos tamquam audientes castigant? podagrici pedibus suis male dicunt, chiragrici manibus, lippi oculis, et qui offenderunt saepe digitos, quicquid doloris habent in pedes deferunt.

What's so unnatural or wrong about working off one's feelings with a little plainspoken abuse? Don't we curse our guts, our teeth, our heads, when they give us trouble? Didn't Ulysses himself have a parley with his heart? Why, the way those heroes in the tragic plays strut around cursing their eyes, you'd think their eyes had ears. Gouty people damn their toes; arthritics curse their joints; the crud-eyed blast their eyes and even toe-stubbers take out their feelings on their feet. (tr. Arrowsmith)

It is at this point that the poem is introduced. The first four lines are as follows:

> Quid me constricta spectatis fronte Catones
>   damnatisque novae simplicitatis opus?
> sermonis puri non tristis gratia ridet
>   quodque facit populus, candida lingua refert.

Why do you censors stare at me with frowning brow and condemn a work of novel simplicity? The lively charm of pure language laughs through it, and what the people do my candid tongue reports.[16]

The continuity of this first part of the verse with the preceding prose passage is seamless. The *Catones*, surely, are the *severioris notae homines* whom we met above. Encolpius is now addressing them directly as if they were present (he is, in fact, soliloquizing) and debating with him on ‖ standards of propriety in speech. The development of the rhetoric is typical of Encolpius, as the narrator (who is, of course, his later self) reveals him to us. In his soliloquy Encolpius moves from the reality of his own impotence to a debate with imaginary adversaries on the propriety of making a declamation out of it. In precisely the same way the earlier oration over the drowned Lichas (115. 8–19) had drifted away from the here and now of the individual corpse on the sea shore to the generalities of a classroom exercise complete with imagined objectors to the line of argument:

At enim fluctibus obruto non contingit sepultura. tamquam intersit, periturum corpus quae ratio consumat, ignis an fluctus an mora. quicquid feceris, omnia haec eodem ventura sunt. ferae tamen corpus lacerabunt. tamquam melius ignis accipiat; immo hanc poenam gravissimam credimus, ubi servis irascimur. (115. 17–18)

But I hear someone object: those who drown at sea die unburied. Lord, lord, as though it mattered how this deathbound flesh should die! Fire or water or the wear and tear of time, what does it matter? Death or death: the end is always the same. But objectors again: wild beasts may mutilate the body. And so? Is the fire that someday cremates your corpse more friendly? Gentle fire, the cruelest death to which an angry master can sentence his slave? (tr. Arrowsmith)

---

[16] My translation here is intentionally as literal as possible. In general, the versions of the published translations are coloured by their common conviction that the poem is Petronius' *apologia* for the *Satyricon* (see esp. Arrowsmith's version).

Surely, then, the 'novae simplicitatis opus' of the poem's second line need be understood as no more than the tirade against the offending member. To accept this interpretation, it is not necessary to believe that the tirade *really is* 'a work of novel simplicity' or that it has in fact all the qualities ascribed to it (purity and candour of language, liveliness and charm). We need only admit that Encolpius himself might well make such a claim. Given his talent for grandiose fantasies (cf. the sacrifice and festival promised to Priapus in 133. 3), the supposition is perfectly plausible. If the term *opus* seems out of all proportion to the few sentences actually recorded, it can be accounted for by Encolpius' exaggerated sense of literary self-importance. Even when first introduced, the tirade is called an *oratio* (the choice of term reflecting, I take it, Encolpius' own estimation at the time): 'erectus igitur in cubitum *hac fere oratione* contumacem vexavi' (132. 9).

On this reading, the expression 'quod facit populus' need be taken to refer to no more than what Encolpius has just been saying that people as a matter of fact habitually do, which is to curse those parts of their bodies which give them trouble. The fourth line of the poem, then, is merely a recapitulation in verse of what has already been argued in detail in prose. Encolpius claims that his tirade has the merit of 'candour' (*candida lingua*) because it reflects the idiom of ordinary people (*quod facit populus*). As he had said earlier (132. 13), he has only relieved his feelings with 'natural invective' (*naturali convicio*).

But, in fact, the expression 'quod facit populus' is usually construed in a ‖ very different sense. Its meaning is generally understood not from what precedes it, but from what follows. For the poem continues (lines 5–8):

> nam quis concubitus, Veneris quis gaudia nescit?
>   quis vetat in tepido membra calere toro?
> ipse pater veri doctos Epicurus amare
>   iussit et hoc vitam dixit habere τέλος.

All men born know of mating and the joys of love; all men are free to let their limbs glow in a warm bed. Epicurus himself, the true father of truth, bade wise men be lovers, and said that herein lay the goal of life. (tr. Heseltine, Loeb)

Reading back from line 5 to 4, it is natural enough to suppose that 'what the people do' is to be understood in the present context as love-making. The inference seems guaranteed by the conjunction *nam*:

> quodque facit populus candida lingua refert.
> nam quis concubitus, Veneris quis gaudia nescit?

Now if this equation of 'quod facit populus' with 'concubitus' and the 'gaudia Veneris' is accepted, it follows that the subject matter of the 'novae simplicitatis opus' is also 'concubitus' and the 'gaudia Veneris'. In that case the 'novae simplicitatis opus' must be construed as something other than Encolpius' tirade, the subject of which was rather different and much more specific, namely his own impotent member. Since there is no other internal candidate for the 'novae simplicitatis opus,' it is tempting to equate it with the *Satyricon* itself and to suppose that the author is here thrusting himself forward to justify his own subject matter.

And yet, as I have argued, this interpretation involves the supposition that here and here only in the entire preserved text does the author choose to violate his otherwise carefully maintained pretense that the *Satyricon* is the continuous autobiography of a narrator with a distinct and definite *persona* of his own. It also involves the supposition of a considerable lacuna immediately prior to the verse to allow first for the change of speakers from Encolpius *in situ* to the author in his own person, and secondly for the shift of subject matter from the propriety of speaking about certain parts of the body to the propriety of treating of sexual matters in general. It is the first of these changes that is the really awkward one. Surely, it is quite inconceivable that at one moment Encolpius the protagonist—not even Encolpius the narrator—should be speaking, and at the next, and without any transition, Petronius in his own voice.[17] And yet it is well-nigh impossible to imagine what form a ‖ transitional sentence or passage, alerting us to the fact that the verse will be the author's own apology, could conceivably take. An easy transition to and from authorial comment is precisely what Petronius has denied himself by the very skill and consistency with which he presents the *Satyricon* exclusively as a story told by his narrator Encolpius.

I suggest, then, that we return to an interpretation of the poem as a continuation of Encolpius' soliloquy, understanding the 'novae simplicitatis opus' as his recent tirade and 'quod facit populus' as the

---

[17] Strangely enough, just such an unsignalled and abrupt switch from Encolpius to the author is implied by both Sullivan (1968a) and Arrowsmith (1959). Both critics believe that the poem is Petronius' own apology, but in their translations neither of them marks a lacuna in front of the verse. Collignon (1892: 53) was more aware of the difficulties involved in reading the poem as authorial comment: 'Ces quatre distiques ne se lient pas étroitement avec ce qui précède. On peut, avec M. Buecheler, supposer une lacune. Ou bien il y a eu transposition de ce morceau primitivement placé ailleurs à l'endroit qu'il occupe aujourd'hui.'

everyday practice, which he has just been discussing, of cursing mis-functioning parts of the body. With this reading we must, of course, postulate a lacuna between lines 4 and 5, since there will now be a *non sequitur* between Encolpius' claim that his speech only reflects the common habit of damning one's faulty members and the rhetorical question 'who is ignorant of love-making?' We may suppose that in the missing section Encolpius developed his argument to the point of demanding from his imaginary opponents the right to speak of sex-ual matters at large, on the grounds of their universality and their prime importance in human life. This intervening prose passage dropped out, and the two verse passages were conflated, with the conjunction *nam* suggesting a sort of spurious continuity. Such a conflation of two pieces of verse can be exactly paralleled in 80. 9, where two separate pairs of couplets have likewise coalesced into a single verse passage, though in that instance the lack of real continuity between the two is more readily apparent.

A significant feature of the verse at 132. 15 (if my interpretation is correct) is the way in which the original tirade is built up in Encolpius' imagination into a full-scale literary *opus*. This quality of exaggeration is also present in the other pieces of verse which are presented as the words or thoughts of the protagonist in action. Significantly, the exaggeration often takes the form of a flight of fancy into the world of literature and myth along much the same lines as the poem on Oenothea's powers (134. 12), which I suggested above should properly be read as the hero's own fantasy projected into the witch's mouth. Thus, in his prayer to Priapus (133. 3) Encolpius commits himself not only to the sacrifice of a goat and a litter of piglets (lines 13–15) but also to an entire festival complete with chorus of suit-ably inebriated and dancing youths (lines 16 f.):

> Spumabit pateris hornus liquor, et ter ovantem
> circa delubrum gressum feret ebria pubes.

New wine will foam in bowls, and thrice around thy shrine the tipsy youth will tread its joyous dance. ‖

The image is that of a rustic revel of the type that features regularly in idealizing poetry about the simple, pious life of the countryside.[18] But it is utterly inappropriate to Encolpius with his radically different *milieu* and style of life. For, in sober fact, how on earth is this city boy

---

[18] Cf. Virg. *Georg.* 1. 338–47, 2. 527–31; Hor. *Odes* 3. 18.

of presumably slender means going to assemble all those dancing yokels to redeem his vow for him? But, clearly, the faithful fulfilment of his promises is not the consideration uppermost in Encolpius' mind.[19] He is indulging in a literary fantasy in which he enters a pastoral world to act as master of ceremonies in a festival modelled on the best poetic stereotypes. Much the same 'trip' into the world of literature is also evident in the verse at 139. 2, though there the realm entered is that of epic and heroic myth. With magnificent hyperbole the impotent Encolpius classes himself, as the victim of Priapus' wrath, with the archetypal victims of divine jealousy, Hercules, Laomedon, Pelias, Telephus, and Ulysses:

> me quoque per terras, per cani Nereos aequor
> Hellespontiaci sequitur gravis ira Priapi.   (lines 7 f.)

Me too over land and grey Nereus' sea the harsh anger of Hellespontine Priapus pursues.

In view of the wide-spread belief that the wrath of Priapus is a major theme in the composition of the *Satyricon* as a whole,[20] it is, I believe, most important to bear in mind that we have only the word of Encolpius the protagonist, not of Encolpius the narrator, as assurance that his sufferings stem from the individual attentions of an outraged god. The hypothesis of divine persecution may well be no more than a fantasy spun by the hero partly to salvage his dignity in the humiliating circumstances || of sexual impotence and partly because, in any case, he is by nature a compulsive spinner of such fantasies.

---

[19] A fair indication of Encolpius' break with reality as his poetic fancy runs away with him is his claim 'non sanguine tristi | perfusus venio, non templis impius hostis | admovi dextram' (lines 6–8). But the crimes of homicide and temple desecration are precisely those that he has recently confessed in his letter to Circe (130. 2): 'hominem occidi, templum violavi.' In the poem, however, Encolpius is deluding himself into the rôle of the guiltless suppliant. Therefore, *by definition of the rôle assumed*, he *cannot* have committed the crimes which in other circumstances he will openly—even somewhat boastfully—admit.

[20] See, for example, the following observations of Sullivan (1968a: 42) and Walsh (1970: 76): 'the wrath of the god . . . provides one of the mainsprings of the plot.' 'The pervasive motif . . . is of a hero beset by the anger of Priapus.' This view was first put forward by Klebs (1889). Strictly speaking, all that we are entitled to claim is, I believe, (a) that Encolpius the protagonist, a character whom we know to be hopelessly prone to fantasy and melodrama, *imagines himself on certain occasions* to be the victim of the anger of Priapus, and (b) that these imaginings are understandable in view of (i) the nature of his ailment at Croton (i.e., impotence) and (ii) his occasional entanglements with people such as Quartilla who are genuinely connected with the cult of Priapus.

So far we have been discussing only those pieces of verse which are presented directly as the words or thoughts of Encolpius *in situ*. A much larger group consists of pieces which Encolpius offers in his rôle of narrator. These pieces are contemporaneous with the prose narrative; they look back on the past adventures from the same later standpoint in time. Most of them are characterized by past tenses: e.g., 'qualis nox *fuit* illa' (79. 8), 'nobilis aestivas platanus *diffuderat* umbras' (131. 8), 'ter *corripui* terribilem manu bipennem' (132. 8), 'non Indum *fulgebat* ebur' (135. 8). When present tenses are used, they tend to be the timeless presents of general propositions: e.g., 'nomen amicitiae sic, quatenus *expedit, haeret*' (80. 9), 'quisquis *habet* nummos, secura *navigat* aura' (137. 9).

Now of all these pieces only a single one actually functions as narrative in advancing the telling of the story. That piece is the verse at 132. 8, which describes Encolpius' attempt at self-mutilation and its failure: 'ter corripui terribilem manu bipennem.' The rest are a medley of background description (e.g., on the beauties of nature as the setting for the meeting with Circe, 131. 8), moralizing (e.g., on the limits of friendship, 80. 9. 1–4), commentary on the action (e.g., the extended simile comparing the sexual failure with Circe to the loss of a hoard of gold that a dreamer experiences on awaking, 128. 6), and literary and mythical allusions (e.g., the comparison between the victory over the geese and the routing of the Stymphalian birds by Hercules and of the Harpies by the Argonauts, 136. 6). Do we conclude, then, that these pieces represent the studied evaluations and literary reflections of the narrator looking back on his past life and adventures? The answer, unfortunately, cannot be a simple yes. For to suppose such would be to ignore a persistent and significant feature of many of these pieces. In perhaps the majority of instances the verse, *taken in context*, is somehow inappropriate, ludicrous, or downright false. Furthermore, the error or absurdity belongs not to Encolpius the narrator, whose concern is to draw attention to it in an oblique and subtle way, but rather to Encolpius the protagonist in action.

Let us take as an example the verse description of Oenothea's cottage (135. 8). The place is characterized as a model of rustic simplicity. The appearance and furnishings are described in terms which are favourable or at least neutral (with the exception, perhaps, of the wine-stained pottery at line 7 and the rather careless application of daub to wattle at lines 8 f.). It is the sort of place, indeed, that prompts thoughts of Hecale, the old woman immortalized by Callimachus as an archetype of peasant hospitality. Now the most striking thing about this verse description is that it is clean contrary to the facts as given in the prose narrative. Oenothea's cottage, as we have seen already, is a ramshackle and filthy hovel and its || owner a slovenly hag (no Hecale she!). The contrast between prose and verse can be seen at its clearest in the edible provisions that each makes mention of. The prose speaks of dirty beans ('grana sordidissimis putaminibus vestita,' 135. 5) and a decaying pig's head, the veteran of countless snacks ('sincipitis vetustissima particula mille plagis dolata,' 135. 4; 'coaequale natalium suorum sinciput,' 136. 1), while the verse describes only fruit and sweet smelling herbs ('mitia sorba | et thymbrae veteres et passis uva racemis | inter odoratas pendebant texta coronas,' lines 12–14). Now the contrast between the sordid reality of the prose and the idealizing fantasies of the verse is too marked, too vivid, and too entertaining to be a matter of chance discrepancy or of careless composition. We must assume, then, that it is an effect intentionally engineered by Encolpius the narrator. It follows, therefore, that the illusions of the verse are not *his* illusions; *he* does not see Oenothea and her shack in the idealizing light of the verse. Whose illusions are they, then? Surely they must represent the poetic fantasies in which, as we have seen already, the narrator's *former* self, Encolpius the protagonist, used constantly to indulge. Though the language of the verse with its past tenses seems to emanate from the narrator looking back in time, the sentiments are very much those of the hero in the thick of his adventures. Like the flight of fancy in the prayer to Priapus (133. 3), the reflections on Oenothea's cottage are clearly the imaginings of the Encolpius who lives half his life in a never-never land of myth and literature and whose imagination is easily triggered into fantastic poetic responses, however inappropriate or even ludicrous. Thus, the mere fact of the *paupertas* of Oenothea's dwelling place (135. 7) is enough to prompt the hero's musings on the commonplace theme of the simple life free from the burden of riches (lines 1–3 of the poem), and by a sort of literary osmosis the shack, despite its all too obvious squalour, is transformed into the rustic and fragrant haunt of a Hecale. The beginnings of this drift into fantasy are caught precisely in the prose sentence that introduces the verse: 'mirabar equidem paupertatis ingenium singularumque rerum quasdam artes.' Though presented in the format of a narrator's description, the verse that follows is clearly a reconstruction of the hero's intrigued reflections ('mirabar equidem') at the time.

Let us look at some of the other passages in which the narrator's verse, by reason of some obviously deliberate contrast with a sordid or ludicrous prose reality, seems to be a reconstruction of Encolpius' fantasies at the time. One such piece is the verse comparing the victory over the geese to the routing of the Stymphalian birds or the Harpies (136. 6). The verb *reor* (line 2 of the verse) should be the narrator's present: 'In just such a way I think the Stymphalian birds . . . fled' (*tales . . . Stymphalidas . . . fugisse* reor). But it reflects, I believe, more the pretensions to mythic grandeur of the hero himself in action. For once again the narrative || makes it abundantly clear that the actual fray is a very different matter from its imagined counterparts, and since the narrator is controlling this contrast between reality and illusion it cannot be he who is the spinner of illusion, except in the sense of *re-creating* his own past fantasies. The passage is a particularly interesting one in that the hero's fantasies are allowed to spill over into the preceding prose (136. 4–5), where we find, often in the same sentence, a subtle mixture of heroic posturing and absurd or very ordinary reality. In the protagonist's imagination his foes are viciously formidable ('impetum in me faciunt foedoque ac veluti rabioso stridore circumsistunt trepidantem') and their leader a sort of Mezentius: 'dux et magister saevitiae.' But probably they are only looking for their midday meal ('qui, ut puto, medio die solebant ab anu diaria exigere'), and part of the injuries which they inflict on Encolpius, the tearing of his tunic and the breaking of his sandal straps, are scarcely compatible with heroic dignity. Again, Encolpius defends himself 'armata manu,' but his weapon is actually a table leg, and a diminutive table leg (*pedem mensulae*) at that! Finally, the battering to death of the *dux* which had been rash enough to bite Encolpius' leg is spoken of as an act of epic vengeance: 'morte me anseris vindicavi.'

Yet another piece of verse in which there is a jarring contrast between the poetry and its prose context is the implied comparison of the love-making with Circe to the ἱερὸς γάμος of Jupiter and Juno (127. 9). The hero's musings ('Idaeo quales fudit de vertice flores | terra parens') are triggered by the varied plant cover on to which Circe lowers him (127. 8): 'implicitumque me bracchiis . . . deduxit in terram vario gramine indutam.' But the love-making itself is a bathetic anticlimax, trailing off into Circe's shrill and vulgar questioning (128. 1): 'numquid te osculum meum offendit? numquid spiritus ieiunio marcens? numquid alarum sum negligens?' What could be more extreme than this contrast between the fantasy of the ἱερὸς γάμος, that most fructiferous of all unions, and the actual impotence of Encolpius' performance, or between the imagined floral idyll and Circe's real anxieties about her personal hygiene? Again, the contrast is clearly an effect produced by the narrator, and the comparison with the ἱερὸς γάμος, so false to the realities of the situation, can only be the fantasy of the hero in the moments before disappointment strikes. The same, surely, is true of the ecstatic poem on the mutual joys of that night which in fact ends so crushingly with Giton's choice of Ascyltus as his 'brother' (79. 8): 'qualis nox fuit illa, di deaeque.' The verse implies a union of souls in the high passion that unites the two bodies: 'et transfudimus hinc et hinc labellis | errantes animas' (lines 3 f.). But as events immediately show, such a union is an illusion: Giton will jilt Encolpius for another man, seemingly at whim. Indeed, in this particular passage the narrator, in what I take to be one of his rare uses of a first person referring to his present rather || than his past self, himself alludes to this very discrepancy between the illusions and the realities of his earlier life. For at the end of the verse the prose resumes with the sentence 'sine causa gratulor mihi' ('but I flatter myself without good cause,' 79. 9). The narrator is here saying that the picture which he has just painted of a highly romantic and, by implication, exclusive passion is unfounded in reality; for Ascyltus, he continues, made off with the boy. The single present ('gratulor'), followed by an immediate switch to past tenses ('nam cum . . . remisissem . . . manus, Ascyltos . . . subduxit mihi . . . puerum et in lectum transtulit suum'), suggests that this is certainly the narrator's comment at the time of narration and not the protagonist's at the time of the original action.[21]

Naturally, not all of the narrator's verse demonstrates the sort of ludicrous contrast with its prose context that would make it unequivocally a reconstruction of the protagonist's musings *in situ*. Some of the pieces are sound and unexceptionable comments on the situations as they really were. For example, the verse on the power of money (137. 9) is an appropriate enough general response to Oenothea's sudden change of attitude over the slaughter of the goose when payment is offered. It would not be inconsistent, then, to imagine that here the verse is the narrator's own commentary, since such a supposition would not contradict what we know of his sophisticated

[21] Such, though, is not the usual reading implied by the translations. Cf., for example, Arrowsmith ('Alas, I boasted of my happiness too soon') and Sullivan ('I congratulated myself too soon').

clear-sightedness. But we can, of course, equally well imagine it to be Encolpius' own reflection at the time, a reflection which for once squarely hits the mark and which is then echoed and endorsed by his later self in the process of narration. The same two options are also open for the verse in which the hero's reaction to the fiasco with Circe is compared to the sense of loss experienced on awaking from a dream of hoarded gold (128. 6). We could take the verse, which is forceful and to the point, either as exclusively the narrator's own composition at the time of narration or else as his reconstruction of a comparison which he made at the time of the original experience. It is impossible to decide for certain, though since we are told that the hero was in fact musing at the time ('ego contra damnatus et quasi quodam visu in horrorem perductus interrogare animum meum coepi, an vera voluptate fraudatus essem;' 128. 5), it is perhaps best to interpret the verse as echoing, in part, the contents of those reflections.[22] ‖

By and large, however, the dominant impression that emerges from the narrator's verse, as from that which is directly attributed to the protagonist *in situ*, is one of a hero who constantly—perhaps even compulsively—indulges in flights of fancy, mainly into a world of literary stereotypes, in contexts which render his fantasies both ludicrous and perversely inappropriate to the prose realities of his life, character, *milieu*, and adventures. The contrast between the hero's fantasies and the real situations in which he lives and moves is established by the narrator through the subtle and humorous juxtaposing of verse and prose. The narrator allows his audience to draw its conclusions about the hero—and about himself—from the contrasts alone. Nowhere does he intrude into his narrative to say in so many words that his protagonist, his own former self, lived much of his life surrounded by an aura of self-induced illusion and literary fantasy. Yet

---

[22] The prose tells us that the theme of Encolpius' self-questioning was 'an vera voluptate fraudatus essem.' If the verse is also taken as re-creating Encolpius' reflections at the time, then the prose summary of his line of inquiry must be understood to mean 'whether it was real (as opposed to illusory or dream-like) pleasure that I had been deprived of.' Encolpius, in other words, is left wondering after Circe's departure whether the whole experience might not have been a dream—or nightmare. I stress this point because the translators for the most part imply that the pleasure was accepted as real enough and that the only question that engages Encolpius' thoughts is whether or not he had lost it: 'wondering if I were now cut off forever from my only hope of joy' (Arrowsmith), 'whether I had been robbed of the chance of true pleasure' (Sullivan). This, I believe, misses the point. The emphatic word in the indirect question is *vera*, which should be understood predicatively.

that is the conclusion that inescapably emerges. It is a conclusion, moreover, that helps us answer the problem with which this study started: the apparent character conflict between Encolpius as the cool and rational sophisticate and Encolpius as the deluded simpleton. The cool and rational sophisticate is the Encolpius who delicately and amusingly shapes his narrative in such a manner as to point up, without specific comment, the fantasies of his subject; the deluded simpleton is the earlier Encolpius who himself dreamt up and experienced the fantasies.

In dealing with the contrast between narrator and protagonist as seen in certain of the verse passages and their prose contexts, one has not, of course, covered (even by implication) the whole topic of the relationship between the two. Much remains to be examined in the prose alone. Much, moreover, remains to be said about the way in which the narrator presents characters other than his own past self. But these topics must wait for separate treatment. For the present I hope that I have established enough to suggest first that a distinction can and should be drawn between Encolpius as narrator and Encolpius as protagonist, and secondly that what Petronius offers us in the *Satyricon* is a portrait of Encolpius the narrator shaping an amusing and sophisticated version of his past life and adventures which includes, as a theme of major interest, a detailed treatment of his own chaotic and fantasy-ridden former self.

To conclude, I should emphasize the fact that both the hero's fantasies and the contrasted 'realities' of his life and adventures as presented in the narrative are constructions of the narrator which may in fact corre- ‖ spond only loosely to the hero's 'actual' fantasies and 'actual' experiences. As I suggested earlier, the narrator's primary concern seems to be to shape his life and adventures into well-organized and entertaining episodes, even on occasions at the expense of realism and verisimilitude. Thus, not only the verse fantasies but also the prose 'realities' may well contain certain deliberate inventions of the narrator designed simply to make the contrast more dramatic. For his aim is not to present an accurate case study of his earlier fantasies but to shape them for our entertainment. What his own feelings towards them actually are, it is difficult to tell (perhaps, in any case, it is the wrong question to ask of such a narrator). But a possible hint is offered by a strange phenomenon which we have already noted: the presentation of most of the protagonist's fantasies in the form of the narrator's own verse compositions looking back from a later standpoint in time. It is as if the narrator were fondly reliving the follies and fantasies of the past by giving expression to them as his own compositions of the present. It is a subtle device. For by identifying with his own past self in this way, the narrator avoids the sort of aloof and heartless ridicule of his subject which would render both himself and his narrative far less attractive than they are. Indeed, I believe that this identification of the narrator with his protagonist contributes in large measure to that atmosphere of good humour and moral sanity which the *Satyricon* somewhat paradoxically maintains. In place of unfeeling condemnation, callous contempt, and unpitying laughter, we are invited to feel sympathy with the young Encolpius as absurdly but gamely he confronts his unedifying experiences with the grand fantasies of myth and literature. To a great extent we feel this sympathy because the older Encolpius who is telling the story retains it himself. ||

AFTERWORD 1997

'Everything makes sense if we accept that the narrator and protagonist is the *only* mediator of the narrative' (Conte 1996: 26). It is heartening to hear this 'Encolpio-centrism' affirmed with great authority and subtlety by Gian Biagio Conte in his recent Sather Lectures almost a quarter-century after I suggested it in this article; heartening too to hear Conte insisting on that view's indispensable concomitant, the distinction between the narrating and experiencing Encolpius.

Conte's study will furnish a useful corrective to the 'reader-response criticism' of Niall Slater's monograph (Slater 1989), which if only by default has held the field in the 1990s. The problem with Slater's study, as I pointed out in my review (Beck 1992), lies not in its own 'readings' of Petronius, which are illuminating and do ample justice to the *Satyrica* as novel, but in the awkward and unnecessary accessing of them through a 'reader' who shifts from the actual to the implied and from the original contemporary to the modern or universal. As I concluded my review, 'I am still more or less convinced by my arguments of a decade ago that a better perspective for integrating the novel is its narrator, not its reader.'

Two things, however, now give me pause concerning the narratological model of this article. One is a single word of the text of the

Satyrica, the narrator's 'exclamat' at 108. 14, which punctuates the flow of Tryphaena's hexameter appeal to the warring factions on shipboard: ' "quis furor", exclamat. "pacem convertit in arma?" ' I failed to see how ill that interjected word fits with my interpretation of Tryphaena's verse, much as Oenothea's at 134. 12, as the fantasy of the experiencing Encolpius projected on to the speaker, in other words, as part of the interior history of the protagonist (the difficulty was pointed out by Slater 1989: 171–3). I am not sure of the remedy, but suspect it lies in shifting the focus somewhat from the experiencing to the narrating Encolpius, in accepting the former as entirely the construct of the latter and not as a fictional being granted an independent history which is then recovered by his subsequent narrating self. My model is perhaps in this respect somewhat anachronistic, as has been suggested to me by Gottskalk Jensson, whose thesis (Jensson 1996) proposes a rather different model based on ancient rhetorical theories of *narratio in personis*. Jensson's work is the other of the two things which now give me pause. No complaints, however. It is a fortunate scholar who both finds his earlier theories accorded renewed currency and sees them developed to the next stage by his student.

On one key issue, though, I remain unrepentant. In the verse at 132. 15 ('Quid me constricta spectatis fronte Catones'), however understood, we are listening to the voice of Encolpius, not of Petronius justifying the *Satyrica*. The mask assumed by our author does not slip.

3

Petronius, *P. Oxy.* 3010, and Menippean Satire

RAYMOND ASTBURY

A papyrus fragment (*P. Oxy.* 3010), first published by Peter Parsons in 1971, contains some fifty lines of a Greek prosimetric novel, a speech of twenty Sotadean lines sandwiched between passages of prose narrative. The subject is not entirely clear, but it is concerned with someone who has been instructed in the rites of Cybele and become a *gallus*, apparently on the advice of his friend Nicon; the *gallus* addresses a certain Iolaus in verse, saying that he has undergone his initiation in order to help Iolaus, whose past history he then recalls 'the story is a sensational one of bastardy, lamentation and intended amours'.[1] The fragment ends with a tag from Euripides on the value of friendship. In his introductory paragraph (53) Parsons commented: 'The verbal interpretation of the text offers considerable difficulties; still more difficult to assign the whole thing to its literary context. I set out the material I have collected, and the speculations which have occurred to me, as a beginning only; the conclusions are intended not as truths but as provocations.' R. Merkelbach[2] has been provoked into further examination of the verbal interpretation, but, so far as I am aware, no one has yet been goaded into further speculations on the literary implications of the fragment. But, as Parsons has said, 'something must be done with it' (66). Clearly the new papyrus will have an effect on our picture of the Greek novel and its development; however, in this article my aim is not to explore the full extent of the fragment's literary implications, but to sketch[3] one line of argument

---

[1] Parsons (1971: 60).   [2] Merkelbach (1973).
[3] Almost every stage of the argument involves matters on which there has been scholarly dispute; I do not propose to re-examine each of these questions but shall be content to state the position I hold on the particular points at issue and to direct the reader to those places where fuller discussions may be found.

which it makes possible—that the *Satyricon* of Petronius has nothing to do with Menippean satire.

I must first make it clear that by Menippean satire I mean the *Saturae Menippeae* of Varro and the *Apocolocyntosis* of Seneca. What we find in Varro is not the continuation in Latin of a genre which had been written in Greek by Menippus[4] but rather something new, created by Varro through ‖ the amalgamation of *prosimetrum* with the subject matter, literary techniques, and purpose of both Greek σπουδαιογέλοιον[5] and Latin *satura*. Varro's description of his works as *Saturae Menippeae*[6] had the effect of relating them in two different directions; the use of the word *satura* enabled the reader to associate them with the *Satires* of Lucilius, with which they share a common purpose and similar methods, while *Menippeae* provided a connection with Menippus. I believe that this latter connection is to be understood in both a specific and a general way; specifically, it refers to his borrowing of the mixture of prose and verse from Menippus,[7] and generally it is to be understood in much the same way as Horace's description of his *Satires* as *Bionei sermones*.[8] Horace did not use the phrase to indicate a close dependence on Bion either as a philosopher or as a writer; Bion's name is used simply as a symbol of τὸ σπουδαιογέλοιον, to suggest the influence which that type of literature had on Horace's *Satires*. In the same way Varro described his

---

[4] I incline to emphasize Varro's originality in his relationship with Menippus, but the argument of this article would not be affected if it were preferred to attach Varro more closely to Menippus, since we know so little about the Greek Cynic. On him, see Wildenow (1881), Helm (1931b), Dudley (1937: 69–74), and Piot (1914: 164–90). I cannot accept the views on the literary relationship of Lucian to Menippus expressed by Helm (1906), and followed by Geffcken (1911) and Scherbantin (1951: 25 ff.). For the arguments against the Helmian hypothesis, see McCarthy (1934) and Bompaire (1958: 550–62); the most we can learn about Menippus from Lucian is a general notion of some of the themes used by the Cynic.

[5] For Menippus as σπουδογέλοιος, see Strabo 16. 2. 29 and Steph. Byz. s.v. Γάδαρα; cf. also Marcus Aurelius 6. 47 and Lucian, *Bis acc.* 33. The comment of Diog. Laert. 6. 99, that Menippus φέρει μὲν οὖν σπουδαῖον οὐδέν τὰ δὲ βιβλία αὐτοῦ πολλοῦ καταγέλωτος γέμει, does not stand up to examination; for example the work of Menippus of which we know most, the Διογένους πρᾶσις (see Helm 1906: 237–53), is clearly σπουδογέλοιος in that the attractive and amusing story of Diogenes' capture by pirates and sale as slave-tutor to the children of Xeniades of Corinth serves as a vehicle for the exposition of the Cynic doctrines of ἀπάθεια, αὐτάρκεια, and παρρησία; of the favorite Cynic comparison between the expertise of the craftsman and the inexpert way in which men conduct their everyday lives; and of ideal Cynic methods of education.   [6] Gell. 2. 18. 7.

[7] I see no reason to dispute the statement of Probus, *ad Verg. Ecl.* 6. 31 that Menippus used *prosimetrum*, though the matter has been much discussed; a summary of opinions will be found in Scherbantin (1951: 48–53).   [8] *Ep.* 2. 2. 60.

satires as Menippean both to indicate that they were a Latin version of Greek popular philosophy and to acknowledge the source of his mixture of prose and verse.

It is part of the conventional wisdom of classical scholarship that the *Satyricon* has a more or less close connection with Menippean satire.[9] Yet there has been little detailed discussion of the precise nature of this connection and the belief in its existence has taken various forms; at the one extreme are those who speak of Varro, Seneca, and Petronius as representatives of the genre 'Menippean satire,' while at the other are those who reluctantly accept that Petronius' *prosimetrum* comes from Varro but regard other literary forms as much more significant in their influence upon the *Satyricon*. Thus, if my attempt to divorce the *Satyricon* from Menippean satire is to succeed, it will be necessary to examine those aspects in which the influence of Varro, or Seneca, or both, upon Petronius either actually has been suggested or appears possible.

A comparison of the language of the three authors produces an extremely meager harvest of instances in which the possibility exists that Petronius || may have borrowed from his predecessors.[10] The proverb *longe fugit qui suos fugit*, which Varro uses as a title, reappears (with *quisquis* for *qui*) in *Satyricon* 43. 5 and is found nowhere else. In fragment 419 Bücheler, Varro has 'barbato rostro,' while Petronius has 'rostrum barbatum' (*Sat.* 75. 10); and Varro's 'dicite labda'[11]

---

[9] Nearly all the scholars whose writings will be cited in later footnotes believe in the influence of Menippean satire on Petronius; see also virtually any literary history of Rome, study of Roman satire, or book on Petronius.

[10] For suggested parallels between Petronius and Varro, see Collignon (1892: 284–86) and Rosenblüth (1909: 30–2); for Petronius and Seneca, see Bagnani (1954: 80–2), following earlier attempts by Collignon (1892: 309–11), and Rosenblüth (1909: 31). I have listed all the instances which I find at all cogent; for the rest let a couple of examples suffice. Collignon finds a parallel between Varro, *Men.* 143 ('. . . in ianuam "cave canem" inscribi iubeo') and Petron. *Sat.* 29. 1 ('ad sinistram enim intrantibus non longe ab ostiarii cella canis ingens, catena vinctus, in pariete erat pictus superque quadrata littera scriptum "cave canem" '). In view of the evidence for such inscriptions in Roman houses, it is gratuitous to suggest that Petronius was 'following' Varro here. Equally, when Rosenblüth seeks to link Varro, *Men.* 146 ('omnes me bilem atram agitare clamitantis') with Petron. *Sat.* 90. 6 ('si eiuras hodiernam bilem'), he will, I think, persuade few that Petronius wrote with the Verronian passage in mind.

[11] The MSS have *labdeae*; *labda* is Bücheler's correction (in the apparatus to the fragment in his 1871 edition of the *Menippeans*); others have preferred *labdae* (taken as a vocative) with Scaliger. For the phrase *labda dicere*, cf. Mart. 11. 58. 11–12 'mentula . . . λαικάζειν cupidae dicet avaritiae'; *Anth. Pal.* 12. 187. 6 (Strato) . . . τοῖς φθονεροῖς Λάμβδα καὶ Ἄλφα λέγε (cf. Maxwell-Stuart 1975); and see Heraeus (1915: 1) and Degani (1962).

(frag. 48) may be reflected in 'laecasin dico' (*Sat.* 42. 2). Lastly, those who accept Bücheler's 'domusioni' in fragment 517 may be prepared to believe that Petronius' use of the word *domusio* (*Sat.* 46. 7, 48. 4) is an echo of Varro; however, I should prefer to follow Vahlen in emending the MSS *dumusioni* to *cum usioni* in Varro fragment 517.[12] A similar paucity of convincing parallels results from the comparison of Seneca and Petronius; of those which have been adduced only four appear to me to suggest the possibility that Petronius echoes Senecan language. The two authors have in common the phrase *animam ebullire*[13] (*A poc.* 4. 2; *Sat.* 42. 3, 62. 10), the proverb *manus manum lavat*[14] (*A poc.* 9. 6; *Sat.* 45. 13), the Greek noun *alogia* (*A poc.* 7. 1; *Sat.* 58. 7), and the similar expressions *non semper Saturnalia erunt* (*A poc.* 12. 2) and *semper Saturnalia agunt* (*Sat.* 44. 3). I do not imagine that anyone will claim that these parallels provide anything approaching proof of use of Varro or Seneca by Petronius.

Equally unconvincing are the attempts which have been made to find significant parallels in subject matter between Varro's *Menippeans* and the *Satyricon*.[15] P. G. Walsh, after an account of the main themes of the *Menippeans*, comments that 'these Varronian discussions on morality, literature and philosophy have many echoes in the *Satyricon*.' He does not, however, ‖ provide the reader with a list of these echoes,[16] and we are driven to seek them ourselves with the help of the list of 'inhaltliche Übereinstimmungen' provided by Martin Rosenblüth. I can find nothing in the *Satyricon* which remotely resembles the Varronian discussions of philosophy. The passages which Rosenblüth cites in this connection are: 88. 7, where philosophy is mentioned (together with dialectic, astronomy, and eloquence) as an art which is dying out because of avarice; 84. 1–3, a similar passage, though the main contrast is between literature and avarice; 104. 3, where Eumolpus tries to dissuade Lichas and Tryphaena from believing their dreams by referring to Epicurus' opinions on the subject; 128. 7, in which Giton compares his relations (or rather lack of them) with Encolpius to Socrates' treatment

---

[12] The lemma under which Nonius cites the frag. on p. 231M reads, 'Usus generis masculini . . . Feminino . . .'   [13] On the phrase, see Treloar (1969).

[14] The proverb has Greek predecessors; cf. Otto (1890: 210).

[15] Very few scholars have been tempted into this area of speculation; the most important are Collignon (1892: 20–6) (though he concludes that there are few, if any, such parallels); Rosenblüth (1909: 22–30); and Walsh (1970: 18 ff.).

[16] But occasional comments in the later part of the work, e.g. 41, 88, 103, 112, 127, provide some indications.

of Alcibiades; 110. 11, an anecdote of obscure significance about Socrates; and 119, where Rosenblüth finds 'Kynische Lehren,' though I can see only commonplace moralizing with no Cynic overtones. In this context I should mention also Oskar Raith's attempt to demonstrate that Petronius was an Epicurean;[17] he does not in my view make his case, though I would not deny that he does find occasional passages (often in fragments of doubtful authenticity) in which Petronius employs certain Epicurean attitudes and ideas. But all these references to philosophers and philosophy amount to little in comparison with the role played by philosophy in Varro's *Menippeans*, where we find 'multa admixta ex intima philosophia.'[18] What there is of philosophy in the *Satyricon* simply reflects the fact that the educated Roman was familiar with the tenets of the main philosophical schools and was able to use his knowledge appositely in appropriate contexts.

No one would deny that on occasion Petronius places moralizing comments into the mouths of his characters. Since the vices which are attacked (luxury, avarice, impiety, etc.) are also among the objects of Varro's criticism, it is hardly surprising that general similarities may be found between these passages of the *Satyricon* and the fragments of the *Menippeans*. But the same general similarities would emerge if we compared Petronius to other writers who show a moralizing tendency, be it the hexameter satirists, or Seneca (in the *Epistulae morales* and *Dialogi*), or others.[19] There is nothing in the relevant parts of Petronius which can be shown to be specifically Varronian in language or ideas. It can therefore be only an assumption that such passages echo those on similar themes in Varro, an assumption apparently based solely on the belief that Petronius took the form of his work from Varro—and on the consequent desire to link as much as possible of what is found in the *Satyricon* to Varro. This is not to deny the essential truth of Walsh's comment that there is considerable ironic humor produced by placing 'stern Varronian moralizing' in the mouths of disreputable ‖ characters. But this remains true if we delete 'Varronian'; there seems to me to be no justification for including the word.

---

[17] Raith (1963).
[18] Cic. *Acad.* 1. 8. On philosophy in Varro's *Menippeans*, see Mosca (1937) and Mras (1914).
[19] It is to be noted that Sullivan (1968a: 193–210) argues that parody of Seneca is to be found in some of these moralizing passages.

The third area in which Walsh believes that Petronius echoes Varro is in the introduction of discussions of literary matters. Here, too, it cannot be denied that Varro introduced such discussions into his satires, but there appears to be no thematic connection between the literary topics discussed by Varro and the debate on contemporary education engaged in by Encolpius and Agamemnon or Eumolpus' reflections on tragedy, epic, and literature in general. We may grant that 'the adoption of the Varronian [I should say "prosimetric"] form for his experiment in fiction . . . allowed easier entry to Petronius' literary discussions'; and it could be argued that Petronius echoes Varro in this respect, in that he saw how his predecessor had used the form for literary discussion and extended the Menippean convention so as to include longer poetic compositions, such as the *Troiae halosis* and *De bello civili*, as an element in his literary criticism. But this approach brings us back to the basic question of the source of Petronius' *prosimetrum*; the inherent potential of the form exists independently of whether Petronius took it from Varro or from elsewhere. It is also a potential which has two aspects: first, the general looseness of structure,[20] which permits the introduction of topics not directly concerned with the plot; and second, the mixture of prose and verse which permits the introduction of verse wherever the writer thinks it appropriate. Now the looseness of structure is not something intrinsic only to Menippean satire; it is also characteristic of the novel form—'of all the recognized literary forms, the romance, or novel, is by nature the most unbounded and the least confined in the range of what it may include.'[21] Thus there is nothing to surprise us in the fact that Petronius, having introduced a *rhetor* as one of the characters in his novel, should have been prepared to go a step further and make this *rhetor* discuss rhetoric and contemporary education with one of the other characters; equally, by making another character a poet he opened the way to discussion of poetic matters. We can see this as an exploitation of the novel form just as easily as we can describe it as an echo of the literary discussions found in Varro's *Menippeans*. The fact that *prosimetrum* is also exploited in this area is a separate matter; I shall argue below that this too is something which did not necessarily come to Petronius from Menippean satire.

'Even more striking,' says Walsh, 'are the parallels between scenes in Petronius' novel and the situations in the satires of Varro.' On closer examination, the three examples which Walsh uses to illustrate this

[20] On this, see Sullivan (1968*a*: 89–91, 267).   [21] Perry (1967: 29).

comment will, I think, prove to be somewhat less cogent than he suggests. First we have 'the theme of the conversational journey,' found in Lucilian satire (Lucilius' *Iter Siculum* in his third book and Horace, *Serm.* I. 5), in Menippean satire (Varro's *Marcipor*) and in Petronius (presumably the journey to Croton in *Sat.* 116 ff., though Walsh does not specifically say so). Leaving aside the question of a relationship between Horace and Petronius here || (about which I am skeptical), I can find no justification for associating Varro's *Marcipor* either with the poems of Lucilius and Horace or with the passage of the *Satyricon.* While fragment 276 of the Varronian satire ('hic in ambivio navem conscendimus palustrem, quam nautici equisones per ulvam ducerent loro') reflects a situation similar to Horace, *Sermones* I. 5. 11 ff., it is to be emphasized that the *Marcipor* is preserved in nineteen fragments and that no estimation of its theme can be formed without an examination of all the fragments. There is nothing in the other eighteen fragments to support the notion that it described a 'conversational journey,'[22] and nothing in any of the extant fragments which suggests any similarity to 'the journey [to Croton] . . . conventionally lightened by an entertainment.'[23]

The second example is Varro's *Eumenides*, which 'is set in a school like the first extant scene of Petronius.' Walsh quotes in support of his view fragment 144: 'et ceteri scholastici saturis auribus scholica dape atque ebriis sophistice aperantologia consurgimus ieiunis oculis'; he might have added fragment 142: 'cum in eo essem occupatus atque in schola curarer, ut scribit Scantius, "horno per Dionysia." ' But these fragments, taken together with the others which survive of this satire, do not show that the satire was set in a school; the setting appears rather to have been a meal (cf. frag. 143: 'quod ea die mea erat praebitio, in ianuam "cave canem" inscribi iubeo') attended by students of philosophy (that *scholastici* is to be so understood is suggested by the fact that the satire deals with a philosophic theme, the nature of madness) at Athens.[24] Thus the parallel suggested by Walsh would appear to be tenuous.

---

[22] So far as I am aware, of the scholars who have studied the Varronian satire, none has found in it a 'conversational journey,' though of course the parallel between frag. 276 and Hor. *Serm.* I. 5. 11 ff. has often been noted. Discussions of the satire may be found in the editions of Varro's *Menippeans* by Riese (1865), Bolisani (1936), and Della Corte (1953); and in Ribbeck (1859), Norden (1892), and Lejay (1911: 140).

[23] Walsh (1970: 104).

[24] The most important attempts to reconstruct the satire, in whole or in part, are those of Popma (1589), Riese, Bolisani, and Della Corte in their editions of the *Menippeans*; and Vahlen (1858: 168–90); Ribbeck (1859: 104–13); Kayser (1860); Boissier (1861: 86–90); Roeper (1862: 41); Bücheler (1865); Havet (1882); Mosca (1937: 55–9).

Finally Walsh suggests that the funeral feast in Varro's Ταφή Μενίππου recalls the 'maudlin finale of the *Cena Trimalchionis*, where the host pronounces his own panegyric.' I do not think that there is to be found here anything but the most general similarity. Varro's satire had as its setting a visit to the tomb of Menippus followed by a meal during which took place the discussion which appears to have formed the main part of the satire.[25] || This was not, I suggest, a funeral feast; ταφή has usually been interpreted as 'funeral,' but there are cogent reasons for not accepting this view. Clearly some, at least, of the participants in the discussion were Romans and Roman topics were discussed (frags. 527–30, 537); it is hard to imagine that Varro would have represented Romans as present at the funeral of Menippus at Thebes in the third century BC. It is therefore preferable to suppose that ταφή has here its less common significance of 'tomb,' 'grave,' and that the setting of the satire was a visit to the tomb of Menippus paid by Romans of Varro's day. It will be seen that there is very little in common between the setting of Varro's satire and Trimalchio's reading of his will, his instructions for his tomb, and his later mock funeral; certainly there is nothing which would suggest that Petronius had the Varronian satire in mind when he wrote the concluding part of the *Cena Trimalchionis*. It has now been shown that it is not possible to demonstrate convincingly borrowings by Petronius of the language or ideas of Menippean satire;[26] thus the discussion of their relationship must be extended to other, more general areas of possible influence, namely form, structure, plot, and purpose.

The *Satyricon* is an extended episodic narrative in the first person.[27] Varro employed narrative, both in the first and third persons, in certain of his satires,[28] and the *Apocolocyntosis* takes the form of a third-person narrative. Since there was thus available to Petronius

[25] Those who have directed their efforts to producing an outline of the satire have, generally speaking, come to similar results: see the editions of Riese, Bolisani, and Della Corte; and also Vahlen (1858: 147–65) (cf. Kayser 1860: 245–6); Ribbeck (1859: 126–8); Havet (1882: 64–8); Riccomagno (1931: 149–50); Mosca (1937: 69–70); Della Corte (1939: 41–3); and Krenkel (1973: 165–71). Note too that Sullivan (1968a: 131–2) has pointed out that close parallels to the relevant parts of the *Satyricon* may be found in Sen. *Epist.* 12. 8 and *Brev. vit.* 20. 3; and indeed Walsh himself (Walsh 1970: 137) cites these passages with the comment: 'It seems impossible that the close of Trimalchio's banquet was not inspired by this celebrated exemplar.' I do not know how this can be reconciled with his earlier suggestion of Varronian influence.

[26] Collignon (1892: 23) compares frags. 370–2 and 375 of Varro's *Papia Papae* with the description of Circe in *Sat.* 126, but it is more likely that the Petronian passage reflects the descriptions of the heroine in the Greek romances; cf. Walsh (1970: 106–7).

[27] Cf. Rosenblüth (1909: 19); Veyne (1964: 301–24); Perry (1967: 325–9).

[28] See McCarthy (1936).

a form of satirical fiction, it is possible to argue that the *Satyricon* is an extended Menippean satire. However, when we consider the remarkable length of the *Satyricon* and its manifest similarity in many respects to the Greek romance, it will appear preferable to look for the source of its structure in the romance, 'the sole type of extended episodic fiction in Greek for which any evidence exists before Petronius; there is no other Greek genre which can be proposed with confidence as having inspired the developed structure of the *Satyricon*.'[29] The fact that Menippean satire presents a form of satirical fiction, whereas the romance has fiction without satire, is not a matter of any significance; given the availability of the form, the question whether it is used in a satiri- || cal way is one which depends on the conscious choice of the individual author and no precedent is required.

As regards plot, insofar as it is useful to look for predecessors in a sphere in which the author's own imagination must play a large part, I can find no connection between Petronius and Varro[30] or Petronius and Seneca, and it is unnecessary to look further than epic[31] and romance[32] as sources for the combination of the *gravis ira Priapi*[33] and the adventures of the homosexual lovers. Of course, other sources come into play for individual episodes and scenes, but it is only epic and romance which affect the overall plot.

Varro's *Menippeans* combined a moral and satirical purpose; he dealt, generally speaking, with what can broadly be described as ethical themes, treating them both positively, in that he attempted to inculcate in his readers the recipe for a better way of life, and negatively, in that he satirized the vices which ruin men's lives and the men who represented views different to his own. Seneca's purpose was also satirical, but his attack on the dead Claudius shows none of the positive moral concern of Varro. On the other hand Petronius, notwithstanding recent attempts to turn him into a serious moralist or

[29] Walsh (1970: 8).
[30] Varro's *Sesquiulixes* has a not entirely clear relationship with the *Odyssey*, but there is no apparent connection between this and the exploitation of epic motifs by Petronius.   [31] Cf. E. Klebs (1889); Sullivan (1968a: 92–8); Cameron (1970).
[32] For various views on the relationship between Petronius and the romance, see Bürger (1892); Heinze (1899); Thomas (1900); Abbott (1911); Mendell (1917); Perry (1925, 1967: 186–210); Courtney (1962); Wehrli (1965); Scobie (1969: 83–90); Walsh (1970: 7–18).
[33] *Sat.* 139. 2. I am not convinced by the recent attempt of Baldwin (1973) to limit the importance of the *offensum numen* motif in the *Satyricon*.

satirist,[34] is a comic writer:[35] he aims to provoke laughter, not contempt, anger, or even pity. Like most comic literature, the *Satyricon* contains potential satiric targets, but they are not converted into ‖ actual objects of attack. The influence of Latin hexameter satire is demonstrable in the *Cena Trimalchionis*[36] and probable in the *captatio* episode at Croton,[37] but the tone in these sections of the work is humorous rather than satirical. Thus Petronius' purpose in the work is quite different from that of Varro and Seneca.

At this stage it is appropriate to give some attention to a recent discussion[38] in which it is contended that 'the *Satyrica* is not only in its frame and many of its episodes a parody of the novel, but . . . within this Petronius intended a whole series of parodies of the most diverse works.' Thus far I raise no objection; but a little further on we read that 'to suit his purpose he chose the form which allowed him to switch from sublime to sordid, from pathos to laughter, from high-flown to relaxed, that of the Menippean satire.' Then E. Courtney goes on to discuss the role of parody and literary allusion in Varro, Seneca, and Petronius.[39] This is not the place to attempt a detailed refutation, but a general comment will serve to indicate my reservations. I grant that the prosimetric form offers scope for parody, and that Seneca and Petronius make considerable use of it. But I do not think that the fragments of Varro's *Menippeans* provide adequate evidence for a similar situation there; I do not deny that parody and literary allusion occur on occasion (what ancient author does not indulge in literary allusion?), but they do not seem to me to be intrinsic to what Varro was doing in the *Menippeans*. I would suggest that the use of parody is something which is personal rather than generic, dependent on the individual choice of each author rather than imposed by a particular form. Thus I prefer to suppose that Seneca exploited the inherent possibilities of Menippean satire for parody, while Petronius saw the similar potential of the prosimetric novel; no predecessor is required for the impulse to parody.

---

[34] Highet (1941); Bacon (1958); Sochatoff (1962); Ehlers in Müller and Ehlers (1965: 440–1); Arrowsmith (1966); Nethercut (1966–7); Sandy (1969); Cameron (1970: 397–425); Zeitlin (1971a: 631–84, 1971b).

[35] See esp. Perry (1925: 34–5, 1967: 200–1); Sage (1969: 215–19); Weinreich (1962: p. lxxx); Sullivan (1967, 1968a: 115–57, 214–31, 255–9); Schmeling (1968–9: 49–50, 64); Walsh (1970: 80–110, 1974: 181–90); Schnur (1972–3: 13–20, esp. 14–15).

[36] Cf. Révay (1922); Shero (1923); Sullivan (1968a: 126–8).

[37] Cf. Schmid (1951).   [38] Courtney (1962: 86–100).

[39] Parody is one of the links between Petronius and Varro suggested by Rosenblüth (1909: 21–2). On parody in Varro, Seneca, and Petronius, see also Cèbe (1966).

The arguments presented so far, if accepted, leave us at last with the use of *prosimetrum* as the only remaining link between Petronius and Menippean satire, and many scholars in the past have reluctantly accepted this matter of external form as the extent of Petronius' debt to Varro and Seneca. Some, it is true, have attempted to break the link by suggesting that other literary influences inspired Petronius' use of *prosimetrum*, such as the Milesian tale[40] and the mime.[41] However, the evidence for the mixture of prose and ‖ verse in these forms is slight, and suggestions based on it have not carried conviction. Ulrich Knoche,[42] with his usual percipience, commented: 'Der Form nach kann man und muss man wahrscheinlich Petrons Roman mit der Menippeischen Satire verbinden, obwohl auch im hellenistischen Roman wahrscheinlich schon hie und da die Erzählung auch ausserhalb der Reden in Verse übergehen konnte. Wir sehen das z.B. im Alexanderroman, in der *Historia Apollonii*, auch ein Vorläufer Charitons hat es vielleicht so gehalten.'[43] The new papyrus enormously strengthens the case for believing that *prosimetrum* was not alien to the Greek romance. It is of the second century after Christ, so it is necessary to hypothesize from it the use of *prosimetrum* in romances earlier than Petronius. This does not appear to be an insuperable obstacle, especially if we recall that, when Richard Heinze first suggested the romance as an influence on Petronius, he was unaware of the evidence for the existence of the romance before Petronius' time; it was only when his article was in the proof stage that he learned of the discovery of the Ninos romance which supported his hypothesis.[44] If we are prepared to accept that *prosimetrum* was probably found in Greek romances before Petronius, we are then faced with two possible sources for the use of the form by Petronius—the romance and Menippean satire. I suggest that, at the very least, it is more economical to find the source in the romance, which, it is clear, influenced Petronius in other respects, than in Menippean satire, with which he has nothing in common other than *prosimetrum*. ‖

    [40] On the possibility of *prosimetrum* in the Milesian tales, see Norden (1915: ii. 756); Perry (1925: 38 n. 2).
    [41] On mime as one of the formative influences on Petronius, see Rosenblüth (1909: 36–55); Preston (1915); Sullivan (1968a: 219–25); Walsh (1970: 24–7); Sandy (1974). For *prosimetrum* in the mime, see Grysar (1854), esp. 263; Reich (1903: 570–4); Norden (1915: ii. 11–12); Scherbantin (1951: 71 ff.); Sandy (1974: 343 n. 34). On the possible implications of this for the *Satyricon*, see Wilamowitz (1905: 192); Abbott (1911: 270); Sandy (1974: 341–3).   [42] Knoche (1971: 74).
    [43] Cf. also Stubbe (1933: 4–6); Rohde (1914: 434–5, 622).
    [44] Heinze (1899: 509 n. 1).

4

Trimalchio on Stage

GIANPIERO ROSATI

The civilizing process set in motion by the Eastern conquests, with its gradual Hellenizing effect on Roman daily life, has as one of its most conspicuous consequences the transformation of the *convivium*. Table manners play a role in the general refinement of different forms of social intercourse. This is how Livy, in the course of singling out the 'semina . . . futurae luxuriae' (39. 6. 8–9), describes the phenomenon:

Tunc psaltriae sambucistriaeque et convivalia alia ludorum oblectamenta addita epulis; epulae quoque ipsae et cura et sumptu maiore apparari coeptae. Tum coquus, vilissimum antiquis mancipium et aestimatione et usu, in pretio esse et quod ministerium fuerat, ars haberi coepta.

Then female players of the lute and the harp and other festal delights of entertainments were made adjuncts to banquets; the banquets themselves, moreover, began to be planned with both greater care and greater expense. At that time the cook, to the ancient Romans the most worthless of slaves, both in their judgement of values and in the use they made of him, began to have value, and what had been merely a necessary service came to be regarded as an art. (tr. Sage 1936)

The proverbially frugal meals of republican Rome give way to elaborate banquets accompanied by *ludorum oblectamenta*. Far from being the mere satisfaction of a natural need, the banquet acquires, in its evolution, various forms of entertainment, and is equipped with the necessary apparatus for putting on a proper show. Another aspect of its evolution is the development of sophisticated gastronomic techniques (which are brought to such a level of refinement that special *leges sumptuariae* are passed to regulate them). The *ministerium* of cooking becomes an *ars*, which demands its own stage and right to perform.[1]

This chapter was translated by Barbara Graziosi.

[1] It is at this time that, due to the social conformity of the upper classes, the great success of famous chefs begins. We get a hint of the existence of this phenomenon in the elder Pliny's discussion of the kind of money needed to pay for such a status symbol (*Nat. hist.* 9. 67).

This apparatus of display, which may be more or less refined and expensive depending on the social and cultural status of the host, characterizes from that point the convivial habits of well-to-do Roman families. The literary evidence for it is extensive and explicit: in his letters Pliny the Younger frequently mentions the various forms of entertainment offered to guests at banquets; once, for example, he expresses his disgust at the 'lautissima cena' where 'scurrae, cinaedi, moriones mensis inerrabant' (9. 17. 1). There were foreign dancers and singers, professional circus artists such as jugglers and acrobats, as well as entire theatre companies which were employed to perform plays or mimes.[2] Guests who were culturally more demanding were entertained, in a less proletarian fashion, with music, poetry, or readings from plays: this is what Pliny promises to offer his guests ('lector, aut lyristes aut comoedus', 1. 15. 2–3); and Juvenal himself, who prepares a 'simple' show in keeping with his modest meals ('nostra dabunt alios hodie convivia ludos', 11. 179), offers readings from Homer and Vergil.[3]

The prime example of the Roman banquet at its ripest, the paradigmatic expression of a society possessed by the *conviviorum furor* which so outrages Seneca (*Ben.* 1. 10. 2) is, as far as we are concerned, Petronius' *Cena Trimalchionis*. Its spectacular impact rests above all on the various forms of entertainment which are set up (juggling, acrobatics, acting, music, etc.) but is enhanced by the staging of the banquet itself: we get the complicated ritual associated with its decoration, the care with which the food is prepared (the meal must please the eye as well as the palate), and the service, which is transformed into a dexterous and acrobatic game. Before discussing further this aspect of Petronius' work, however, one or two points need to be clarified. The theatrical aspects of the *Cena Trimalchionis* are well known, but have, in general, been studied and singled out in a rather narrow-minded fashion. The main focus has been the analogy with subjects or procedures characteristic of theatre or mime. The latter's close link with Petronius' text, from the point of view of content, language, and style, as well as the shape and editing of the scenes, has

---

[2] A relevant passage is Cornelius Nepos' *Vita Attici* 14. 1, where it is said that reading was the only *acroama* offered by Atticus to his friends as a *delectatio animi*. For futher references see Sherwin-White (1966: *ad* 1. 15. 2–3) and, above all, Blümner (1911: 410 ff.).

[3] Juvenal's Satire 11 is, in its entirety, an important document for contemporary *convivia*. The author expresses his critical attitude towards such banquets, in contrasting them with his own simple table.

often been commented on. However, as has more recently been re-marked[4] (though there have been some perceptive earlier anticipa-tions),[5] the theatrical character of the *Cena* has a wider scope and needs to be considered in a broader sense; every single aspect of the banquet is spectacular, from the preparation of food to its ceremonial presentation, from the *coups de théâtre* to the theatrical reactions they provoke. The theatricality of the banquet's description is confirmed by its organization: as we shall see, Trimalchio stages the play of his own life inside his *triclinium*.

I

The stage, namely the *triclinium* itself, has been equipped with in-genious machinery which ensures that, at the appropriate time, the ceiling is opened and the *apophoreta* descend upon their intended recipients, that is, the astonished guests (60. 1–4). The meal itself, more-over, turns into a series of performances: now a new amazing course holds the stage and is the object of general attention, then we are con-fronted with a 'cultural' display on Trimalchio's part, then again with a breathtaking story told by a guest. Every element which makes up the *Cena* is potentially spectacular, as is the very figure of Trimalchio: from his first appearance, when he indulges in showing off his *lautitiae*, which stupefy and amaze Encolpius, the text suggests that he should be read in this key: 'nec tam pueri nos, quamquam erat operae pretium, ad *spectaculum* duxerant, quam ipse pater familias' (27. 2). However, we should in fact see the whole banquet in this light: Menelaus takes Trimalchio's entrance to be anticipating the banquet itself: 'et quidem iam principium cenae videtis' (27. 4).[6]

The banquet-show is articulated into a series of courses whose staging follows well-established procedures. These are well known to all habitual guests, whereas the poor and naive Encolpius ignores,

---

[4] Two notable studies on this issue are Sandy (1974), a detailed and rich work whose only drawback is a rather rigid analysis of the *Cena*'s structure; and Barchiesi (1981), which is the text of a lecture delivered in 1975 and published *post mortem*. Sandy (1974: 329 n. 1) also offers an extensive bibliography on the role of the theatre, and in par-ticular of mime and other minor genres, in Petronius' work.

[5] I am thinking in particular of Thomas (1912: 144 f. and 150 f.).

[6] This remark is a proper 'stage-direction', as Barchiesi (1981: 129) calls it.

for a while, the staging directions which govern the banquet. The courses are made and presented in solemn and spectacular fashion: a good example of this is the showpiece where the peacock eggs covered by the fake hen are delivered (33. 3–8). This is perfectly orchestrated by overemphatic servants, a *symphonia strepens*; while Trimalchio, the main actor, delivers the key lines in the scene.[7] Here, more than elsewhere, the text draws attention to the theatrical combination of culinary techniques with staging devices: 'convertit ad hanc *scaenam* Trimalchio vultum . . .' (5).

A particularly useful example in order to illustrate the aesthetic character of the banquet's ceremonies and their theatrical models is the description of the *scissor*'s actions. He is called to carve, in front of everyone, the food which makes up the astonishing Zodiac dish:

Processit statim scissor, et ad symphoniam gesticulatus ita laceravit obsonium, ut putares essedarium hydraule cantante pugnare. (36. 6)

Together with the theatricality of his gesture, we get a pun on his name: he is called *Carpus*; thus, as an experienced guest explains to Encolpius, every time Trimalchio 'dicit "Carpe", eodem verbo et vocat et imperat' (36. 8). Both name and gesture are show tricks ('at ille, qui saepius eiusmodi *ludos spectaverat* . . .').

But let us go back to the carver's elaborate movements: Encolpius compares him to an *essedarius* who moves to the notes of a water organ (Nero was fascinated by the mechanics of this instrument; cf. Suet. *Nero* 41). Thus, though the *scissor*'s movements serve a practical function, they seem to be determined, above all, by aesthetic considerations. The service becomes a show. His unusual gestures, which are accompanied by music, are interpreted as the performance of an actor who has mastered his role to perfection. A similar passage in Juvenal's *Virronis cena* evokes a delightfully theatrical setting:

---

[7] A similar procedure serves to introduce Trimalchio's lines a little later: a servant brings in the *larva argentea*, thus offering Trimalchio the opportunity of delivering his lines on life's fleeting nature (34. 8–10). The theatrical character of the presentation of the *larva* should not be forgotten: the commentaries' admittedly relevant comparisons with passages from Herodotus and Plutarch on a similar Egyptian costume tend to obscure the theatrical impact of the scene. We are dealing here with a *catenatio mobilis* such that 'articuli eius vertebraeque laxatae in omnem partem flecterentur': nothing of the sort characterized Egyptian mummies. Moreover, the *figurae* it performs almost suggest that a capable magician is using a *neurospaston*. Barchiesi (1981: 135) sees this aspect of the scene and calls it 'a silent pantomime on the human condition'.

Structorem interea, ne qua indignatio desit,
saltantem spectes et *chironomunta* volanti
cultello, donec peragat dictata magistri
omnia; nec minimo sane discrimine refert
quo gestu lepores et quo gallina secetur.   (5. 120–4)

Meanwhile, just to ensure that your cup of anger is brimming, watch the carver waving his arms like an Indian dancer, flashing his knife until he has finished all of his teacher's programme. Yes, for of course it's a matter of vital importance what flourish is right for slicing a hare and what for a hen. (tr. Rudd 1992)

The formalized nature of the gesture, its ritual and aesthetic character, which serve to transform a servant's action into a ballet performance, are implicitly recognized by the poet and become the object of his sarcasm. Juvenal repeatedly insists on how artificial and unnatural such spectacular dinner parties are, and contrasts them with his own genuine and simple meals.

But there is an episode in the *Cena* where the connection between *ministerium* and theatre is actually explicitly made, namely during the performance of 'Ajax's madness'. After the Homeristae have been introduced (59. 2 ff.) and Trimalchio has announced the subject of their performance (which turns out to be an amazing plot based on myth, whose final outcome is precisely Ajax's madness),[8] a huge boiled calf is delivered to the table. It is *et quidem galeatus*, as if to represent the enemy:

Secutus est Aiax strictoque gladio, tanquam insaniret, concidit, ac modo versa modo supina gesticulatus, mucrone frusta collegit mirantibusque vitulum partitus est. (59. 7)

Here the two levels coincide perfectly, and the show's success lies precisely in taking the theatricality of the service to extremes; thus the play's stage, where these emphatic gestures are performed, comes to be identified with the 'culinary stage', where the food is displayed.

In the first century BC the Roman banquet seems to reach its apex, and the development of cooking techniques leads to narrower and more specialized roles for those who work with food. The *ministerium* of

---

[8] Ajax's madness must have been a popular subject for minor genres of performance. Cf. Lucian, *Salt.* 46 and, above all, Suet. *Nero* 21. 3, who refers to it as to a favourite performance theme of Nero.

cooking comes to be divided among specialists,[9] and there are even schools which train people in the main specialities, one being the *scissor*'s job: his performance in front of the guests must be dexterous and simply perfect.[10] One may compare a description of it found in Seneca:

Alius pretiosas aves scindit: per pectus et clunes certis ductibus circumferens eruditam manum frusta excutit, infelix, qui huic uni rei vivit, ut altilia *decenter* secet . . . (*Ep.* 47. 6)

Another carves costly birds: plying his expert hand in set actions over the breast and rump, he shoots out morsels—unhappy man, who lives for this one thing, to cut up chickens gracefully . . .

Here as elsewhere (cf. *Brev. vit.* 12. 5: 'quanta arte scindantur aves in frusta non enormia'), the moralist's attention is caught by the gesture's *decus* and *ars*, that is, by its aesthetic impact. A number of centuries later in Renaissance banquets the *scissor*'s gestures would once again be accorded artistic status in treatises such as Vincenzo Cervio's *Il trinciante* (Venice, 1581). Thus, not just the *cocus'* job (as Livy had already observed, see above, p. 85) but also all the other jobs connected with the banquet's *ministerium* have risen to the status of *ars* ('Quare ars apud te ministrare'; Sen. *Brev. vit.* 17. 2). Whoever aspires to be called elegant must establish his reputation on the banquet's stage ('ex his elegantiae lautitiaeque fama captatur . . . ut nec bibant sine *ambitione* nec edant'; Sen. *Brev. vit.* 12. 5); he must make sure that the *glabri* who move across the *triclinium* are delicate and graceful in their eagerness to serve, that the arrangement of the plate is perfect ('nec temere et ut libet conlocatur argentum sed perite struitur'; Sen. *Brev. vit.* 17. 2), and that the entire apparatus is meticulously set up. Eating becomes an art, a show of refined elegance, and thus turns theatrical ('ambitio et luxuria et impotentia *scaenam* desiderant'; Sen. *Ep.* 94. 71).

Let us turn, now, to Trimalchio's *mise-en-scène*. The musical accompaniment seems to be the unifying element of the whole show and serves, throughout the dinner party, to articulate its various stages and underline its most important moments. Already before the banquet, when Trimalchio comes out of the bath on his litter, he

---

[9] Cf. Marquardt (1879: i. 144 f.) and Blümner (1911: 395 ff.).

[10] An apt description of a training course for *scissores* in a chefs' school, where the appropriate gestures for the most exotic and disparate animals are meticulously described and prescribed, can be found in Juv. 11. 136–41.

is accompanied by a *symphoniacus* who 'toto itinere cantavit' (28. 5). Trimalchio then makes his star appearance 'ad symphoniam' (32. 1), and the guests are welcomed by the servants with the sound of music. Even Encolpius cannot fail to notice how theatrical the banquet is:

Pantomimi chorum, non patris familiae triclinium crederes. (31. 7)

The banquet's last act, directed by a progressively more drunken host, is a sort of collective show: Trimalchio acts out his own *parentalia* and, to this purpose, calls in a *novum acroama* and *cornicines* and encourages his guests to participate in the acting ('Putate vos, ait, ad parentalia mea invitatos esse . . . Fingite me, inquit, mortuum esse. Dicite aliquid belli'; 78. 4–5).

As we have said, the entire dinner party can be seen as a series of performances. Trimalchio is its irrepressible director and principal actor, and thus mostly holds the stage. He shows off among his clapping guests with his coarse puns, his poetry (e.g. 34. 10, 55. 3), his cultural talk and his philosophy (56. 7, 39. 4 ff.), as well as his acting (52. 9, 64. 5) and singing (35. 6, 73. 3). But all this takes place in a context where, as we have seen, entire theatre companies or groups of artistes, such as the Homeristae (59. 2 ff.) or the acrobats (53. 11 ff.), also are at home. These professionals' shows may be followed by a mime performed by one of the *famuli* (for example, the 'puer Alexandrinus' of 68. 3 who 'luscinias coepit imitari'),[11] or by, *ecce alius ludus*, the show put on by Habinnas' slave, who goes through his entire repertoire of gags (68. 4–7, 69. 4–5) or by tricks performed by the cook Daedalus (70. 7, 13) or by the guests themselves (e.g. 64. 2–5).

Another element of the *Cena* which is typical of theatre is the applause, a natural reaction to any successful performance. Thus, for example, a general applause, set off by a claque, follows the entrance of one of the most sumptuous courses: 'damus omnes plausum a familia inceptum' (36. 4). But, in his relentless exhibitionism, the host in fact attracts most of the clapping: his insipid jokes and depressing puns meet with his guests' ostentatious and unrestrained admiration (e.g. 48.7: 'Haec aliaque cum effusissimis prosequeremur laudationibus . . .'; 41. 8, etc.) while his theatrical-culinary gimmicks are received with triumphal acclamations:

---

[11] The imitation of animal voices must have been a typical form of entertainment at the theatrical *ludi*. Cf. e.g. Phaedrus 5. 5.

Plausum post hoc automatum familia dedit et 'Gaio feliciter' conclamavit.
(50. 1)

But also when Trimalchio shows off his culture, as is the case
when he interprets the Zodiac dish, his audience reacts with equal
enthusiasm:

'Sophos!' universi clamamus, et sublatis manibus ad cameram iuramus
Hipparchum Aratumque comparandos illi homines non fuisse. (40. 1)

The guests' cry, which is typical of theatres (like our 'bravo!'),[12] and
the lifted arms in sign of extreme admiration[13] are the appropriate
reaction to the act which provoked it. Trimalchio's gesture is indeed
theatrical in that it is aimed at impressing the audience and at inspiring their admiring amazement.

Amazement is in fact a recurrent theme in the *Cena*. Before even
entering the *triclinium*, at the very moment he first encounters
Trimalchio and his *lautitiae*, Encolpius and his followers are 'admiratione iam saturi' (28. 6), but their admiring amazement grows
steadily as they explore this new and extraordinary scene ('dum omnia
stupeo', 29. 1; 'miratus sum', 30. 1; 'his repleti voluptatibus', 30. 5).[14]
Trimalchio's entire show is created for this purpose and the surprise
and amazement of the 'audience' regularly reappears at the most salient
moments, as a reaction to the host's most ingenious tricks: 'nobis
lautitias mirantibus' (34. 8); 'mirantibus' the spectacle provided

---

[12] See Citroni (1975: *ad* 1. 3. 7). An interesting comparison is to be found in a letter
by Pliny (2. 14. 5). He tells us of an amusing nickname given to applause-hunters like
Trimalchio, common in judicial circles: 'inde iam non inurbane σοφοκλεῖς vocantur,
isdem Latinum nomen impositum est Laudiceni': 'from this they are now rather wit-
tily called *Sophocles*, and the same are labelled with the Latin name Laudiceni'. The term
Laudiceni puns on the parasite's habit of earning a dinner by flattery, while σοφοκλεῖς
is explained by ἀπὸ τοῦ σοφῶς καὶ καλεῖσθαι, a gloss which had entered into the text
(or at least this is the view expressed in Sherwin-White 1966: *ad loc.*, but there is still
some room for doubt here).

[13] Cf. e.g. Cic. *Acad.* 2. 63; *Fam.* 7. 5. 2; Catull. 53. 4; Hor. *Sat.* 2. 5. 97; see also Sittl
(1890: 269 ff.).

[14] The two unusual expressions 'admiratione . . . saturi' and 'repleti voluptatibus'
should perhaps be underlined. They extend the feeling of satiety (which is already
perceived before the dinner has begun) from food to the other form of entertainment
constantly offered by Trimalchio, namely a mixture of shows and *lautitiae* which
thoroughly overwhelms the guests. The same theme reappears in this wider meaning
at the end of the *Cena*, where the guests feel nauseated (78. 3: 'Ibat res ad summam
nauseam . . .'). This is the usual outcome of too much food, and special strategies in
the order and arrangement of courses were developed to avoid it.

by Ajax's madness (59. 7); and again 'mirari . . . tam elegantes strophas' (60. 1); 'mirantes' the ceiling which opens automatically (60. 2). Amazement is also provoked by actors' performances: the reaction to the end of Nicero's werewolf story is 'attonitis admiratione universis' (63. 1), and the audience wonders, 'miramur nos' (64. 1), at the end of Trimalchio's story of witches.

Thus, a number of different indications suggest that the 'show' element, in its various aspects, from theatre to the circus to gladiatorial *munera*, is central to the *Satyricon*. Apart from the fact that various professional performers attend the *triclinium*, the guests and the *Satyricon* itself display extreme familiarity with the *ludi*. Trimalchio, above all, loudly expresses his enthusiasm for mimes (35. 6, 52. 9, 73. 3) and, even more vehemently, for acrobats (53. 12) and gladiators (29. 9, 52. 3). He even goes as far as imitating his favourite champion's feats on his own funeral monument (71. 6). But the servants too (70. 13) and the guests (45. 4–8, 10–13) are fans of the circus and the amphitheatre; even Encolpius, the narrator, often reveals his familiarity with the *ludi* (31. 7, 36. 6, 47. 9),[15] and uses it to try and decode the allusions orchestrated by the dinner party's director. Thus, sometimes, when the references to performance are more specific than usual, Encolpius does not fail to notice it. This is the case, for example, at 34. 4: 'Subinde intraverunt duo Aethiopes capillati cum pusillis utribus, quales solent esse qui harenam in amphitheatro spargunt . . .'.[16]

But in order to understand the internal organization of the text, another observation needs to be made: not only does Encolpius prove to be sensitive to the theatrical character of the dinner and to insist on this characteristic feature; his attention to shows and theatre, thoroughly understandable in the context of this particular dinner, seems intrinsic to his perspective as a narrator and to his very way of

---

[15] He also uses the theatrical term *catastropha* at 54. 3 (cf. *TLL* iii. 598. 38 ff.; and in particular *Schol. ad Iuv.* 4. 122).

[16] Although Encolpius does not explictly comment on it, the process described at 68. 1, where the servants 'scorbem . . . croco et minio tinctam sparserunt et, quod numquam ante videram, ex lapide speculari pulverem tritum', was regularly carried out in the circus, as we know from Plin., *Nat. hist.* 33. 90, 36. 162; Suet. *Cal.* 18. 3. Moreover, at 60. 6 a machine wafts off crocus fragrance during the *nova ludorum remissio*: this was common practice in theatres, see Lucr. 2. 416; Hor. *Ep.* 2. 1. 79; Prop. 4. 1. 16; Ov. *Ars am.* 1. 103; Plin., *Nat. hist.* 21. 33; Mart. 5. 25. 8, etc. Deonna and Renard (1961: 45), however, link the use of saffron to religious ceremonies mainly on the basis of the context where it appears. They also underline the religious significance of the red lead at 68. 1, and mention its employment in triumphs. Indeed, as we shall see later, the solemn spectacle of public ceremonies is clearly a model for Trimalchio's banquet.

perceiving the world. To sum up, Encolpius' eye, which is Petronius' filter, seems particularly inclined to focus on the more theatrical aspects of reality, and to interpret the world through categories learned by going to the theatre. This is confirmed in other parts of the *Satyricon*: one need only recall how his language evokes the theatre. This is the case, for example, at 19. 1: 'omnia mimico risu exsonuerant'. It is also worth remembering Encolpius' descriptions of emphatic or paratragic gestures, such as Quartilla's tears 'ad ostentationem doloris paratas', which are called an 'ambitiosus imber' (17. 2–3); or of the various attempted mutilations and suicides: 'audacius tamen ille *tragoediam* implebat' (108. 11), 'nec Eumolpus interpellaverat *mimicam mortem*' (94. 15). He actually reinforces the latter observation a little later at 95. 1: 'dum haec *fabula* inter amantes luditur . . .'. Last but not least, remarkable in this context is the verse passage inserted as commentary when Encolpius is cruelly abandoned by Giton: the stage once again plays a part when the instability of friendship and good fortune is illustrated: friendship is as variable as the change from the fiction on stage to the harsh reality which re-emerges after the play is over (80. 9. 5–9).

The knowledge of the *scaena* and *ludi* which permeates the society to which Trimalchio and Petronius belong seems thus to function as a code which, given the guests' and, respectively, the readers' competence, ensures that the banquet's set-up and its connotations and further meanings are understood. We can now try to decode some of these further meanings, which in fact serve to uncover Trimalchio's intentions.

II

Every single element in the dinner's set-up is carefully orchestrated for specific symbolic or allusive purposes: the 'director' himself, Trimalchio, declares as much when he says, 'nihil sine ratione facio' (39. 14). Dining loses all the spontaneity of the necessary satisfaction of a natural need, and tends to become a rhetorical act, as well as an intensely ritual performance. Trimalchio turns the banquet into an occasion to show off his alleged culture and to amaze his guests with his *lautitiae* and wit. Even what does not happen according to plan, but rather casually and spontaneously, must achieve spectacular or paradoxical effects: thus the acrobat who falls onto Trimalchio takes advantage of the accident[17] to display his 'genial' spirit (54. 1–5).[18] In the same spirit the casual is made theatrical in the scene of the fake fight between the servants, though here the 'casual' has actually been planned: the servants ignore Trimalchio's verdict and break one another's amphorae, thus ensuring that yet more delicacies are being distributed (70. 4–6).

A similar basic principle governs the meal's scenic aspect. It is a well-known feature of Roman gastronomy that the food is presented in such a way that its main ingredients are not recognized.[19] As a passage in Cicero, *Fam.* 7. 26. 2, makes clear, the *leges sumptuariae* seem in fact to have encouraged greater refinement in cooking: the restrictions imposed on the variety and sophistication of the ingredients had to be compensated by more refined ways of processing them. Thus, the ability of Trimalchio's cook to serve a number of dishes which imitated different types of food but were actually made with the same ingredient is highly valued (70. 1). It almost seems to have been a challenge to the guests' taste and sight: Apicius 4. 2. 11 recommends a recipe by pointing out that 'nemo agnoscet quid manducet'.[20]

Clearly, this habit of dissimulating the real ingredients of a dish under false pretences fits quite well with the highly artistic and artificial presentation of the food itself. This was the responsibility of the *structor*, who was in charge of *fercula docte componere*.[21] Thus presented, the food was meant to convey highly symbolic meanings. Perhaps the most illuminating example of this is provided by the passage that describes the dish representing the Zodiac, probably the most elaborate in the entire dinner. When it first appears, it disappoints the guests' expectations: 'laudationem ferculum est insecutum plane non pro expectatione magnum' (35. 1); and they proceed to taste, without too much enthusiasm, the simple foods placed on every Zodiac sign:

---

[17] I do think that this is an accident rather than a planned occurrence. One indication that this is the case is that the *aulaeum* in Horace's *Cena, Sat.* 2. 8. 64 ff., undoubtedly the model of this passage, falls by accident. Cf. Révay (1922: 209) and Shero (1923: 136 ff.).

[18] Early on, before entering into the *triclinium*, Trimalchio similarly takes advantage of the incident of the wine spilled by fighting masseurs, and interprets it as a good omen for himself (28. 3). Barchiesi (1981: 140 f.) talks about the absence of the chance element in the *Cena*.   [19] See e.g. lines 26–8 in Horace's *Cena, Sat.* 2. 8.

[20] Cf. e.g. Mart. 11. 31; other relevant passages are quoted by André (1965: 108).

[21] Juv. 7. 184 f. On Trimalchio's *structor*, see especially 35. 2. There are frequent references in Petronius to the chef's *doctrina*: see e.g. Trimalchio's compliments at 70. 1 ff. as well as Encolpius' subtle irony at 70. 7: 'ingeniosus cocus'; and at 74. 5: 'ab illo doctissimo coco'.

'tristiores ad tam viles accessimus cibos' (35. 7). But Trimalchio, far from failing to notice this initial disappointment, has certainly planned it.[22] It is meant as a foil to the spectacular entrance of the dancing cooks accompanied by music (36. 1), who suddenly lift the lid and provoke a general applause: 'damus omnes plausum a familia inceptum et res electissimas ridentes aggredimur' (36. 4). Trimalchio is satisfied with the outcome of his gag: 'eiusmodi methodio laetus' (36. 5); and later reveals the principles which govern his direction, begging his guests not to consider him witless or his dinner unrefined:

Rogo, me putatis illa cena esse contentum, quam in theca repositorii videratis? 'Sic notus Ulixes?' Quid ergo est? Oportet etiam inter cenandum philologiam nosse. (39. 3–4)[23]

Trimalchio boasts that his dinner parties are cultural occasions. Later he points out that he does not serve food fit for *rustici* (47. 10). At his home, even the natural activity of eating is sublimated into a highly symbolic and intellectual enterprise, where the various scenic elements build up into a complex performance.

Trimalchio is turned on by the human ability to control and manipulate nature, and takes it as evidence for the triumph of culture and as a reassuring sign of his own genius. His enthusiasm for the chef's virtuoso performance is significant: the cook's ability to manipulate with his *ars* the most basic ingredients inspires Trimalchio, who names him Daedalus (70. 2), like the eponymous hero of civilization and mechanics. The 'machine' theme, in its various forms, runs through the *Cena*,[24] and represents an aspect of the more general 'show' element. It is indeed well known that machines played an important role in theatres and circuses and were conspicuous in Petronius' extravagant times. One is reminded of Seneca's words, when he

---

[22] Ciaffi (1955: 47) rightly makes this point in his analysis of the scene.

[23] As Cameron (1970: 406) and Fedeli (1981: 100 f.) have pointed out, it is remarkable that, by quoting the Vergilian line, Trimalchio claims for himself Ulixes' multiform ingenuity. He implicitly compares the principle which governs his spectacular courses to the trick of the fatal wooden horse: they too hide an unexpected truth under their deceiving appearances. But this comparison with the Trojan horse must have been more common than we might expect: Macrobius 3. 13. 13 informs us that already in the second century BCE a dish called *porcus Troianus* was very popular in Rome: 'quem illi ideo sic vocabant, quasi aliis inclusis animalibus gravidum, ut ille Troianus "equus gravidus armatis" fuit': 'which they named such for this reason, as being pregnant with other creatures shut inside it, just as the famous Trojan horse was "pregnant with armed men" '. This dish must have been remarkably similar to those offered in our *Cena*.

[24] Barchiesi (1981: 134, 139 f., 142 f.) makes some valuable observations on this aspect.

contrasts Diogenes with his opposite, Daedalus, and considers technical progress as responsible for the corruption of the modern man:

qui invenit quemadmodum in immensam altitudinem crocum latentibus fistulis exprimat, qui curipos subito aquarum impetu implet aut siccat et ver satilia cenationum laquearia ita coagmentat ut subinde alia facies atque alia succedat et totiens tecta quotiens fercula mutentur. (*Ep.* 90. 15)

The one who discovers a means of spraying saffron perfumes to a tremendous height from hidden pipes, who fills or empties channels in one sudden rush of water, who constructs a set of interchangeable ceilings for a dining-room in such a way as to produce a constant set of different patterns, with a change of ceiling at each course . . . (tr. Campbell 1969)

The enthusiasm of Claudius and Nero for *automata* is well attested (Suet. *Cl.* 21. 6 and 34. 2; and *Nero* 34. 2); and the most famous examples of *cenationes* with mechanized ceilings are those in Nero's *domus aurea*:

cenationes laqueatae tabulis eburneis versatilibus, ut flores, fistulatis, ut unguenta desuper spargerentur; praecipua cenationum rotunda, quae perpetuo diebus ac noctibus vice mundi circumageretur. (*Nero* 31. 2)

All the dining-rooms had ceilings of fretted ivory, the panels of which could slide back and let a rain of flowers, or of perfume from hidden sprinklers, shower upon his guests. The main dining-room was circular, and its roof revolved slowly, day and night, in time with the sky. (tr. Graves 1957)

Just as Nero loves to put on a show consisting of the world which rotates around its ruler, namely Nero himself, so Trimalchio also wants to simulate his own universe where the thundering gods send gifts down from heaven (60. 1–3). He uses the technology available to him and meticulously plans the choreography of the dinner, which seems to include, in its complex symbolism, a series of allusions to public ceremonies and religious rituals.[25] A passage from Sallust preserved by Macrobius can be used to clarify the intention behind the employment of an *automatum* such as the one on the ceiling.[26] Sallust (*Hist.* 2 fr. 59 McGushin) describes the impressive banquets organized for Quintus Caecilius Metellus Pius, which were exceptionally sumptuous: 'ultra Romanum ac mortalium etiam morem'; the room was draped and adorned and a stage was set up 'ad ostentationem histrionum':

---

[25] This is confirmed, among other passages, by the technical expression 'de caelo nuntiaretur', which belongs to the language of augurs. For the religious connotations of this scene, see Grondona (1980: 83 ff.), who offers a number of parallels and a bibliography.   [26] Macrobius 3. 13. 7–9 (= Sall. *Hist.* 2. 59 McGushin).

simul croco sparsa humus et alia in modum templi celeberrimi. Praeterea tum sedenti in transenna demissum Victoriae simulacrum cum machinato strepitu tonitruum coronam ei imponebat, tum venienti ture quasi deo supplicabatur.[27]

The floor was strewn with saffron, and other features recalled the magnificence of a temple. In addition to that, when he was seated, a statue of Victory, let down by a rope and accompanied by the artificially produced sound of thunder, used to place a crown on his head; then when he ventured abroad he was worshipped with incense as if a god. (tr. McGushin 1992)

But I shall return later to this type of allusion in Trimalchio's banquet.

For the time being, let us focus more closely on the overall principle which governs the banquet's culinary show. The sublimation of nature which, in this case, is represented by the food is achieved through an illusory imitation of nature itself, that is, of the food in its original form, or at some stage in its processing. It goes without saying that the fake dissimulation of food processing actually celebrates its success; as the principle of mimetic aesthetics prescribes, *ars est celare artem*. Thus the sausages are, of course, served already cooked and still *ferventia*, but at the same time the cooking process is reproduced by placing under the silver grate some 'Syriaca pruna cum granis Punici mali', which represent coal embers (31. 11). Similarly, the bread offered by the page at 35. 6 is carried in inside a silver *clibanus*, which represents its oven.[28] The intention seems to be that of representing under the eye of the guests the entire process of cooking from its very first stages; thus we get the pretence that, during the banquet, a pig is chosen, killed, and immediately cooked (47. 8 ff.). This pig, which in the space of a fleeting moment reappears on the table perfectly cooked,

---

[27] Cf. Val. Max. 9. 1. 5: 'Palmata veste convivia celebrabat demissasque lacunaribus aureas coronas velut caelesti capite recipiebat.'

[28] All this is also done in accordance with another fashion of the times, that for 'open cooking': the food was served while extremely hot and almost still cooking. This seems to be an attempt to go back to nature, and a regression to a more 'primitive' cultural stage; see Sen. *Ep.* 78, where the cooks are described as 'ipsos cum opsoniis focos transferentium' so that 'cenam culina prosequitur'. It was fashionable, for example, to cook fish that had just been caught at the banquet itself: 'in cubili natant pisces et sub ipsa mensa capitur que statim transferatur in mensam' (Sen. *NQ* 3. 17. 2); '... in ipso ferculo exspiret' (3. 18. 2). Apart from the eating itself, this ensured the further pleasure of watching the animals' death. Cf. Sen. *NQ* 3. 18. 1: 'Hoc ... tam pulchro spectaculo'; and 3. 18. 7: 'Non sunt ad popinam dentibus et ventre et ore contenti; oculis quoque gulosi sunt.' In fact, Seneca's entire chapter insists on these perverse pleasures of sight. For a list of sources and a discussion of this subject, see Citroni Marchetti (1983: 76 ff.).

serves to introduce one of the most appreciated *automata* (50. 1): Trimalchio pretends that the chef has forgotten to take out the pig's entrails and the absent-minded cook is therefore called in and asked to *exinterare* the creature there and then. Here, too, the illusionist trick imitates reality: the intestine yields perfectly processed entrails, in the form of sausages and black puddings (49. 10). The same principle holds for the pastry eggs covered by a wooden hen. The gimmick is based on the idea that 'in all likelihood' the eggs should by now contain a chick. At 33. 5 Trimalchio says, 'timeo ne iam concepti sint', and Encolpius is about to throw out his serving 'nam videbatur . . . iam in pullum coisse' (33. 7). And sure enough the guests find out that they contain a small bird: 'pinguissimam ficedulam . . . piperato vitello circumdatam' (33. 8).

These last two tricks suggest a further observation: by pursuing this 'fake realism' in its minutest detail, yet another theatrical effect is achieved. To disembowel a pig in front of one's guests cannot exactly be called elegant. It is an open and crass breach of an elementary norm of behaviour: one ought to offer a 'finished product' and dissimulate the more unpleasant and, in some cases, revolting aspects of the *ars* which accomplished it. (One is reminded of a famous passage in Ovid's *Ars amatoria*: 3. 209–34.) It is equally obvious that impregnated eggs should not be served at a dinner party. However, just as soon as the guests experience the thrills of transgression or of embarassment, as when they are 'consternati' by the insolence of two servants towards Trimalchio (70. 5–6), the supposed gaffe turns out to be a brilliant way of deepening the guests' astonishment and admiration. Another episode which is remarkable for its shifting ground between fiction and reality is the staging of the boar-course described at chapter 40. This is a sort of *venatio* foreshadowed by its symbolic and allusive setting: 'advenerunt ministri ac toralia praeposuerunt toris, in quibus retia erant picta subsessoresque cum venabulis et totus venationis apparatus' (40. 1). Against this background we witness a proper hunt with barking dogs (40. 2), and with fowlers ready to catch the thrushes which fly out of the boar's belly: 'Parati aucupes cum harundinibus fuerunt, et eos circa triclinium volitantes momento exceperunt' (40. 6).

The spectacular character of Trimalchio's dinner party essentially lies in this mediation of nature through culture: rather than being served as it is, nature seems to be 'staged' and processed through a symbolic and ritual filter. It is precisely as a show that the banquet serves to

establish Trimalchio's culture and power in front of a selected audience. This takes us once again to some Renaissance court banquets
which were conceived as proper shows and included theatre performances, concerts, dances, as well as buffoons' and acrobats'
sketches. One need only think of the famous wedding of Cosimo II at
Florence in 1608. On this occasion, the Salone dei Cinquecento in the
Palazzo Vecchio was turned into an amphitheatre. The guests sat on
the stairs arranged along the walls and the banquet–show occupied
the middle of the hall. Equally famous is the wedding banquet for
Marie de' Medici in 1600, which was orchestrated by Buontalenti, the
great master of stage machinery. He worked out a series of amazing
automata, such as revolving tables or triumphal carts which crossed
the stage. We find exactly the same ceremonial solemnity, the same
combination of engineering and high cuisine, of machinery and
music, in Trimalchio's dinner party. The banquet finds its sublimation against an ideal-symbolic background and turns into the triumph
of its most liberal of hosts.

III

Apart from scenic dishes accomplished by the chef's sophisticated
techniques, another characteristic feature of Roman banquets, like
Trimalchio's, is the ceremonial service which is invariably solemn and
impeccable. This is carried out by the most good-looking, and usually
Asiatic, pages: Juvenal calls them the 'flos Asiae' (5. 56). In their hands
the food becomes a glorious trophy. Take the lobster served to Virro:

> Aspice quam longo distinguat pectore lancem
> quae fertur domino squilla, et quibus undique saepta
> asparagis qua despiciat convivia cauda,
> dum venit excelsi manibus sublata ministri.
>
> (Juv. 5. 80–3)[29]

That lobster there, adorning the dish on its way to the master—look at
the length of its body and how it is walled around with choice asparagus; see
how its tail looks down on the party as it enters, borne aloft by the hands of
a towering waiter. (tr. Rudd 1992)

---

[29] For the importance of the food's visual impact, its *species*, cf. Hor. *Sat.* 2. 2. 35 ('ducit
te species') and 39 f. ('Porrectum magno magnum spectare catino | vellem'), as well as
2. 4. 76 f.

The *ministerium* of the servants allocated to serving at the dinner table seems to be modelled on the ritual solemnity of public religious ceremonies. Remarkable, in this context, is a passage from Horace's *Cena Nasidieni*, where the servants' solemn parade is compared to processions in honour of Demeter:

> ut Attica virgo
> cum sacris Cereris procedit fuscus Hydaspes
> Caecuba vina ferens, Alcon Chium maris expers.

> *(Sat. 2. 8. 13–15)*

Like the Athenian maiden with the sacred objects of Ceres, the dusky Hydaspes advanced bearing Caecuban wine, Alcon brought Chian wine which had never seen the sea.

In describing a banquet of the imperial age Macrobius also insists on the ceremonial and almost religious way in which a fish is served: 'a coronatis . . . cum tibicinis cantu, quasi quaedam non deliciarum sed numinis pompa' (3. 16. 8).[30]

As far as Trimalchio's banquet is concerned, it has already been mentioned that its pomp seems at times to assume a specifically religious connotation; and it is on the show's religious character, rather than on the infinitely large number of religious and superstitious elements in the *Satyricon*, that we shall now focus.[31] One clear example is provided by the section which precedes a traditional ceremony at banquets: the libation to the Lares and the emperor. After a machine 'miraculously' opens up the ceiling and a *repositorium* full of fruit and cakes is introduced, precisely as the guests are about to lay hands on this solemn course, 'ad pompam' (60. 5), another *automatum* wafts out saffron.[32] At this point, the guests are convinced that they are facing a sacred meal and begin to invoke the emperor:

Rati ergo sacrum esse ferculum tam religioso apparatu perfusum, consurreximus altius et Augusto, patri patriae, feliciter diximus. (60. 7)

Encolpius himself explicitly comments on the analogy between this course and a religious ceremony. This analogy becomes all the more evident if we compare a description of the *ministerium* typically

---

[30] Also in Sen. *Tranq. an.* 1. 8, the model for the servants' pomposity seems to be provided by public ceremonies: 'diligentius quam in tralatu vestita et auro culta mancipia'.

[31] For religion and superstition in the *Satyricon*, see Deonna and Renard (1961) and the more recent and more specific Grondona (1980).

[32] Deonna and Renard comment on the religious connotation of this detail, see above, n. 16.

associated with Arval rites: 'mor[e] pompae . . . fercula . . . transierunt' (*Acta Arv.* p. 27 Herzen),[33] or descriptions of other public ceremonies, and especially of triumphs.[34]

The same models, namely official public and religious ceremonies, seem to lie behind another characteristic feature of Trimalchio's behaviour: namely, his passion for inscriptions, his tendency to record with scrupulous solemnity, and to comment in verse, the events which happen in his own little world.[35] Remarkable, in this context, are the words in which Trimalchio expresses his wish to write down the 'moral' of the accident of the fallen acrobat drawn by his guests: 'Ita . . . non oportet hunc casum sine inscriptione transire' (55. 2).[36] Trimalchio loves to make formal records of his strict provisions as the master of the house: 'quisquis servus sine dominico iussu foras exierit, accipiet plagas centum' (28. 7), or even, quite simply, of his actions, for example, when he 'foras cenat' (30. 3). He seems to want to make them official and ensure that they are remembered.[37] Proud as he is of his own greatness, Trimalchio shows off, within his little domestic universe, the symbols of his success and of the honours he received, as if they were trophies.[38] He also repeatedly affirms his

---

[33] Cf. P. Paris s.v. *ferculum*, in Daremberg *et al.* (1817–1919: 1041), and Grondona (1980: 84 n. 250), who studies the influence of religion on Petronius' language.

[34] It is perhaps worth noting that the term *ferculum*, which in Petronius denotes the sumptuous courses served at the banquet, is more commonly used of the carts and other instruments used to carry images of gods, trophies, or other appropriate objects during the solemn processions at public ceremonies, and in particular at triumphs. In this latter meaning it often occurs together with *pompa* (see *TLL* vi. 1. 491. 35 ff.) and this connection may have facilitated its usage in the context of dining.

[35] On this point, see the overall discussion offered by Tremoli (1960), who underlines the official and solemn aspect of Trimalchio's inscriptions, which can sometimes be detected in their very layout. Grondona (1980: 37 f.) compares Trimalchio's taste for inscriptions with the references to religious ceremonies and triumphal *tabulae*.

[36] The celebration of avoided peril clearly parodies a quite traditional model which was especially common in epigrams. See Citroni (1975: 53 f.).

[37] As Tremoli (1960: 27) points out, 'the inscriptions are for him the marble and lasting record of public life'.

[38] In fact, in showing off his position, Trimalchio takes as his models much higher offices than the one of *sevir* which he actually holds. This is true also of Habinnas, see 65.3–4, for which a remarkable parallel is Hor. *Sat.* 1. 5. 34–6. In Trimalchio's case, we may notice that, whereas in a Roman house trophies were usually displayed in the *vestibulum* (see Blümner 1911: 14 n. 4, for evidence), he places the *fasces*, which are symbolic of consular status, on the doorposts of the *triclinium*. His *fasces* end with ship *rostra* made of bronze: these are an allusion to Trimalchio's 'sea victories', that is, to his success in trading. Thus, the freedman pays homage to and appropriates the official symbols of aristocratic *honores* in order to express his own market ideology. For a discussion of the most conspicuous ways in which Trimalchio imitates social statuses higher than his own, namely the equestrian and senatorial classes, see Narducci (1984), who discusses the chapter on Petronius in D'Arms (1981).

absolute power by passing decrees (54. 5), delivers verdicts about fake controversies (70. 5); or makes an *actuarius* read out an account of what happens in his 'empire', 'tamquam Urbis acta' (53. 1 ff.). This is as solemn as an Italian *Gazzetta ufficiale*, which is in fact modelled on the Roman *acta* of Caesar's times.[39] Thus, to sum up, Trimalchio tends to appropriate for himself, more or less explicitly, the prestige of the ruling classes and to claim all types of power, indeed almost to the ultimate extent of styling himself an emperor.[40]

Within his little universe Trimalchio exploits every opportunity to act out his own life. And the banquet, with the audience it provides, is quite a good one. The orders he gives to Habinnas concerning the scenes, taken from his own life, which are to decorate his funerary monument seem particularly significant, in that he wants his public image and his acts of extreme, imperial generosity to be given special priority (71. 9–11). After his funeral, which must be as solemn as his prestige requires ('ego gloriosus volo efferri, ut totus mihi populus bene imprecetur', 78. 2), his very tomb will constitute the final act of the show which is Trimalchio's life. He expects it to secure immortal glory for him: 'ut quisquis horas inspiciet, velit nolit, nomen meum legat' (71. 11); 'ut mihi contingat tuo beneficio post mortem vivere' (71. 6). However, Trimalchio is not going to wait until his own funeral to make himself the object of fine art: the most important moments of his life and his triumphal successes are already the subjects of paintings inside his house (29. 3–6). The narrative character of these paintings, their realistic portrayal of specific events, their educational function, and their obvious allegories seem to suggest that they are modelled on paintings of triumphs,[41] whose main purpose was to display to the people the great achievements of the main

---

[39] Trimalchio's *acta* are solemn also in their language; see for example, in the formulaic expression 'quod est T.' at 53. 2. Cf. Smith (1975: *ad loc.*), who rightly does not accept Müller's athetesis. Another example of linguistic solemnity is provided by the archaic 'Sextiles', which rather than simply being 'a little quaint', as Smith writes, seems to emphasize the dignified and official character of the document. Tremoli (1960: 18) points out that Trimalchio 'wishes to assume the tone and the gravity of the ancient Roman'. In Trimalchio's confused and multiform ideology there is a place also for the archaic element. It emerges, for example, in the revealing passage where Trimalchio composes his own epitaph: after having praised himself for the wealth he has accumulated, he adds, 'nec umquam philosophum audivit' (71. 12), which, in an archaizing context that reminds us of Cato, is also taken to be a merit. This point is well brought out by Tremoli (1960: 23 f.).

[40] See Smith (1975: 142) and Narducci (1984). Trimalchio's satisfaction with his own αὐτάρκεια (see 48. 2–3, quoted by Narducci, and also the speech of the guest sitting next to Encolpius, especially at 37. 8–38. 6) also seems to indicate that he aspires to absolute power, much like the emperor.   [41] Cf. Becatti (1951: 169 f.).

public figures in Rome. Two particular scenes deserve to be singled out: one is the triumphal arrival of the young Trimalchio at Rome, which alludes to the iconography of the *adventus Augusti*;[42] and the other is the representation of Trimalchio as he is invested with the office of *sevir Augustalis*. He has chosen to be represented in a solemn pose as he is led by Mercury towards the *tribunal excelsum* to which the *sevir* had a right in his role as *editor ludorum*. The scene is styled on the apotheosis of emperors, the model of which can be traced back to the iconography of Alexander.[43] It is also significant that here too Trimalchio insists on his public role, and in particular on his role as organizer of *ludi*, which was a highly popular and prestigious public office. Clearly, Trimalchio puts on stage his entire existence and models this show on public institutions and ceremonies. Particularly remarkable is the occasional appearance of the imperial model. His favourite stage, however, remains the banquet, which is at the same time theatre and triumph: σύνδειπνον, τουτέστι πομπὴ καὶ θέατρον, as Plutarch would say.[44] There he fulfils his highest aspiration: that of offering and admiring the show of his very own self.[45]

[42] Cf. Becatti (1951: 170) and Magi (1971: 88 ff.).

[43] See the analysis of this passage by Campanile (1964: 123–6). Another trace of 'Trimalchio's 'apotheosis' can perhaps be detected also at 29. 3, where Trimalchio is given Mercury's staff. This suggests an identification between him and his guardian god, since the god-to-be was often assimilated to a divinity simply in that he had acquired its specific attributes. [44] *Cupid. div.* 528b.

[45] For the popularity of the *scaena* in Petronius' time I recommend once more the fine study by Barchiesi (1981, esp. 132 ff.).

5

Environment, Linguistic Situation, and Levels of Style in Petronius' *Satyrica*

HUBERT PETERSMANN

I. Date, Intention, and Title of the Work

Any student of Petronius notices on every page of his novel the author's linguistic art. For, more than any other ancient writer, Petronius, who sets his narrative in his own, that is the Neronian, era,[1] has the capacity to represent in an adequate style the environment he is describing. The author's genius consists in his ability to use the language of his characters to give a realistic picture of the society of the early empire and its typical representatives. Characters depicted in vivid colours illustrate the various aspects of the intellectual and material ambience of their epoch.

By contrast with most Greek novels of love and adventure, however, Petronius' heroes are not high-ranking persons, but rather middle- and lower-class people, such as students, teachers, rich freedmen, and a would-be-poet. Hence, Petronius gives up the idealized, pseudo-historical setting of the conventional Greek novel of love and advent-ure and puts his characters into a wholly realistic environment, his own, with which his contemporary readers are familiar. Accordingly, the distant locations in which most novels are set have been replaced by well-known places in the Roman empire. Thus the bulk of the preserved fragments—Petronius' work perhaps consisted of twenty-four books originally—is set in south Italy. Cumae or Puteoli are the most

This chapter was translated by Martin Revermann.

[1] Criteria of content and parody, e.g. the relations between the work of Petronius and the poetry of Lucian, Seneca, and other authors, make it certain that the author of our novel is identical with the *arbiter elegantiae* at Nero's court who is described by Tacitus at *Ann.* 16. 17–18. Cf. the detailed discussion in Rose (1971), Müller and Ehlers (1983: 485 ff.), Coffey (1976: 178 ff.), Petersmann (1977: 27 f.), and, most recently with further literature, Sullivan (1985*b*: 1666 ff.).

likely candidates for the setting of the *Cena Trimalchionis*: there are several references to the location as a 'colonia' (44. 12, 16, 57. 9, etc.), while at 81. 3 we find 'Graeca urbs'; 116 ff., on the other hand, is set at Croton.[2] This realistic world harmonizes with the linguistic style of the characters. Consequently, Petronius' novel not only provides a realistic portrait of customs and manners in the early empire; it also bears most valuable testimony to contemporary colloquial and vulgar speech.

One of the author's primary aims, however, is to mock his contemporary world and its shortcomings by accurately describing them.[3] This parodic intention is already evident in the title: from the form 'Satyricon' transmitted in the oldest preserved manuscript of Petronius, the Bernensis (B), it is to be inferred that Petronius entitled his work not, as was formerly believed, 'Satirae' or 'Satyricon', but 'Satyrica'.[4] On the one hand, the title 'Satyrica' refers parodically to the titles of the Greek novel of love and adventure, such as Lollianus' *Phoinikika*, Xenophon's *Ephesiaka*, Heliodorus' *Aithiopika*, etc.; on the other hand, it hints at the shameless and frivolous stories of the hero Encolpius and his friends, who like satyrs led a leisurely, unrestrained life full of escapades and love affairs, thus recalling Aristides' erotic novel *Milesiaka*. For Petronius not only made his characters experience the standard involuntary adventures of the Greek novels—pursuit by an angry god, sea-storm and shipwreck, apparent death, etc.—he also let them voluntarily lead the disreputable and good-for-nothing life of satyrs, in order to provide a contrast with the traditional heroes of the novel. Petronius' *Satyrica* is thus the earliest picaresque novel in world literature.

But there was yet another reason for choosing the title 'Satyrica': it was meant to be associated with Roman satire, whose main characteristic had originally been great variety of content and form—a *mélange*, that is to say, which in Petronius is augmented in a unique and unprecedented fashion by the variety of different levels of language and style. Since Lucilius there was also satire in our sense of the word, the tendency to mock and ridicule, a feature which is also essential

---

[2] I would therefore take issue with, for example, Walsh (1970: 76), who argues for a wholly fictitious setting; see also Smith (1975: pp. xviii ff.).

[3] Cf. especially Sullivan (1968*a*: 158 ff.); Courtney (1962: 86 ff.); and Burck (1979*a*: 202 ff.).

[4] Thus rightly Müller and Ehlers (1983: 491 f.) and Walsh (1970: 72), as already Henriksson (1956: 74 ff.); van Rooy (1965: 154), however, maintains the singular *Satyricon*.

to the Greek post-classical satyr play. Thus the title 'Satyrica' refers not only to Roman satire, but also to Greek satyr play.

With its mixture of prose and verse—which, however, is also found in the older type of novel,[5] even if to a lesser extent—the *Satyrica* appears to be a *satura Menippea*. Named after its first great representative, Menippos of Gadara (third century BC), Menippean satire had been introduced into Roman literature by Varro. One of its chief characteristics is the occasional interspersion of Greek passages, which also occurs in Petronius, though to a much lesser degree. In one respect, however, Petronius' work is markedly different from the typical *satura Menippea*. The *Menippea* is short, often of fantastic nature, focuses on a single subject, and has didactic aims in the manner of Cynic popular philosophy. The *Satyrica*, on the other hand, is firmly embedded in reality, has several subjects, and, on the whole, is written in Latin, with the exception of a few Greek expressions, which have a clear stylistic function as social markers. Furthermore, Petronius eschews the part of a moralist; on the contrary, he makes fun of the society he is describing, its follies and vices, its constant lying, and its language too, by rendering them in full detail as a result of accurate observation. Owing to this faithful and realistic depiction of the characters, their environment, situation, and style, the *Satyrica* presents itself as a mime with a satirical tendency.

II. PETRONIUS AND PERIPATETIC THEORIES OF STYLE

In order to achieve his satirical purpose the author makes use of the entire linguistic repertoire at his disposal. Petronius' forte is not only that he, more than any other ancient author, has a uniquely fine ear for the language of his environment and is therefore able to portray it accurately, but also that he employs the appropriate stylistic means at the right moment within the plot. So he succeeds in achieving

[5] For the first time in Chariton's *Callirhoe*, probably the oldest completely preserved sample of the Greek erotic novel, dating from the end of the first century BC. While Chariton's verse insertions are no longer than four lines and are mainly quotations from Homer, Petronius' are long and original. Another difference between Petronius and Chariton is that the latter's poetic insertions serve to underline emotions like pain, joy, and astonishment, whereas Petronius' poetic passages are independent of the rest of the work: their main purpose is to demonstrate the author's skill in writing poetry. The prosimetrum of the Iolaus fragment, on the other hand, may be more like Petronius: see Barchiesi (1986), translated in this volume (Ch. 6).

correspondence between content, characters, and their style, something unrivalled in the whole of ancient literature. In that respect
Petronius reveals an excellent knowledge of the Peripatetic theories
of style, for he applies their postulates to the style of his characters,
sometimes even in a perverted form, thus creating a comic impact,
achieving what Aristotle describes at *Rhet.* 3. 7. 1–2 (= 1408ª10 ff.):
'The *lexis* [linguistic register] will be appropriate if it expresses
emotion and characater and is proportional to the subject-matter.
Proportion exists if there is discussion neither of weighty matters in
a casual way nor of shoddy things solemnly, and if ornament is not
attached to a shoddy word. Otherwise, the result seems comedy . . .'
(tr. Kennedy 1991). Aristotle's pupil Theophrastus mentions the two
relations which every utterance has, to the hearers and to the things
mentioned; cf. fr. 64 (ed. Wimmer), 'since the utterance has two relations, one to its listeners, the other to its subject-matter', and fr. 65
(ed. Wimmer), 'the attitude of the utterance is twofold, as the philosopher Theophrastus has defined, that towards the listeners to whom
it is communicating something, and that towards the subject-matter,
of which the speaker aims to persuade his listeners'. These views are
found frequently in later rhetoricians.[6] See, for instance, Theon, *Prog.*
235 (*Rhetores Graeci*, ii, Spengel) in his discussion of prosopopoeia:
'Prosopopoeia is the introduction of a character speaking words
unambiguously suited to himself and to the prevailing situation.'
And in the following chapter Theon mentions those factors which
are to be taken into account in a fictitious speech (236): 'And first it
is necessary to consider the nature of the speaker's character, and
to whom the speech is directed, and the age of those present, and
the occasion, and the place, and the chance circumstances, and the
underlying subject of the words intended to be spoken.'

III. The Peculiarity of Petronius' Language in
Comparison with Other Authors

No other ancient author applied the so-called 'pragmatic'[7] postulates
of the Peripatetic theoreticians of style, who have only recently been
rediscovered and rephrased by modern linguistic psychology, to such

---

[6] Cf. also later Joh. Sard., *Comment. in Aphthon. progymn.*, pp. 19621 ff. (ed. Rabe).
[7] On the term 'pragmatic' in textual linguistics, see the detailed discussion in
Petersmann (1983: 95 ff.) with further modern literature.

an extent and so persistently as Petronius. Intent on creating realistic portrayals, Petronius represents the uneducated main characters as talking in a linguistically lower style, which reflects the *sermo vulgaris* of his time. This is particularly the case for the freedmen's speeches in the *Cena Trimalchionis*. By deliberately imitating their *sermo*, he is providing us with a much clearer and more faithful testimony to popular language than many other authors, who may in effect be writing in vulgar Latin, but who are actually attempting unsuccessfully to express themselves in a refined style. In consequence, according to their social rank and education, the style of such authors is greatly influenced by the artificial language of high literature. One example is the *Iter Egeriae*, whose language is not vulgar but, as Löfstedt[8] has pointed out, completely stylized. A high degree of stylization, caused not least by the metre, is also encountered in Plautus' diction, which in terms of everyday language does not have the same value as that of Trimalchio and his friends in Petronius' novel. Plautus is not concerned with depicting everyday language. His aim is not parody, which Petronius achieves through peculiarity of diction, but comedy through action. This is why Plautus generally makes all his characters talk in a barely differentiated *sermo*. Thus those who belong to free and higher classes, even gods, tend not to talk in a manner different from slaves, prostitutes, pimps, or soldiers.[9] Nor are members of a socially lower stratum specifically characterized by means of language, as happens, for instance, in the *Metamorphoses* of Apuleius, a text composed in a rhetorically stilted style. The same also applies to the language of the main characters in the surviving Greek novels. This is not to say that the diction of these authors is always uniform: they too employ linguistic devices, but it is only specific situations and particular desired effects which give a certain and momentary colour to the generally uniform language of the characters.

It hardly needs to be mentioned that the same factors are vital in Petronius. But strangely enough, it is just these psychological aspects of language which have not been sufficiently taken into account for the constitution of the text and the exegesis of the sophisticated prose of our author.

---

[8] Löfstedt (1911: 9 ff.).
[9] Recent studies on Plautus, however, have shown that he, too, differentiates the language of his characters according to social class and origin, sex, and age: see Maltby (1979, 1985); Gilleland (1979); Stockert (1982); Adams (1984); Jocelyn (1993); Petersmann (1995c, 1996–7).

III.1. The sermo urbanus

Since Bücheler's[10] fundamental recension of the text more than a
hundred years ago, those prose passages which are spoken by the
narrator Encolpius and his educated friends have been called 'sophisticated'. A series of editors and linguists have wanted to separate
too strictly the sophisticated from the vulgar parts of the *Satyrica*: in
the wake of Bücheler, among others, Heraeus,[11] Stefenelli,[12] and, most
recently, Smith.[13] These scholars accepted vulgarisms in the lexical
area,[14] but usually did not tolerate deviations from the norms of
grammar in the case of the narrator Encolpius and the other educated
characters, and thus resorted to conjectural solutions. This attitude
is to be discarded along with the opposite view, advocated especially by Marmorale[15] and Swanson,[16] who argue for a largely uniform
prose style of the *Satyrica* and are inclined to regard it as vulgar
throughout. Both views are extreme, since sophisticated prose is a highly
complex stylistic phenomenon: in fact, Petronius employs various
kinds of diction according to his artistic intentions and the specific situation.[17] Müller in the third edition of his excellent Tusculum text (with
a German translation by Ehlers[18]) takes this fact fully into account,
in contrast with the text of the *editio maior* which was greatly influenced by Fraenkel.[19]

III.1.1. The Rhetorical Style

As one might expect, the style of Encolpius' declamation on the
decline of oratory at the beginning of the novel is rhetorical:

(1. 1) num alio genere furiarum declamatores inquietantur, qui clamant: 'haec
vulnera pro libertate publica excepi, hunc oculum pro vobis impendi; date mihi
[ducem] qui me ducat ad liberos meos, nam succisi poplites membra non sustin-
ent'? (2) haec ipsa tolerabilia essent, si ad eloquentiam ituris viam facerent.

---

[10] Bücheler (1862).   [11] Bücheler (1922).
[12] Stefenelli (1962) is too categorical in declaring that all parts not belonging to the
speeches of Trimalchio and his uneducated guests are composed in an elevated and
elegant style. Cf. against this Risch (1963: 211 ff.), who adduces the vulgar colour of a
speech of an administrator called Bargates in *Sat.* 96. 7.
[13] Smith (1975); cf. also the literature quoted in the bibliography of Petersmann
(1977: 13 ff.).
[14] Cf. Heraeus (1899), corrected and augmented in Heraeus (1937: 52 ff.), and my
treatment of lexical vulgarisms below (pp. 116–18).
[15] Marmorale (1948: 198–223, 1961).   [16] Swanson (1963: p. xxxi).
[17] Cf. Petersmann (1977: 23 ff.).   [18] Müller and Ehlers (1983).
[19] Müller (1961).

nunc et rerum tumore et sententiarum vanissimo strepitu hoc tantum proficiunt, ut cum in forum venerint, putent se in alium orbem terrarum delatos. (3) et ideo ego adulescentulos existimo in scholis stultissimos fieri, quia nihil ex his quae in usu habemus aut audiunt aut vident, sed piratas cum catenis in litore stantes, sed tyrannos edicta scribentes quibus imperent filiis ut patrum suorum capita praecidant, sed responsa in pestilentiam data ut virgines tres aut plures immolentur, sed mellitos verborum globulos et omnia dicta factaque quasi papavere et sesamo sparsa.

(2. 1) qui inter haec nutriuntur non magis sapere possunt quam bene olere qui in culina habitant. (2) pace vestra liceat dixisse, primi omnium eloquentiam perdidistis. levibus enim atque inanibus sonis ludibria quaedam excitando effecistis ut corpus orationis enervaretur et caderet. (3) nondum iuvenes declamationibus continebantur, cum Sophocles aut Euripides invenerunt verba quibus deberent loqui. (4) nondum umbraticus doctor ingenia deleverat, cum Pindarus novemque lyrici Homericis versibus canere timuerunt. (5) et ne poetas [quidem] ad testimonium citem, certe neque Platona neque Demosthenem ad hoc genus exercitationis accessisse video. (6) grandis ut ita dicam pudica oratio non est maculosa nec turgida, sed naturali pulchritudine exsurgit. (7) nuper ventosa istaec et enormis loquacitas Athenas ex Asia commigravit animosque iuvenum ad magna surgentes veluti pestilenti quodam sidere afflavit, semelque corrupta eloquentiae regula . . . stetit et obmutuit. (8) quis postea ad summam Thucydidis, quis Hyperidis ad famam processit? ac ne carmen quidem sani coloris enituit, sed omnia quasi eodem cibo pasta non potuerunt usque ad senectutem canescere. (9) pictura quoque non alium exitum fecit, postquam Aegyptiorum audacia tam magnae artis compendiariam invenit.

This, surely, is the same band of Furies goading our teachers of rhetoric when they cry: 'These wounds have I sustained for our country's liberty, this eye have I forfeited in your service. Give me a helping hand to escort me to my children, for my legs are hamstrung and cannot support my body's weight.' Utterances even as bad as this we could stomach if they advanced students on the path to eloquence. But in reality all they achieve with their turgid themes and their utterly pointless and empty crackle of epigrams is that when they set foot in court they find themselves transported into another world. That is why I believe that our hapless youngsters are turned into total idiots in the schools of rhetoric, because their ears and eyes are trained not on everyday issues, but on pirates in chains on the seashore, or on tyrants signing edicts bidding sons decapitate their fathers, or on oracular responses in time of plague urging the sacrifice of three or more maidens. These are nothing but verbal gobstoppers coated in honey, every word and every deed sprinkled with poppy seed and sesame!

Students fed on this fare can no more acquire good sense than cooks living in the kitchen can smell of roses. Forgive my saying so, but you teachers of rhetoric more than any others have been the death of eloquence. Your lightweight, empty bleatings have merely encouraged frivolity, with the result that oratory has lost all its vigour, and has collapsed. Young man were not as yet straitjacketed with declamations when Sophocles and Euripides devised the language they needed. No professor in his ivory tower had as yet expunged all genius when Pindar and the nine lyric poets shied from Homeric measures in singing their songs. Not that I need to cite the poets in evidence; so far as I am aware, neither Plato nor Demosthenes had recourse to this kind of exercise. Lofty and what one may call chaste eloquence is not blotchy or turgid; its inherent beauty lends it sublimity. But of late this flatulent, disordered garrulity of yours has decamped from Asia to Athens. A wind as from some baleful star has descended on the eager spirits of our youth, as they seek to rise to greatness, and eloquence has been stopped in its tracks and struck dumb, once its norms were perverted. In short, who in these later days has attained the renown of Thucydides or Hyperides? Even poetry has not maintained the brilliance of its complexion unimpaired; it has all been fed on the same diet, and has not been able to survive to grey-haired old age. Painting too came to a similar end, once the shameless Egyptians devised short cuts to so noble a pursuit. (tr. Walsh 1996)

But this rhetorically well-balanced discussion by the pupil Encolpius is interrupted[20] by an extremely pompous speech of his rhetoric teacher, Agamemnon, who hypocritically imposes on his students ethical and linguistic demands which he himself does not meet:

(3. 1) non est passus Agamemnon me diutius exclamare in porticu quam ipse in schola sudaverat, 'sed' adulescens' inquit 'quoniam sermonem habes non publici saporis et, quod rarissimum est, amas bonam mentem, non fraudabo te arte secreta. (2) nil mirum <si> in his exercitationibus doctores peccant, qui necesse habent cum insanientibus furere. nam nisi dicerint quae adulescentuli probent, ut ait Cicero, 'soli in scholis relinquentur'. (3) sicut ficti adulatores cum cenas divitum captant nihil prius meditantur quam id quod putant gravissimum auditoribus fore (nec enim aliter impetrabunt quod petunt nisi quasdam insidias auribus fecerint), (4) sic eloquentiae magister, nisi tamquam piscator eam imposuerit hamis escam, quam scierit appetituros esse pisculos, sine spe praedae moratur in scopulo.

(4. 1) quid ergo est? parentes obiurgatione digni sunt, qui nolunt liberos suos severa lege proficere. (2) primum enim sic ut omnia, spes quoque suas ambitioni donant. deinde cum ad vota properant, cruda adhuc studia in forum [im]pellunt et eloquentiam, qua nihil esse maius confitentur, pueris induunt adhuc nascentibus. (3) quod si paterentur laborum gradus fieri, ut studiosi iuvenes lectione severa irrigarentur, ut sapientiae praeceptis animos

[20] Cf. Kissel (1978: 320 ff.) with a stylistic analysis of Encolpius' discussion.

componerent, ut verba Attico stilo effoderent, ut quod vellent imitari diu audirent, <si persuaderent> sibi nihil esse magnificum quod pueris placeret, iam illa grandis oratio haberet maiestatis suae pondus. (4) nunc pueri in scholis ludunt, iuvenes ridentur in foro, et quod utroque turpius est, quod quisque perperam <di> dicit, in senectute confiteri non vult. (5) sed ne me putes improbasse schedium Lucilianae humilitatis, quod sentio et ipse carmine effingam.

Agamemnon refused to allow me to deliver in the colonnade a declamation longer than the one which had raised sweat on him in the school. 'Young man,' he said, 'your speech reflects no ordinary taste, and you are uniquely gifted with love of good sense, so I shall not withhold from you the secrets of the trade. It is hardly surprising that teachers are at fault in these school exercises; they have to go along with lunatics, and play the madman. Unless their speeches meet with the approval of their young pupils, they will in Cicero's words be left high and dry in the schools. Our plight is like that of flatterers on the stage who cadge dinners from the rich; their chief preoccupation is what they think will please their hearers most, for they will attain their aim only by laying traps for their ears. Likewise, unless the teacher of eloquence turns angler and baits his hook with the morsel which he knows the fish will bite on, he stands idle on the rock with no hope of a catch.

So what is the moral? It is the parents who deserve censure for refusing to allow stern discipline to ensure the progress of their children. To begin with, they sacrifice their young hopefuls, like everything else, on the altar of ambition. Then, in their haste to achieve their goals, they bundle them into the courts while their learning is still undigested. When their sons are still in their cradles, they swaddle them with eloquence, believing that eloquence is the be-all and end-all. Whereas if they allowed them to struggle step by step, making the youngsters work hard, steep themselves in serious study, order their minds with the maxims of philosophy, score out with ruthless pen what they had first written, lend patient ears to the models which they wished to imitate, convince themselves that nothing admired by boys can be of intrinsic worth—then the lofty utterance of old would maintain its weight and splendour. But as things stand, as boys they fool around in school, and then as young men attract derision in the courts, and what is more shameful than either of these, in old age they are unwilling to acknowledge the defects of their education. But I would not have you think that I have been carping at the impromptu commonplace utterances of a Lucilius, so like him I shall express my feelings in verses. (tr. Walsh 1996)

And the same discrepancy between principle and personal practice is continued in Agamemnon's ensuing verses.[21]

---

[21] See my treatment in Sect. III. 3 below.

III.1.2. The Poetically Coloured Style

A suitable illustration of poetically coloured style is, for instance, provided by the description of the beauty of a young woman called Circe at 126. 13 ff.:

... dominam ... producit ... mulierem omnibus simulacris emendatiorem. nulla vox est, quae formam eius possit comprehendere, nam quicquid dixero, minus erit. crines ingenio suo flexi per totos se umeros effuderant, frons minima et quae radices capillorum retro flexerat ... oculi clariores stellis extra lunam fulgentibus, nares paululum inflexae et osculum quale Praxiteles habere Dianam credidit. iam mentum, iam cervix, iam manus, iam pedum candor intra auri gracile vinculum positus: Parium marmor extinxerat.

Her mistress ... she escorted ... No statue could match her perfection, no words could do justice to her beauty; any description of mine would be an understatement. Her hair fell in natural waves all over her shoulders; from her narrow forehead her hairline receded in curls ... Those eyes were brighter than the stars which twinkle beyond the range of the moon's light; her nose was delicately curved; her diminutive mouth was like that which Praxiteles envisaged for Diana. And what a chin, and neck, and hands—and her gleaming foot circled with a slender golden band! Parian marble by comparison lost its sheen. (tr. Walsh 1996)

The description of magnificent paintings depicting mythological scenes is similarly poetically coloured (83. 1 ff.). There is parody of tragedy and epic, among other genres, in the frivolous Milesian short story about the Widow of Ephesus (111. 1 ff.), in which the language deliberately contrasts with the everyday style of the rest of the narrative.

III.1.3. The Different Levels of Colloquial Style

Colloquial style, often of a rather unreflective kind, is encountered in Encolpius' chatty narrative and in the speeches of ordinary content. The *sermo cottidianus*, however, is not a uniform phenomenon, but encompasses many gradations and colours.[22] In the passages of sophisticated prose we therefore encounter a multitude of levels of expression ranging from a refined style to vulgarisms;[23] this is also true of the freedmen's speeches, which cannot always be branded categorically as vulgar. I should like to focus on a few illustrative examples, starting with a passage from a freedman's speech:

---

[22] Cf. especially Reichenkron (1965: 55)'s treatment on the boundaries between classical and vulgar Latin.   [23] Cf. Petersmann (1977).

(a) Sophisticated Elements in the Speech of the Freedmen

In 44. 18 the freedman Ganymedes, contrasting contemporary impiety with former piety, tries to make the style of his words match the solemn content:

> antea stolatae ibant nudis pedibus in clivum, passis capillis, mentibus puris et Iovem aqu(am) exorabant. itaque statim urceatim plovebat: aut tunc aut numquam: et omnes redibant udi tamquam mures. itaque dii pedes lanatos habent, quia nos religiosi non sumus. agri iacent . . .

> At one time the women wore long dresses, and walked barefoot up the hill with their hair unbound and their clothes washed dazzling white, praying to Jupiter for rain. At once it came down in buckets; otherwise it never rained. They would all go home looking like drowned rats. So this is why the gods wrap their feet in wool; it's because we don't keep the faith. The fields lie fallow . . . (tr. Walsh 1996)

Apart from the deliberate rhythm, the word *antea* at the beginning of the sentence is to be noted; this is the more elevated form of the word *ante*[24] and occurs only here in Petronius; elsewhere the author uses *ante*, even in 'sophisticated' passages. A solemn effect is also achieved by *stolatae* in the meaning of *mulieres stolatae*, for which the dictionaries quote only this passage, and *aqua* meaning 'rain', which also occurs, for example, at Ov. *Fast.* 4. 386 and Hor. *Ep.* 2. 1. 135. The double accusative with *exorare*, which Nelson[25] regards as vulgar because of its occurrence in old Latin (Plautus and Terence), should rather be considered as archaic–poetical: it can still be found in post-classical rhetorical prose at Seneca, *Contr.* 1. 2 and in poetry at Stat. *Silv.* 2. 7. 121. The refinement of diction is in addition underlined by the chiasmus and the rhythmical clausulae: the resolved arsis in the first of the ditrochees expresses the initially relatively swift movement of the procession towards the mountain (*pedìbùs ín clívúm*; then things become more solemn and slow: a normal ditrochee (*passís càpíllís*) and cretic + trochee (*méntìbús púrís*) are followed by a heavy ditrochee *(éxórábánt)*. But Ganymedes is unable to keep up this high level of style. The content and style of his speech subsequently deteriorate drastically: 'itaque statim urceatim plovebat: aut tunc aut numquam: et omnes redibant udi tamquam mures'. The parody lies exactly in his failure to keep up the high level of language, and in the sudden decline of both subject and style—which, however, is ridiculously

---

[24] Cf. Hofmann and Szantyr (1965: 223).　　　[25] Nelson (1947: 144).

contrasted with the heavy ditrochee *támquám múrés*. It is continued in the following, non-rhythmical, sentence which is about the gods who have their feet bandaged with wool.[26] Normally in Petronius the pure vulgar language of the uneducated characters is not rhythmical, as Müller notes in his excellent section on prose rhythm.[27]

Things are, however, different with the *sermo urbanus*. The passages spoken by the narrator Encolpius and his companions are rhythmical in various degrees[28] depending on the mood and situation, and one can note a multitude of levels of style, which can range from the poetic and rhetorically refined to the vulgar. Thus, one should not be surprised by the occasional use of downright vulgar diction in sophisticated passages. This can be observed in the fields of morphology, syntax, and lexicography.

(b) Elements of Vulgar Style in Sophisticated Prose

By analogy with the poetic expressions in the freedman's speech quoted above, I should like to give some examples of vulgarisms in sophisticated prose which are due to a special linguistic situation. In 53. 12 and 78. 6 the form *cornices* instead of the nominative plural *cornicines* (of *cornicen*) is transmitted. We know from glosses, inscriptions, and other sources[29] that *cornices* is a vulgar variant. In both passages editors have conjectured the correct form *cornicines*, since Encolpius himself uses it in his narrative at 78. 5. In view of this, emendation to *cornicines* appears to be justified at 78. 6, but not at 53. 12. For here *cornices* is found in conjunction with the vulgar variant *acromata*[30] instead of *acroamata* in Encolpius' account of a remark made by Trimalchio, which Encolpius renders thus: 'ceterum duo esse in rebus humanis quae libentissime spectaret, petauristarios et cornices; reliqua animalia acromata tricas meras esse'. This suggests that Petronius allows his narrator Encolpius to lampoon his host's diction by mockingly imitating his violations of correct accidence.

Traits of vulgar speech are even more frequent in the style and syntax of the sophisticated prose. Owing to our deficient knowledge of Latin everyday language, many of these have mistakenly been removed by editorial conjecture. Very many of the syntactic vulgarisms in

---

[26] Albrecht (1983: 152 ff., esp. 158).   [27] Müller and Ehlers (1983: 449).
[28] Müller and Ehlers (1983: 449).
[29] For references, see *TLL* iv. 956. 10 ff. See also Heraeus (1937: 148 f.) and Leumann (1977: 235).
[30] On *acroma* instead of *acroama*, see Heraeus (1937: 149) and *TLL* i. 433. 15 ff.

the sophisticated prose can be explained by Petronius' intention to create a realistic portrait of the colloquial speech of his time, in which certain phenomena, which up to then had been confined to the *sermo vulgaris*, gradually began to intrude. In 41. 2, for instance, the *codex Traguriensis* has Encolpius say: 'duravi interrogare illum interpretem meum, quid me torqueret'. Nearly all editors change *quid* to *quod*, an easily explicable conjecture palaeographically, in order to produce the expected relative clause. But it is psychologically more natural that the verb *interrogare* is followed by an indirect question; besides, the extensive use of interrogative instead of relative pronouns in vulgar Latin, shown in the freedmen's conversations in Petronius, epigraphic evidence, and the Romance languages, provides a strong case for not changing *quid* to *quod* in this passage. In the Greek *koine* the relative pronoun was similarly challenged by τίς and τί, a tendency which probably begins as early as the classical period—e.g. at Soph. *El.* 316 (there again typically after a *verbum interrogandi*) ὡς νῦν ἀπόντος ἱστόρει, τί σοι φίλον.[31]

Less disputed are the vulgarisms in the vocabulary of the sophisticated passages, in the case of which even Heraeus admits that 'in Petronius sophisticated speech is not without influence from the lower sphere in which the work is set'.[32] Thus in his sophisticated prose Petronius uses, for example, the word *cocio* ('dealer') three times (14. 7, 15. 4, 8). The use of this word is expressly criticized for being ordinary and vulgar by the mime-writer Laberius (fr. 63 Ribbeck[3]) in Gellius 16. 7. 12: ' "cocionem" pervulgate dicit, quem veteres "arrilatorem" dixerunt'. It is telling that only the term *cocio* continues to exist in the Romance languages. The same applies, for instance, to *sternutare* ('to sneeze'), which Encolpius uses at 98. 4 when narrating a funny trick:

dum haec ego iam credenti persuadeo, Giton collectione spritus plenus ter continuo ita sternutavit, ut grabatum concuteret.

My persuasion was just winning his trust when Giton could no longer withstand the pressure of air in his nose, and he sneezed three times in rapid succession, so violently that the bed shook. (tr. Walsh 1996)

Sternutare also occurs at 102. 10 in a slightly indignant (direct) speech of Encolpius:

---

[31] See the detailed discussion in Petersmann (1977: 266 ff.) with further literature.
[32] Heraeus (1937: 55).

'ita vero' inquam ego 'tamquam solidos alligaturus, quibus non soleat venter iniuriam facere? an tamquam eos qui sternutare non soleamus nec sternere . . . ?'

'Is that your plan?' I asked. 'To tie us up as though we're solid all the way through, as though our bowels won't do the dirty on us? Are we the sort of creatures who neither sneeze nor snore?' (tr. Walsh 1996)

The frequentative instead of the simple *sternuere* belongs to the lower linguistic stratum; this is evident from its occurrence in the Pompeian inscriptions, a criticism in the grammarian Caper (vii. III. 13 *GLK*), and the fact that it is the only form which survives in the Romance languages.[33] In Petronius the use of this somewhat vulgar word is motivated by the respective situations—in the first case by the description of Giton, who has been hiding underneath the bed (*grabatum* too is a crude word of everyday language) in order to play a trick on Eumolpius, but who cannot hold his breath any longer and is forced to sneeze. In the second case the strong *sternutare* is to be explained psychologically both by the crude and trivial context and by the narrator's irritation and excitement. Here the diction is automatically assimilated to the content of the passage and the narrator's mood.

III.2. The sermo vulgaris

As mentioned above, by assimilating linguistic expression to linguistic reality the *Satyrica*, especially in the *Cena Trimalchionis*, comes close to a mime. In this mimic aspect Petronius adds some local colour to the diction of his uneducated characters, particularly to that of Trimalchio and his friends. In this respect the author of the *Satyrica* seems to have been inspired by comedy and by the indigenous form of humorous theatre, the *fabula Atellana*. Aristophanes already represents people from foreign regions as speaking in their vernacular (in the *Acharnians*, the *Lysistrata*, and the *Thesmophoriazusae*), as do Eubulus and Alexis in Middle Comedy (frs. 12, 142 Kock). Similarly in Menander's *Aspis* a fake doctor speaks Doric, and in Plautus' *Poenulus* a character speaks Punic. Similarly, Petronius gave Trimalchio and his friends, whose dinner party is set in a small town in south Italy, a series of expressions whose specifically south Italian provenance Wagner was able to demonstrate[34] through their survival in those regions up to the present day, just as in general the *sermo plebeius* of

---

[33] Meyer-Lübke (1935: no. 8250).   [34] Wagner (1933).

the *Cena* corresponds to the Pompeian inscriptions. This congruence is important, because it provides an important clue not only for the date of the *Satyrica* but also for a series of phenomena of the contemporary *langue parlée*.

I should like to give a few examples. As regards phonology, the mutation of *au* into the monophthong *o* is not a general characteristic of popular Latin, but primarily a feature of rustic language.[35] In Petronius this happens only in the freedmen's speeches; at 44. 12 the form *coda* occurs, whereas in the poetry of 89. 38 *cauda* is used instead; at 39. 12 we find *copones* as, for instance, in *Corpus inscriptionum Latinarum* iv. 3948 and 6700, but at 98. 1, in Encolpius' narrative, *cauponi*; similarly at 45. 13 *plodo* is found in a freedman's speech, but at 79. 10 Encolpius uses *plaudebat*.

Moreover, it is striking that in Petronius the simple dative of the object is never periphrased by *ad* + accusative, even if the beginnings of this periphrasis, which is to become so popular in later Latin, can be traced back to archaic Latin.[36] From this Süss[37] inferred that for some inexplicable reason Petronius deliberately avoided this sort of periphrasis, which he assumes to have been commonly used by the time of the early empire. Väänänen's research, however, shows that the above-mentioned replacement of the dative is also absent in the Pompeian inscriptions.[38] This leads to the conclusion that this periphrasis for the dative, which originated in the archaic *sermo cottidianus*, was not developed until fairly late and only in the western part of the empire, since in Romanian the dative has been preserved in its full function. It therefore seems to be a reasonable assumption that at the time of the colonization of Dacia the use of the dative as a synthetic case was still widespread among the language of the common people. Thus, because of its geographical marginalization, the Latin which was spoken in Dacia did not adopt the periphrasis for the dative, a feature which began only fairly late and started from the centre of the empire. The popularity of the dative in the Eastern territories is proved by the fact that in Romanian it can even be used instead of the genitive in order to denote a possessive relation. Thus people say, for instance, *casa vecinului*, that is *casa vicino illi*, 'the house to the neighbour',[39] very similar to the German colloquialism

---

[35] Leumann (1977: 72 f.); Sommer and Pfister (1977: 68 f.); Väänänen (1966: 30 f.).
[36] References in Petersmann (1977: 78 n. 35).   [37] Süss (1926: 24).
[38] Väänänen (1966).   [39] Meyer-Lübke (1899: 49 ff.).

'dem Nachbarn sein Haus'. Petronius also provides examples of this
sort of dative, cf. 39. 4, where Trimalchio wishes 'patrono meo ossa
bene quiescant'.

III. 3. The Poetic Insertions

The observations made above on vulgar and sophisticated language
also apply to the diction of the poetic insertions. Here, too, the language is conditioned by the topic as well as by the intention of the
speaker, in accordance with Peripatetic principles of style. The same
factors determine also the choice of the metre. This can be seen most
clearly in the first poetic insertion (4. 5–5. 1), in which the rhetoric
teacher Agamemnon describes his ideal programme for rhetorical
training. Having spoken in prose up to now, he changes to poetry,
praising Lucilius' simple style and his poetic *humilitas*, which (however) he himself does not choose to follow:

4. . . . (5) sed ne me putes improbasse schedium Lucilianae humanitatis,
quod sentio et ipse carmine effingam:

> 5. artis severae si quis ambit effectus
> mentemque magnis applicat, prius mores
> frugalitatis lege poliat exacta.
> nec curet alto regiam trucem vultu
> cliensque cenas impotentium captet,
> nec perditis addictus obruat vino
> mentis calorem, neve plausor in scaenam
> sedeat redemptus histrionis ad rictus.
> sed sive armigerae rident Tritonidis arces
> seu Lacedaemonio tellus habitata colono
> Sirenumque domus, det primos versibus annos
> Maeoniumque bibat felici pectore fontem.
> mox et Socratico plenus grege mittat habenas
> liber et ingentis quatiat Demosthenis arma.
> hinc Romana manus circumfluat et modo Graio
> + exonerata + sono mutet suffusa saporem.
> interdum subducta foro det pagina cursum
> et fortuna sonet celeri distincta meatu;
> dent epulas et bella truci memorata canore,
> grandiaque indomiti Ciceronis verba minentur.
> his animum succinge bonis: sic flumine largo
> plenus Pierio defundes pectore verba.

But I would not have you think that I have been carping at the impromptu commonplace utterances of a Lucilius, so like him I shall express my feelings in verses:

> 'The man who seeks success in austere Art,
> And sets his thoughts on mighty enterprises,
> Must first refine his ways by rigid laws
> Of serious living. Let him not aspire
> To insolent palace with its lofty stare;
> Nor as dependent scheme to gain admission
> To dinners of intemperate hosts. Nor must he
> Attach himself to wastrels, and with wine
> Submerge his mind's hot flame, nor yet again
> Sit as a hired claqueur before the stage,
> Applauding the actor's grin.
> > What *must* he do?
> > Whether the smiling citadel
> Of armed Tritonis guards him there,
> Or where the Spartan immigrant dwells,
> Or where the Sirens have their lair,
> To poetry let him first commit
> His earliest years, drink at the pool
> Maeonian, to his heart's delight.
> Next have his fill of Socrates' school,
> Then loose his reins, and riding free
> Wield great Demosthenes' armoury.
> Then, Roman poets circling round,
> From Greece's measures newly freed,
> Must well up in him, and transform
> His taste-buds. Still must he secede
> From lawcourts. Let his page run free,
> Proclaiming Fortune in its clear, swift course,
> Recounting feasts, and war's harsh blasts
> With lofty Ciceronian force.
> Virtues like these must clothe your soul;
> Your river of eloquence then is full,
> Words will well forth at the Muses' call'.

(tr. Walsh 1996)

In the first part, which deals with symposia and everyday entertainments, Agamemnon uses the iambic metre, which by its origin and nature was usually employed for ridicule in everyday style. But the diction of these verses is by contrast extraordinarily baroque and artificial. In the second part of the poem, which is about the different kinds of literary training, particularly study in Greece, the Homeric epics, and philosophy and rhetoric, the metre changes to bombastic dactylic hexameters. The contrast between literary principle and its non-implementation, which attracted Petronius' satirical parody, corresponds, as mentioned above,[40] to the moral behaviour of Agamemnon. This contrast was often the subject of criticism, since in antiquity tastelessness and barbarism in the conduct of one's life was considered worse than in one's speech.[41] The hypocrisy and absurdity of Agamemnon's behaviour—he appears later as an enthusiastic participant in Trimalchio's tasteless and lavish symposium and even takes his students along to it—are also reflected in the insincerity of his language.

IV. PETRONIUS AND HIS AUDIENCE

Apart from the mimetic-parodic and psychological factors, there are, according to Peripatetic principles of style, further aspects determining the variety of Petronius' language: the literary genre and the audience to which the *Satyrica* is addressed. Although Petronius' work follows the Greek novel of love and adventure, his artistic intention is significantly different. Petronius wrote for a highly educated readership, whom he wished to entertain by demonstrating their follies, shortcomings, and hypocrisies. In doing so the author also sought to show his universal literary talent, even in the area of high poetry. And this diversity of persons, so realistically described, had to be matched by the variety of their levels of language and style. At the same time a deliberate contrast had to be created to the rather uniform style of the conventional idealized Greek novel of love and adventure.

V. SUMMARY

In conclusion, we may say that Petronius' work is original in its intention to be at the same time a novel and a *satura Menippea*. The author simultaneously draws on both literary genres, but succeeds in making a creative use of their standard motifs. In a playful and parodic

---

[40] See my treatment of Agamemnon's speech in Sect. III. 1.1 above.
[41] On this, see Dihle (1977: 162).

manner he varies, combines, and rehandles the traditional literary elements, thus creating a completely new work of art which has been justly described as 'the most peculiar phenomenon in the whole literature of the Empire'.[42] The ingenuity and modernity of Petronius' fiction is also exhibited by the way in which his characters are depicted linguistically in keeping with their social status, education, and mentality. Sociolinguistically, too, Petronius' *Satyrica* provides testimony unique in the ancient world.[43]

---

[42] Schanz and Hosius (1935: 516).

[43] Since the publication of this article in 1985, several contributions have appeared which confirm its findings—see esp. Petersmann (1995a,b) and Gerschner (1997).

6

Traces of Greek Narrative and the Roman Novel: A Survey

ALESSANDRO BARCHIESI

A Greek *Satyricon?* The question, at least in this form, seems completely out of date; but Leo's, Wilamowitz's, Norden's, and Heinze's versions of it are still full of interest today.[1] The hunt for lost Greek models reveals in Petronius' case the unusual feature that a disparity of value must be assumed. As Wilamowitz rightly pointed out, our refined and cosmopolitan Petronius must have looked down on his narrative models in a manner similar, perhaps, to Vergil's condescension towards Nicander; so we too must look downwards to find Petronius' models. In his attempt to trace a lost *roman comique*, Wilamowitz assembled pale images of popular genres lost to us: clowns and mimes, *phlyakes* and *cinaedi*, *aretalogoi*, as well as the picaresque characters depicted in the Villa Farnesina, and the caricatures found on ancient pottery: 'das ist die Gesellschaft Petrons'. All these clues should point to a type of novel, now lost, which somehow contained all these scattered pieces of evidence. In his great analysis of the relationship between Petronius and the 'idealized' Greek novel, Heinze reached similar, or at any rate compatible, conclusions. He certainly did not exclude the possibility that lost *Satyrica* had existed: on the contrary, he believed in the existence of a comic precedent for Petronius, a literary parody which, however, would not have displayed the highly innovative formal arrangement of the *Satyricon*, namely its free and original mixture of verse and prose. With greater caution, but, as we shall see,

I wish to thank all the friends who took part in the Petronius seminar led by Gian Biagio Conte at Pisa in 1984–5, and in particular Dr Roberto Andreotti and the *normalista* Luigi Galasso. I would also like to thank Prof. Antonio Carlini for his patient advice on the bibliography for the new papyrus finds. This chapter was translated by Barbara Graziosi.

[1] Leo (1912: 459); Wilamowitz, in Leo (1912: 190); Gercke and Norden (1910: 520); Heinze (1899: 494 ff. = 1960: 417 ff.).

with extreme perceptiveness, Norden underlined the importance of some forms of entertainment, for example the *kinaidologoi*, licentious one-man shows performed by *cinaedi*.

The *Satyricon*, wrote Paul Veyne,[2] is that work whose contents are everywhere and whose form is nowhere at all; which was a way of saying that, in the sieve of the source-hunter, thematic parallels are always to be found, whereas parallel structures and narrative modes cannot be discovered. It is, therefore, understandable that Heinze studied the relationship between Petronius and the Greek romance from the point of view of content.[3] He described, in a basic typology, the recurrent themes of the idealized Greek novel: the adventures of divided and harassed lovers, their suicide attempts, wanderings, ship-wrecks, rivals, prophetic dreams, threatened virginity, and misunder-standings. He then rediscovered this web of themes in a distorted and parodic form in Petronius' own work. Of course, Heinze's brilliant criticism was based on the clear and important similarities which identify as a group the few Greek romances which have come to us through the Byzantine tradition. The basic resemblance between the Greek novels is so strong that, from a functional point of view, they could be analysed and dissected along Proppian lines: they have, for example, been called *Märchenromane mit leidendem Helden*, 'fairy tale novels with a passive hero'.[4] This kind of analysis would not give as clear and satisfactory results in the case of Petronius' novel. As far as we can tell, the *Satyricon* lacks the one element which, in the Greek novels, sets in motion the whole narrative and which, because of its importance, cannot be put on a level with other typological parallels: the initial separation of the two lovers, which, by itself, establishes their status as the main characters.

The homogeneity of the sample studied by Heinze, however, is not random and therefore is also not necessarily reliable. This group of novels has been pre-selected for us. We still have Xenophon's *Ephesiaka*, but not the *Rhodiaka* by Philip of Amphipolis, which the Suda describes as 'utterly obscene'. It is in fact strange that, despite his great knowledge of the ancient novel, Perry claimed that Petronius is more

---

[2] Veyne (1964: 310). No matter how much we may wish to disagree with Veyne's conclusions, it must be acknowledged that Veyne rightly saw the first-person narrat-ive as a central issue in trying to define the *Satyricon*'s literary status. Much progress on this question (also from a methodological point of view) has been made by two recent studies: Beck (1973) and Aragosti (1979).

[3] Heinze (1899: 494 ff. = 1960: 417 ff.).   [4] Nolting-Hauff (1974: 417–55).

obscene than any Greek novelist we know of, although he himself makes
the better point elsewhere in his study that the absence of direct
testimonies on the ancient novel proves very little.[5] A couple of years
ago a papyrus fragment appeared purporting to contain the erotic
memoirs of the famous Ionic courtesan Philaenis.[6] This must have been
a very popular book—a sort of forerunner of *Fanny Hill*; and as we
know, Ovid explicitly quotes works of this sort (*Tristia* 2. 413–18). When
seen against this background of erotica, Petronius' sexual realism
becomes less surprising than his literary complexity.

It is puzzling that Heinze on the whole disregarded the evidence
from papyri. Though the papyrus fragments of novels which were
beginning to be published in his time on the whole create more problems than they solve, Heinze went so far as to treat even the Ninus
romance only superficially, although the mere fact of its publication had considerably weakened Rohde's view on the origins of the
novel.[7] All this was taking place at the end of the last century; since
then a number of papyrus fragments have turned up which, interestingly, fit in extremely well with Heinze's overall picture. The new
fragments display for us more distressed heroines, attempted suicides,
dreams, shipwrecks, incognito lovers (among whom is an impressive
Pharaoh), and discussions on the nature of love. All these elements
point towards the stylized and somewhat abstract world already displayed in the narratives of Chariton and Xenophon of Ephesus.[8]

The main advantage of Heinze's view lies, as often happens, in
the fact that he allowed for exceptions and lacunae, maintaining a
relaxed, open-minded approach. It is true that he focused mainly on
the parodic relation between the *Satyricon* and the idealized Greek novel.
If one pursued this line, the *Satyricon* could be seen as an occasional
answer to a popular literary genre; such an answer would be individual,
whether parodic or antiphrastic, and comparable to *Shamela*'s relation to the sentimental romance or *Northanger Abbey*'s to the Gothic
novel. This type of parody, by its very nature, needs no precedent: it
is conceived as a pastiche criticizing and trying to subvert a well-
established tradition.[9] If this were Heinze's view of the *Satyricon*—and

---

[5] Perry (1925: 47, 39 respectively).   [6] Tsantsanoglou (1973).

[7] Only two years after Heinze's article there was another important publication,
Wilcken (1901), which was, however, damaged and delayed by a fire in Hamburg harbour.

[8] Apart from the fundamental work by Rattenbury (1933), a useful bibliography on
the most interesting finds can be found in Hägg (1983: 238).

[9] This type of parody should, of course, be distinguished from the Homeric or
Vergilian parodies found in the *Satyricon*. On the compatibility of these two types of
parodies, see e.g. Scobie (1969: 83–90).

his work often suggests as much—then his analysis would seem today extremely fragile and one-sided. However, as I have already pointed out, he did not exclude the possibility that other types of model had existed, in the form, for example, of lighter and less idealized narratives. In fact, speculations about Apuleius' possible Greek models suggested to him that this was a distinct possibility. To forget this point would result in an uncharitable view of his work.

One of the narratives which certainly cannot be called idealized is the novel published in 1971 by Albert Henrichs: Lollianus' *Phoinikika*.[10] The existence of works of this kind was foreseeable and had, indeed, been predicted by many.

The fragments suggest that, as Henrichs claims, the *Phoinikika* are our first example of a middlebrow novel of entertainment. In the first fragment, which belonged to the first book, a man, conceivably the main character in the novel, tells the story of his first sexual experience. His partner's name, Persis, is inappropriate for a heroine in a romance; moreover, the behaviour of the two lovers and some realistic details in the story do not suit the typical couple of the idealized Greek novel. Also, unlike in romances,[11] loss of virginity apparently does not seem to constitute a problem: in fact, Persis interestingly seems to offer the man some remuneration for the loss of his virginity. Furthermore, the man does not seem likely to follow the chaste and pure career appropriate to a romance hero. The general thrust of the episode seems to contravene not only the norms of behaviour encoded in the romance but also the most basic social rules which pertain to such matters: that a *man* be paid for his sexual services clearly subverts expectation. We do not know to what extent this episode was integral to the exotic setting of the story, which is implied by the title, *Phoinikika*; but it is interesting that there are some parallels in Petronius. It should also be remembered that similar *initiamenta Veneris* similarly appear in the early stages of the plot in the *Metamorphoses* and in the *Onos*.[12]

---

[10] Henrichs (1972); among the many discussions which followed, particularly notable is Winkler's acute analysis (1980).

[11] The protection of virginity is a central theme which unifies the novels' plots. See the balanced observations of Reardon (1971: 400–2, 1969: 291–309).

[12] As we know, somewhat similar erotic episodes have often been postulated for Sisenna's work on the basis of fragments such as 'nisi comminus excidisset. "Quanti dantur?" "Tanti" inquit Olumpias, simul haec dicens suavium dedit' (fr. 8 Bücheler) and 'proin dato aliquid, quod domi habebis, quod tibi non magno stabit' (fr. 9 Bücheler). I am tempted to put these two fragments together with Lollianus, since here too we find the name of an obliging maid (Olympias; cf. Palaestra, Photis, and now Persis in *Onos*; Apuleius and Lollianus respectively), a situation where flirting is going

We have another fragment from the *Phoinikika*, whose position within the work is unknown. A wayfarer named Glauketes meets a ghost during the night, who requests that he and a beautiful murdered girl may be buried. Glauketes, who is frightened, does not stop but continues his journey. He crosses a river and arrives at a village, where he finds an open stable. While he is trying to fall asleep on the straw, a woman comes down from the floor above . . . and here the papyrus breaks off.

Violence and strong emotions colour another fragment, which is quite long and must come somewhere after the erotic encounter with Persis.[13] A certain Androtimus, presumably the main character, is held captive by a band. He is forced to witness an orgy and a human sacrifice, and has to take part in a cannibal feast. The text describes in great detail the cooking of human flesh and crudely lingers on the guests' physical reactions to the banquet—vomiting, wind-breaking, and the smells and noises thereof. Such colourful details belong to the mime and some 'low' episodes in Petronius,[14] but certainly not to the polite elegance of the romantic novel. But it is precisely these farcical details that set us on the track of a distinguished model: after all, Odysseus himself had been a prisoner of a cannibal who, in his drunkenness, belched and threw up human flesh. And yet there is no indication that the Cyclops episode constitutes an active and lively model for Lollianus. (One would be hard pressed to find specific allusions to the *Odyssey* or to Attic satyr play.) It is well known that the connection of this type of literature with its single exemplary model is mediated and watered down through generic archetypes. Being the prisoner of uncivilized brutes is a typical situation in a novel, be it low or refined, and it certainly need not be a reference to or a parody of epic. Themes and stories travel without declaring their place of origin, and the narrators themselves have no interest in revealing from where they picked up their story.

A family tree of the ancient novel based purely on resemblances of theme and situation would actually prove very little. Fritz Wehrli, for

on, and a discussion of the gifts which should be offered in compensation for erotic services (cf. Lollianus fr. A2ʳ, pp. 84. 20 ff. Henrichs). These texts may share a common theme. However, we do not know whether the two fragments by Sisenna are connected with one another; and the outcome of earlier speculations on fragments of Milesian novels warns us against the dangers of comparing *obscura* with *obscuriora*.

[13] The episode must have straddled two books. See Henrichs (1972: 92 ff.).
[14] Cf. Petronius, *Sat.* 117. 2 ff. The connections between the episode and staged performances, such as Aristophanes, Italic farce, and mimes, have long been recognized.

example—in a work whose very respectable overall aim is that of showing that idealized and comic-realistic novels should not be seen as sharply distinguished and mutually exclusive categories—tries to bring Petronius and Xenophon of Ephesus closer together by pointing out that both novels take place, in part, in Magna Graecia.[15] The problem with this kind of comparison of detail is that the chain of similarities, once it is conceived in this way, is endless: if resemblance of theme or detail is used to establish a relation, then there is no reason to restrict ourselves to the narrow Graeco-Roman world. It would be possible to find just as many points of contact by comparing the *Satyricon* to the *One Thousand and One Nights* or to Sanskrit animal fables.[16] Of course, proving whether these similarities are in any way functional is a different matter altogether.

And in fact I believe that it is precisely *functional* similarities which provide a more useful starting-point for interpretation. A brief example from Petronius should serve to illustrate this.

In *Satyricon* 79. 8–80. 1 Encolpius becomes the victim of a cruel fraud, precisely as he is enjoying the culminating point of his love story with Giton. Ascyltus removes the boy from Encolpius' bed and takes him to his own. In his outrage, Encolpius tries to throw Ascyltus out, but the latter draws his sword:

'age' inquit 'nunc et puerum dividamus'. iocari putabam discedentem. at ille gladium parricidali manu strinxit et 'non frueris' inquit 'hac praeda, super quam solus incumbis. partem meam necessest vel hoc gladio contemptus abscindam'.

The whole scene is calibrated by a series of parodic allusions. It is a relentless sequence: Encolpius, in his precarious happiness as a lover, bursts out in Catullan hendecasyllables, Giton compares the quarrelling friends to Eteocles and Polyneices, and then intervenes to divide them like the Sabine women who stood as a prize between the two fighting nations: elegy, tragedy, and historical *exempla* follow one another in an exhilarating series of debunking transformations. And there is more: the entire episode is even more entertaining if it is seen as the parodic reworking of an underlying model which is in fact very familiar to us. During the night a *puer* is moved from one bed to another, and it is then suggested that he should be cut up into two: the model

---

[15] Wehrli (1965: 134).
[16] The most adventurous explorer of these routes has, in fact, admitted to feeling a little like Sinbad the sailor: Anderson (1984: p. vi).

is not elegy, tragedy, or historiography, nor does it belong to Greek
or Roman literature: it is the story of the judgement of Solomon, from
the Book of Kings. It seems impossible to prove a historical connection between the two texts. However, the evidence provided by the
very structure of Petronius' work should not be underestimated. A parodic transformation of a serious text is precisely what the structure
of our text seems to require at this point: it seems hard to resist such
an amusing counterpoint. Moreover, what we know about Petronius'
work encourages us in this interpretation.

    However, we are still facing the problem of a parody without an
acceptable model. Or are we? A text dated to the second century BCE,
studied by Eric Turner and published only in the last decade,[17] tells
us that 'Philiscus of Miletus [the well-known fourth-century prose-
writer, pupil of Isocrates and teacher of Timaeus] wrote about a baby
who was the object of contention between two women; since both
claimed that he was their own son, he [we do not know the identity
of the subject of this clause] gave orders that the child be cut into two
and that each woman have half of him.' Voilà: here is our story of the
divided boy; the connection with Petronius, which did not seem
plausible on the basis of the texts once known to us,[18] becomes much
more plausible. This parallel does not weaken an *internal* interpretation of Petronius' text. The paradox inherent to the idea of
dividing the boy is clearly at the centre of Petronius' elaboration:
'nunc et puerum dividamus . . . iocari putabam . . . partem meam . . .
hoc gladio . . . abscindam'. In fact, as Encolpius' first reaction shows
(he thinks the suggestion is a joke), the very verb *dividere*, which
constitutes the meeting-point between Petronius' text and his model,
suggests a sexual *double entendre*. In a homosexual context *dividere* can
be taken as a rather straightforward metaphor (cf. Plaut. *Aul.* 283 ff.).
And here begins the perversion of the model.[19]

    [17] Turner (1973: 8–14). The possibility that this text can be connected with
Petronius has not escaped Winkler (1980: 157 n. 7).
    [18] Lucas (1903), however, had bravely believed in this connection on the basis of
an iconographical find: the 'judgement of the two mothers' at the Farnesina, found in
1879. Among other paintings found then, there is also a *Schelmengeschichte* which can
also be compared with the *Satyricon*: two men are quarrelling for the possession of a
cloak. See Robert (1901: 364–8). Wilamowitz was certainly thinking about this sort of
analogy when he quoted the Farnesina in connection with Petronius. See p. 124. I wish
to thank Cesare Questa for suggesting this connection to me, before I had a chance to
read Lucas's work, which is now difficult to find.
    [19] This technique of undermining a famous text from within, by focusing on a
possible sexual double meaning, is quite frequent in Homeric parodies. It is a feature
common to *Priapea* and Sotadean parody and attested also elsewhere in Petronius.

This example gives us a glimpse of the possibilities that open up, once we take into consideration the thematic correspondences between Petronius and the ancient novel. Such correspondences need not just be used in order to establish Petronius' genealogy. For example, the similarities of theme found with the *Phoinikika* are essential in order to understand the level and tone of this newly discovered work and be able to place it properly within the tradition. Conversely, Petronius and Apuleius progressively seem less isolated. Stories of bandits and ghosts inserted within a wider narrative of adventures clearly resemble Apuleius' novel;[20] a passive hero, victim of violent and erotic adventures, again takes us to Apuleius; but, to a certain extent, it also reminds us of Petronius. In the *Satyricon*, moreover, the grotesque parody of mystery cults plays an important role. On the other hand, the sensational adventures of the hero, who is ensnared into witnessing a weird mystery orgy of cannibals, serve to establish, by contrast, the 'bourgeois' atmosphere in the *Satyricon*: the hero is captive to a lascivious lady, and the cannibals are the inhabitants of the very civilized (and Pythagorean) city of Croton. It thus becomes clearer and clearer that Petronius' irony and realism undermines the sensational element typical of the novel of entertainment.

To sum up: Heinze's method of looking for thematic parallels still seems viable, provided we do not rigidly distinguish between romance, comic novel, and, perhaps, Milesian tale. These sharp distinctions seem now extremely questionable, but the scepticism should not extend to the usefulness of thematic comparisons *per se*. One wonders, moreover, whether the discovery of other texts may serve to break down another traditional distinction, that drawn between the *Satyricon*'s content and its form—whether the latter be called Menippean, prosimetric, or satiric. One is tempted to ask whether its form really is 'nowhere at all'. A new approach, wholly independent of the usual references to Menippus' ghost and Varro's trifles, has been suggested by the publication of the so-called 'Iolaus romance'.[21]

For example, the 'funerata est illa pars corporis, qua quondam Achilles eram' at 129. 1 is even funnier if one thinks of the most epic attribute of Achilles, his 'mighty spear' (cf. *Iliad* 16. 143, 22. 133, and Sotades fr. 4 Powell).

[20] A typical feature of Petronius' poetics is that ghost stories and other themes which belong to sensational and popular literature are rigorously restricted to heterodiegetic narrative. The social and cultural status of the speakers is used by Petronius in order to distance himself ironically. Also in this context new finds such as the *Phoinikika* help to clarify the complex relation between Petronius and the phantasy world of entertainment literature.   [21] *P. Oxy.* 3010; Parsons (1971, 1974).

The contents of this fragment, which contains about fifty lines of prose and verse, can be reconstructed on the basis of one assumption: that we are dealing with the initiatory mysteries of Cybele and with her low-ranking priests, the Galli, eunuchs dressed up as women, who travel from city to city and perform in the streets. They sing in their high-pitched voices, dance, wound, and flagellate themselves, and prophesy or sell magic potions. Their social status is very low and their activities range from ecstatic performances like those of whirling Dervishes, to more or less open forms of prostitution, enhanced by their feminine appearance. They are effeminate dancers, exactly like the *cinaedi*, with whom they are in fact often associated.

Since these Galli were the objects of scorn and contempt throughout antiquity, it is reasonable to suppose that our papyrus belonged to a comic or satiric work. It deals with a man, Iolaus, who seems to have been the main character in the story. He has a grand name, the same as Heracles' companion, but he hangs out with a disreputable lot. We read of a friend of his who seeks initiation into Cybele's mysteries in order to come to Iolaus' rescue. After having become a Gallus, though we do not know to what extent, this friend returns to Iolaus and addresses him in verse, in about twenty Sotadean lines which sum up the knowledge derived from the initiation and put it at Iolaus' disposal while at the same time displaying the friend's competence. At the end of the fragment both Iolaus, who has heard the mysteries, and his friend, who is called, with ambiguous sarcasm, a τέλειος Γάλλος, 'a Gallus through and through', seem to be quite satisfied. A quotation on the value of friendship, appropriately taken from Euripides' *Orestes*, sententiously puts an end to the episode and to our papyrus. The subject-matter, as reconstructed, is totally appropriate for a comic novel or short story. The Gallus tells Iolaus a complicated story which probably refers to the antecedents of our plot. Terms such as oath, bastard, mother, lamenting father, suggest a new comedy type of plot. But crucial for us is the Gallus hint at Iolaus' plans: ὅτι δόλῳ σὺ βεινεῖν μέλλεις. βεινεῖν, as Parsons points out, 'is not a nice word'. It determines on its own the narrative situation, as well as defining the register of the work. The overall aim of the intrigue is to go to bed with someone. And a story of uninhibited and secret sex takes us to a world shared by mime, the so-called Milesian tale and Petronius.

Dodds compared the structure of this plot to Terence's *Eunuchus*. We could perhaps add a comparison with satire, which is closer in time to the date assigned to the papyrus. In a passage known as the Oxford fragment (6. 020–026), Juvenal warns husbands not to be deceived by appearances: the more effeminate the eunuch, the likelier he is to turn out to be a vigorous adulterer. Leave the dancer Thais with your wife, and she'll turn into Triphallus. Juvenal himself calls this situation 'a mime'.[22]

But this new fragment is not only interesting from a thematic point of view. As Parsons acutely observes, the new fragment's atmosphere and theme, but also, and above all, its form, recall the *Satyricon*. The story, which seems to focus on Iolaus' secretive love affairs, allows for a remarkable freedom of expression, which could be roughly described as prosimetric. The *cinaedus* expresses himself in Sotadean lines, exactly like the *cinaedus* in *Satyricon* 23. 3;[23] the speaking voice inserts a Euripidean *gnome* as a commentary to the story; and the scribe singles it out as a poetic quotation by leaving a blank space, although he does not indent it like the Gallus' Sotadean lines. Thus, two characteristics, which until now had seemed peculiar to Petronius, are in fact attested elsewhere: the use of verse within speeches (or, as is the case here, of entire speeches in verse) and the employment of poetry to comment on the action.

Of course, the statements so far made must remain tentative, especially in view of the small size of the preserved fragment, and a number of qualifications need to be made. The Sotadean lines in the papyrus are metrically irregular and the dialogue extremely colloquial, but the narrative frame seems, as far as we can tell, equally plain and far from stylistically pure. We may want to believe, with Parsons, that there must have been a contrast in style between the Sotadean tirade and the narrative frame, but I have not actually been able to detect any evidence for this. The analogy with Petronius would be more convincing if we had a narrative frame in, say, a refined Atticizing style, that is, a restrained middle register which would emphasize other stylistic levels by contrast. Such levels could be either lower, for example the characters' words, or higher, as in the case of literary insertions.

Moreover, the Sotadean lines delivered by Iolaus' friend are totally justified by the plot and perfectly functional within the narrative

---

[22] The employment of mystery rituals for covert sexual aims reminds us of the Quartilla episode in Petronius. For mystery cults in the Iolaos romance, see the useful but sometimes overburdened analysis by Merkelbach (1973).

[23] Here too, Parsons's (1971) analysis is essential. The comparison is elaborated by Bettini (1982: 90–2) in relation to a new perspective on the Sotadean tradition.

frame. We may well suppose that these lines effect some sort of comic estrangement. Iolaus' helper goes through initiation and when he comes back he talks in verse: he could not be expected to do anything else since by now he has become a *cinaedus* through and through, a Gallus who has been properly initiated. Prophecies, mimes,[24] and *kinaidologoi* are expressed in Sotadean lines, and the author of our text uses them to express a farcical mystery revelation uttered by a *cinaedus*. Speaking in Sotadean verse is the most immediate proof of initiation. Thus, the reasons behind the employment of these lines are too specific and context-dependent to allow for wide-ranging speculations about the overall form of the Iolaus romance. This single insertion of verses does not prove that the alternation of prose and verse was a formalized feature of the novel, which is the case with Petronius' work, in that prose and verse are equally determining for its overall form. The case of the Iolaus romance is different: a novel which includes an opera-singer as one of its characters need not be an opera.

The employment of a quotation from poetry *controlled by the narrator*, though perhaps at a first glance not as striking a feature, is in some ways more interesting. Though, on the whole, Petronius does not use quotations in order to comment upon the narrative, a recurrent feature of the *Satyricon* is the insertion of brief passages in verse which comment upon the action. Such passages may themselves contain quotations or, more precisely, be formulated as pastiches. They

---

[24] It is precisely a prosimetric mime, the so-called Mime of Charition, which provides another parallel for the Sotadean lines delivered by Petronius' *cinaedus*. This low but amusing farce (*P. Oxy.* 413ʳ) has a plot based on high models such as the *Iphigenia in Tauris* and the serious novel, but it is soaked in an atmosphere which recalls the music hall. Within this papyrus we should perhaps mention a barbarian king who among limping or incomprehensible lines manages to deliver four decently constructed Sotadean verses: 'βάρβαρον ἀνάγω χορὸν ἄπλετον, θεὰ Σελήνη, | πρὸς ῥυθμὸν ἀνέτῳ βήματι βαρβάρῳ προβαίνων; | Ἰνδῶν δὲ πρόμοι πρὸς ἱερόθρουν δότε τυμπανισμόν, | Σηρικὸν ἰδίως θεαστικὸν βῆμα παραλλάξ' ('I lead on the numberless barbarian chorus, goddess Selene, stepping to the rhythm with loose barbarian step; you, the foremost of the Indians, give us as well the cymbal sound of sacred noise, and in your own strange manner give us alternately your god-inspired (?) Seric step'.).

So, the theme of this show is an invitation to dance in a paratragic register: there are a number of Euripidean reminiscences. This is an interesting parallel for the farcical lines delivered by Petronius' *cinaedus* (*Sat.* 23. 3):

> huc huc convenite nunc, spatalocinaedi,
> pede tendite, cursum addite, convolate planta
> femore facili, clune agili et manu procaces,
> molles, veteres, Deliaci manu recisi.

Thus, these songs seem to be genuine mime arias.

are, one may say, the opposite of apocryphal texts: they are composed *ad hoc* by Petronius, but they are marked off, in the narrative context, as pseudo-quotations. For example, in *Sat.* 80 the narrator comments on Ascyltus' and Giton's escapade, with a gnomic verse passage where he reflects upon the precariousness of friendship. Similarly, in the Iolaus romance, the narrator's voice employs a Euripidean saying which illustrates the advantages of friendship; but while Euripides' line deals with the heroic friendship between Orestes and Pylades, the situation outlined in the romance seems to show that, in the name of friendship, one can become a eunuch of Cybele. Thus the quotation may serve as a comic contrast, as well as a comment on the scene.

The snippet of comparative evidence provided by the Iolaus romance can be inserted within a more specific context. Petronius scholars tend to take for granted a sharp distinction between two types of literary influence. The *Satyricon's* narrative structure recalls the Greek romance, as well as the comic novel and short story, which are, to us, far less known.[25] On the other hand, the *Satyricon's* narrative form, with its free mixture of prose and verse, takes us to Menippus. At first sight, these two literary traditions seem clearly distinct. We have no evidence that Milesian tales contained passages in verse, not even in the form of quotations. On the contrary, we are perhaps in a position to underline Petronius' own innovation. He adapts the plot of a Greek licentious story about a widow and interweaves it with typically Latin intertextual references: above all, Dido's story in the *Aeneid.* The Vergilian quotes are the most obvious feature of Petronius' reworking of the story. As for Weinreich's suggestion that the Greek model too may have played with a web of poetic quotations which Petronius would have replaced and Romanized, it seems utterly inconceivable.[26]

---

[25] When talking about literature of entertainment it is particularly advisable not to assume a different readership for Greek and Latin works. For example, Plut. *Crass.* 32 is often taken as evidence of *Sisenna's* success. However, since the Parthians cannot have been fluent Latin speakers, whereas Roman officials presumably read Greek, the episode may well not refer to the success of texts written in Latin: attributing these low novels to Sisenna is as uncertain as taking them, say, as the original works of Aristeides of Miletus. The increasing popularity of Latin translations from the first century BCE only shows that Greek narratives of love and adventure were already in some measure successful in Rome. The consumption of this sort of literature in educated circles is an important presupposition for Petronius' 'ironic' poetics.

[26] On this point, see the reliable contribution by Müller (1980: 103–21, esp. 119). Sisenna's fr. 1 Bücheler, which consists of only two words, 'nocte vagatrix', has often been quoted as evidence for poetic insertions in the Milesian tale, but it is difficult to draw any conclusions on the basis of such a short fragment.

Quotations from elevated poetry play a role of some importance in the pseudo-Lucianic *Onos* and probably also in its Greek original, but these are just minor decorations completely integrated within the narrative. They are never metrically recognizable or shown up in context, or in some way isolated from the main body of the story.

It would, however, be dangerous to generalize too much. As we know, verse passages do not seem to play a substantial role in the Greek romance either.[27] However, the earliest complete novel, Chariton's romance, deserves special attention. Chariton's work is usually described as a simpler and less decorated version of the traditional idealized romance. The dating of the text has been dramatically changed due to some papyrus findings. The new dating is confirmed by some internal features which had not, perhaps, been given sufficient attention: Chariton's style shows no trace of Atticism. It thus constitutes the only complete example of a Greek novel of a 'pre-sophistic' period: it could be dated within the first century CE. It is interesting that Heinze, who disregarded the dating of the idealized novels which was current in his times, confidently ascribed Petronius' lost models precisely to the first century CE.

In this context it is interesting that Chariton frequently used *quotations from poetry* (nothing of the sort can be found in much more refined and complex writers, such as Achilles Tatius or Heliodorus). Roughly thirty Homeric quotations are inserted in the narrative and replace the narrator's voice at emotional or otherwise crucial points

---

[27] On the prosimetric tradition in Greek and Latin there are two overall, though perhaps not exhaustive, studies: Immisch (1921: 409 ff.), who insists too much on the connection between aretalogy and the *Satyricon*; and Bartonkova (1976: 65–92). (See now Relihan 1993—ed.) The most reliable reference work for *prosimetrum* in Petronius remains the *Apocolocyntosis*. My observations on *prosimetrum* in *narrative* texts are not intended to devalue or substitute this line of enquiry. It should be noted that the vulgate title *Apotheosis per saturam* may allude to the mixture of prose and verse as a characterizing feature of the work. See Reeve (1984: 305–7). I find unacceptable the mechanical opposition between 'Menippean' and 'narrative' *prosimetrum* set up by Astbury (1977: 22 ff.) (above, Ch. 3), although Astbury presents good arguments against the characterization of Petronius' *prosimetrum* as 'Menippean'; this characterization is often based on vague and general references to Varro's satire. One would also hope that the somewhat metaphysical character of the term 'Menippean', derived from Bakhtin's deservedly successful theoretical work, will not further confuse the issue. Systematic research on the varying status of ancient *prosimetrum*, accompanied by a necessary methodological clarification of the very category of *prosimetrum*, would be extremely useful in trying to put some order into this matter. (See now Relihan 1993—ed.)

in the story. Homer provides a pathetic vocabulary which is almost never integrated or diffused within the narrative discourse (allusions of this sort would clash with Chariton's plain and unassuming style); rather, Homer's voice makes a brief appearance, without losing its identity, and without interrupting the narrative flow of the story.[28]

Clearly, Chariton is no Homerid, and does not boast that he is one. When Chaereas' mother wants to keep him away from danger and shows him her breast to inspire pity, Hecuba's words to her son come naturally in that context (3. 5. 6). When a character undergoes some emotional trauma, the narrative's pathetic expressions, its swooning laments—which are so typical of a *larmoyante* narrative— consistently rely on Homer (cf. 1. 1. 14, 1. 4. 6, 3. 6. 3, 4. 5. 9, 5. 2. 4). This does not mean that the characters ask to be compared to their great predecessors, or that Chariton's work naively presents itself as the direct heir of epic poetry at its greatest. Chariton is straightforward, perhaps, but not naive. He invites a comparison on the basis of similarities of situation, but does not suggest a continuity of genre.

At the same time these allusive indications must be taken seriously. Chariton does not bring an Achilles or a Penelope on stage, but neither does he employ his quotations in order to create a mock-heroic atmosphere. His characters do not live in heroic times, but they are nevertheless highly dignified and belong to a nobler past. His novel is peopled with kings and great generals. His lovers' feelings, moreover, are never portrayed in ironic terms. In the end we must take the quotations at face value: they are authoritative lines which aid the author in telling the story. Naturally, the intertextual effects thereby achieved are rather monotonous and limited. These Homeric quotations rarely contain subtle psychological nuances: Homer rather provides pathetic gestures and formulas which are complete in themselves. It is up to the reader, if anyone, to integrate the comparison evoked by the quotation.

And yet sometimes subtler and wider effects are accomplished. The long separation between Chaereas and Callirhoe has often evoked the *Odyssey*'s narrative structure, and the final reunion suggests to the reader the bedroom in Ithaca. And predictably at 8. 1. 17, we get the quotation of *Odyssey* 23. 296, which many important scholars have considered the natural conclusion of Odysseus' and Penelope's story.

---

[28] The most detailed study of Homeric quotations in Chariton is Müller (1976).

Such narrative effects are harder to achieve when the *Iliad* constitutes the model, since it cannot contribute much to the narrative structure of a love story full of separations and adventures. However, Chariton, very appropriately, often singles out from the *Iliad* Achilles' feelings for Patroclus. In his brave disregard for any differences of sex, Chariton shows that he sees in the episode between Patroclus and Achilles the only hint of romantic love within the *Iliad*'s plot.

Why Homer is the quotable author *par excellence* can perhaps most clearly be seen by looking at 6. 4. 6. While out hunting, a king is inspired by Love to form a mental picture of his beloved in hunting gear. Such a fantasy is elegiac, but it actually resolves, almost at once, into the image of the hunting Artemis at *Od.* 6. 102–4. Just like Nausicaa and Dido in *Aeneid* 1. 498 ff., this vision of a woman deserves to be given a mythical counterpart. The model belongs to a discourse shared not only by author and audience, but also by the characters in the story: it is a cohesive element in the text. The same principle is responsible for Encolpius' belief that his (most unfortunate) rendezvous with Circe resembles Zeus' and Hera's meeting on mount Ida. The only difference is that the appropriation is in this case ironic, rather than neutral: in Chariton an epic formula such as οὔπω πᾶν εἴρητο ἔπος is used as a pretentious ending for a speech (3. 4. 4), while Petronius saves the analogous Latin clause 'haec ubi dicta dedit' for the end of the most vulgar, odd, and unstructured tirade of his entire novel (61. 5).

Needless to say, such analogies do not presuppose any direct or exclusive link between Petronius and Chariton. But the presence of quotations from poetry in the idealized novel had to be pointed out. If Chariton's romance represents only one surviving example of a widespread type of novel (and it is difficult to imagine this conventional work outside such generic boundaries), then the existence of 'counter-models' to the *Satyricon* becomes all the more plausible. Petronius sets himself up against this tradition not only through the content of his work (as Heinze argued), but also through the ironic and devious usage of the *Verseinlagen.*

Serious and idealized novels written in sober and restrained language are embellished with Homeric quotations, which are free from even the faintest hint of irony. Comic novels or narratives, written in a colloquial and realistic style, are decorated with Euripidean *gnomai*. Narratives interposed with strange and varied verse sections keep being found: the Sotadean lines in the Iolaus papyrus, but also the weird iambic cataleptic tetrameters in a narrative text which has been published even more recently.[29] The contents deal, perhaps, with a eunuch, an unfaithful wife, and a prophet. The Greek lines are treated metrically like the Latin iambic septenarii in Plautus' or Varro's Menippeans. While we are waiting to be in a better position to define the different status of prosimetrum in narrative texts, we must already admit that there is no longer any reason to see the novel and Menippus as two sharply distinguishable influences in the *Satyricon*. Such boundaries can be very easily broken down when it comes to the lowest levels of entertainment literature in the first century CE. And it is in this area that the most exciting experiments can be carried out.

If the *Satyricon*'s poetics, as has been rightly pointed out,[30] entails a degree of self-parody, this is precisely because it incorporates those 'low' genres which are the basis of the irony. Thus, no low texts, no down-and-outs of literature, should frighten off the Petronius scholar.

As must have become clear, these tortuous and indirect studies and the fragmentary nature of the evidence do not inspire much easy enthusiasm. The best one can do in collecting fragments is gradually to shed some light on the grey areas which surround the *Satyricon*. By now the colourful company, the picaresque *Gesellschaft* which Wilamowitz aimed at singling out, has acquired one or two new characters: *cinaedi* who speak like oracles, cannibal bandits with painted faces, and even judgements of Solomon. Every new finding warns us more and more clearly that we must distinguish between the nature of the model and the use Petronius makes of it. On the one hand, we must get a better understanding of the para-literature which provided Petronius with material for his composition. On the other hand, the new fragments of Greek novels also serve as a point of contrast. They help us to define what Petronius could *not* have found in the great pool of the lost novels.

No other ancient novel has such a complex narratological structure. We find a narrator almost totally involved in the illusions of the past, an author who juggles with literary and cultural codes, with the readers' expectations they entail, at the expense of the characters and even of the narrator himself, and some passages written in verse which are perfectly functional within this narrative device and which often serve to interpose a diaphragm of false consciousness, illusion, and bad faith between the characters and the story as it is told.

---

[29] *P. Turner* 8 in Haslam (1981: 35 ff.).   [30] Veyne (1964: 308).

These passages in verse stand between the author's superiority, as manifested by his ability to insert such refined literary codes in the narrative, and the narrator's inferiority, as a captive to his illusions. These passages represent the intersection, the moment of crystallization and contact between the two levels. It is precisely this stratification which allows Petronius to draw his material from the most disparate cultural levels: between the literary complexity of the work and its profession of its low character, there opens up a space for conflict and irony. Any study of the novel and short story as sources for Petronius' work must necessarily become all the more convincing if it takes his great transformation into account.

AFTERWORD 1997

After some years the dust round Iolaos seems to have settled, and two features have emerged as the most important: the use of initiation references in the context of a coarse sexual adventure ('a crafty fuck': Stephens and Winkler 1995; 371; 'to cunningly lay': Holzberg 1995: 63; 'to screw by deceit': Tatum 1994: 3) according to the stylistic preferences of translators, plus the decisive contextualization of the plot (cf. Menander, *Androgynos*; Terence, *Eunuchus*) made by Dodds in Parsons (1971).

I am still very interested in the problem of *prosimetrum*, but here difficulties are increasing. The discussion by Stephens and Winkler (1995: 363–6) is much more sceptical than mine, and the Tinouphis fragment is a problematic parallel, especially because of its metrical enigma.

Regarding Iolaos, I reiterate the point that the contextual motivation of the Sotadean lines differs from the conventions of Petronius: thematic motivation in Iolaos formal motivation (one has to assume) for most poetic inserts, and quotations in the *Satyrica*. I would now add that the *Orestes* quotation comes from the classical text which was most often used in school exercises: *sententiae* about friendship, especially from Euripides, appear to have been the staple diet of an average school education (cf. Cribiore 1996: 512).

This confirms that Iolaos does not belong in the same world of literary sophistication and stratification as Petronius; and we still have no clue about the chronology of this text—with its implied tradition of Greek, criminal-satiric-cum-verse narrative—relative to

Petronius. In my view it is still possible that Petronius knew, and cared about, previous traditions of Greek pulp fiction, and totally transformed them, above all by creating a cultural gap between the narrating voice(s) and the low-life situations, by using high poetry as a distorting lens, and by including, but holding at a distance, lowbrow Greek narrative through *mise-en-abyme* and metadiegesis. I also refer to the tantalizing scraps unearthed from the *Etymologicum genuinum* by Alpers (1996). These seem to constitute a narrative which combines a word such as *binein* (see above for modern translations), a character named Protagoras, and a journey to Abdera. Alpers, who at page 32 refuses to translate *binein*, notes at pages 42 ff. that the character Protagoras not only has an impressive literary name, but is also related to the very birthplace of the 'Archeget der Sophistik'; then at pages 53–4 he invokes Petronius for the mix of learning and sexual goings-on. Curiously, Petronius has not only the impressively named Eumolpus, but even two characters named after masters of classical rhetoric: Corax and Gorgias.

For a reappraisal of the complexity of *prosimetrum* in the *Satyrica* I recommend Schmeling (1996c) and Connors (1998).[31]

---

[31] This version of the original publication is dedicated to the memory of Luigi Pepe, who did so much to modernize the study of ancient fiction in Italy, and who organized the Perugia conference where my paper was presented in 1985.

7

On the Unity of Apuleius' *Metamorphoses*

ANTONIE WLOSOK

In his *Metamorphoses* Apuleius of Madauros, who called himself 'philosophus Platonicus',[1] employed the adventure story of the ass-man Lucius for the purposes of religious propaganda. He had the story itself before him in its Greek version—the first two books of the *Metamorphoses* by Lucius of Patrae[2]—of which we have a substantial excerpt among Lucian's works, entitled Λούκιος ἢ Ὄνος.[3] In general, Apuleius adheres closely to its plot.[4] One major change, however, has been made: he turns the retransformation of the ass into an act of redemption brought about by the goddess Isis and into a prelude to the real metamorphosis, i.e. apotheosis in the mysteries of this goddess.

Even if the Greek version with its natural and burlesque ending is disregarded, this final turn of the plot in Apuleius comes as a surprise. For the preceding ten books of the *Metamorphoses* contain a loose series of very various and worldly adventures, narratives which are in part

---

Lecture delivered at the 10th meeting of the *Mommsengesellschaft* in Münster on 6 June 1968 and (slightly abridged) as a probationary lecture in Heidelberg on 15 July 1964. I may be allowed to remark that I encountered the problem I am dealing with here in connection with my work on Lactantius and the Gnosis, and that the solution I suggest was basically reached during a seminar on Apuleius in the winter semester of 1959–60. This chapter was translated by Martin Revermann.

[1] *Apol.* 10. 6; cf. 64. 3 ('Platonica familia'); *Flor.* 15. 26 (pages from *Met.*, *Apol.*, and *Flor.* are quoted according to the editions of Robertson and Vallette 1956 and Vallette 1960).

[2] Photius was still able to read and compare it to the Lucianic *Onos*: *Bibl.* cod. 129 (p. 96b12 Bekker), cf. after Bürger (1887) especially Perry (1926) and Lesky (1941).

[3] This can today be regarded as the solution to the problem of how the three versions of the ass novels relate to each other; see Perry (1926) and Lesky (1941: 43–50), and further Helm (1961) and Burck (1961: 275 = 1966: 393).

[4] On the relation between Apuleius and his model, see above all Perry (1923) and Junghanns (1932); on the question of insertions, in particular Lesky (1941: 43–68) and Mazzarino (1950).

loosely inserted into the main plot and which in tone and temper stand out markedly from the solemn seriousness of the final Isis book. Nothing seems to prepare for the religious denouement. Apuleius' ass reflects neither about the meaning of his path of suffering, nor about the cause for his unfortunate metamorphosis, which is the result of his own bold actions. Nor does he show the slightest sign of an increased inner maturity or even of a catharsis which would lead him towards being chosen for serving Isis. He remains stupid, lecherous, gluttonous, and curious, and in the end has learnt nothing new.

This fact makes it also impossible to understand the *Metamorphoses* as a 'novel of development', as has been repeatedly attempted over the past decades. I mention above all Paratore, Wittmann, and Riefstahl.[5] If we use the idea of development, the unity of the work cannot be understood, and this has already been emphasized by critics.[6] Accordingly, the question has been repeatedly raised whether Apuleius was ever aiming at an internal connection between the adventures of Lucius-ass and his redemption, that is between the main part of the *Metamorphoses* and the Isis book. Up to the present date opinions are divided, although a number of considered and very plausible arguments in support of a homogeneous conception of this novel have been advanced.[7] Besides these, however, there are a number of somewhat speculative or at least awkward explanations, particularly using the history of religion, but also using philosophy and literary theory, which may have aroused suspicion towards any attempt at a unifying interpretation.[8] In consequence, recent editors

[5] Paratore (1928); Wittmann (1938, esp. 8, 151); Riefstahl (1938).

[6] Especially Lesky (1941: 69 f.). On Paratore (1928), see in particular Helm (1928); on Riefstahl (1938), Pfister (1940) and Rüdiger (1963: 59 n. 3).

[7] See above all Junghanns (1932: 159–65) and Dornseiff (1938). The most important arguments adduced are: (1) the parallelism of the fates of Lucius and Psyche; (2) the motif of *curiositas*; (3) the motif of evil *fortuna* and her role as the counterpart of Isis; (4) the relation of the ass figure to the cult of Isis. It is undisputably the merit of Reitzenstein (1906, esp. 32–4) to have pointed out that an intention of religious edification or even proselytizing goes well with that of entertainment and thrilling amusement, and that even in such serious works as the *Acta Ioannis* or the *Life of Paul* by Jerome amusing interludes of a miraculous or even erotic–lascivious kind are not dispensed with. See also Pfister (1940: 540) and Weinreich (1962a: 226).

[8] This applies above all to the interpretation of the *Metamorphoses* within the wider framework of a derivation of the novel from mystery cult as attempted by Kerenyí (1962) and Merkelbach (1958), and to further ineffective attempts at explanation like those propounded by Landi (1929) or Riefstahl (1938). Despite several good observations in detail, Morelli (1913, 1915), Scazzoso (1951), and Moreschini (1965), among others, may be classed amongst unmethodical and over-imaginative (and therefore rather unattractive) interpretations.

and translators[9] have firmly refused in their introductions to accept any internal unity of the novel as a whole. At the same time they have denied any profound and serious intention on the author's part and characterized the *Metamorphoses* as an amusing novel of entertainment, made up of heterogeneous elements which are loosely bound together. From this point of view the religious ending must be regarded as disturbing, and to a scholar like Rudolf Helm, who has done great service in Apuleian research, the Isis book has appeared to be 'a dark patch on a many-coloured piece of cloth'.[10]

By contrast with these views and impressions I wish to show in the following that the whole work is based on a clear and carefully planned structure, which is rooted in its author's philosophical and religious views and which provides insight into the reasons which lead Apuleius to write propaganda for the Isis religion. Up to now the acknowledgement of such an interpretative route has been hindered by the fact that Apuleius neither sets out his purpose didactically nor pursues it with systematic rigour. But he has marked it by using certain concepts as a leitmotiv, and he has illustrated it by mythical analogies and expressed it by other artistic means in his presentation and composition.

The concept on which our demonstration is to hinge is the word *curiositas*,[11] which has long been recognized and discussed by scholars

[9] Robertson and Vallette (1956: 35); Helm (1928: 20–2); Brandt and Ehlers (1958: 503 ff.); Burck (1966). Rode (1956) and Grabar-Passek (1956) do not deal with the question of unity at all (I owe this reference to E. G. Schmidt).   [10] Helm (1961).

[11] References to the important role of *curiositas* for the conception of the *Metamorphoses* are already made by Junghanns (1932: 161 f.) and Wittmann (1938: 81) (on which see Dornseiff 1938: 233). Cf. also Lesky (1941: 71), who emphasizes the ambivalence of the concept in the *Metamorphoses* and therefore accepts the function of *curiositas* as a leitmotiv only in a limited way. Rüdiger (1963: 57–82), on the other hand, emphasizes both its employment as a leitmotiv and its ambivalence, and rightly sees the significance of Apuleian *curiositas* in its 'fatal tendency towards the forbidden' and the 'inquisitive violation of the numinous' (69; see also his afterword to Rode 1960: 531–8). Fundamental for the mental history of this concept, which in Latin culture occurs first in Apuleius, is Mette (1956; see also 1962). Further important contributions to the history of *curiositas* are Blumenberg (1962, 1961 (where Apuleius, however, is omitted, referring the reader to Schneider 1954: 445)) and Labhardt (1960) (wrong criticism of Mette's categorization combined with misguided attempts of derivation in Joly 1961: 33–44). Most effort to apply the concept to the work of Apuleius has, it appears to me, been made by Lancel (1961, esp. 25–33) (even if I cannot agree with his equation, inspired by Merkelbach, of Eros-Cupid with Harpocrates-Horos and, in consequence, a mystical-theurgical interpretation of the Amor and Psyche story; but see p. n.28 below). Riefstahl (1938: 29), Merkelbach (1958) (cf. Merkelbach 1962: 1 ff., 19–22, 42 ff.), and, in passing, Schneider (1954) have also adduced the notion of *curiositas* for an interpretation of the novel as a whole. The following have most recently argued against any

as the leitmotiv of the *Metamorphoses*. It hardly ever occurs before Apuleius.[12] In the *Metamorphoses* it denotes from the very beginning a fundamental disposition of Lucius. In the course of the narrative he himself repeatedly talks of his *familiaris, genuina*, or *ingenita curiositas*.[13] And in the revelation speech of the priest of Isis (11. 15) the priest names precisely this characteristic as the prime cause of his unfortunate transformation into an ass[14]: 'curiositatis inprosperae sinistrum praemium reportasti'. What is meant by *curiositas* here? And why is it condemned from the viewpoint of the Isis religion?

According to Lucius' own account his *curiositas* is a deep and all-embracing desire for knowledge. He is 'thirsting for news', 'he wishes to know everything or at least very much', he is 'very eager to get to know rare and miraculous things'. In this or similar ways he introduces himself to the reader in the first chapters.[15] It emerges very quickly, however, that this drive for knowledge has its specific direction: towards magic.[16] Lucius is representing a particularly enhanced form of human desire for knowledge: he is 'coram magiae noscendae ardentissimus cupitor' (3. 19. 4).

For Lucius magic is a *divina disciplina*, a secret art, which deals with the hidden divine powers in nature and the cosmos. To him it appears to be the perfect example of knowledge, as the culmination of human wisdom and of intellectual capacity. The magic powers of Thessalian witches are repeatedly praised in hymnlike enumerations.[17] In the end it is always the same: they possess power over the stars and the elements, over ghosts and the gods, that is to say over

unifying function and significant use of the motif: Brandt and Ehlers (1958: 503) (*curiositas* in the *Metamorphoses* is nothing but a 'dramaturgical motif') and Burck (1961: 285) (on Lucius' desire for knowledge: 'this is nothing but a part of narrative technique, a literary ploy').

[12] Its only occurrence is Cic. *Att.* 2. 12. 2 (from 59 BC), on which see Labhardt (1960: 209), who makes it appear probable that it is a spontaneous new creation of Cicero which he himself forgot again.

[13] 'familiaris curiositas' (3. 14. 1, 9. 12. 2; cf. 1. 2. 6, 2. 6. 1); 'genuina curiositas' (9. 15. 3); 'ingenita curiositas' (9. 13. 3).

[14] See Junghanns (1932: 162 n. 73); Wittmann (1938: 81); Mette (1956: 229 f.); Lancel (1961: 32).

[15] 1. 2. 6: 'sititor . . . novitatis . . . qui velim scire vel cuncta vel certe plurima'; 2. 1. 1: 'nimis cupidus cognoscendi quae rara miraque sunt . . .'.

[16] As is set out at 2. 6.

[17] 1. 8. 4: 'caelum deponere, terram suspendere, fontes durare, montes diluere, manes sublimare, deos infimare, sidera extinguere, Tartarum ipsum inluminare'; 3. 15. 4: 'quibus obaudiunt manes, turbantur sidera, coguntur numina, serviunt elementa'; cf. 2. 5. 4 and 1. 3. 1.

the cosmos as such. The believer in miracles calls the witch 'divini potens' (1. 8. 4). She has the divine element at her disposal, inasmuch as it is present and effective in the cosmos by its powers. From this point of view access to magic is tantamount to the mysterious access to the divine. Magic enables the surpassing of human boundaries, and grants participation in divine power.

In view of these aims Lucius' *curiositas* is nothing but his own decision to penetrate into areas of knowledge from which humans are barred by their very nature. Yet from the viewpoint of a religion of revelation—and such the Isis religion is—it is not just curiosity but *hybris*.[18] This religious aspect of *curiositas* is crucial for Apuleius. He makes this clear twice in the course of the narrative: the first time at the beginning of book 2 by confronting Lucius with the statue of Actaeon,[19] who is described as the mythical *exemplum* of presumptuous curiosity; the second time in the middle of the story by the inserted story of Psyche's fate, a downfall similarly caused by a *curiositas* explicitly condemned by a god.

First, the unhappy fate of Actaeon is emphatically demonstrated in the introduction to Lucius' adventures in the Thessalian city Hypata. It is the motto, as it were, for the subsequent events. The situation is, in brief, the following. On the first morning after his arrival Lucius is having a look at the Thessalian city full of curiosity (*curiose*). By chance he meets a relative from his mother's side, Byrrhena, a noble lady from the family of the philosopher Plutarch, as is specifically remarked. She leads him into her house. In the middle of the atrium there is a magnificent marble sculptural group, which attracts the view of Lucius as he enters. It represents Diana going to bathe, accompanied by dogs and being stared at by Actaeon. Apuleius devotes an extensive and rhetorically refined description to this work of art. It is clearly modelled on Ovid's description in the *Metamorphoses*

---

[18] Wittmann (1938: 81 f.), Lancel (1961: 28–32), and, more generally, Blumenberg (1961: 53) (and elsewhere).

[19] As I found out after having completed this article, this interpretation has already been advanced by Lancel (1961: 31). Riefstahl (1938: 67–9) too noted the importance of the Diana–Actaeon group and applied it to Lucius' fate. He, nevertheless, misunderstood the character of this *curiositas*. Mette (1956: 231) also briefly points to the 'predictive' character of the scene. Less to the point is Merkelbach (1962: 339 n. 3), who, probably in the wake of his mystery interpretation of the *curiositas* in Apuleius, which he refers to the secret of mysteries and the initiand's duty of silence (19–22, 42 f., 48; cf. Merkelbach 1958: 109 f., 113), speaks of the 'punishment of the eavesdropper'.

(3. 138 ff.)[20] and seems to presuppose a knowledge of it. In comparison with Ovid, however, two things are remarkable. Apuleius stresses the nobility of the goddess on the one hand, and the urgent *curiositas* of the human on the other. In Ovid, who seems to follow a common version of the myth,[21] Actaeon comes upon the goddess' bath by chance.[22] Apuleius, however, describes how he leans forward, curiously looking (*curioso optutu*) at the goddess: already turning into a deer, he is observing the goddess, who is about to take a bath (2. 4. 10). The punishment, his transformation into an animal, is therefore due to Actaeon's *curiositas*, and this *curiositas* is characterized as presumptuous curiosity, which intends to penetrate into the secrets of the divine, and to behold them without permission.

The very deviation from Ovid's version of the myth shows that Apuleius wishes to give more than a mere artistic ekphrasis of a work of art.[23] The inserted description is, as we saw, very carefully fitted into the frame and has an important statement to make within the whole. This becomes particularly clear through the way it is connected with the plot as a whole. While they are inspecting the work of art, Byrrhena warns Lucius of the magic powers of his hostess Pamphile, directly invoking the goddess depicted in marble: 'per hanc deam . . . cave tibi, sed cave fortiter' (2. 5. 3). This is saying that here Diana is to be viewed as the goddess of magic.[24] Actaeon, then, becomes the mythical embodiment of the human being who attempts to gain divine power by means of magic and is punished and destroyed for this *hybris*. Beside the momentary interpretation of the pictorial situation, his fate, in the

---

[20] Cf. Ov. *Met.* 3. 158 f.: 'simulaverunt artem | ingenio natura suo' with Apuleius' remark: 'quae ars aemula naturae veritati similes explicuit' (2. 4. 7) and Ov. *Met.* 3. 200: 'ut vero vultus et cornua vidit in unda' with Apuleius: 'Actaeon simulacrum et in saxo simul et in fonte . . . visitur' (2. 4. 10). Riefstahl (1938: 68 f.) points to correspondences in the description of Lucius' metamorphosis in Apuleius and that of Actaeon in Ovid.

[21] Cf. Call. H. 5. 113 f. (οὐκ ἐθέλων); Hygin. *Fab.* 181: 'in conspectum deae incidit'.

[22] Emphasized in lines 141 f. and 174 f.; cf. *Trist.* 2. 103 f. ('inscius Actaeon vidit'). Riefstahl (1938: 68) completely overlooked this fundamental difference.

[23] Thus Bernhard (1927: 280) regards this description, together with those at 4. 6 (the robbers' cave) and 5. 1 (Amor's palace), only as 'description of a locale'. Ehlers (1983: 515) has it among his examples of 'high poetry', 'poetical gloss', and 'rhetorical twists'. Similarly, Burck (1961: 398) counts it as one of the artistic showpieces of the 'flamboyant orator Apuleius'.

[24] As such she is, for instance, invoked in Catullus' hymn (34. 15: 'tu potens Trivia . . . es dicta'). In the sixth book of the *Aeneid* Vergil also calls Apollo's divine sister Trivia (*Aen.* 6. 9–13, 35, and, above all, 69).

present context, also serves as a strong warning, which menacingly underlies the superficial meaning of Byrrhena's words.

Lucius is blind to these connections, and this is an essential characteristic of his *curiositas*, which is a form of *hybris*. Byrrhena's express warning causes the opposite outcome: his appetite for magic becomes an obsession (in hindsight he calls himself 'vecors animi' and 'amenti similis', 2. 6. 3 ff.). Of Byrrhena's words he picks up only the possibility of an acquaintance with magic in the house where he is staying, and in passionate blindness he plunges headlong into disaster.

A second illustration of Lucius' *curiositas* is given in the most extensive inserted story of the *Metamorphoses*, the so-called fable of Amor and Psyche.[25] An old woman tells it in the robbers' cave to the captured bride Charite in order to console her. The ass is listening. In the story the two separated lovers are reunited after a long and painful separation—this is the consolatory hint at Charite's liberation. Further parallels between the fates of the two couples can only be constructed with much strain and are hardly intended by the author.[26] The real meaning of the Psyche story lies, as has repeatedly been said,[27] in its symbolic relation to the main plot. Psyche's fate mirrors that of Lucius and serves to illustrate it. I regard as the decisive parallel both the reason for the downfall and the subsequent path of suffering of the two heroes: Psyche is succumbing to the same *curiositas* as Lucius.

Despite several warnings and strict prohibition (5. 6. 3, 11. 3–6, 12. 3 ff.) she is possessed by the desire to find out the secret of her unknown husband, who approaches her only in the darkness of the night. While he is sleeping she gazes curiously at him in the light of a lamp (5. 22 ff.). She looks and tremblingly recognizes the radiant god.[28]

[25] 4. 28–6. 24. Note the edition with notes by Grimal (1963), with an overview of the various attempts of interpretation (6–21). The most important literature is now in Binder and Merkelbach (1968). As regards more recent literature I wish to point to Portogalli (1963) and Moreschini (1965), who see the story as a philosophical allegory in terms of a Middle Platonic and Apuleian demonology.

[26] Against Merkelbach (1958; cf. 1962: 1–3), who states that 'the content of the stories of Psyche, Charite and of Lucius are the same in the end. Psyche and Charite are separated from the beloved and, after some ordeals, are reunited with him again. Charite is liberated from the robbers' hands, Lucius from being an ass. Like Psyche, he is united with the divinity after long ordeals.'

[27] By Junghanns (1932: 159–65) and Dornseiff (1938: 225).

[28] 'divini vultus intuetur pulchritudinem'. In this section Cupid is called 'deus' seven times. As far as his appearance is concerned, the effect of light is particularly mentioned. In this respect we are in fact dealing with an enforced contemplation of the divine, an epiphany, and in this sense with theurgy. To this extent I regard the 'theurgical' interpretation of the scene, which Lancel (1961: 35 ff.) proposes, as worth consideration.

As had been predicted, this indeed destroys her happiness. The god himself had previously condemned Psyche's 'curiosity for the forbidden sight', the 'vultus curiositas' (5. 19. 3), as 'sacrilega curiositas' (5. 6. 6). Psyche falls prey to *curiositas* a second time, at the end of her path of suffering. This means that she too does not learn anything new; she does not mature in view of what has happened to her. She has already accomplished her difficult task and fetched unopened from the underworld the box containing 'divine beauty', i.e. a magic device, when she is seized by a rash desire—'mentem capitur temeraria curiositate' (6. 20. 5)—and opens the box so as to acquire some of the divine beauty. This deed of *curiositas* is presumptuous clutching at divine power or the magic device.[29] Only by Amor's intervention is Psyche saved from death. The god sums up: 'ecce rursum perieras, misella, simili curiositate'. Thus in the story of Psyche *curiositas* is taken apart into its main components: presumptuous desire to behold or understand the divine and presumptuous greed for divine power.

Tellingly, the story fails to have an effect on the ass. He sees it as nothing but a 'nice little story', *bella fabella* (6. 25. 1). He is very far from learning from it. For this he will need the priest's revelation.

Here we have arrived at the most important point of Apuleius' conception. He does not make the person himself gain the insight that his *curiositas* is a misdeed, even a sort of original sin, but has a priest pronounce this. This insight is already a part of the revelation; *curiositas* and revelation are antithetically related to each other. Thus the prehistory of the Apuleian concept of *curiositas* leads us into the area of Hellenistic gnosis, more exactly into the kind of Jewish and pagan philosophy of revelation as represented by Philo of Alexandria and the Hermetic tradition.[30] This has already been seen by Wittmann[31] and, more clearly, Mette[32] in his sketch of the history of

---

[29] Here again the forceful warning of the tower precedes (6. 19. 7).

[30] On this see Wlosok (1960).

[31] Wittmann (1938: 81 f.). In order to show the negative evaluation of human desire for knowledge from the viewpoint of a theology of revelation, Wittmann has already adduced the hermetic Asclepius (14 = *Corp. Herm.*, ed. Nock–Festugière, ii. 312. 16 ff.) and also pointed to the role of *curiositas* in the Latin church fathers, especially Tertullian and Augustine.

[32] Mette (1956: 227–35), who makes the important reference to the Momos speech of Kore Kosmou (*Corp. Herm.*, ed. Nock–Festugière, ii. 312. 16 ff.). Less to the point is the use of Philo, *Migr. Abr.* 216 ff. Passages like *Migr. Abr.* 184–7 (on which see Blumenberg 1961: 58 f.), *Somn.* 1. 52 ff., *Mut. nom.* 66–76, and *Ebriet.* 167 should rather be adduced. Further, the description of περίεργοι in Vettius Valens should be considered (e.g. p. 7. 30 Kroll, 37. 29, 42. 33).

the concept *curiositas*. From this provenance of the concept we can explain the striking fact that after Apuleius' time the word and the concept are to be found mainly in the Christian theologians, starting with Tertullian up to Augustine,[33] for whom *curiositas* is part of a supreme triad of desires, i.e. one of the cardinal sins.[34]

How deliberately Apuleius is aiming at the idea of revelation can be demonstrated by a comparison with the Greek *Onos*.[35] Here the motif of *periergia*—the Greek equivalent of *curiositas*[36]—is already present. But it is neither stressed nor evaluated in any way, and is always used in the sense of everyday curiosity or at most a thirst for new experiences and a desire to learn new things. In the three passages of the pseudo-Lucianic version which feature the word[37] there is a jocular play on the proverbial curiosity of the ass.[38] There is, then, a touch

[33] The passages are in *TLL* (Schwering), even if not always assigned to the correct lemma. On their evaluation see Mette (1956), Blumenberg (1961, 1962), and, in particular detail, Labhardt (1960).

[34] Cf. Theiler (1933 = 1966: 205–12), Labhardt (1960: 221–3), and Blumenberg (1962: 296). The attempt to deduce this triad from Porphyry has been called into question by Labhardt.

[35] Made also by Mette (1956: 229 f.). The differences, however, are not made clear with the necessary precision, nor is *curiositas* in Apuleius determined with sufficient accuracy. Above all, too little has been made of the material for evaluating Apuleius' conception.

[36] The first firm occurrence is provided only by Apuleius in the *Metamorphoses*. Quintilian (*Inst.* 8. 3. 55) still glosses περιεργία by *supervacua operositas*. In the *Itala* translation of *Acta* 19. 19 (τῶν τὰ περίεργα πραξάντων = qui curiositates gesserunt; *TLL* iv. 1491. 7), *curiositas* has already acquired the precise sense of magical practice and superstitious activity. The adjective *curiosus*, on the other hand, is used in comedy since Plautus as a rendering of περίεργος (besides πολυπράγμων); see Labhardt (1960: 207 f.). Has Apuleius really freshly created the word *curiositas* in analogy to the Greek pair περίεργος–περιεργία without any relation to Cicero's earlier coinage (see n. 12 above), as Labhardt suspects?

[37] (a) *Onos* 15: the curse of the narrator's own περιεργία, which has led to the unfortunate metamorphosis, missing in the corresponding passage in Apuleius, instead being transposed to the priest's speech at 11. 15. 1. (b) *Onos* 45: the curious behaviour of the ass while in a gardener's service, which leads to the creation of the proverb: ἐξ ὄνου παρακύψεως, exact correspondence with *Met.* 9. 42; (c) *Onos* 56 (the end of the story, Lucius after his retransformation and return): 'There I made sacrifices and set up memorials to the gods who had preserved me, since after so long and so narrowly I had escaped home, not by God, "from the ass of a dog", as the saying goes, but from the snooping of an ass' (tr. Sullivan, in Reardon 1989: 618). In Apuleius this is similarly transformed and integrated into the theological context of the Isis book.

[38] The proverbial expression ἐξ ὄνου παρακύψεως (first occurrence: Men. fr. 211 Körte; cf. Otto 1890: 41 f., *asinus* no. 8, and Mette 1962: 398) is based on the characteristic curiosity of the ass, which tends to poke its nose into everything, usually at the wrong time. This is shown by aetiologies such as can be found at *Onos* 45 and Apuleius 9. 42. 2 and 4 ('unde etiam de prospectu et umbra asini natum est frequens proverbium'). For a proper understanding of the Greek ass novel and of the opportunities for

of tragicomic self-knowledge in the Greek Lucius uttering the follow-ing execration after his transformation (15): 'Oh, what mistimed meddling! (*periergias*)' (tr. Sullivan 1989).[39] In this passage, the de-scription of the transformation, Apuleius agrees in every detail with the *Onos*. But he omits exactly this self-critical remark. Apparently he has been saving it for the priest's speech (11. 15. 1), in which the accusation is literally repeated: 'curiositatis improsperae'.

A last example is to show that, and how, Apuleius is playing off magic against redemption through the mysteries, *curiositas* against revelation. The magic transformation in the third book of the *Metamorphoses* is clearly stylized as an initiation,[40] and the introduc-tion into magic is obviously modelled on a mystery initiation. By this means the magical transformation, as a sort of magical mystery, is in deliberate contrast with the Isis initiation later on. The comparison is demanded by the author through striking cross-references and antithetical correspondences. Only the most important may be men-tioned here.

Lucius caps his decision to gain access to magic at any cost with the formula: 'quod bonum felix et faustum itaque, licet salutare non erit' (2. 6. 8). This formula returns, significantly varied, in the priest's mouth in book 11 before the final initiation: 'quod felix itaque ac faustum salutareque tibi sit' (11. 29. 5). The two events are thus com-bined and at the same time separated from each other. The earlier self-authorized decision is contrasted with election by the goddess, and the wrong initiation, the disastrous mystery, is confronted with the true mystery of redemption.

By this the two main aspects of the comparison have been pointed out too. Magic is to be unmasked as a rival to and a perversion of reli-gion. One way is to characterize it as sacrilege, another as the road

---

associations which it was offering to an author such as Apuleius it may be important that for quite some time the ass had become an 'allegorical animal' (a phrase of Ernst Zinn *per litteras*): see also Mette (1962) as above.

[39] More closely defined at 13: 'for I wished to find out by experiment whether, changed from my human shape, I would have the soul of a bird also' (tr. Sullivan). It is thus primarily desire for knowledge which resorts to magic for the sake of experi-ment rather than self-elevation, as is done by Apuleius' Lucius, who in the same con-text thinks of the 'dignitas pinnarum' (3. 23. 1).

[40] It consists of two parts: (1) a sort of prelude, 3. 13–20, which contains the rev-elation of the arcana of the house or Lucius' first initiation as a preparation for the magic part proper; that is to say, (2), the nocturnal magic scene, 3. 21–4, which is divided into (a) a magic contemplation (metamorphosis of Pamphile) and (b) Lucius' magic metamorphosis.

to disaster. This is why the scene of transformation is stylized in such a way that parallels in terminology and subject-matter that are as far-reaching as possible are established, but its impact is represented as exactly the opposite of a redemption.

One of the parallels is, for instance, that the servant Photis is behaving like a mystagogue whose role is to disclose divine secrets;[41] that she is asking her initiate Lucius to keep silent, expressly referring to other initiations,[42] and that she is regarding outsiders as uninitiated.[43] Others are that she praises the overwhelming power of the witch, her mistress,[44] using attributes which return in the Isis hymn of book 11,[45] and that Lucius voluntarily declares himself her servant,[46] whereas later on he is obliged to obey the rules of the Isis religion at all costs.[47]

Above all, the main elements of the magical mystery are assimilated to the cultic one:[48] Lucius is participating in both a vision and a

---

[41] Above all 3. 14 ff.; cf. esp. 3. 15. 3: 'arcana dominae meae revelare secreta'; 3. 15. 7: 'erae meae miranda secreta'. I think it possible that the change of the servant's name (in the Greek version she is called Palaistra, which is significant in another way) is to allude to her magic-mystagogical role. As opposed to Isis, the true inspiration with her salvation-bringing 'light' (see n. 58 below), Photis would thus be a light which leads astray, a fatal 'illumination'. Similarly also Lancel (1961: 46).

[42] 3. 15. 4 ff.: 'qui . . . sacris pluribus initiatus profecto nostri sanctam silentii fidem, quaecumque itaque comisero huius religiosi pectoris tui penetralibus, semper haec intra conseptum claustra custodias, oro, et simplicitatem relationis meae tenacitate taciturnitatis tuae remunerare'; 3. 20. 2: 'rei tantae fidem silentiumque tribue'. Cf. 11. 21. 7, 22. 1, 23. 4, 24. 7.   [43] This becomes very obvious at 3. 15. 1 and 6 f.

[44] 3. 15. 7: 'erae meae miranda secreta, quibus obaudiunt manes, turbantur sidera, coguntur numina, serviunt elementa'.

[45] 11. 25. 3: 'tibi respondent sidera . . . gaudent numina, serviunt elementa'; previously: 'te observant inferi' and similar expressions.

[46] 3. 19. 5: 'in servilem modum addictum atque mancipatum teneas volentem'; 22. 5 when asking for the magic ointment: 'tuumque mancipium inremunerabili beneficio sic tibi perpetuo pignera . . .'; cf. 23. 2: 'per dulcem istum capilli tui nodulum, quo meum vinxisti spiritum'.

[47] 11. 6. 5: 'plane memineris . . . mihi reliqua vitae tuae curricula adusque terminos ultimi spiritus vadata. nec iniurium, cuius beneficio redieris ad homines, ei totum debere, quod vives'; 7: 'quodsi sedulis obsequiis et religiosis ministeriis et tenacibus castimoniis numen nostrum promoveris'; in addition 15. 5: 'da nomen sanctae huic militiae, cuius non olim sacramento etiam rogabaris, teque iam nunc obsequio religionis nostrae dedica et ministerii iugum subi voluntarium. nam cum coeperis deae servire . . .'; 16. 4: 'statim sacrorum obsequio desponderetur'. On 3. 22. 5, cf. esp. 11. 24. 5: 'inremunerabili beneficio pigneratus'.

[48] Described 11. 23–4. Of central importance are the symbolically encoded events of the mystery night at 11. 23. 7, narrated from the perspective of personal experience (death and resurrection, contemplation of the divine light, communication with the gods). Further, described in more detail at 11. 24, the initiand's resurrection as image of the god on the following day, through which the initiand's apotheosis (as rebirth; cf. 11. 21. 7) is demonstrated. On the details, see Dibelius (1917), Berreth (1931), Wittmann (1938); cf. Reitzenstein (1927: 19 ff., 220 ff.), Hopfner (1940–1), Merkelbach (1962) (who has further literature on pp. 6 f.).

transformation. But here the reversal starts. The magic transformation does not cause him to become a god but an animal, and that of
the humblest sort, which is at the same time the most remote from the
divine, for, as is expressly said later on, the ass is associated with
the opponent of Isis, the evil god Typhon.[49] The content of the vision
is not constituted by noble gods and their effects, but by the naked
old witch and her metamorphosis into an eagle owl, that is to say into
a bird of night and of the dead. The consequences for Lucius are his
wanderings and sufferings as an ass, who, enslaved and driven about
without respite, is subject to the mercilessness of blind *Fortuna*.[50] The
Isis religion, however, leads to 'the haven of tranquillity' and 'the altar
of mercy' (11. 15. 1); it protects its adherents by the shelter of the
all-powerful and all-wise 'saviour-goddess'[51] *Fortuna videns*, whose
mystery of rebirth brings about the true metamorphosis.

This juxtaposition of magic and religion, of the works of man and
redemption, is inherent already in the title, if it is correctly referred
to its content. For Apuleius called his work *Metamorphoses*—in the
plural!—without giving a collection of transformation stories, as we
know them from Ovid and as, according to the testimony of Photius,[52]

---

[49] 11. 6. 2, spoken by Isis: 'pessimae mihique detestabilis iam dudum beluae istius
corio te protinus exue'. The relation of the ass to Typhon (Seth) is testified, among
others, by Plutarch, *Isis* 362f, 363c. Further passages in Hopfner (1940: 137 ('ass' as
a name of Seth), 21 n. 9). Representations of Seth-Typhon with an ass's head occur,
for example, in the magical papyri (illustrations in Preisendanz 1931, table. II fig. 11).
To me it seems to be worth noting that Seth-Typhon was associated with bad or black
magic, whereas Isis is called 'the great magician' in the laudatory sense (Hopfner 1940:
137 f.). On the Egyptian Seth, see now Te Velde (1967). The 'Typhonian role of the ass'
is also recognized by Kerényi (1927: 184–6) as well as Merkelbach (1962: 1) ('the shape
of the ass represents life without Isis'); see already Morelli (1913: 153) and Junghanns
(1939: 104).

[50] 7. 2–3, 16. 1, 17. 1, 25. 3, 8. 24. 1, 9. 1. 5, 11. 12. 1, 15. 2–4. The motif of Fortuna
(cf. after Morelli 1913, 1915, above all, Junghanns 1932: 163 f.) as a power hostile to
man is used as a leitmotiv in the *Metamorphoses*. It is particularly prominent in the later
books (from 7 onwards), in which the *curiositas* motif could no longer be applied as
well. It thus takes over its unifying function and, like the *curiositas* motif, is taken up
by the priest's speech at 11. 15 and interpreted in a theological sense, so that Fortuna
and her blindness as well as malice seem integrated into the divine salvation plan, the
Isidis magnae providentia, and serve as an instrument of salvation (11. 15. 2; cf. 12. 1).
Beyond that the motif is also used for ring composition. At the beginning, in the first
inserted story, it is demonstrated in the figure of the pitiable Socrates, who serves as a
warning *exemplum*: like Lucius later on, he had, albeit unwittingly, started a sexual relationship with a witch (on the combination of 'eroticism' and magic, see Lancel 1961:
32 ff.). Socrates becomes 'the trophy of triumphant Fortuna' (1. 7. 1). With this corresponds at the end the counterweight of the redeemed Lucius, who, as the protégé of
Isis, now 'triumphs over Fortuna' (11. 15. 4)!

[51] Isis as 'sospitatrix dea': 11. 9. 1, 15. 4; at 11. 25. 1 she is praised as 'humani generis
sospitatrix perpetua'.   [52] See n. 2 above.

also occurred in the work of Lucius of Patras.[53] In Apuleius the diversity of *Metamorphoses* occurring in Ovid is reduced to two contrary types: the transformation of human being into animal, which is attributed to the area of magic, and the sacred apotheosis of the human being, which is reserved for the Isis religion.

In this confrontation magic is the exemplary area of human *curiositas*, which in its blind and perverse drive for knowledge is reaching out towards powers held by the divine. Religion, by contrast, appears to be the space in which the divine graciously descends towards the human being, reveals itself to him, and gives him that which he is not capable of achieving on his own. Thus the selection of Lucius starts with the epiphany and self-introduction of Isis, who reveals herself as the all-powerful goddess and ruler of the cosmos (11. 3, 5). The end is constituted by the highest revelation of the divine, the epiphany of Osiris, which is not described because it is indescribable, and whose loftiness can only be denoted by stammering and ever greater attributes.[54]

The magic metamorphosis, the transformation into an ass, shows how the divine withdraws from the pressing clutches of the human and how, as I tried to demonstrate using Actaeon and the words of the Isis priests quoted above as examples, this *curiositas* is condemned as a grave sin. Before Lucius is selected for the first initiation Apuleius spends a whole speech by a priest (11. 21) in condemning any sort of human impetuosity and urging as wrongdoing. The pious attitude which he is preaching is characterized by patient waiting and humble quietude, accompanied by ascetic exercise and contemplative preparation. In this context there are expressions like 'patientia',[55] 'mitis quies', 'taciturnitas' (11. 22. 1). In contemporary religious speculation, however, patient quietude, silence, and tranquillity of the soul are the fundamental conditions of mystical unification with the divine.[56]

---

[53] Apuleius' title is usually explained as sheer borrowing from the Greek model (thus, most recently, Burck 1961: 288 f.). By contrast, Reitzenstein (1927: 262) and Junghanns (1932: 180 f.) already counted the mystery transformation as a metamorphosis.

[54] 11. 30. 3: 'deus deum magnorum potior et maiorum summus et summorum maximus et maximorum regnator Osiris'.

[55] 11. 21. 5; by contrast with the specifically Roman meaning of the word *patientia*, the word here already has the sense which is found in Christian authors such as Tertullian and Cyprian; see Kunick (1955).

[56] Cf. e.g. Philo, *Fuga* 132–6, *Heres* 263 ff., *Somn.* 1. 119; Max. Tyr. 11, 10; on which, see Wlosok (1960: 93. 255 f.).

After all this it does not come as a surprise that Apuleius describes the experiences of the night of the mysteries as an enlightenment[57] and the Isis religion as 'sobria' and 'purissima religio' (11. 21. 3, 9), i.e. as a spiritual religion, that he calls Isis 'the seeing one' and the great 'illumination',[58] and that he recommends her religion as the field for philosophical contemplation, now unfolding on the basis of the revelation. Turning to the doctrine of revelation is only the corollary to the negative evaluation of *curiositas* and the human drive towards knowledge which it represents.

The question from which we started, whether the Isis book is in some way or other closely interconnected with the whole of the *Metamorphoses*, may thus be positively answered. But our scholarly *curiositas* does not allow us to stop as yet. At the end of the *Metamorphoses* Apuleius identifies himself with the Isis initiate Lucius (11. 27. 9). This is more than a literary commonplace of authentication. For this celebrated man, who was already honoured with statues during his lifetime,[59] is thus making a stand for the Isis religion and its theology of revelation by virtue of his person and authority. The same Apuleius had already proudly confessed himself a 'philosophus Platonicus'[60] in his earlier writings, and through his activities as an author and translator disseminated contemporary Platonic doctrines in the Latin-speaking world. One is therefore forced to address the question: is there a connection between Apuleius' Platonism and his belief in the mysteries?

The answer is hinted at in the *Metamorphoses* by the author himself. The narrator, behind whom the author is hiding, claims descent from 'the famous philosopher Plutarch' on his mother's side. This is claimed twice, in the self-introduction right at the beginning of the work (1. 2. 1) and again on the occasion of Lucius' meeting with his aunt Byrrhena,[61] who then plays an important role as a warning figure. This remark makes sense only if understood as a confession of Plutarch's philosophical denomination. In our context one may think in particular of Plutarch's work on Isis and Osiris, in which the myth and rites of this Egyptian mystery religion are philosophically

---

[57] 11. 23. 7: '. . . nocte media vidi solem candido coruscantem lumine'.

[58] 11. 15. 3 '. . . videntis, quae suae lucis splendore ceteros etiam deos illuminat'.

[59] We know of several statues, e.g. two in Carthage (Ap. *Flor.* 16. 1 and 39 ff.) and one in Oea (Aug. *Ep.* 138. 19).

[60] See above, n. 1. Nowadays it is commonly accepted that the *Metamorphoses* belong to the later works of Apuleius and were written after the *Apologia* (c.160). On the date, most recently Carratello (1963).   [61] See above, p. 146.

interpreted in various ways.[62] Its introduction is most telling.[63] It
contains Plutarch's justification of the Isis religion on the basis of a
conviction which corresponds to the one hinted at by Apuleius. Thus
in Plutarch Isis is the 'wise and wisdom-loving goddess' (351e). She
leads her adherents, who devote themselves to her in pure and
spiritual veneration, to the truth and to understanding of the highest god.[64] Her temple and her cult are the places of revelation (352a).
Here the initiates receive 'the sacred lore about the gods' (352b), free
of *deisidaimonia* and *periergia*, as is expressly noted. Here, finally, in the
mysteries of the chief god, Osiris, the contemplation of being takes place,
of the first, initial, transfigured, supreme *noeton*. For this contemplation Plutarch uses the well-known description of enlightenment[65]
from Plato's seventh letter,[66] thus transposing the last philosophical
insight into the mysteries and making philosophy reach its fulfilment
in the mystery initiation. In this Apuleius seems to follow him. In his
philosophical writings we find the view expressed that the supreme
god heralded by Plato in his *Timaeus* (28c) is only accessible via a mystic contemplation, a mystery of enlightenment.[67] In the *Metamorphoses*
the practical experience of mysteries, the nocturnal contemplation
of mysteries, is interpreted in the sense of such an enlightenment
(11. 23. 1). Like Plutarch, therefore, Apuleius, as a Platonizing philosopher, is open to a theology of revelation and could regard the Isis
religion as the fulfilment and perfection of his Platonism.

[62] Cf. Hopfner (1941), on which Wlosok (1960: 56–9 with n. 38).
[63] Chs. 2 and 3 = 351e–352c.
[64] About worshipping her 351f says: 'the end of which is the knowledge of the first,
the sovereign, the intelligible'.
[65] 373a–e, 382c–d; cf. 351f–352a, 372e, and other passages.
[66] Plato, *Ep.* 7. 344b; cf. Wlosok (1960: 58 with n. 35).
[67] *De deo Socr.* 3: 'When Plato . . . very frequently proclaims that this being alone,
through its extraordinary and ineffable excessive greatness, cannot be even to a small
degree comprehended in any discourse, owing to the poverty of human language; even
for men of wisdom, when they have separated themselves from their bodies as far as
possible by force of mind, the understanding of this god only sometimes flashes, like a
bright light with the swiftest of flickering in the depths of darkness'; on which, see Wlosok
(1960, n. 226, 255).

8

The Tales in Apuleius' *Metamorphoses*

JAMES TATUM

There is no unanimity of opinion among modern scholars as to whether Apuleius' *Metamorphoses* is as successfully composed as its golden title might suggest.[1] It is not, for example, strictly a romance or satire.[2] Moreover, comparison with other works of ancient and modern fiction has not entirely resolved the question of which genre it belongs to.[3] The peculiar Latin and the account of the initiation of the hero Lucius into the cult of Isis in the final book have attracted considerable attention, but it is above all the tales scattered throughout the work which have caused many to wonder how we can reconcile the incontestably serious ending of book 11 with the tales and their oft-stated purpose of 'entertaining' the reader.[4]

Perhaps the frivolity of these stories is exaggerated because of association with later authors' use of them (e.g. the Tale of the Tub in Boccaccio), or perhaps the idea that the work is nothing but a series of Milesian tales ('sermone isto Milesio', 1. 1) makes us expect nothing but entertainment. Yet most of these tales are neither mundane nor || light-hearted. If they are told only for our delectation, one marvels at the tastes they would appeal to, for they usually end in the humiliation and death of the characters involved.

It has been a conventional practice in analyzing the *Metamorphoses* to deal with all the so-called *Einlagen*, or episodes and tales which do

---

I am grateful to the editor of *TAPA* and to Douglas Marshall for many suggestions toward the improvement of this essay.

[1] For a recent survey of all Apuleian scholarship, see Schlam (1968b: 4–31); and for a brief discussion of the contrary results reached in assessing its composition, see Tatum (1969b: 6–14).   [2] See Perry (1967).

[3] For comparison with ancient works, see Mazzarino (1950) and Ciaffi (1960); for modern literature, Riefstahl (1938) and Heine (1962).

[4] e.g. Perry (1967: 233–4, 242–3); and Burck (1966: 399–400).

not appear in the Pseudo-Lucianic *Loukios or the Ass*.[5] A consideration of only the tales might have some advantage over such analysis,
for Apuleius' formal identification of the constituent parts of his work
extends only to these *fabulae* ('varias fabulas conseram', 1. 1), and not
to other kinds of additions he may have made to the story of Lucius,
such as long speeches or a description of a piece of sculpture. Taking
all the *Einlagen* together also obscures the fact that the tales form most
of the work. Their prominence argues that they cannot be taken
merely as pleasant interruptions in the wanderings of Lucius. Some
have been studied for their beauty,[6] and others for their flaws,[7] but
they also merit attention to see whether all of them, and not just the
story of Cupid and Psyche, have an intelligible and serious role in relation to the final book. If they do have some bearing on the story of
Lucius and the 'Isiac' interpretation of his experiences in book 11, then
it will be possible to maintain that the *Metamorphoses* is a disciplined,
purposeful composition throughout.

Before considering the tales, I offer here a summary of the religious
interpretation which the eleventh book gives the first ten.

At the end of book 10, Lucius flees the amphitheater and gallops
for his life, not only because he is ashamed of copulating with a condemned woman in public, but also because he fears that the beasts
sent to slay the woman will not be 'civilized' enough to spare him.
Both Apuleius and the author of the Greek epitome shape the subsequent action on the basis of an understandable fear of death, but
with very different || results.[8] Loukios eats the roses and returns to
his original form (*Onos* 54), and his dilemma, as well as his story, are
resolved by his re-transformation. Apuleius' Lucius flees the theater,
however, and makes his way to Cenchreae (10. 35). His concern for
salus becomes the transitional idea to the final book, and the basis for
his appeal for salvation to the 'Regina caeli' (11. 2). As is possible with

[5] For a list of the various *Einlagen* categorized by form, see Bernhard (1927: 259);
Lesky (1941) offers the best example of the analytical method of studying the origin of
various *Einlagen*.

[6] e.g. the Cupid and Psyche story; see Grimal (1963: 1–29), for a comprehensive summary of the many studies on this tale.

[7] e.g. the tales of Thelyphron and Aristomenes; cf. Perry (1929*a,b*).

[8] Cf. *Onos* 54, ἐγὼ δὲ ἅμα μὲν ἡδούμην ἐν τῷ θεάτρῳ κατακείμενος, ἅμα δὲ
ἐδεδίειν μή που ἄρκτος ἢ λέων ἀναπηδήσεται, and 10. 34, 'quaecumque ad exitium
mulieris bestia fuisset immissa non adeo vel prudentia sollers vel artificio docta vel abstin-
entia frugi posset provenire.'

the word *salus*,[9] the idea of momentary freedom from danger is transformed into *salus* in a religious sense, or 'salvation.' This leaves the
original idea of escape from momentary personal danger, which at first
is identical with the situation in the *Onos*, far behind indeed. The
perils of the arena are regarded as only the last in a long series of
misfortunes:

tu meis iam nunc extremis aerumnis subsiste, tu fortunam conlapsam adfirma,
tu saevis exanclatis casibus pausam pacemque tribue. (11. 2)

This appeal recalls Lucius' earlier statements about his experiences.[10] Further, we see here the same language which Isis, her
priest, and Lucius himself will use as he becomes an initiate into the
cult.[11] In this way does the first half of book 11 refer to Lucius' story,
so that the priest's speech in the center of the book (11. 15) is a continuation of an established point of view. His adventures were an
unpleasant alternative to life without Isis, and his 'Odyssean' wanderings, which he ‖ once boasted made him at least a 'much-knowing'
man (9. 13), are now regarded as nothing but one trial after another
under evil fortune.

Because of such interpretative consistency, the speech at 11. 15
is the most important statement of an 'Isiac' view of the entire
Metamorphoses.[12] The priest's language recalls remarks in the first part
of the book, and adds more besides. He explains why Lucius endured
what he did, and also to what point those experiences have now brought
him. Interpretation of past experience and initiation into the cult are
so closely linked together that this speech is nothing less than a
signification of the story in books 1 through 10 into the morality of

[9] For the religious concept of *salus*, cf. Nilsson (1961: 159, 689 (on *soteria*), and
624–39); Latte (1960: 227 n. 3, 234–5); and Nock (1963: 9 ff.).

[10] The word *aerumna* in particular is often used to describe Lucius' tribulations;
cf. 3. 29 ('tot aerumnis me liberare'), 7. 16 ('talibus aerumnis edomitum novis fortuna
saeva tradidit cruciatibus'), 8. 26 ('iam meas futuras novas cogitabam aerumnas'), 7. 2
('veteris fortunae et illius beati Lucii praesentisque aerumnae et infelicis asini facta
comparatione'), 7. 27 ('nec aerumnae meae miseretur').

[11] Cf. 11. 5, 'adsum tuos miserata casus, adsum favens et propitia, mitte iam fletus
et lamentationes, depelle maerorem; iam tibi providentia mea inlucescit dies salutaris'
(Isis); 11. 15, 'multis et variis exanclatis laboribus magnisque Fortunae tempestatibus
et maximis actus procellis ad portum Quietis et aram Misericordiae tandem, Luci,
venisti . . . en ecce pristinis aerumnis absolutus Isidis magnae providentia gaudens Lucius
de sua Fortuna triumphat' (the priest of Isis); and 11. 19, 'adfatis itaque ex officio sin-
gulis narratisque meis propere et pristinis aerumnis et praesentibus gaudiis me rursum
ad deae gratissimum mihi refero conspectum' (Lucius).

[12] See Wittmann (1938: 77) and Lesky (1941: 72).

the worshipers of Isis. What the priest says here is by no means an
isolated display piece set down in an effort to link book 11 with the
rest of the work.[13]

Throughout the *Metamorphoses* there are repeated professions of
pleasing the reader or of telling a 'charming' story,[14] but what the priest
says does not make either Lucius' travels or the tales which he heard
sound trivial. His trials really were the 'storms of fortune' of which
the priest speaks. The very phraseology echoes the words which were
used earlier in the book to describe his 'labors' and 'disasters.'[15] The
'port of quiet' and the 'altar of mercy' which Lucius has reached are
the answers to his plea for *salus* in 11. 1–2. ‖ Cenchreae, the 'surest
port for all vessels,' becomes the 'surest port' for Lucius, too, as the
site of his conversion.[16]

As the priest says, the reason for Lucius' sufffering is that, in spite
of his book-learning and good background,[17] he was addicted to
'servile pleasures' ('serviles voluptates'), and was punished for his
'unlucky curiosity' ('curiositatis inprosperae sinistrum praemium
reportasti'). This criticism is only just; indeed Lucius' *curiositas* is frequently acknowledged as the most notable feature of his character.[18]

---

[13] For a different opinion see Perry (1967: 242).

[14] Cf. 1. 20, 'sed ego huic et credo hercules et gratas gratias memini, quod lepidae
fabulae festivitate nos avocavit, asperam denique ac prolixam viam sine labore ac tae-
dio evasi'; 2. 20, 'immo mi Thelyphron,' Byrrhena inquiet, 'et subsiste paulisper et more
tuae urbanitatis fabulam illam tuam remetire, ut et filius meus iste Lucius lepidi sermonis tui perfruatur comitate'; 4. 27, 'sed ego te narrationibus lepidis anilibusque fabulis protinus avocabo'; 9. 4, 'cognoscimus lepidam de adulterio cuiusdam pauperis
fabulam, quam vos etiam cognoscatis volo'; and 9. 14, 'fabulam denique bonam prae
ceteris, suavem, comptam ad auris vestras adferre decrevi, et en occipio.' All these
reasons for telling a story follow the theme of the reader's entertainment which is
announced so elaborately in 1. 1 (esp. 'auresque tuas benivolas lepido susurro permulceam' and the concluding exhortation, 'lector intende: laetaberis'); and the last example, 9. 14, in particular echoes the opening words of the *Metamorphoses* ('auresque
tuas benivolas,' 'fabulam . . . comptam ad auris vestras').

[15] Cf. 11. 2, 'tu meis iam nunc extremis aerumnis subsiste, tu fortunam conlapsam
adfirma, tu saevis exanclatis casibus pausam pacemque tribue; sit satis laborum, sit satis
periculorum'; and 11. 15, 'multis et variis exanclatis laboribus . . . pessimis periculis
. . . pristinis aerumnis.'

[16] Cf. 10. 35, 'portus etiam tutissimum navium receptaculum,' and 11. 15, 'ad portum Quietis et aram Misericordiae tandem, Luci, venisti.'

[17] An observation frequently made while Lucius was a man; cf. 1. 20, 1. 23, 2. 5,
and esp. 3. 11 (his noble background), 3. 15 (his learning).

[18] The most recent study is by Schlam (1968a). The meaning and implications of
the word *curiositas* have been studied with considerable thoroughness; see for this also
the excellent study of the history of the word by Labhardt (1960); Joly (1961); Lancel
(1961); Mette (1956); (1963).

This abandonment to 'servile' pleasures is a condemnation of double significance. Sexual gratification is on a 'lower' level than the divine, and *servilis* also recalls that Lucius was quite literally abandoned to sex with a serving-girl, Fotis, up to the moment of his metamorphosis. His appeal to Fotis to reveal her mistress Pamphile's magic arts was tied very explicitly to their mutual pleasures.[19] As he accepts the worship of Isis, he will adopt something altogether different from such promiscuous living, for service to her offers a 'higher' pleasure (without sex), and also a complete rejection of any curiosity about her mysteries.

Throughout the speech, fortune is continually said to be the agent of Lucius' sufferings, and in fact the half-proverbial, half-real Tyche of the Greek Romance[20] is conceived of everywhere in the *Meta-* ‖ *morphoses* as an almost visible foe against whom Lucius and many others bitterly complain.[21] Thus is 'blind Fortune' transformed into a 'seeing' Fortune, or Isis-Tyche, one of Isis' numerous manifestations.

in tutelam iam receptus es fortunae, sed videntis, quae suae lucis splendore ceteros etiam deos illuminat. (II. 15)

This change resembles that in *voluptas*, which we saw move from the 'servile' pleasures of Fotis to the spiritual joy of worshiping Isis. So also does Lucius exchange his former servitude as an animal of burden for the voluntary yoke of a servant of Isis ('ministerii iugum subi voluntarium'). The more he serves her, paradoxically, the freer he shall become ('nam cum coeperis deae servire tunc magis senties fructum tuae libertatis').[22]

[19] Lucius himself says that he is a slave to his passions for Fotis: 'in servilem modum addictum' (3. 19).

[20] Cf. the description of Tyche by Rohde (1914: 303): 'Im trüben Spiegel lassen sie (sc. die Romane) uns gleichwohl mit unerfreulicher Deutlichkeit erkennen, wie jenen Zeiten das Gesamtbild des menschlichen Daseins erschien. Durch Länder und über Meere treibt die "neidische Tyche," wie sie immer gennant wird, ihre Helden vom Gluck in das Elend und immer neue Not; meint man endlich, nun sei des Unglücks Gipfel überstiegen, so schleudert ein Zufall, eine neue Laune des Dämons die Armen wieder zurück.' This description could have been taken from Lucius' own remarks on *fortuna* at 7. 2.

[21] e.g. Socrates (1. 7), Aristomenes (1. 16), Cupido (5. 5), Charite (6. 28), and most of all, Lucius (7. 2, 7. 17, 7. 20, 7. 25, 8. 1, 8. 24, and 10. 4).

[22] A comparison with the *Onos* shows that the *periergia* of Loukios is not as sinister as the *curiositas* of Apuleius; e.g. *Onos* 15, 'Oh, what mistimed meddling!' (tr. Sullivan 1989). The counterpart of *fortuna*, *tychē*, is used only in a proverbial and innocent fashion, as at *Onos* 47, 'Seeing that fortune was fondly smiling on me and realizing that only this piece of comedy would save me', and 19, 'But some evil demon, aware of my designs, turned them right around.' In neither case does *periergia* or *tychē* undergo the kind of transformation in meaning which we see in Apuleius.

As the speech ends, those standing around are impressed by the 'innocence' and 'faith' which must have marked Lucius' earlier life for him to merit such honor.[23] He is 'reborn' into the services of the goddess, and soon shows his new self by rejecting the very faults which had previously been so much a part of his character. In the latter half of book 11, he is careful to guard the secrets of Isis' cult from the uninitiated, is solicitous about keeping his readers free from the dangers of 'rash curiosity,' and adopts the asceticism of a priest of Isis.[24] ||

The changes in meaning of *fortuna, voluptas,* and *servitium,* and Lucius' total rejection of *curiositas,* suggest that books 1 through 10 need not be 'religious' at all, or rather that they may be so only by an enthusiastic, but unsuccessful, attempt to affirm a point of view opposed to the doctrine preached in book 11. Thus, the more vulgar and sensual the experiences, or the tales, the more 'moral,' ultimately, they may prove to be. Presumably we need not wait until book 11 to recognize that *curiositas* or the baser *voluptas* are wrong. Such vices, if presented cleverly, will discredit themselves in the telling.

If this proves true, I realize I am tending towards a moralistic interpretation of these stories—perhaps even a humorless one. But the priest of Isis does exactly this in 11. 15. Apuleius never mentions the reader's edification, but, unless the tales are drastically out of harmony with the religious interpretation of this work which I have outlined, a purpose deeper than mere entertainment should be discernible in the stories.

THE TALES OF ARISTOMENES AND THELYPHRON

The tale of Aristomenes, the first in the *Metamorphoses,* introduces the reader into the strange world of Thessalian magic.[25] Lucius meets two men on the road and urges one of them to tell a story which the

---

[23] This comment about Lucius' character is not ironic or a slip on Apuleius' part, but an accurate explanation of his credulity and inability to recognize evil; cf. below, p. 180.

[24] His address to the reader at 11. 23 reveals a complete reversal in character: 'Quaeras forsitan satis anxie, studiose lector, quid deinde dictum, quid factum; dicerem, si dicere liceret, cognosceres, si liceret audire. sed parem noxam contraherent et aures et linguae illae temerariae curiositatis.' And this from a man who, at the beginning of his travels, could say of himself, 'non quidem curiosum, sed qui velim scire vel cuncta vel certe plurima' (1. 2)!

[25] See Perry (1967: 259–64); Ciaffi (1960: 9–52, esp. 9–17, 38–41); Feldbrugge (1939: 4–11); and Junghanns (1932: 121–2).

other finds quite unbelievable. This tale is designed to pass the time of a tedious journey, but there proves to be little enough festivity in it.

Aristomenes begins, as do Lucius (1. 1) and Thelyphron (2. 21), with a brief reference to himself and what caused him to enter upon such a situation (1. 5). His description of the appearance of Socrates forcefully establishes the image of *fortuna* as a malign power:

> humi sedebat scissili palliastro semiamictus, paene alius lurore, ad miseram maciem deformatus, qualia solent fortunae decermina stipes in triviis erogare. (1. 6) ‖

The first words of Socrates, the 'refuse' of fortune, are a warning to Aristomenes not to ignore her unpredictability:

> 'Aristomene,' inquit, 'ne tu fortunarum lubricas ambages et instabiles incursiones et reciprocas vicissitudines ignoras.' (1. 6)

He is nothing but a 'trophy' of fortune:

> at ille, ut erat, capite velato, 'sine, sine,' inquit, 'fruatur diutius tropaeo Fortuna, quod fixit ipsa.' (1. 7)

Socrates ends his account of his troubles by blaming the witch Meroe and fortune for his lot. This is the same *fortuna* which shall torment Lucius, but of which he is as yet ignorant. At the same time, it should be noted that Socrates' explanation of his troubles reveals that he himself bears some responsibility for all this, for he enjoyed Meroe's favors not unwillingly: 'Meroen, anum sed admodum scitulam' (1. 7).

Just as fortune first appears vividly in the description and lamentations of Socrates, so also a negative conception of *voluptas* is established. Aristomenes scolds Socrates for placing sexual pleasures before the welfare of his own family:

> 'pol quidem tu dignus,' inquam, 'es extrema sustinere, si quid est tamen novissimo extremius, qui voluptatem Veneriam et scortum scorteum Lari et liberis praetulisti.' (1. 8)

Socrates does not bother to refute this charge of *voluptas Veneria* and *scortum scorteum*, but only cautions Aristomenes not to criticize the morals of the 'divine' Meroe, who has punished many people before for such indiscreet talk. Thus a close association, which reappears throughout the *Metamorphoses*, is established from the very beginning between magic and its use for the gratification of sexual desires, and

revenge for their frustration.[26] This outburst against Socrates' dalliance
with Meroe is the only explicit condemnation of *voluptas* ever made
until the priest at 11. 15 mentions Lucius' 'servile pleasures.' ‖

In spite of his distaste for Socrates' conduct, Aristomenes recognizes
the savage as well as the miraculous nature of Meroe's arts: ' "Mira,"
inquam, "nec minus saeva, mi Socrates, memoras" ' (1. 11). But this
does not save him from their wrath when witches finally appear.
He is named an accomplice in Socrates' desertion of Meroe, and is threatened with punishment for his *dicacitas* and *curiositas*: 'faxo eum sero,
immo statim, immo vero iam nunc, ut et praecedentis dicacitatis et
instantis curiositatis paeniteat' (1. 12). *Dicacitas* is more apparently a
fault of Socrates than Aristomenes, and neither of them is as clearly
a *curiosus* as Lucius. But regardless of the justification, *curiositas*, like
fortuna and *voluptas*, is unmistakably identified and punished.

Panthia suggests to Meroe that Aristomenes be castrated,[27] but
he is spared in order to bury his friend. Socrates' throat is cut, like
an animal's at a sacrifice, 'a victimae religione' (1. 13). When the
witches leave, Aristomenes' fear of being blamed for this murder
leads him to attempt escape, but the gatekeeper refuses to let him out.
He then attempts suicide, but the bed on which he jumps falls to pieces,
and his search for *salus* in death is thwarted. At that moment, the
janitor enters and Socrates springs up alive, accusing him of being a
curiosus intent on stealing something (1. 17).

This is a miraculous deliverance from a somewhat contrived, but
nonetheless horrifying dilemma. Aristomenes is apparently saved from
prosecution, and Socrates seems more robust than ever. This proves,
however, to be a false deliverance. A similar turn of events occurs in
the tale of Thelyphron in book 2, where there is likewise a seemingly
happy resolution to what appears a hopeless situation (2. 26). There,

---

[26] Meroe changes various lovers into other forms and uses her magic for evil purposes, as does Pamphile (cf. 2. 5); and the evil wife in the tale at 9. 14–31 calls on a
witch's help either to return her to her husband's good graces, or to kill him (9. 29).
Note esp. the virtually identical phraseology which describes the woman in book 9 and
Meroe: 'saga . . . et divina potens' and 'saga illa et divini potens.' Lucius decides to learn
about magic by using the maid Fotis to accomplish his ends: 'verum enim vero Fotis
famula petatur enixe. nam et forma scitula et moribus ludicra et prorsus argutula est'
(2. 6).

[27] The motif of mutilation and castration is not so pronounced a theme as *curiositas* or *voluptas*, but it does recur later in the work; Lucius is so threatened by the
robbers and the evil boy in book 7. For a Freudian interpretation of castration as a
literary motif in another author, see Sullivan (1968*b*: 232–54, esp. 248, on castration).
In the Isis–Osiris myth the member of the god Osiris is cut off and thrown into the
Nile; cf. Plutarch, *De Iside et Osiride* 18.

by falling asleep on the job of watching a corpse, Thelyphron does the one thing he ought not to have done. At the very moment he awakes, the widow and her attendants enter and discover the corpse unharmed. He, too, is overcome with joy at his sudden luck, and is in fact so beside himself that he makes a rather tactless remark which results in his expulsion. In both tales there is a deceptively happy ‖ resolution to a situation of extreme peril, but this is soon 'corrected' by a surprising and horrifying conclusion. Socrates will soon 'die' a second time, and Thelyphron will discover at what cost the corpse remained untouched.

Such mercurial changes in luck are what Lucius shall experience in book 3. At his trial in the Risus Festival, his fortunes sink to their lowest point, and, like Aristomenes and Thelyphron before him, he stands at the very jaws of Hades (3. 9). He then has a sudden change in luck ('quae fortunarum mearum repentina mutatio?'), for his robbers prove to be only wine-bags, and, in the words of Fotis, he is not a homicide, but a 'utricide' (3. 18). Yet both Aristomenes and Thelyphron are examples, in their own stories, that such a dramatic deliverance may not be fortune's last turn, and shortly afterwards Lucius is transformed into an ass. These changes reflect the *Metamorphoses'* peculiar theme of multiple changes in fortunes as well as forms, for bad luck (a cut throat for Socrates, failure and mutilation for Thelyphron) appears for a time to have been miraculously deflected, 'in alias imagines,' 'to other appearances.' Finally it returns to its original, true state, 'rursum in se.'[28] In the words of Socrates (1. 6), we should not ignore the rapid and unpredictable changes of fortune, but, to our cost, we too often do.

This first tale ends in Socrates' death; as he bends over a running stream for a drink, Meroe's warning not to do so is realized, and Aristomenes is compelled to flee his former life and take up a new one:

ipse trepidus et eximie metuens mihi per diversas et avias solitudines aufugi et quasi conscius mihi caedis humanae relicta patria et lare ultroneum exilium amplexus nunc Aetoliam novo contracto matrimonio colo. (1. 19)

The same fate, exile, is also reserved for Thelyphron at the end of his tale, as he flees and adopts a disguise for fear of being *ridiculus*:

---

[28] A similar turn of fortune comes in the story of Charite and Tlepolemos when the apparently happy resolution of their story is reversed in the tale at the beginning of book 8. Conversely, the 'tragedy' in book 10 of the wicked step-mother, in spite of a portentous introduction to the contrary, ends quite happily for all concerned.

nec postea debilis ac sic ridiculus Lari me patrio reddere potui, sed capillis hinc inde laterum deiectis aurium vulnera celavi, nasi vero dedecus linteolo isto pressim adglutinato decenter obtexi. (2. 30) ‖

Just how accurately the conclusion of these two tales predicts Lucius' fate becomes apparent shortly before his own metamorphosis. His curiosity and indulgence in sex are there so strong that he renounces his home and former life to gain his desires: 'iam denique nec larem requiro nec domuitionem paro et nocte ista nihil antepono' (3. 19). These desires are soon fulfilled.

In addition to these forebodings, there are a number of echolalic responsions between this tale and its setting which are of considerable subtlety. For example, the contrast drawn between the sceptical *comes* and the credulous Lucius is repeated within the tale itself. Since Aristomenes tells the story, this detail of its plot is very likely to be taken as a rejoinder to his sarcastic companion. When he professes disbelief in Socrates' account of Meroe's powers, Socrates gives her abilities in a list of *adynata* (1. 8) which recalls the earlier list his companion had made as of things merely preposterous and hyperbolical (1. 3). At this point a character is said to have the very powers which barely five chapters before had seemed only ridicule. Both lists involve reversals of the natural order of things:

I. 3	I. 8
amnes agiles reverti	caelum deponere
mare pigrum conligari	terram suspendere
ventos inanimes exspirare	fontes durare
solem inhiberi	montes diluere
lunam despumari	manes sublimare
stellas evelli	deos infimare
diem tolli	sidera extinguere
noctem teneri	Tartarum ipsum inluminare

This sarcastic echo within the tale conforms to Lucius' earlier dictum (1. 3), that things which seem very difficult at first hearing may prove easily done after all.

An even more subtle connection between the tale and its setting lies in Lucius' unusual anecdote which he tells to encourage Aristomenes to tell his story. He almost choked to death on a piece of cheese, but he saw a man in Athens swallow a sword and remain unharmed. This bizarre story anticipates the two 'deaths' of Socrates in the tale, for though he seems to survive having his throat cut, by eating a ‖ piece of cheese and attempting to quench his thirst—as innocuous an action as Lucius'—he dies.[29] As we shall see with most tales in the *Metamorphoses*, the story of Aristomenes reflects a good rhetorician's concern to suit his speech to the taste and predisposition of his audience.

Even after only the first of the 'variae fabulae' of the *Metamorphoses*, the elaborate reiteration of the theme of 'entertainment,' with which the episode closes (1. 20), has a sardonic sound to it. It is not necessary to assume that merely because a tale is introduced for 'entertainment' or 'distraction' it is at odds with the interpretation given in book 11. Neither should we take Apuleius so literally when he speaks of our 'delectation.' If we can perceive nothing more than *iucunditas*, *festivitas*, or a *lepida fabula* in this story, then we have grasped nothing more than Lucius himself.

Aristomenes does not fail to see the savagery of magic, which Lucius cannot perceive. His inability to recognize evil, even when face to face with it, along with an unshakable faith that no matter how strange a thing may be, it can still be proven true,[30] are every bit as typical of him as his curiosity. These qualities remain with him right up to his metamorphosis at 3. 24. It is these faults to which the crowd refers when it speaks of the *innocentia* and *fides* of his former life (11. 16).

Events within the tale answer to the setting in which it is told. It appeals to all that is essential in Lucius' character: his curiosity, his faith in the miraculous, and that strange innocence, even naivete, which prevents him from recognizing evil when he sees it.

Most importantly, the story is thematically and interpretatively in harmony with the final book. *Fortuna*'s power is strongly emphasized (1. 6–7); *voluptas* is identified and condemned for the first and only time until book 11 (1. 8); the dangers inherent in magic, the perils of *dicacitas* and *curiositas*, are identified and, like sexual promiscuity, *voluptas veneria*, punished (1. 12–13). Thus the tale establishes very strongly in our minds, before Lucius' involvement with magic begins, ‖ all the themes mentioned in book 11, and it establishes them in the

---

[29] Schlam (1968*b*: 55–7).

[30] His remarks at the end of the tale show that he is a fit subject for the experiences he is about to undergo: 'ego vero,' inquam, 'nihil impossibile arbitror, sed utcumque fata decreverint, ita cuncta mortalibus provenire: nam et mihi et tibi et cunctis hominibus multa usu venire mira et paene infecta, quae tamen ignaro relata fidem perdant' (1. 20). There is clearly enough *fides* here to qualify him for faith in Isis.

same system of values applied by the priest at 11. 15. Aristomenes has
anticipated not only the events in books 1 to 3 which lead up to Lucius'
metamorphosis, nor merely the atmosphere of magic and intrigue
therein,[31] but also the ultimate interpretation of the entire work. This
tale is, in practical terms, an extension of the prologue, an expansion
of the essential theme of *figuras fortunasque* in the first chapter.[32] Not
even in the Cupid and Psyche story are such explicit statements
made about all the themes mentioned in book 11.

After this tale, Lucius' involvement in magic deepens—his interest
whetted, no doubt, by the outlandish story of Aristomenes. He is particularly interested in metamorphosis, and imagines that everything
he sees—rocks, birds, statues, or whatever—are wavering back and
forth from one form to another (2. 1). The statue of Actaeon and Diana
in Byrrhena's house is interpreted as an example of the *punishment* of
curiosity by metamorphosis. Actaeon is portrayed at the moment he
is transformed into a stag for spying on Diana with a 'curious stare':
'inter medias frondes lapidis Actaeon simulacrum curioso optutu in
deam proiectus' (2. 4).[33] Byrrhena follows the description with 'tua
. . . sunt cuncta, quae vides' (2. 5), a phrase with double meaning. It
includes her house with its sculpture of Actaeon's metamorphosis, but
also the warning implicit in that sculpture. She then swears by the
very goddess, Diana, who destroyed Actaeon for his *curiositas* (2. 5)!

Later in book 2, Lucius recalls that a prophet Diophanes had predicted his future renown (2. 12). At the beginning of book 3, he
remembers this prophecy, but forgets altogether what Byrrhena had
said, and pays no attention to the warnings of Fotis. He has a talent
for hearing only what he wants to hear. ‖

It is in this deepening atmosphere of Lucius' interest in metamorphosis and ominous predictions that Thelyphron tells his story.[34]
If Aristomenes' tale anticipates an 'Isiac' interpretation of all these
experiences, then Thelyphron's is even more to the point in the way

---

[31] Junghanns (1932: 122).

[32] I have in mind here a symbolic anticipation of the whole work not unlike that
which Viktor Pöschl demonstrated in the opening of the *Aeneid* (1964: 23–56).

[33] Compare this to Ovid, who explicitly attributes Actaeon's metamorphosis to a case
of bad luck: 'Fortunae crimen in illo, non scelus invenies; quod enim scelus error habebat?'
(*Met.* 3. 141–2) and also 3. 146, 'illum fata ferebant.' See Riefstahl (1938: 67–9) and
Mette (1956: 231), who sees this as a 'vorbedeutende Szene.'

[34] See Junghanns (1932: 132, 140); Feldbrugge (1939: 11–19); Ciaffi (1960:
53–108); de Jonge (1941: 2–6); Brotherton (1934, esp. 47–50); Perry (1967: 264–73);
also Perry (1949) (a review of de Jonge and an amplification of points made in Perry
(1929b).

it shows the punishment of a brash young man who failed to heed warnings about the dangers of magic and suffered the consequences. In charity, we might ascribe this misfortune to his innocence. He, like Lucius, seems to be incapable of heeding any warning, no matter how direct.

Themes such as *curiositas, voluptas,* or *fortuna* do not appear as explicitly in this tale as before, but if not actually stated, they are implied by the actions of the characters. Thus Thelyphron attends the public inquisition into the young man's death and looks on the scene with 'curious eyes' (2. 29), and at the end of the tale he decides to 'tempt fortune' (2. 30) by seeing if his ears and nose really were cut off.[35] The wife who is charged with poisoning her husband is an example of the corrosive power of *voluptas*, and she is the kind of woman who appears frequently in books 9 and 10. The most clever of Apuleius' sly hints at book 11 is the appearance of the Egyptian priest Zatchlas. His 'divine'[36] providence is accorded great respect, ‖ and the miracle of resurrecting the dead for a good purpose, *veritas*, stands in the strongest possible contrast to the evil magic practiced by the witches on Socrates or Thelyphron. There is a very important difference between the two 'resurrections' in these tales: Socrates is revived by black magic for the purpose of revenge, but in Thelyphron's tale the young husband is brought back to prove his wife's guilt.[37] Thus

[35] Most modern texts have the emendation of Gruter to *formam*, even though the manuscripts read *fortunam*; however, earlier editors were able to see *fortunam* here. Oudendorp (1786, *ad loc.*) suggested that *fortunam* is appropriate because of the thematic importance of 'figuras fortunasque' in the prologue, and certainly 'fortunam adgredior temptare' would conform to the thematic usage of the word. Perry (1967) 272 follows the reading *fortunam* in his translation of this passage. To 'test fortune,' 'temptare fortunam,' is a common phrase (*TLL* 6. 1. 1185. 11–12), but 'temptare formam' seems without parallel (*TLL* 6. 1. 1069. 15–37).

[36] *Divinus*, unless used by such men of doubtful wisdom as Socrates, is reserved for philosophers ('senex [sc. Socrates] divinae providentiae,' 10. 33, and 'divinus Pythagoras,' 11. 1), a wise man such as the doctor who saves the little boy's life ('providentiae divinae condignum . . . exitium,' 10. 12), and above all for Isis (with *vox* 11. 4; *promissio,* 11. 12; *vadimonium,* 11. 23; *simulacrum,* 11. 24; *vultus,* 11. 25; and *somnium,* 11. 30). Zatchlas has that same 'divine providence' which Lucius rates so highly, and which few others possess.

[37] The 'resurrection' of a character occurs often enough that it is very likely a motif related to Lucius' own 'rebirth' in book 11 (cf. 11. 16, 11. 21, and 11. 23). Socrates, the young husband in this tale, the boy in the 'tragedy' of book 10, and Psyche are each involved in one kind of 'rebirth.' Socrates shows the motif as an example of the evil powers of black magic; the young husband, as an example of the benign powers of an Egyptian priest; Psyche, as the benefit of divine intervention (in this case by rather congenial, but nonetheless immortal, Olympians); and the young boy, as a sham

there is a contrast in the tales, but not in the main narrative, of supernatural powers used for good and for evil. Zatchlas hardly seems a part
of this Thessalian world of black magic and human folly.

As in Aristomenes' tale, there are echolalic responsions between the
tale and its setting. The conversation at the dinner table (2. 20)
anticipates the plot of Thelyphron's story, for Lucius has heard of
the mutilation of the dead, and Thelyphron is a living example of it.
Lucius' apprehensive remark about magic, 'oppido formido caecas et
inevitabiles latebras magicae disciplinae' (2. 20), is echoed within the
tale, where the same curiously rhyming phrase, 'oppido formido,' occurs
in the words of Thelyphron: 'mihique oppido formido cumulatior
quidem' (2. 25).

Nor is Lucius the only person to whom Thelyphron so subtly
refers. Byrrhena urged her guest to tell his story—one somewhat embarrassing to say the least—and prevailed only after Thelyphron's
protest over the coarse laughter and humiliation he received from the
guests (2. 20).[38] Within the tale, the servant maid who accompanies
the adulterous ‖ and probably murderous widow is named 'Myrrhene'
(2. 24),[39] and this sounds, but for the initial letter, suspiciously like
the unusual name of Lucius' aunt, Byrrhena.

In the series of increasingly explicit warnings which lead up to Lucius'
metamorphosis at 3. 24, the tale of Thelyphron is more 'localized' than
that of Aristomenes, in that it tells of fair warnings ignored, and the
consequences. Thus, to set Thelyphron's story apart from all other warnings Lucius receives would distort its function. The description of
Actaeon, the prophecy of Diophanes, and the warnings of Fotis and
Byrrhena are all of a piece, and it would be somewhat artificial to

resurrection, in which the motif is almost irreverently treated, by a false death and
rebirth ('adulescentium duorum pater repente factus est,' 10. 12). The contrast of
all these to Lucius' spiritual resurrection is clear, and, as in the case of the *providentia,
voluptas,* and *fortuna* of Isis, there is no doubt that his 'rebirth' under her grace is by
far the more desirable.

[38] The laughter which greets the tales of Aristomenes and Thelyphron ('alto exerto
cachinno,' 1. 2; 'convivium totum in licentiosos cachinnos effunditur,' 2. 20; and 'com-
potores vino madidi rursum cachinnum integrant,' 2. 31) anticipates the derision and
ridicule to which Lucius will be exposed in his 'trial' in book 3 ('risu cachinnabili
diffluebant' and 'exitium meum cachinnat,' 3. 7; cf. also 3. 10). *Cachinnus* was
regarded as onomatopoetic by the ancients (cf. Porph. Hor. *Ars* 113, 'verbum secundum [ὀνοματοποιίαν] fictum a sono risus'; see also Ernout and Meillet (1951: 80) and
Walde and Hofmann (1930–55: 126), and well describes the *Schadenfreude* which
Thelyphron and Lucius suffer.

[39] The standard reading now of *Myrrhine* is an emendation of Beroaldus from
Myrrhene.

abstract this second story from the series of warnings to which it so clearly belongs.

Although the pretense of our 'entertainment' has been scrupulously observed by the author at every point, I hope we do not fail to see more to both these tales than meets Lucius' eye.

ROBBER STORIES

After Lucius' metamorphosis and his abduction by a band of robbers, he is driven to a mountain lair where he hears the story of three bandits who each suffered gruesome deaths.[40]

Just as Aristomenes and Thelyphron began their tales faced with a challenge to their credibility and dignity, so too an unnamed bandit ('unus ex illo posteriore numero,' 4. 9) defends himself and his fellows against another bandit's charges of cowardice—even of crawling through an old woman's bedroom. The thief who makes this charge praises Lamachus' 'excessive courage' (4. 8), which will earn him a place alongside the most famous kings and generals. Such grandiose praise abounds in every robber's speech. Lamachus' *virtus* is never questioned, paradigm for robbers that he is, but the survivors have to make some explanation for returning safe and sound. To answer || this attack it is essential to show that the other robbers in the band performed deeds just as meritorious as Lamachus, and lost their lives just as willingly.

The villain in the case of Lamachus was a miser named Chryseros, 'Mr. Gold-love,' who nailed Lamachus' hand to the door as he tried to break in. The robbers were forced in desperation to cut off his arm at the shoulder to escape, and then ran off with 'the rest of Lamachus.'[41] He begged them to put him out of his misery 'by the right hand of Mars,' their patron god (a somewhat incongruous oath, as he had just lost one of his own hands). But no one can be persuaded to commit *parricidium* (a word indicative of Lamachus' 'paternal' standing among them),[42] even though he says that no robber should

---

[40] See Junghanns (1932: 61–78, 141–3 (for 4. 9–22) and 156–65 (for 7. 5–9)); Lesky (1941: 50–61); and MacKay (1963).

[41] An exceptional use of *ceterus* (cf. *TLL* 3. 966. 27–9), which is at once funny and cruel; for a description of this mixture of terror and grotesque humor, see below, n. 73.

[42] Cf. Sommers (1967: 166–7). *Parricidium* indicates that he is regarded as the *paterfamilias* of the band.

outlive the hand 'by which he was accustomed to rob and murder.'
As he says, any bandit would be lucky to die by a comrade's hand.
Enthusiastic to the last, he kisses his sword passionately and plunges
it through his breast. His story ends with his burial at sea, in a manner reminiscent of famous, but more respectable, heroes: 'et nunc iacet
noster Lamachus elemento toto sepultus' (4. 11).[43]

By this heroic death, Lamachus shows that bravery and self-
control in extreme pain and mortal danger, along with a selfless concern for the welfare of one's fellow *latrones*, constitute the highest good,
for the very bad. But in spite of this inspiring and sanguinary tale, the
narrator cannot obscure the fact that Lamachus failed, however
much *virtus* he had.

No such inspiration can be drawn from the second story (4. 12). In
contrast to Lamachus, who died rich in maxims, one sentence
describes Alcimus' wretched end. Compared to the lengthy praise of
the 'heroes' in the first and third tales, this middle tale seems laconic.
But to make the best of a poor showing, the narrator introduces the ‖
tale simply as an example of bad luck: 'enim vero Alcimus sollertibus
coeptis tamen saevum Fortunae nutum non potuit adducere.' This
'hero' has little else to recommend him besides his credulity and spectacular death. Even more incautious than Lamachus, he is pushed from
an upstairs window by an old woman, who tricked him into looking
next door for the neighbors' fortunes.[44] He is given a hero's burial, as
a 'good follower' of Lamachus.

The legacy of Alcimus, however, is something other than the narrator intended to impart. The narrator must of course excuse *all* fail-
ures, but the effect of this brief story sandwiched between the two long
tales of Lamachus and Thrasyleon is to suggest that it is only one more
in a series of heroic deeds, which of course it cannot possibly be. Alcimus

---

[43] e.g. the famous sentence in Thucydides 2. 43 (that the whole earth is the grave
of famous men) or Lucan 8. 858–9. 11 (the description of Pompey's eternal fame).

[44] Only in book 4 does *fortuna* occur in the sense of 'money' or 'wealth.' But would
it be possible for the word *fortuna*, even when meaning 'money,' to be mentioned without one's thinking of *fortuna saeva*? The usage previous to book 4 should of necessity
color the meaning of the word. Thus Alcimus the robber is a victim of the 'savage nod
of fortune' because he was 'thinking about the fortunes' of others. Another example
of such word-play is at 8. 20: 'per fortunas vestrosque genios.' Although the phrase
'per fortunas' apparently means only something like 'for heaven's sake' (cf. Cicero,
Att. 5. 11. 1), the old man who says it later turns into a snake and devours a youth.
He called them 'by their fortunes,' and the result was *mala fortuna* for one. In this way
Apuleius exploits the ambiguity which is possible with *fortuna*; this of course the Greek
tychē cannot do.

accomplishes nothing at all, and meets his end in an absent-minded and stupid way. His death is blamed on *fortuna*, and what better way to show the 'nobility' of any robber than have him slain by an act of treachery?[45] It is the peculiar standard among these thieves that they find virtue and immortality in robbery or murder, but treachery in the frustration of their enterprises: both Chryseros and the old woman who pushes Alcimus from a window, for example, are called *nequissimus* (4. 10 and 12).

The third tale explains the most imaginative of all their attempts at robbery, but it is as unsuccessful. A rich man Demochares provided an easier target for robbers than their other victims (cf. 4. 9). One robber volunteered to dress in the skin of a dead bear and was placed inside the house with other animals collected for a spectacle. He is ‖ introduced in the formulaic way of all robbers,[46] with the added virtue not merely of strength in body, but in spirit as well. Thrasyleon, 'Bold-lion,' submits himself to this ordeal with the calm face of a noble hero ('vultu sereno,' 4. 15). His disguise in the bear-skin becomes an oblique reference to the theme of metamorphosis. Once dressed in it, he seems to have been transformed into a bear: 'fortissimum socium nostrum prorsus bestiam factum' (4. 14). When he is discovered at night wandering about Demochares' house and is exposed to mortal danger, he remains faithful to his disguise to the end. We read not of the death of a man, but of a *bear*: 'lanceam mediis iniecit ursae praecordiis' (4. 21). Even after his death, people are afraid to approach the 'bear's' corpse. Thus he gains his share of 'immortality' among thieves. For one time at least, the robbers proceeded with caution, but bad luck ('scaevus eventus') did have a role in this story.

The one thing all three tales have in common is the failure and death of each 'hero.' Why does Apuleius tell three such stories in a row?[47] No amount of praise for their virtue, glory, or immortality can

---

[45] MacKay (1963: 152). No character in the *Metamorphoses* ever admits as much, but Apuleius acknowledged elsewhere, in a discussion of *fatum* and *fortuna* (*De Platone* I. 12), that not everything can be blamed on fortune: 'nec sane omnia referenda esse ad vim fati putat, sed esse aliquid in nobis et in fortuna esse non nihil.'

[46] Cf. 4. 8 ('unus, qui robore ceteros antistabat'), 4. 9 ('unus ex illo posteriore numero'), 6. 31 ('unus omnium'), and 6. 30 ('unus e numero').

[47] Cf. Junghanns (1932: 141): 'Den Rahmen der Räubermahlzeit benützt Apuleius, wie die Vorlage (= *Onos*), dazu, das Räubertum durch Darstellung eines Gesprächs zu illustrieren.' He assigns a similar purpose to the tale of Aristomenes (cf. n. 31, above). In neither case is he incorrect, but I do not think that a simple elaboration of a scene was the primary reason for the tale. Lesky (1941: 60) does see a connection between the tales in book 4 and book 7, and points out that the robber stories in 4 make it

obscure the fact that in each case these bandits died wretchedly—and in Alcimus' case, most ingloriously. The point is that equal praise for unequal acts discredits all such praise, even when it is genuinely deserved.

Apuleius never tells a story only to expand a particular scene, or to reiterate something already present in the main narrative. The tales of Aristomenes and Thelyphron incidentally contributed to the atmosphere of magic and intrigue, but we have seen that they deal more ‖ than anything else with the characters of certain people as they contrast and complement Lucius' own personality. The one thing that is *not* created by these three stories is an aura of authenticity or realism about the robbers.[48] Perhaps they are caricatures of real life, or of the Greek Romance, in which they were a fixture,[49] but it will be noticed that, for all their dire threats, they never quite get around to killing anyone, and are more boasting and talk than action. They are the only characters in the *Metamorphoses* who are untouched by, and apparently unconcerned with, *voluptas*. Much like the Pirates of Penzance, or underworld characters in the 'Beggar's Opera,' they are stereotyped, romantic, but hardly realistic. Like everyone else in the *Metamorphoses*, they are addicted to excusing their short-comings by blaming fortune. Also like the characters in most other tales, their escapades end in complete futility and death. To this extent, they are very much a part of Lucius' uncertain and cruel world.

But they are hysterically overdrawn. The hymn to their *virtus*, their immortality, bravery, loyalty, and their *disciplina* of robbery (cf. 4. 9) loses all its solemnity, and gains much in silliness, by its repetition. One story, of Lamachus, is inspiring; Alcimus' tale is embarrassing; and Thrasyleon's, ingenious and depressing. Yet to hear three times of varied adventures, with but one dismal conclusion, only confirms our opinion of the robbers' ineptitude and gullibility.

I believe that the speech of 'Haemus' (7. 5–8) is fundamentally a parody of the values set forth in these tales in book 4. From the first sentence onwards, it exaggerates the outlandish sentiments of

plausible for Haemus to join the band in book 7: they have lost men, and also their leader, Lamachus, and need a new one. But this does not altogether explain why we also hear about Alcimus and Thrasyleon, who are only members of the band, not leaders. The interpretation of Haemus' speech as a satire based on the stories in book 4 would account for the two additional tales.

[48] Cf. MacKay (1963: 150).

[49] Cf. Rohde (1914: 385–86, on the noble robber); Junghanns (1932: 150); and MacKay (1963: 148).

such sentences of Lamachus as 'sat se beatum qui manu socia volens occumberet,' and 'manu reliqua sumptum gladium suum diuque deosculatum' (4. 11). Now they hear a leader who would rather be wounded than take money—one who even prefers death to life itself (7. 5). Such irony and exaggeration play upon their gullibility, their bravery, and their fatalistic addiction to bad luck, all with considerable art. Much of what Haemus says is barely credible, and certainly funny, but for them it is a convincing manifestation of their 'heroism.' They are deceived even as they hear the truth. ‖

Haemus, 'Mr. Blood,' outdoes all their names by his selection of 'Haemus' (*haima*), and his etymological explanation that he was 'nursed on human blood,' 'humano sanguine nutritus' (7. 5). An ancestral *virtus* makes him an aristocrat among thieves.[50] His speech is a rhetorician's exercise in appealing to the special interests of the group hearing it. In this respect it resembles the tales of Aristomenes and Thelyphron, which told Lucius exactly what he wanted to hear, and appealed to his predilection for magic and metamorphosis. Like those tales, however, this speech, with its story of 'Plotina,' has a veiled warning, and an anticipation of the eventual capture of the thieves. It says as much about the audience as it does about the people in the story.

The larger part of the speech is an account of the virtues of Plotina, who stayed faithful to her husband and was his companion in all his misfortunes. Haemus justifies this praise of her virtue, which seems out of place amidst robbers, by saying piously that he must tell the story because 'the truth has to be told,' 'vera enim dicenda sunt' (7. 7). He echoes a similar phrase from book 4, 'vera quae dicta sunt credens' (4. 12) 'believing that what was said was true,' which accounted for the deception of Alcimus by an old woman. This is yet another echolalic responsion, in this case between two widely separated tales. The story does not arouse the robbers' suspicion, yet it is *vera* in a way they cannot know, for they will be foiled by disguise and deception just as the enemies of 'Plotina' were. Even Haemus himself used a disguise to escape his enemies (7. 8), but his story of earlier disguises does not put them on their guard. Like other bandit heroes, he was at the jaws of death (7. 7), but unlike them, escaped by disguise and deception. He claims as much respect alive as was given Lamachus or Thrasyleon only when they were dead.

---

[50] MacKay (1963: 151).

The bandits are suitably impressed. Is it any wonder they acclaim him as their new leader? He seems to embody every virtue they have, and unfortunately for them, he also knows their weaknesses as well: the weaknesses which were outlined so clearly in the tales of book 4. Like Lucius, they receive some warning about what will happen from the story of Plotina, but perhaps this was all too subtle. In any case, ‖ their capture and death are as bare of detail and as ignominious as that of Alcimus.

The tale of the wifely devotion of Plotina has an additional point which its narrator could hardly be expected to know. Tlepolemos seems for the moment to be master of the situation, but he too will soon prove no more immune from treachery than his victims. He is shortly betrayed and slain by his friend Thrasyllus. It is then left to his wife Charite to take revenge on the murderer. The tale of Plotina seems at first hearing to be nothing more than a private joke told to flatter Charite's sense of her own virtue,[51] but in recollection we shall see that it more accurately foreshadows her role in revenging Tlepolemos.

Coming as it does after the Cupid and Psyche story, the speech of Haemus is the last of the anticipative tales in the *Metamorphoses*, and, with the stories in book 4, continues Apuleius' parable of human foibles. His characters have an apparently unlimited capacity for self-deception and over-confidence. This speech also forms an important transition to the theme of the tales in books 8 to 10, for there deception plays a part in every story, and the outcome is rarely any more certain, ultimately, than Haemus' momentary triumph.

The grim picture of life without Isis in book 11 is not contradicted here. By including even his light-hearted thieves in the 'Isiac' scheme of things, Apuleius has left no episode and no set of characters untouched by his pessimistic and consistent view of life: most men, if left to themselves, are not likely to make things come out right.

CUPID AND PSYCHE

The old woman who looks after the band of robbers tells a story to distract the captive bride Charite from her unfortunate situation. Her tale, the story of Cupid and Psyche (4. 28–6. 24), is the longest in the

---

[51] It is a highly developed one; note her speeches at 4. 34, 6. 28–9, and esp. 8. 12.

Metamorphoses, and is the most admired and studied part of the whole work. I intend here only to examine its thematic connection with the interpretation in book 11, and to take it as only one more tale (albeit the longest) among many. ‖

The opening recalls the purpose of so many stories in the *Metamorphoses*, the distraction of the audience. But this immediate purpose is soon superseded and the tale becomes much more than the 'bella fabula' which Lucius calls it at the end. The story may be a consolation to Charite, but Psyche's struggles with *curiositas* and *fortuna*, and the unusual length and central position of her story suggest that this is an allegory of Lucius' own adventures, too.[52] Further, while the reader of the *Metamorphoses* soon grows accustomed to the 'redende Namen' which occur in many tales,[53] in this story he encounters simple personifications: not only Psyche and Cupido, but also Sobrietas (5. 30), Consuetudo (6. 8), Sollicitudo (6. 9), Tristities (6. 9), Voluptas (6. 9), and Providentia (6. 15).

It is the name and character of Psyche, however, which concern us most, for Cupid, like Fotis or Byrrhena, disappears from the scene and leaves Psyche to face her ordeal alone (5. 25–6. 21). Word-play even more elaborate than with Cupido is employed with the equivalent words for ψυχή in Latin, *animus* and *anima*.[54] The latter word, the semantic equivalent of *Psychē*,[55] appears together with her name in such phrases as 'tuae Psychae dulcis anima' (5. 6), 'Psychae animam gaudio recrea' (5. 13), and 'miserandae Psyches animae' (6. 2). All these are spoken by Psyche herself, in pleas to Cupido and Ceres. *Animus* often describes the weak character and emotional states of Psyche. This is most distinct at 5. 22, where she finally looks upon her husband for the first time. There her faintness in resolve and body, her shock ‖

---

[52] For the most recent example of this interpretation, see Schlam (1968c).

[53] e.g. the pun on *thēlu-* in Thelyphron's name at 2. 23, 'animum meum *conmasculo*,' and the character of Thrasyllus (*thrasus*) revealed in 8. 8, 'sed Thrasyllus, praeceps alioquin et *de ipso nomine temerarius*.'

[54] For *cupido* see especially 5. 6. A clear distinction between *animus* and *anima* is not always observed, though the ancients attempted to draw one: e.g. Accius, *Trag.* 296, 'sapimus animo, fruimur anima; sine animo anima est debilis'; and Nonius Marcellus 426. 27, 'animus est quo sapimus, anima qua vivimus.' But *animus* is occasionally used in Cicero in place of *anima*, as an equivalent to *psychē: De sen* . 21. 77, 'credo deos immortales sparsisse animos in corpora humana, ut essent qui terras tuerentur,' and *Tusc.* 5. 13. 38, 'humanus animus decerptus ex mente divina.' Cf. also the association in Lucretius 1. 131, 'tunc cum primis ratione sagaci, unde anima atque animi constet natura videndum.' Whatever distinctions we may wish to draw, Apuleius undoubtedly plays on the relationship between the two words by describing Psyche's torments continually in terms of her *animus*.   [55] Ernout and Meillet (1951: 32).

at first seeing Cupido, and, finally, her recovery are all expressed
in terms of her *animus*: 'tunc Psyche, et corporis et *animi* alioquin
infirma . . . Psyche tanto aspectu deterrita et impos *animi* . . . re-
creatur *animi*.' The repetition of the genitive accentuates this pun.

To show parallels between Lucius and Psyche, the tendency has been
to treat her as a character whose chief similarity to Lucius is her *curiositas*.[56] This equation is undoubtedly correct, for she loses her husband
and fails her last test under Venus by succumbing to that fault and
opening the *pyxis* of Proserpina.[57] But there is, as we have seen, more
to Lucius' character than curiosity, and the same is true of Psyche.
In this tale of the soul, *psychē*, Apuleius also treats other aspects of
Lucius' character as well. In such an allegory, *curiositas*, or anything
else, may be taken not merely as the flaw of one character, but
instead something to be found in all men.

Just as any soul can be helpless before the multifarious changes of
fortune with her many dangers, so is Psyche. Like Lucius and many
others, she is vulnerable to the deceptions of her sisters and cannot
recognize their threat to her. In spite of repeated warnings from her
husband, who likens their threat to the storming of a citadel (5. 12),

dies ultima et casus extremus, et sexus infestus et sanguis inimicus iam
sumpsit arma et castra commovit et aciem direxit et classicum personavit; iam
mucrone destricto iugulum tuum nefariae tuae sorores petunt,

the 'citadel' falls before the assault of its enemies (5. 15):

tunc nanctae iam portis patentibus nudatum sororis animum facinerosae
mulieres, omissis tectae machinae latibulis, destrictis gladiis fraudium sim-
plicis puellae paventes cogitationes invadunt.

These warnings are as explicit as those Lucius received in books 1
to 3. Psyche's vulnerability to curiosity helps to 'elevate' the whole
conception of *curiositas* to a higher level than mere 'nosiness.' It
embraces not merely trivial desires, or longing to learn the secrets of
evil and supernatural arts, but now the identity of a *god*. The gravity
of this fault, of course, depends entirely on the object of such ‖ curiosity. If it is *curiositas* about everyday affairs, perhaps it will prove only
annoying; if about magic, it could be foolish and dangerous; and
if about a god whose form is forbidden to men's eyes, it may be a

---

[56] See above, n. 18.

[57] Note that as Psyche succumbs to *curiositas* by opening a *pyxis* (6. 21), so too does
Lucius, when Fotis opens and uses the contents of the wrong box: 'me trepidatio simul
et festinatio fefellit et pyxidum similitudo decepit' (3. 25; cf. also 3. 21).

mortal sin. The fault remains the same, and is, I think, at all points meant to be reprehensible. We may only measure its gravity by the circumstances; whether Lucius recognizes all this or not is very doubtful—at least not until book 11.

Neither Psyche nor Lucius have the foresight which Cupid urges, and they cannot comprehend the nature of the forces which threaten them. They are both curiously myopic about such dangers, whether it be black magic or jealous sisters, and both innocently persevere in their desire to know. The tale of Psyche is Apuleius' explanation of why they are so strangely innocent.

Psyche cannot grasp these direct warnings because of her *simplicitas*, 'naïveté, ingenuousness.' To no purpose does Cupido warn her of the consequences of betrayal. He speaks of his *secreta* in the same way Fotis earlier spoke of the secrets of magic to Lucius; she also was fearful of revealing anything, but when pressed, begged him not to disclose the 'mysteries' (3. 15). Similar warnings against betrayal appear again in the final book of the *Metamorphoses*, where Lucius commits himself at last to silence and respect for the *secreta* of Isis (11. 23). This concern to guard from the knowledge of the uninitiated the *secreta* of a cult typifies the Lucius of book 11, as much as its absence does the old Lucius before his metamorphosis.

Although *simplicitas* may be applied in exasperation, as when Cupid calls Psyche *simplicissima* (5. 22; at that moment it is only just, as she has just looked at him for the first time), it is by no means a fault to be regretted. When Psyche tries to lie to her sisters, she fails because of her 'excessive innocence' (5. 15), and we cannot really find much fault with that. This *simplicitas* is 'naïveté' in a good sense. Thus the reed which advises Psyche in the second of her labors is 'simplex et humana'; such an association of *humanitas* and *simplicitas* is a virtue which Apuleius regarded as appropriate to a philosopher.[58] It is a ‖ highly desirable quality for any convert to have, as uncomprehending innocence must inevitably be in the face of evil. If *curiositas* is the chief fault of Psyche, then surely *simplicitas* is her chief virtue.[59]

---

[58] Cf. *Apologia* 43: 'quin et illud mecum reputo posse animum humanum, praesertim puerilem et simplicem, seu carminum avocamento sive odorum delenimento soporari et ad oblivionem praesentium externari.' The author of the *Asclepius* (14) comments that one engages in devotion to a deity with an attitude of *simplicitas* in mind and spirit: 'simplici enim mente et anima divinitatem colere eiusque facta venerari, agere etiam dei voluntati gratias, quae est bonitatis sola plenissima, haec est nulla nimia importuna curiositas violata philosophia.'

[59] Cf. Grimal (1963: 64): 'C'est là une des qualités essentielles de Psyché, cette "naïveté," cette "honnêteté," qui finalement lui assurera l'affection d'Amour.'

How else than with *simplicitas* can we explain that curious, selective innocence of Lucius, who in many respects is very wise in the ways of this world (as with Fotis), yet so oddly careless and ignorant in others?[60] Such simplicity requires some outside intervention, be it by Jupiter or Isis, if such people are ever to be saved from themselves. Quite simply, Lucius and Psyche deserve the protection they finally receive because neither can learn to be evil.

Thus the character of Psyche as developed in this tale is an important key to understanding Lucius' story. There are also more mundane, but nonetheless important narrative parallels. For example, when Psyche falls victim to Venus, her trials under the goddess of love resemble his own under *fortuna*. She very quickly earns the enmity of Venus for her beauty, and, like Charite, is called *infortunatissima*.[61] In her role as an unceasing and vindictive tormentor, Venus becomes in the course of the tale identified with *fortuna*, who is in fact not mentioned after Venus begins her persecution of Psyche.[62] Psyche's trials lead her towards the *salus* and *tutela* which Lucius eventually desires. She seeks first the protection of Ceres, and then Juno. When pleading to Juno, she refers to her trials in practically the same language which Lucius will use in book 11: ||

sis meis extremis casibus Iuno Sospita meque in tantis exanclatis laboribus defessam imminentis periculi metu libera. (6. 4)

tu meis iam nunc extremis aerumnis subsiste, tu fortunam conlapsam adfirma, tu saevis exanclatis casibus pausam pacemque tribue. (11. 2)

When Psyche's final plea is rejected, we read that all hope of safety is dashed, 'tota spe salutis deposita' (6. 5). 'Spes salutis,' the mere 'hope of safety,' is the same thing Lucius desires at the beginning of book 11. The whole point of the labors under Venus in book 6, with

---

[60] See above, p. 162.

[61] This superlative form appears only in the *Metamorphoses* (cf. *TLL* 7. 1480. 70), and is another example of a responsion between a tale and the conversation preceding it. Charite speaks of the name of her 'most unfortunate husband' ('infortunatissimi mariti nomen,' 4. 27), and the old woman who narrates the story calls Psyche's father 'the most wretched father of a most unfortunate daughter' ('infortunatissimae filiae miserrimus pater,' 4. 32).

[62] The same epithet, *saeviens*, is applied to both Venus and *fortuna*; cf. 5. 31 ('Veneris iram saevientem sic adortae'), 6. 2 ('deae tantae saeviens ira'), 6. 5 ('saevientes impetus [sc. Veneris] eius mitigas?'), 6. 16 ('nec tamen nutum deae saevientis vel tunc expiare potuit'). For *saeviens* with *fortuna*, cf. 6. 28, 10. 4, and 11. 15. See Junghanns (1932: 161 n. 70) and Schlam (1968b: 139).

each one increasing in difficulty, is that they are completely hopeless, and without end. Nothing Psyche accomplishes there can satisfy Venus, for she can no more be propitiated than *fortuna* herself.

She learns nothing from her trials, and Lucius acquires no safeguards against unpredictable changes of fortune. The grim series of events dealing with the death or dramatic reversal in the fortunes of various people in books 8 to 10 leads nowhere and is not 'educational' in any way. And of course it must not be, if Isis is to be of any help. No preparation or caution can account for fortune; Venus is as vindictive, for her 'savage nod' (6. 16) can never be avoided.[63]

Psyche finds a deliverance similar to Lucius' in almost every respect. He is saved only by Isis' intervention, and she finds *salus* only when Cupido intervenes (6. 22) and Jupiter commands the other gods to accept her on Olympus. All the gods welcome her, including her former tormentor Venus, who now even dances in her honor (6. 24). This dramatic reversal in role, turning one's worst enemy into part of the celebration, is precisely what the priest of Isis will say to Lucius about *fortuna* in book 11: 'in tutelam iam receptus es fortunae, sed videntis, quae suae lucis splendore ceteros etiam deos illuminat.'

Finally, there is the birth of a child named 'Voluptas,' 'joy' or 'pleasure,' with which Psyche's tale ends (6. 24). It will be recalled that Lucius' indulgence in *voluptas* is condemned by the priest of Isis at 11. 15. Is there then some sinister meaning in the birth of a child named Voluptas to Psyche? If so, this would be a curious way indeed to end what is supposed to be a happy story. Fortunately, such is ‖ not the case, for, depending on its context, *voluptas* can express either sensual or spiritual pleasure. Cicero's distinction (*De fin.* 1. 11. 37) is the clearest; namely, that the kind of pleasure spoken of depends on whether the mind or the body is referred to:

huic verbo [sc. voluptas] omnes qui Latine sciunt duas res subiciunt, laetitiam in animo, commotionem suavem iucunditatis in corpore.

Laetitia in animo is the *voluptas* which Lucius feels, for example, in his contemplation of Isis' image at 11. 24, 'paucis dehinc ibidem commoratus diebus inexplicabili voluptate simulacri divini perfruebar'; while *commotio suavis iucunditatis in corpore* describes the *serviles voluptates* which he enjoys with Fotis, and which the priest refers to in 11. 15.

---

[63] The 'nod of Venus,' 'nec tamen nutum deae saevientis vel tunc expiare potuit' (6. 16), is described almost exactly like the 'nod' of *fortuna*: 'feralem fortunae nutum latere non potuerunt' (10. 24).

The birth of a child with this name, as the happy resolution to the tale of Psyche, represents the soul's discovery of spiritual joy at its deliverance from the power of blind fortune (in Psyche's tale, represented by Venus). Just as the intervention of Jupiter anticipates the appearance of Isis to Lucius, so does the birth of Voluptas anticipate the spiritual pleasure Lucius will feel in his salvation in Isis. In book 11, he is 'reborn' in spirit, and his own tale, like Psyche's, ends happily as he goes forth clothed in the garb of a priest: 'sed quoquoversus obvio, gaudens obibam.' These final words of the *Metamorphoses*, '*gaudens obibam*,' recall the ending of the story of Cupid and Psyche, '*quam Voluptatem* nominamus.'

TALES OF REVENGE AND ADULTERY

In discussing the latter part of the *Metamorphoses*, Franz Dornseiff observed an 'infernal' development in books 8 and 9 which leads toward the 'purgatory' of book 11.[64] I believe this description could be extended to book 10 as well. But where exactly does this 'Inferno' lie: in Lucius' experiences, or the tales?

After Lucius' deliverance from the robbers (7. 12), contrary to the rewards he had expected, he is abandoned to a cruel boy who tortures him most wickedly. After the boy is eaten by a bear (7. 26), Lucius ‖ then works for various masters, who mark off four stages in his wanderings: the corrupt priests of the Dea Syria (8. 23–9. 10), the miller (9. 11–31), the gardener and the soldier (9. 32–10. 12), and the baker and cook (10. 13–35).[65] Essentially the same progression of events occurs in the *Onos*,[66] but I do not think one could term the adventures of Loukios there as an 'Inferno': perhaps it is bizarre poetic justice, but otherwise hardly worthy of Dornseiff's term. The 'infernal' aspect of books 8 to 10 is in fact created by Apuleius' *Einlagen*, and principally by the tales. The themes of adultery and revenge, and the effect of *fortuna* on other people's lives, are examined in ever greater depth and with a continually worsening cast of characters.

---

[64] Dornseiff (1938: 226).

[65] Cf. Schlam (1968b: 47): 'The experience of the Ass at each of these stages emphasizes a different aspect of the evils of this world.'

[66] *Onos* 29–33 (Loukios' suffering under a *paidarion akatharton*), 35–43 (Loukios with the priests), 43–6 (with the miller), and 46 ff. (with the cooks).

After many personal dangers in book 8, Lucius does comparatively well in books 9 and 10. The 'storms' of fortune, against which he complains so long and bitterly at 7. 2–3, turn from him and concentrate their fury on other people. He observes the misfortunes of others with a kind of 'Odyssean' detachment, just as he heard with equanimity the unfortunate stories of Socrates and Thelyphron before his metamorphosis in book 3.

In all the *Metamorphoses*, there is only one tale which in itself seems to have no sinister overtones: the Tale of the Tub (9. 5–7). After that story, Lucius is moved by the pitiful sight of the suffering of slaves and his fellow animals at the mill to explain to the reader that the one advantage he derived from his asinine form was an unhindered ability to observe the actions and conversation of men (9. 18); he had, in other words, a perfect means to indulge in the same old *curiositas*. In the middle of the story of the miller's faithless wife, he comments on the advantages which a 'curious' man has in the form of a beast (9. 30):

sed forsitan lector scrupulosus reprehendens narratum meum sic argumentaberis: 'unde autem tu, astutule asine, intra terminos pistrini contentus, quid secreto, ut adfirmas, mulieres gesserint, scire potuisti?' accipe igitur, quem ad modum homo curiosus iumenti faciem sustinens cuncta, quae in perniciem pistoris mei gesta sunt, cognovi. ||

He later humorously likens himself to a philosopher, at the end of the enactment of the *iudicium Paridis* in the arena. After observing the similarities between his present situation and the trial and condemnation of Socrates, he breaks off that disgression with a self-flattering remark (10. 33):

sed nequis indignationis meae reprehendat impetum secum sic reputans: 'ecce nunc patiemur philosophantem nobis asinum,' rursus, unde decessi, revertar ad fabulam.

These comments show that, until the moment comes for Lucius to copulate with a condemned woman in the arena (10. 34), he clearly relishes this role as an observer untouched by the horrors in the tales he hears. He may occasionally involve himself by exposing wrongdoers to justice: he brays so loudly that the priests of the Dea Syria are exposed while debauching a village youth (8. 29–30); he intervenes in the tale of the baker's wife by crushing the fingers of the adulterer Philesitherus (9. 27); and he unwittingly betrays his master the gardener by 'curiously' showing his shadow to a search party of soldiers (9. 42). In this way he is an 'agent' of justice. But when he is about to meet the *matrona* in the arena, he loses all taste for this role, and also the one consolation he believed he had, that of being an animal with a man's intelligence.

We may now turn to the final series of tales which this impartial observer, this 'philosophizing' ass, tells us.

In the *Onos* (34), a messenger brings the news of the death of the young bride and her husband who had been with Loukios among the robbers:

When it was deep night, a messenger came to the estate and farm from the village with a report about the newly-wed bride, the one who had been captured by the robbers, and her groom. Around late evening they had been taking a walk on the seashore, and suddenly the sea had risen and carried them away out of sight, and they had met their end in disaster and death.

In Apuleius, too, a messenger arrives and reports evil tidings (8. 1), but in contrast to the *Onos*, the deaths of Tlepolemos and Charite are explicitly attributed to fortune and the corrupting power of *voluptas*, as seen in the adulterous suitor, Thrasyllus. The plain bad news of ‖ their deaths is expanded into a tale of adultery and the revenge which it inspires. The messenger tells this story so that it may be recorded by those 'doctiores, quibus stilos fortuna subministrat' (8. 1).

If Lucius' speech at 7. 2–3 is an indication of his growing awareness of the power of *fortuna* in his life,[67] and a prelude to the grim experiences which he must endure, then this tale of Charite's revenge is just as much a prelude to the stories which appear in books 8 to 10. The wretched ending of this happy couple is a 'correction,' as it were, of their once happy fortune. This is not the first time, of course, that we have observed someone's fortune undergo an unpredictable change.[68] It seems that the old woman's tale about the happy ending of the Cupid and Psyche story, with its birth of Voluptas to the re-united pair, was a fate not destined to be fulfilled by Charite and Tlepolemos, after all.

With this tale of a *faithful* wife (a great rarity indeed in the *Metamorphoses*), Apuleius introduces his tales in books 8 to 10 with a reversal, in a kind of negative exposure, of the plots of the subsequent stories. Thrasyllus is emblematic of the women in the tales that will follow, for he is deceitful and driven to his crimes by lust:

---

[67] Wittmann (1938: 7).   [68] Cf. above, pp. 164–5.

in profundam ruinam Cupidinis sese paulatim nescius praecipitaverat. quidni, cum flamma saevi amoris parva quidem primo vapore delectet, sed fomentis consuetudinis exaestuans inmodicis ardoribus totos amburat homines (8. 2). . . . ecce rursus nuper fervide voluptatis detestabilis petitor aures obseratas de nuptiis obtundens aderat. (8. 9)

He is eventually defeated by his own weapons of dissimulation and treachery, for Charite tricks him into her power and then scratches out his eyes with a hairpin.

The tragedy of Charite, an embodiment of grace (*charis*), is that by a bitter turn of fortune she is compelled to change her spirit and harden herself to a task of bloody revenge. Not unlike the matron 'Plotina' in the speech of 'Haemus,' she becomes 'worthy of a man' in her resolve. She is made into as cruel a creature as many another woman in the *Metamorphoses*; indeed she seems almost another character, altogether different from the young girl who heard the tale of Cupid and Psyche. She stands above the unconscious Thrasyllus, ‖ whom she drugged by means of a sleeping potion, with a man's resolve (8. 11): 'iamque eo ad omnes iniurias exposito ac supinato introvocata Charite *masculis animis* impetuque diro fremens invadit ac supersistit sicarium.' When she commits suicide at her husband's tomb, she 'breathes out a manly soul': 'efflavit *animam virilem*' (8. 14). In her revenge of her husband, she resembles Plotina, who even adopted the dress and manners of a man: 'tonso capillo *in masculinam faciem* reformato habitu' (7. 6). Like Charite, Plotina acted a man's part in dealing with her adversaries: 'cunctorum periculorum particeps et pro mariti salute pervigilem curam sustinens, aerumnas adsiduas *ingenio masculo* sustinebat' (7. 6). This change of sex, figurative perhaps in the case of Charite, but in outward appearance quite literally true for Plotina, constitutes a kind of 'metamorphosis' of the two heroines, for both play the role of a man when their husbands are no longer able to defend them. Thus, by her fidelity to her husband, Charite recalls the heroines Plotina and Psyche, and by her revenge she also anticipates the character of the rather less pleasant ladies in the tales which follow.

Before Lucius enjoys the relative calm and decent masters of books 9 and 10, he passes through a series of terrible experiences in book 8 which are complementary to the tale of Charite. At one point he hears of a horrible crime of adultery and revenge. This 'facinus oppido memorabile' (8. 22) is the shortest tale in the *Metamorphoses*, and tells very succinctly of the punishment of a slave for adultery with a neighbor's wife. The slave's wife not only burns up all his records,

but also kills herself and her own child. His master holds him to
account for all this and punishes him by feeding him to a bed of *ants*.
The horror of the tale is accentuated by its brevity. It is almost as if
an outline of a story were being sketched. But the last sentences
describes the manner of his death in fastidious and vivid detail: '. . .
parvis quidem sed numerosis et continuis morsiunculis penitus
inhaerentes [sc. formicae].'

This tale has been accounted as simply one more in a series of horrors, but beyond this, there has been a reluctance to attribute much
more to it than a deepening of the mood of horror and despair.[69]
Certainly || the tale does this. Along with the attack by the villagers
and dogs on Lucius' party (8. 16), the warnings of a villager from the
ominous perch of a cypress tree (9. 18), and the strange meeting with
an old man who turns into a snake and devours a youth (8. 20–1),
this story contributes to the mood of terror which deepens throughout the book, and which ends only after the most grotesque and fearful adventures with Lucius' sale to the depraved priests of the Dea Syria.
But it also resembles the darkest of the tales of adultery and revenge,
the story in book 10 of the 'vilis aliqua' who mistakes her husband's
innocent sister for his lover, and sets off on an orgy of poisoning that
eventually claims five victims. Thrasyllus' passion is very finely
drawn as the madness of love, and Charite's revenge is, if bloody,
at least justified, but the *facinus* at 8. 22 conveys only two things in
its brevity: the corrupting power of *voluptas*, and the terrible forms
which revenge for adultery may take. In both tales of book 8, adultery is so savagely punished that we should be mistrustful, to say the
least, when we read Lucius' remarks about the first of the 'charming'
stories of adultery in book 9: 'cognoscimus *lepidam* de adulterio
cuiusdam pauperis fabulam' (9. 4).

The tales in books 9 and 10 bring to a climax the 'infernal' development of the plot. Four stories are formally introduced as such: the
'lepida fabula' (9. 4–7), the 'fabula denique bona prae ceteris suavis'
(9. 14–31), the 'tragoedia non fabula' (10. 2–12), and the story of
the 'vilis aliqua' (10. 23–8). In addition to these parallel stories of revenge
and adultery, the account of the death of three brothers at 9. 33–42
continues the gloomy theme of fortune's power ('puncto brevissimo
dilapsae domus fortunam,' 9. 39), and leads into the theme of the final
stories, revenge.

[69] See Junghanns (1932: 166–7 and n. 80) and Paratore (1942: 272 n. 37).

As I have already noted, the Tale of the Tub (9. 4–7) is the only story in the *Metamorphoses*, aside from that of Cupid and Psyche, which has a happy conclusion, with no sinister implications; unlike every other tale in books 8 to 10, there is no death. Yet this solitary tale discredits adultery, an aspect of *voluptas*, in the strongest possible way. Adultery appears at first as an amusing foible of men and women, but does not remain as pleasant or as harmless as we might wish. The genial conclusion of this tale is 'corrected' almost at once by a very elaborate story which is parallel in most respects. The same narrative ‖ technique of arousing false hopes which Apuleius used *within* the tales of Aristomenes and Thelyphron is now applied to the conclusion of a tale. The dramatic reversal of fortune comes in a second story with a similar plot. The careful parallelism in the tales of books 9 and 10 is Apuleius' most extensive development of his theme of fortune's unpredictability: 'ne tu fortunarum lubricas ambages et instabiles incursiones et reciprocas vicissitudines ignoras' (1. 6).

The second tale in book 9, 'good beyond any other,' is structurally the most complicated of all the tales. It is a *tour de force* in irony and surprise endings. These two things, always a feature of any tale in Apuleius, are carried to their most elaborate point by the two tales told within the main story. The account of Philesitherus and his successful cuckolding of Barbarus is an encouragement to the Baker's wife in her own affair, and, like the Tale of the Tub, seems to augur well for her success. The second tale-within-the-tale, the Baker's gloomy report of the adultery of a neighbor's wife, is told in ignorance of his own betrayal ('ignarus suorum, domus alienae percenset infortunium,' 9. 23), and anticipates the tragic conclusion to his own story. The four adultery stories in book 9 unfold in an interlocking series of deceptively happy conclusions:

> Tale of the Tub: happy conclusion
> Tale of the Baker's wife: ultimately an unhappy conclusion
>> Tale of Philesitherus: happy conclusion
>> Tale of the Neighbor's wife: unhappy conclusion.

The Baker's account of his neighbor's troubles reminds us at a crucial moment that adultery is more likely to result in an ending like the tales in book 8, than the Tale of the Tub.

The spirit of this story which Apuleius calls 'good beyond all others' is identical with that of the first story in book 9—at least up to the moment the Baker discovers Philesitherus. But the ending is very different from what we might have imagined. The Baker addresses the frightened lad with a 'serene brow and a calm face' (9. 27), and his explanation for such calm embodies clever references to each of the two preceding tales: 'non sum barbarus [i.e. either literally a barbarian or the husband Barbarus], nec agresti morum squalore praeditus [an expanded phrase equaling *barbarus*], nec ad ‖ exemplar naccinae truculentiae te necabo [a reference to his own account of the Neighbor's wife].' The adulterer is punished by another, more depraved kind of *voluptas* (buttock-beating and buggery), and such use of *voluptas* as a punishment darkens the motif of 'servile pleasures' considerably. The husband is shortly thereafter slain by magic. The savage end of the tale reintroduces the idea of the use of magic as a punishment for the frustration of *voluptas*, which, it will be recalled, we also saw in the tales of Aristomenes and Thelyphron. In this way the tales in book 9 go a long way towards effecting a 'religious' view of *voluptas*: they completely discredit the idea of sexual pleasure as a desirable thing.

A similar parallelism of plot lies in the tales of book 10. The first one, a 'Phaedra-Hippolytus' story,[70] tells of a step-mother who attempts to take revenge on her step-son for refusing her advances, but is foiled by the providence of a physician. The last one, about a 'certain vile woman,' tells how she avenged herself by slaying her husband, his sister, a doctor and his wife, and even her own child. Apuleius carefully introduces the first tale as a 'scelestum ac nefarium facinus' (10. 2) and provides a solemn introduction which sets the tale apart from all the others: 'scito te tragoediam, non fabulam legere et a socco ad coturnum ascendere' (10. 2). The plot of the tale does recall the *Hippolytus* of Euripides and its tragic end, but these words are as deliberately misleading and ironic as the elaborately cheerful introduction to the tale at 9. 14–31 as a 'charming' story. In this case, what is introduced as a 'tragedy' ends with an unexpected reversal of fortune, and a happy ending (10. 12).

The cast of characters in these stories is similar. In both, for example, a doctor plays an important role. It is the 'divine providence' of the first one which saves the situation (10. 12), whereas the doctor in the second tale not only helps the evil woman poison others, but, with little providence for his own interests, himself falls victim to her crime (10. 26). The jealous wife's attempts at murder are foiled

[70] Both the description of love as a sickness at 9. 2–3 (by far Apuleius' most elaborate and sympathetic description of a woman in the grip of passion) and the chaste stepson who refuses to 'cure' his step-mother recall Euripides' *Hippolytus*.

completely in the first tale, and are altogether successful in the second, so that the arbitrary nature of blind fortune is nowhere more evident || than in these tales. It causes what seems almost certainly a tragedy to have an unexpectedly happy outcome; yet again the same situation also leads to the death of everyone but the guilty person.

The second tale of book 10, and the last in the *Metamorphoses*, amply justifies Lucius' desire for *salus*. Here the Greek and Latin authors agree at least in broad outline. In the *Onos*, Loukios is about to have intercourse with a condemned woman in the arena, and no more is said of her than that she is 'one of those condemned to die,' τινα τῶν γυναικῶν, ἥτις κατεκέκριτο θηρίοις ἀποθανεῖν. In Apuleius, by contrast, a wife's crimes are described in the last and, I think, most dreadful of all the tales: at least in sheer number of deaths (5), it outdoes any other. She is beyond question the wickedest woman in the *Metamorphoses*, and her story forms a significant expansion of the simple description in the *Onos*. At the conclusion of this tale, Lucius remarks that it is with such a woman as *this* that he must lie (10. 29). Little wonder that he would regard copulation with her as a *contagium* (10. 34). Now he is to dispense justice in a way far different from his punishment of Philesitherus or the priests of the Dea Syria, and it is a brand of justice, *voluptas* as punishment, which he cannot be eager for. The prospect of her favors also discredits whatever pleasure Lucius found with his kindly *matrona* in the first part of book 10.

By the end of book 10, *voluptas*, and indeed everything about Lucius' old character, is utterly discredited. The lesson which the priests of Isis have to give us in book 11 is, in large measure, a lesson already taught, for the treatment of sexual pleasures in these latter tales reflects clearly the ascetic doctrine of book 11, with its 'higher' and more 'spiritual' pleasures.

There is a clear parallelism between these tales, and an easily perceivable progression in human degradation.[71] Apuleius carries his

---

[71] While the wife in the Tale of the Tub is an adulteress, and scandalously deceitful, the woman in the long tale at 9. 14–31 is every bit as bad, but resorts to murder and magic as well. Cf. the description of the first wife at 9. 5: 'uxorcula etiam satis quidem tenuis et ipsa, verum tamen postrema lascivia famigerabilis.' This is mild, however, when compared to the scabrous description of the wife in the second tale (9. 14), of which perhaps the most vivid part is the finely phrased comparison of her to a latrine: 'sed omnia prorsus ut in quandam caenosam latrinam in eius animum flagitia confluxerant.' The unnatural passion of the step-mother in book 10 is more sympathetically portrayed; Apuleius hesitates whether to blame an innate depravity for her love, or simply fate: 'seu naturaliter impudica seu fato ad extremum impulsa flagitium' (10. 2). But there is no doubt at all about the 'vilis aliqua' (10. 23) of the last tale in

custom- ‖ ary technique of responsion between one tale and the next, or between a tale and its setting, to its greatest length in books 9 and 10. Now tales deliberately anticipate or, on the other hand, contradict one another, so that one does not know what conclusion to expect. One enthusiastic sensual experience is followed by a similar one which 'corrects' it, and prepares for a kind of doctrine which shall reject all such things. Showing the wages of sin is not something original to Apuleius, but it is undeniably effective. If this is all mortal *voluptas* can offer us, we would do well to pass it up.

Surprisingly, as we near the end of Lucius' travels, his personal torments cease altogether. In book 10, his masters are indulgent to a remarkable degree, and he enjoys physical pleasures of every kind. It is only in the tales that something appears to be increasingly wrong with this hedonistic Odyssey.

If book 11's interpretation is to be relevant to the tales, there should be at least two things observable as we near the end of Lucius' adventures: an eventual need for a *salus*, which again and again is shown to be never surely attainable by men on their own, and a desire for something better than sensual *voluptas*. I believe this is clearly the case. The stronger the justification for the 'purer' *voluptas* of Isis, the more convincing the conversion to her worship will be. These horror-stories about the misfortunes of other people effect exactly such a justification, but *not* the experiences of Lucius himself. If left to himself, he could have continued indefinitely in his ways, for in book 10 he enjoys nothing but one kind master after another. And in book 9, he obviously relishes the role of an unknown observer of human affairs: an ideal role for a *curiosus*. There he was still the man who said he would like to know 'everything or certainly as much as possible.'

But the imminent appearance of the condemned woman shatters this foolish euphoria. The steadily declining cast of characters in the tales, with all their moral depravity, is now about to intersect with ‖ Lucius himself. He always believed himself immune from example, just as when he was a man, yet with this last story he is to be made into the final chapter, as it were, of the tale of the wicked step-mother. He is to be her punishment, and share her *contagium*.

In the same way that the respective fates of Aristomenes, Thelyphron, and Actaeon finally intersect with Lucius in book 3, so

---

book 10. The change in her character is as rapid as it is extreme: 'coepit puellam velut aemulam tori succubamque primo suspicari, dehinc detestari, dehinc crudelissimis laqueis mortis insidiari' (10. 24).

now does the moral condemnation of adultery and sexual pleasures, which *only* the tales generate, eventually overtake Lucius in book 10. Far from being extraneous to the plot, these last tales are the very means by which Lucius' adventures are led towards the salvation of Isis in book 11. They are the reason why that salvation is credible and desirable.

SUMMARY

The tales in the *Metamorphoses* serve a number of purposes. They often anticipate a later event in the main narrative, and all without exception have a didactic purpose in harmony with book 11. Although often introduced as entertainment or diversion, on the whole, the tales are as much instruction as amusement. It is a matter of taste how far one may go in reconciling the heterogeneous elements in this work, for I do not deny that they exist. The *Metamorphoses* is a well-composed work, and an immensely complicated one; but that fact, in itself, says nothing about its bizarre and often disturbing mixture of moods.[72]

There is not so much a rigid, formal unity here as an interpretative harmony between the final book and the first ten, with thematic connections between all parts, and all tales. The author who added the tales is also the author who concluded his work with the 'Isis book,' || and I do not find it so surprising that the tales are consistent with that last book's interpretation.

It has been necessary, of course, to discriminate between various types of stories. Thus, the magic stories in books 1 to 3 are admonitory, warning Lucius about what is to happen to him; the robber tales in book 4 anticipate the deception of the bandits in book 7, yet the speech there of Haemus says more than even he knows about the fate of himself and Charite; the story of Cupid and Psyche allegorizes

[72] Cf. Auerbach (1957: 52–3): 'With an extreme emphasis on desire, which all the spices of rhetorico-realistic art are employed to arouse in the reader too, there is a complete absence of human warmth and intimacy. There is always an admixture of something spectrally sadistic; desire is mixed with fear and horror; though to be sure there is a good deal of silliness, too. And this runs through the entire book: it is full of fear, lust and silliness.' I find this an excellent appraisal of books 1–10, but, significantly I hope, not of book 11. It is from this mad world which Auerbach describes that Isis frees Lucius. All 'fear, lust and silliness' are left far behind when we enter the eleventh book, and its tone is throughout elevated, religious, and serene. The harsher the contrast between Isis' world and Lucius' old one, the better.

Lucius' experience, and predicts the happy intervention of Isis; and the tales of revenge and adultery create the need in Lucius for a salvation in Isis by discrediting the kind of indulgence which marked his life as a man. Such stories thus make for a flexible and highly adaptable narrative style.

Very broadly, the tales achieve this much for the story of Lucius: they emphasize the inability of human beings to improve their luck on their own, and, by the picture they give of the foibles and weaknesses of others, they widen the range of humanity beyond a single character, Lucius, to suggest that *all* men act this way. Lucius himself is placed in a ludicrous position. He has the itinerary of an Odysseus, with no heroic stature. He has a range of experiences as bizarre as any hero ever had, but, because he is, after all, an ass, he is continually denied the glory of a real hero—however much he pretends to be one. In other characters likewise there is a disparity between what is actually the truth of the situation, and what they think it to be. Human perception is consistently presented as a very limited thing, and though there be occasional flashes of *providentia*, the elaborate parallel of the provident and the stupid doctors in book 10 shows that it comes more often by accident than design.

All the while that the tales contribute to this depressing view, they also seem, innocently enough, to fulfil the promise of 'entertaining' the reader. Apuleius evidently enjoyed the irony of maintaining this pose, for he never admits openly that the tales do more than amuse us.

Thus, by anticipation of later events; by sensitivity to the narrative 'environment'; by extremely subtle interrelationships between characters in a tale, and the people hearing it; and by thematic relationship to the final 'Isis book,' the tales are not simply relevant to the main story, they are in fact essential to its conclusion and its philosophy of ‖ human life in relation to Isis. It is not the 'Isis book' which solemnizes and holds together this new work which Apuleius created;[73] rather, the tales themselves are the principal means whereby the author changed a frivolous and entertaining story, such as we see in the *Onos*, into the mystical and religious work which the *Metamorphoses* so clearly is.

In this discussion I have been led to treat more than anything else the character of the people in the tales. We continually find careful representation, even allegorization, of faults and imperfections in

----

[73] See Perry (1967: 244) for a different opinion.

Lucius' character which lead him, and presumably us, to see the error of his ways. Indeed, this story is more for our benefit than his, since through much of the work he is oblivious to the 'message.'

Because of the 'Isiac' point of view, which is never very far away in the tales, it is only fair to say that, if Apuleius is a student of human nature, he is so only as far as the doctrine he preaches in book 11 allows him to be. Women, for example, are wholly sensual creatures, susceptible to corruption and capable of great wickedness; the rare exception (Charite) is likely to be corrupted or betrayed. This world is a dangerous, crazy place, made even more uncertain by the malevolent and supernatural powers of magic. If pure chance (*fortuna*) does not ruin us, then we shall probably do it ourselves, and blame fortune in the bargain.

Undoubtedly there is complexity in the telling of this story, but I do not feel it is ever very profound. Certainly there are *types* of people, who are used chiefly to exemplify the inherent evils of greed, lust, or treachery, but they never really seem fleshed-out, believable characters. We are taught to expect very little of other men, or of ourselves, so that we may expect all the more of Isis. Such is the simplistic, pessimistic lesson of a mystic with no high regard for men's capabilities or their achievements. Some will perhaps think this justified; others may find it intellectually and humanly repugnant. I hope to have shown merely that it is never anything less than a lesson well taught.

Lucius' personal experiences do not differ greatly from those of his Greek counterpart in the *Onos*, yet two more different conclusions to || the same story could scarcely be imagined. In the *Onos*, the hero tries again to indulge in sexual pleasures after his return to human form, but is repulsed because his penis is too small. He lost 'that great characteristic of the ass,' τὸ μέγα τοῦ ὄνου σύμβολον, and the *Onos* ends with thanks to the gods and an allusion to a vulgar proverb (56):

There I made sacrifices and set up memorials to the gods who had preserved me, since after so long and so narrowly I had escaped home, not, by God, 'from the ass of a dog', as the saying goes, but from the snooping of an ass.

The *Metamorphoses* ends not with a vote of thanks to 'the gods who saved him,' but with Lucius' grateful participation as a priest in the service of one particular goddess, Isis, a deity opposed to everything his former life stood for. In direct contrast to the sensualist he was before, and which the Greek Loukios remains to the end, Lucius openly rejoices in this new life, and its asceticism:

rursus denique quam raso capillo collegii vetustissimi et sub illis Syllae tem-
poribus conditi munia, non obumbrato vel obtecto calvitio sed quoquoversus
obvio, gaudens obibam.

The last transformation we read of, of Lucius into a priest, is as a literary achievement more remarkable than any effected by magic, and
it is chiefly because of the tales in the *Metamorphoses* that this most
significant metamorphosis of all is so convincing. ‖

9

The Narrative Voice in Apuleius'
Metamorphoses

WARREN S. SMITH, JR.

While few critics today would follow St Augustine in his famous assumption that author and narrator of Apuleius' *Metamorphoses* are identical, it has not yet been systematically shown in what way Apuleius limits his narrator's perspective and how such limitations affect the character of the work in general. Such a demonstration must take into account the psychology of the narrator, Lucius, and how his personality may be related to his role as narrator. While I do not propose here to treat in detail the entire problem of the relationship between the narrative *persona* and the story, I hope that some of my conclusions may encourage the setting up of new guidelines in critical approaches to Apuleius' narrative method as a whole. We will start with an analysis of the narrative voice in the cryptic 'prologue' to the first book of the novel, in which the narrator introduces himself to the reader and makes certain claims about the nature of the forthcoming work. Critics who discuss this prologue have tended to emphasize its vagueness, the apparent inadequacy of its information, and its bombastic language; some have dismissed it as a joke intended to amuse by the absurdity of its claims, or, less charitably, have taken it as evidence for Apuleius' proletarian literary tastes.[1] I wish to argue that the prologue does in fact make definite hints about the complex nature of the ensuing narrative, but that it does so in a playful, allusive manner which owes something to the prologues of Plautus. In the

I am indebted to Profs. Thomas Cole of Yale University and Harvey Klevar of Luther College for helpful suggestions in the preparation of successive versions of this paper. In part it derives from my dissertation (Smith 1968).

[1] For a sample of such views, see Bürger (1888: 492); Perry (1926: 259); Walsh (1970: 142); Ebel (1970: 161). More reliable analyses of the prologue are those of Calonghi (1915) and Vallette (1965: vol. i, pp. xii–xv).

second section, I will ‖ show how the prologue anticipates subsequent explicit comments made by the narrator about specific *fabulae* to which he introduces the reader. Finally, we will consider how the narrative point of view is transformed in the closing book of the novel.

I. THE PROLOGUE

The prologue begins as follows:

At ego tibi sermone isto Milesio varias fabulas conseram auresque tuas benivolas lepido susurro permulceam, modo si papyrum Aegyptiam argutia Nilotici calami inscriptam non spreveris inspicere, figuras fortunasque hominum in alias imagines conversas et in se rursum mutuo nexu refectas ut mireris.[2]

In this sentence the narrator promises to delight the receptive listener with various *fabulae* told in 'a Milesian manner of speech' (*Milesio sermone*), but adds the hope that the reader will not be 'put off' ('modo si . . . non spreveris inspicere') at reading 'an Egyptian papyrus written with the *argutia* ('cleverness,' or better, 'sharp point' in a double sense) of a reed from the Nile. There are two major things to observe about this part of the sentence. First, the author implies a distinction between an oral narrative (*fabulae* which will 'delight the ear') and a written one (the papyrus inscribed by the Nile reed). Second, these two parts (or aspects?) of the novel will be likely to cause opposite reactions in the reader: he is sure to be delighted by the first, but he may be put off by the second. Both parts of the novel, the narrator goes on, will be based on the theme of the magical metamorphoses of the 'figures and fortunes of men into other shapes.'

It seems unavoidable to conclude that in this sentence Apuleius refers, however imprecisely, both to a light-hearted and to a more serious aspect of his novel. The 'Milesian' aspect would include racy tales such as those for which Aristides and Sisenna were known[3] (in *Met.* 4. 32 even the 'Cupid and Psyche tale' seems to be called Milesian, but the claim is made suspect by its context in a joke), whereas the ‖ 'Egyptian' aspect, whatever its exact nature, might be expected to inculcate religious or philosophical edification, with which the Egyptians were

---

[2] The text of the *Metamorphoses* cited throughout is Helm (1965). In the passage here quoted I have substituted commas for Helm's dashes before *modo* and after *inspicere*.

[3] For discussions of this literary sub-genre, see Perry (1967: 90–5); Walsh (1970: 10–18).

closely associated.[4] Note that the unexpected word *argutia*, 'sharpness,' is used here partly for the sake of contrast with the soft 'whispering' (*susurrus*) of the Milesian tales.

We will later consider some further implications of the contrast which is posited in this opening sentence. First note, however, that by drawing an apparent distinction between lighter and more serious aspects of his comic novel, Apuleius is following a not uncommon practice of ancient writers of light fiction. Closely parallel is Lucian's introduction to his *True History*, where he tells the reader that he will offer him various diverting fictitious stories, but also urges him to be on the lookout for something more worthy of serious contemplation (θεωρίαν οὐκ ἄμουσον ἐπιδείξεται).[5] Other parallels can be drawn from Longus' *Daphnis and Chloe* and from Varro's *Menippeae*.[6] Apuleius' opening sentence differs from the comments of these other writers, however, by his turgid and allusive language — an allusiveness which continues throughout his prologue. In the next sentence, the narrator promises to begin his story at once (*exordior*) but pauses to answer a supposed demand by the reader for a personal introduction ('Quis ille?'). 'Here is a short answer for you!' replies the narrator enthusiastically, but instead he launches into a wordy and high-flown Greek geography lesson: 'The Attic Mt Hymettus, the Isthmus of Corinth' (called by its less common name, 'Ephyra'), 'and the Spartan [town of] Taenarus —lucky realms, which are immortally described in books luckier than this one—are where my family comes from.' He means to say, of course, 'I am from Greece;' but does so by using vague circumlocutions for three of its principal cities: Athens, Corinth, and Sparta.[7] The vagueness of the phrases, and their failure to convey the expected information adequately, are used comically in ‖ a manner recalling Plautus. The Plautine *prologus* is apt to tease his audience by promising to dispatch his *argumentum* in a few words, and then disappointing their expectations by drawing out his prefatory remarks or telling a joke. The parallel with the *Menaechmi* is especially close:

---

[4] Cf. *Met.* 11. 5; *Asclepius* 24; *Florida* 15 (p. 21. 16–20 Helm); Heliodorus, *Aethiopica* 3. 16. 4.

[5] *True History* 2. Walsh (1970: 3–4) misleadingly describes this dichotomy in Lucian's introduction as one between content ('trivial and escapist') and style ('elegant and bookish').

[6] *Daphnis and Chloe, prooimion* 2; cf. Chalk (1960: 32); Varro, *Inglorius* (περὶ φθόνου), fr. 218 Bücheler, where the contrast is between *voluptas* and *litteras*.

[7] For a similar circumlocution, cf. Petronius 6. 1; Walsh (1970: 86).

Nunc argumentum accipite atque animum advortite:
Quam potero in verba conferam paucissima.
Atque hoc poetae faciunt in comoedis:
Omnis res gestas esse Athenis autumant,
Quo illud vobis graecum videatur magis;
Ego nusquam dicam nisi ubi factum dicitur.[8]

Now here's the plot, pay close attention:
I'll set it forth as briefly as I can.
Now here's what authors do in every comic play:
'It all takes place in Athens, folks,' is what they say.
So this way everything will seem *more Greek* to you.
But I reveal the true locations when I speak to you.[9]

Like the buffoon showman who introduces a play of Plautus, Apuleius' narrator appears to be laughing with his audience at the dramatic convention he is forced to observe; and he at once goes on in the same light vein to hint that he makes no claims for the lasting literary value of his efforts, nor does he claim any genius for himself:

There [in Greece] I gained [knowledge of] the Attic tongue [as a reward] for the first service of boyhood [presumably this means, 'in my studies at school']. Soon thereafter, in the city of Latium [Rome], a stranger to Roman studies, I approached the native language and learned it after hard work with no teacher to guide me. And by the way, I ask your pardon if I give any offense as an unaccustomed speaker of a foreign and alien language.

This vague 'autobiography' cannot be related precisely either to the experiences of the narrator, Lucius, in the remainder of the *Metamorphoses* or to known experiences in the life of Apuleius himself. Lucius, it is true, is Greek; more precisely, he is from Corinth, which we are not told in the prologue and learn later only indirectly (books 1. 22, 2. 12); he does make a journey from Greece to Rome (book 11. 26), || but under circumstances which seem hardly reconcilable with the above reference. In any case the statement of the prologue is deliberately absurd; it conjures up the disarming, but somehow ludicrous, picture of a Greek boy bent over his books in school laboring to learn his own native language, followed by an equally arduous stint in Rome (this time with no help from a teacher) in which he struggles with only partial success to learn Latin. It is clear that Apuleius, who was

---

[8] *Men.* 5–10. Cf. *Captivi* 1–2; *Poenulus* 46 ff.
[9] The translation of the last four lines is from Segal (1968a: 36–7).

proud of his skill in both Greek and Latin,[10] could not be seriously apologizing for a crude or unrefined style in his own novel. But if the statement about the narrator's background is worthless as a piece of biographical information, it may at least make a legitimate literary point: Apuleius wishes to emphasize that the forthcoming story has been adapted from a Greek original, and his statement perhaps hints that the reader can expect plenty of typical Greek raciness in it. Likewise, in the *Florida*, when Apuleius is about to start a story in Latin, having previously spoken in Greek, he uses a geographical term: '. . . satis oratio nostra atticissaverit. Tempus est in Latium demigrare de Graecia.'[11] (We may also compare the opening sentence of the prologue, where the novel is said to be set on two 'fronts,' Miletus and Egypt.) The novel is shown to have had a Greek genesis but to have put on a Roman dress, namely its present form in Latin. It may be argued that Apuleius chooses a cumbersome method to convey a bit of simple information, but this is to miss the spirit of buffoonery. The comic parallel is again to be sought in Plautus, who always refers to the Romans as *barbari* and who pretends to excuse immoral conduct on the grounds that his plays are set in Greece.[12] In Apuleius, the narrator ironically groans over the back-breaking work of translating into a 'foreign tongue' and begs to be excused in advance for inadvertent solecisms. His claims, when taken literally, are a comic sham (just as are Plautus' excuses about the setting of his plays), and yet his disarming modesty, though tinged with irony, wins our sympathy both here and many times later when he addresses the reader.

The meaning of the next sentence in the prologue has been much disputed: 'Iam haec equidem ipsa vocis immutatio *desultoriae scientiae* stilo ‖ quem accessimus respondet.' 'This very change of language' must mean 'this use of the Latin language to translate a Greek story.' This 'change' is said to correspond to the style which we have undertaken of a *desultoria scientia*. Scholars have been divided on the interpretation of the italicized words, which seem to mean 'a knowledge which jumps from one horse to the next;' does the phrase refer to the metamorphosis produced by witchcraft, in which the bodies of men are miraculously changed into different shapes?[13] Or could it refer to

---

[10] *Apologia* 38 (pp. 43. 19–44. 1 Helm); *Florida* 18 (p. 38. 16–26 Helm).
[11] Printed as preface to *De Deo Socrate* (5. 6–7 Thomas); cf. Plautus, *Men.* 11–12, 49, 56.
[12] e.g. *Stichus* 446–8; other examples and discussion in Segal (1968: 31–8).
[13] As argued by Hildebrand (1842: 1. 12); Molt (1938: 29).

the variety of the Milesian tales (cf. *varias fabulas conseram*), which quickly move from one subject to the next?[14] The first of these theories can be dismissed, I think, on the grounds that, while metamorphosis is a subject frequently treated in the novel, it cannot be equated with a style of composition. The second theory is more plausible, but still difficult; I cannot see any obvious close correspondence between a transition from Greece to Rome (or from the Greek to the Latin language), on the one hand, and the telling of widely varied tales on the other. In order for the second member of the comparison to correspond to the first, it must be based on a *single* transition of some sort. Now Apuleius several times in the *Metamorphoses* and elsewhere uses the word *stilus* in the sense of a method of composition —specifically, a method employed by authors talented enough to write serious literature, as opposed to the purely narrative talent of an oral storyteller (a *fabulator*), whose tales may be stylistically crude. Speakers in the novel twice attribute *stilus* only to men who are 'better educated' (*doctiores*) than they—men, that is, who are fortunate enough to be able to compose written *historiae*, as opposed to oral *fabulae*.[15] We now recall the distinction which the first sentence of the prologue makes between two aspects of the forthcoming book: the Milesian tales, which are, strictly speaking, stories told *orally*;[16] and the 'Egyptian papyrus,' ‖ which will not produce the same delighted reaction as the tales but may fall in a genre closer to serious literature. Although this distinction is vague, it is the closest which the narrator comes in the prologue to a specific explanation of his narrative method, and it must be this explanation to which he refers at the close of the prologue. Now in order for *desultoriae scientiae stilus* to 'correspond' to *immutatio vocis*, it must refer to 'a literary method which is based on a (single) jump from one (area of) knowledge to another,' in the same way that the narrator himself has made the transition from Greek to Latin. The phrase must refer, then, to the narrator's *two kinds of narrative ability* which have resulted in a single composition:

---

[14] Cf. Leo (1905: 605); Calonghi (1915: 23).

[15] 6. 29. 7, 8. 1. 11; cf. *Florida* 9 (p. 13. 23 Helm). The reference in 2. 12 to 'historiam magnam et incredundam fabulam et libros' would seem, like the statement in the prologue, to be a hint at the bipartite style of the *Metamorphoses*. But the distinction between *fabula* and *historia* is not one which Apuleius attempts to press everywhere, as witnessed by the reference (at the end of the prologue) to the novel as a *fabula Graecanica*.

[16] It is helpful here to remember Lucian's description of Aristides *listening* with delight to the recitation of Milesian tales (*Amores* 1).

first, the ability to invent oral, entertaining *fabulae* told in the Milesian manner; second, the ability to compose polished literature which is worthy of being written down ('papyrum . . . inscriptam'): specifically, literature which deals with an Egyptian, and therefore possibly religious, motif. Metaphorically the phrase *desultoria scientia* recalls the geographical jump which the novel will make from Miletus to Egypt, corresponding to the move which the narrator himself claims to have made from Greece to Rome. Furthermore, the anticipated reaction of the reader to each of these 'jumps' is parallel: just as he may be 'put off' ('modo is . . . non spreveris inspicere') by the 'Egyptian' aspect of the book, he may also be 'offended' ('siquid . . . offendero') by the narrator's inexperience in the Latin language.

At the end of the prologue, the narrator allows a veil to fall over whatever distinctions and contrasts he has made in regard to his novel, as he issues a summons to the reader to have a good time:

Fabulam Graecanicam incipimus. Lector intende: laetaberis.

We begin a tale told in the Greek manner. Pay close attention, reader; you will be delighted!

This wording again recalls the opening of a comic play. Compare Plautus' *Asinaria*:

Inest lepos ludusque in hac comoedia:
Ridicula res est. Date benigne operam mihi . . .[17]

Be so kind as to pay attention to me, and you'll find
that this comedy contains a lot of wit and fun; the plot is side-splitting. ||

Thus, to round out his introduction the narrator ceases to attempt any meaningful explication of the novel; he echoes his opening words as he acts as pitchman summoning an audience to attention, a role which he is to repeat several times later. Like the Plautine *prologus* he drums up interest in the story, makes a pointed reference to its exotic origin, and promises a reward to those who listen carefully.

II. The Ass and the Gentle Reader

It is perhaps significant that the prologue to the *Metamorphoses* closes with a warning to pay close attention. For Apuleius' narrator does not

---

[17] *Asin.* 13–14.

simply step off the stage after his opening words, allowing the reader
to view and judge the subsequent action for himself; he will be there
both to present and to interpret all of the remainder of the novel for
us, not as an omniscient author but rather as an actor in his own story,
with a viewpoint which is almost always strictly limited to what he
can see at the moment. In this respect, Apuleius may have modelled
his comic narrator in part on Encolpius, the narrator of Petronius'
Satyricon: the readers of both Latin novels confront each new bizarre
twist in plot with none but the narrator's own hasty reaction to them
as a guide.[18] However, Encolpius, for all his mistakes, is at least a somewhat more reliable guide than is Lucius: we laugh at him when, in
dining with Trimalchio, he emulates what he takes to be the *urban-
itas* of his host,[19] but his taste on purely literary matters is generally
sound and probably coincides with that of Petronius himself. For
example, he is disgusted when listening to a farcical rendering of Vergil, and he offers a heartfelt plea for a return to the simplicity of the
classics as literary models.[20] Moreover Encolpius, at least in the
surviving portions of the *Satyricon*, never steps out of character to
address the reader directly (in contrast with Lucius' confidential
asides: see below); nor does he offer his own views about such creative efforts as the Matron of Ephesus tale (111–12) ‖ or Eumolpus'
poem on the Civil War (119–24). Apuleius rarely allows his own
stories to pass without comment; his narrator often plays the role of
salesman for the varied fare of the *Metamorphoses*, either alerting the
reader ahead of time that an exciting tale is forthcoming (9. 4; 9. 13–14;
10. 2) or applauding such a tale at its conclusion (1. 20; 6. 25). He
passes judgment on people as well as tales, but usually finds that
his first impressions of his acquaintances have to be revised. For
example, in Hypata Lucius develops a real, if misguided, affection for
Milo's servant-girl Fotis (3. 19), but after Fotis accidentally causes
him to be changed into an ass he decides that she is 'the most worthless and evil of women' (3. 26). Later, Lucius is prepared to damn the
whole female sex when he is outraged at the supposed promiscuity of
the captive maiden Charite (7. 10), until he discovers that the robber

---

[18] Two examples from Petronius: *Sat.* 7 (Encolpius' belief that the old bawd is a witch);
Sat. 19 (his terror at Quartilla's incomprehensible merriment).

[19] *Sat.* 41; cf. Sullivan (1968a: 158–9).

[20] *Sat.* 68 and 1–2; see Sullivan (1968a: 163–4). Walsh (1970) argues, 84–5, that
even the latter passage, while it 'may well represent Petronius' own judgment,'
humorously contradicts its own message through its overwritten style.

who has proposed selling her into prostitution is actually her husband Tlepolemus in disguise (7. 12). Far from promiscuous, Charite emerges as one of the few wives in the novel whose virtue cannot be bought.

If Lucius' judgment about people and events is suspect, it naturally follows that we cannot always believe his analyses of the *fabulae* to which he introduces the reader. In fact in the bulk of the novel the narrative *persona* largely speaks without even the sporadic subtleties it evidences in the prologue, retaining only the prologue's efforts to impress the reader and in large part dropping its efforts to inform him. Lucius the ass cannot invent tales for his acquaintances to hear, nor would such invention match his role as a mere observer of the world through which he travels. Instead he is a recorder and categorizer of material passed on by others. The shallowness and superficiality of his understanding of this material recalls that of Dionysus in Aristophanes' *Frogs*, and prefigures the naiveté of Chaucer the pilgrim in the *Canterbury Tales*, who ironically is given the worst literary taste of all his comrades and recites the travesty 'Sir Thopas,' his one 'original' poem, to prove it. The sweeping categories in which Lucius glibly places most of the tales are at best less than helpful in guiding the reader's reaction to them. For example, Lucius sums up the Cupid and Psyche tale, one of the richest and most complex sections of the *Metamorphoses*, by calling it a mere 'pretty little story,' a view which is obviously not to be taken as Apuleius' own final word on this major || section of the novel;[21] in this instance, the suspect nature of the comment is highlighted by the fact that in the same breath the narrator laments that this pretty story has been lost to the world forever due to his lack of a pen and tablets to use in writing it down. This is Apuleius' buffoonery at its best; we are startled to discover that we were not really listening to the ass report this tale to us after all, but were fellow listeners along with him; however, the solicitous ass, not willing to relinquish his role as narrator, lamely supposes for the moment that if only he had had writing materials, he would somehow have been able to grasp them in his hooves and take dictation.

---

[21] *bellam fabellam*, 6. 25; Helm (*RE* 23, col. 1438) insists on taking the comment seriously, but contrast the attitude of Tatum (1969: 498) (in reference to the tale of Aristomenes): 'If we perceive nothing more than . . . a *lepida fabula* in this story, then we have grasped nothing more than Lucius himself.' I note sadly Tatum's comment elsewhere (493) that he may be tending toward a 'humorless' interpretation of Apuleius' tales.

The passage illustrates the elements of surprise, mock-naiveté, and incongruity which are essential to Apuleius' wit, and which both here and in the prologue are combined in an appeal to the reader's sympathy and for his attention. We laugh as we are brought down from Olympus with a jolt. In his refusal to set up explicit guidelines to his tales, Apuleius allows Lucius to classify 'Cupid and Psyche' with such widely disparate tales as the witchcraft story of Aristomenes (1. 5–20) and the bedroom farce, 'The Lover and the Tub' (9. 5–7), both of which he calls *lepidae fabulae*. Lucius hopes that the reader will share his amusement at all such tales, but he himself never profits from them, even when (as is true of the tales of Aristomenes and Cupid and Psyche) they seem to imply morals which are applicable to him.[22]

Even when Lucius does attempt to be more precise in categorizing the tales, his prefatory comments are of only minimal help to the reader. Thus, at the start of the Wicked Stepmother tale (10. 2–12) we are told to take off our comic slippers and to put on the tragic buskin. The story which follows does appear to set tragic events in motion: in the manner of the Hippolytus legend, a boy is unjustly ‖ accused of raping his stepmother, while another accidentally takes poison intended for his brother. We are surprised, however, by a joyous ending, when the first boy is acquitted of the crime and the second is restored to his father from the dead.[23] An opposite surprise occurs at the end of the tale of the Baker's Wife (9. 14–31). Here Lucius tells us at the start that we must not miss out on a tale which will be 'the best one of all—delightful, with all the trimmings.' There follows a 'framework story' of adultery, interrupted by two internal tales on a similar theme; the first of these secondary tales (9. 17–21) ends with the escape of the lover, while the wronged husband remains undeceived; the second (9. 24–5) ends more ominously if still ambiguously, as the husband and wife reach an uneasy temporary truce. In the 'framework story,' however, the adultery leads to disaster: the cuckold baker

---

[22] See Tatum (1969a: 493–502) (on Aristomenes and Thelyphron). It is particularly appropriate to Lucius' character that he draws no moral from 'Psyche,' which certainly recalls some of Lucius' past experiences and hints at his eventual salvation, though it is too much to say that it is an 'allegory of Lucius' own adventures' (Tatum's phrase, 509) in any extended detail.

[23] Walsh (1970) claims that 'our author seems hardly to have known how his story was going to end when he launched it. . . .' (171). Both Walsh and Perry (1967, e.g. 254) are unable to appreciate Apuleius' skillful use of misleading clues and surprise twists in plot. For a discussion of Apuleius' method of deceiving the reader with false expectations, see Junghanns (1932, esp. 73–4).

punishes his wife's lover and the enraged wife hires a witch to murder her husband; the closing note is one of nightmarish gloom. In Apuleius' masterly use of the grotesque, violence and tragedy can follow close on, or coexist with, fun and frivolity, and the author delights in surprising those who expect only a laugh. Metamorphosis is truly the reigning god in this novel, and its effect on us is enhanced by the narrator's seeming inability (or the author's own puckish refusal) to provide the reader in advance with precise roadsigns.

Now to be constantly confronted with a series of roadsigns which raise false expectations might be a bewildering rather than a comic experience if the author did not provide us with some clues as to the true state of affairs. Otherwise Apuleius, rather than his narrator, might be justifiably charged with simple blundering, or with lack of concern for exact literary classification. But in fact Lucius the ass implicitly warns the reader, time and again, that to say the least he is no expert on the subjects of literature or human nature; and in some cases the reader is depicted actually interrupting the narrative in order to call Lucius to task for a statement. In the prologue, as we saw, when || it looks as though the narrator is about to begin his story without properly introducing himself, the reader calls him short with a question ('Quis ille?'), but is rewarded only by a reply in which the narrator manages to avoid mentioning either his name or his native city. In book 9, when telling the tale of the Baker's Wife, Lucius carelessly omits any reference to how he, an ass, could have found out all about the machinations of his mistress; the reader interrupts him again: 'Wait a minute, you clever ass—if you were tied up behind the bread–mill, how could you know about the goings-on of these women, which were done in secret, as you admit?' and the ass is forced to add a hasty explanation (9. 30).[24] Again, in book 10 Lucius is treated to the view of a lascivious mime in which actors depict the judgment of Paris. He reacts indignantly (10. 33) to the immorality of the lesson which the mime supposedly conveys; if, at the beginning of the world, says Lucius, the judge Paris preferred sexual gratification to any of the other treasures which the goddesses offered him, why should we wonder if judges now

---

[24] Cf. Plautus, *Captivi* 10–13 (Nixon (1916)'s translation): 'Now you take me? Very good! Bless my soul! that gentleman at the back says he does not. Let him step this way. In case there is no opportunity to take a seat, sir, you can take a stroll, seeing you insist on making an actor turn beggar.' Laurence Sterne, *Tristram Shandy* (1940) 56: 'How could you, Madam, be so inattentive in reading the last chapter? I told you in it, *that my mother was not a papist.*—Papist! You told me no such thing, Sir.'

are so easily bought, or if various famous men—Palamedes, Ajax, or Socrates—were all unjustly condemned by the juries trying them? The juxtaposition of the names of these three famous Greeks was no doubt suggested to Apuleius by a reference in Plato's *Apology*, and Lucius' tirade here may stem from a guilty conscience resulting from his own earlier choice of Fotis as a lover (which proved as unfortunate a choice as that of Venus by Paris). Nevertheless, the connection between the Judgment of Paris and an Athenian jury's condemnation of Socrates is a tenuous one at best; such unenlightening drawing of analogies is the ass' way of parading his cleverness, and the dubious relevance of his outburst to its specific stimulus is all too obvious.[25] Apuleius is clearly aware of this and ‖ allows Lucius to sense dimly his own absurdity: 'But I'm afraid that some of you will criticize the extent of my indignation and think, "What is this? are we going to let this ass spout philosophy at us?" '[26] He then calls a retreat: 'I'll get back to the point of my story where I left off.'

Lucius' enthusiasm for learning is indomitable despite his frequent setbacks, and, though aware of his mental limitations and of the absurdity of his plight, he is not deterred from intellectual pretensions which can verge on the lofty. In a revealing aside soon after he has gone to work in the mill (9. 13), Lucius reflects on what his experience as an ass has meant to him:

The only comfort which I could find in my wretched existence derived from my natural curiosity; for no one took note of my presence and they all spoke and acted freely in front of me. How true it was, what that noble old Greek author said! For when he was describing a man of the highest intelligence (*summae prudentiae*), he sang of how he attained the highest virtues through his wanderings among many countries and acquaintance with varied peoples. Yes, I gave thanks a thousand times for being an ass; for the ass, while he did not make me so very wise (*minus prudentem*), at least made me

---

[25] See Schlam (1970: 485–6); Plato, *Apology* 41b. The narrator's pride in his philosophical predilection is clear almost from the start of the novel; in 1. 2 he boasts of his descent from 'the famous Plutarch and his nephew Sextus the philosopher'; but even there the claim is deflated, for with disregard for geographical accuracy he places the Boeotian Plutarch in Thessaly. See also 2. 3, 8. 27 *fin*. In 1. 4, when he converses with two travellers on the road to Hypata, Lucius again gets carried away by his love for making far-fetched 'analogies.' In order to illustrate the existence of unexplained wonders, he first tells of his own difficulties in swallowing a piece of cheese, then describes a sword-swallower in Athens, and then an acrobatic boy who climbed up the sword—and in a final ingenious irrelevance, compares this sight to the serpent-entwined staff of the god of medicine.

[26] Cf. 6. 26: 'haec quidem inepta et prorsus asinina cogitatio. . . .'

acquainted with many things (*multiscium*), through being concealed in his skin and experiencing varied fortunes.

This analogy between the wanderings of Odysseus and those of an ass is not rendered less absurd by Lucius' professed refusal to compare his own wisdom with that of Homer's hero. For in fact Lucius often prides himself on his 'cleverness,' or 'wisdom,' while inside the skin of the ass: it is the *prudens asinus* who is able to discern the truth about Charite and Tlepolemus (7. 12), and who has just boasted again about his *prudentia* (9. 11) only a few pages before the passage quoted above. Furthermore, the *curiositas* from which Lucius pretends to derive so much comfort[27] is, as the reader knows, actually one of Lucius' greatest || handicaps: under the control of curiosity he ignored repeated warnings about witchcraft and was changed into an ass when he tampered with magic.[28] The denouement of the novel will again call to our minds how poorly Lucius learns from his experiences, for the priest of Isis in book 11. 15 reminds Lucius that all his troubles derived from *curiositas*. Further, the priest adds pointedly that the divine *prudentia* of Isis (in implied contrast with Lucius' own folly) is the factor which will bring about his salvation.[29] In the context of our discussion, however, the point to note most carefully about Lucius' 'confession' in 9. 13 is that it immediately precedes the introduction to the tale of the Baker's Wife which, as we saw (above, p. 187), Lucius misleadingly claims as the most delightful of all his tales despite its surprise tragic denouement. Apuleius nowhere gives us a better clue as to how the reader should weigh the judgments passed on to him by the narrator; just for the moment, he lets Lucius inadvertently confess the truth to us: I, the much-travelled ass, have learned many things but am a bad interpreter of all of them; now listen to the most delightful tale of all. The veil is lifted only to be immediately dropped again, but the careful reader will sense that a surprise is in store in the ensuing tale.

[27] This is actually only one of a series of mutually contradictory claims in which Lucius tries ironically to look on the bright side of his condition: in 3. 24 he says that the only *solacium* of becoming an ass was the increased size of his sexual member, to serve Fotis; in 9. 15 he cites his big *ears* as his *unicum solacium*.

[28] For a recent discussion of this theme, see Schlam (1968c: 120–5).

[29] Here I follow the reading of the MSS at 11. 15. 22; modern editors follow Colvius in emending *prudentia* to *providentia*, but cf. *De deo Socratis* 15 (p. 24. 11–14 Thomas): 'quippe tantum eos deos appellant, qui . . . iuste ac *prudenter* curriculo vitae gubernato . . . vulgo advertuntur;' *Asclepius* 34 (p. 74. 18–20 Thomas): 'omnia enim deus et ab eo omnia et eius omnia voluntatis. quod totum est bonum decens et *prudens*. . . .' See also Hildebrand (1842)'s arguments in defense of *prudentia, ad loc.*

III. THE NARRATIVE VOICE AND APULEIUS' DRAMATIC
METHOD; ALTERATION OF TONE IN BOOK II

Many of the effects described above can be well compared with those
of a great modern satirical novel. In discussing Laurence Sterne's
Tristram Shandy, Martin Price refers to

the self-consciousness that is constantly subverting the larger forms of the
book itself—insisting upon it as a printed thing . . . calling attention to the
artifice of fictional time or to the process of reading itself, or, most of all, ‖ to
the author's exercise of control. . . . Sterne insists upon making us conscious
of all we have commonly taken for granted. By pretending incompetence or
indecision, by teasing us with false leads or cheating our logical expectations,
he exposes the forms at every point.[30]

Calling attention to normally accepted conventions; cheating the
reader's logical expectations at every turn—these elements are
essential to Apuleius' narrative method, as well as to Sterne's. Both
authors, for example, borrow the comic dramatists' trick (of which
ancient dramatists are so fond[31]) of temporarily shattering the dramatic mood by claiming to anticipate some interest or objection on
the part of the audience. Because of his limited wit, an ass has to work
harder than would a human narrator in holding the reader's attention; and Apuleius never lets us lose sight of his narrator's efforts
to present his material in a manner acceptable to the reader. Thus,
the narrator will self-consciously stress the absurdity of an ass as the
author of a book (6. 25. 1–4), or the nuisance of having to translate
the words of all of his Greek characters into Latin (1. 1. 10–12, 4. 32),
or the task of whipping up his characters' *fabulae* into proper literary shape (6. 29. 6–8, 8. 1. 9–12). Like Sterne, Apuleius allows the
reader to interrupt the story in order to point out logical inconsistencies (cf. above, n. 24). His solicitous asides to the reader, ostensibly
meant to guide him or hold his attention, instead lead him down
blind alleys.[32]

---

[30] Price (1965: 327).
[31] e.g. Aristophanes, *Peace* 43–8; Plautus, *Poenulus* 550–2; and see above, p. 199 and
n. 12.
[32] Cf. Sterne (1940: 283): 'So much for my chapter upon chapters, which I hold to
be the best chapter in my whole work; and take my word, whoever reads it, is full as
well employed, as in picking straws.' Sterne's mocking statement of purpose (301–2)
can be helpfully compared with Apuleius' prologue.

New and startling twists on convention are especially important in Apuleius' tales, which, because of their unexpected turns of plot, false clues, apparent inconsistencies, and surprise endings, are sometimes thought to be hastily constructed hybrids.[33] It is not sloppy writing, but deliberate use of misleading hints, which falsely raises the expectation that Telephron's mutilation will come about as a punishment for his dereliction in the duty of guarding a corpse (2. 22), or which turns Charite from a modest, unassuming wife into a scheming virago (8. 1–14), or which causes the tale of the Baker's Wife to lose its ‖ Milesian raciness and to end on a note of horror (9. 30–1). Similarly, the reader is often surprised by the intrusion of parodies of standard dramatic devices, which embrace a variety of genres, so that we are treated to burlesques of stock declamations from tragedy and the Greek romance, and of themes from mythology,[34] all of which depend largely for their humor on their introduction at ludicrously inappropriate moments. In a novel of magical metamorphosis, nothing remains what it seems to be; and this factor of sudden change should be considered central to an explanation of the most unexpected surprise of all in the novel, the transformation of the *Metamorphoses* itself from a collection of anecdotes providing varied edification and entertainment into a fable about the journey of the soul through life. Such a transformation becomes possible through the sudden elevation of perspective in book 11, when Lucius learns the meaning of his former life and chooses to turn away from that life.

In order to appreciate fully this leap in perspective in book 11, the reader has to see how the limited perspective of the pre-Isis world in the novel is tied to the narrator's own humorously distorted and limited judgment. At the start of the novel, Lucius, a cloistered young scholar (cf. 2. 10. 5, 3. 19. 13–14) is poorly equipped to comprehend the dangers of his own misdirected adolescent emotions, nor is he skillful at comprehending the true motives of others toward him. Lucius is disconcerted by the forwardness of the well-meaning Byrrhaena, and rejects her good advice about staying away from Pamphile; he persists in fidelity to the miserly and self-serving Milo and, feeling the need for a protective and authoritative father-substitute, maintains a filial

---

[33] Cf. Walsh (1970: 153–4, 158 n. 2, 161, 201), and see above, n. 23.

[34] Tragedy: Socrates' speech, 1. 8. 10–13; Romance: Aristomenes' speech to his bed, 1. 16. 4–8 (cf. Chaireas' speech in Chariton, 'Chaireas and Callirrhoe' 5. 6); Mythology: Odysseus, 9. 13. 13–20, and Pasiphae, 10. 22. 16–21. Further examples of parodies in Walsh (1970: 52–60).

devotion to him even after Milo has been instrumental in betray-
ing him to public humiliation in the Festival of Laughter.[35] Above all,
Lucius goes beyond the bounds of all reason in his slavish infatuation
with Fotis. Apuleius brilliantly reveals the ludicrousness and actual
superficiality of this grand passion by causing Lucius to deliver an
overblown || sophistic encomium on the beauty of Fotis' hair, and on
the nobility of hair in general (2. 8–9). Surely in this passage, if any-
where, we feel the limitations of an outlook on life which can never
see below the surface of people, and which never looks for anything
in their discourses beyond banal titillation. At the end of book 10, when
Lucius breaks away from a circus and finds refuge in the soft bosom
of the sand on the beach at Cenchreae—like Psyche's sleep in the flowers
outside Cupid's palace—he is on the verge of discovering a new and
receptive power that can free him from his former hostile world, a world
which sought only to exploit him or to put him on display as a freak.
But more importantly, Lucius is now ready to throw off his old asinine self and to discover a heavenly *voluptas* which will enable him,
like Chaucer's Troilus after his death,[36] to laugh at his old life as he
discovers how trivial are all the values he once considered important.

   In book 11 Lucius truly becomes a man, in a sense that goes far
beyond the mere question of his external form. Apuleius suggests this
widening of his theme by causing Lucius to lose sight of the limitations of the ass's perspective even before his actual retransformation.
When Lucius attempts to describe Isis rising out of the sea, he
expresses the fear that the *paupertas oris humani* may not be sufficient
to convey her divine beauty (11. 3. 7–11): a remarkable aside, in sharp
contrast to his usual joke about the absurdity of an *ass* attempting to
treat weighty matters. The beginning of the subsequent description
of Isis, which refers to her long, flowing hair, surprisingly echoes Lucius'
earlier encomium on the beauty of Fotis' hair. This touch, whether
deliberate or not, is psychologically profound: the suggestion of Fotis'
beauty being present in the august deity indicates that Lucius' earlier misconceived attraction has been sublimated and transferred to
a meaningful object—to the goddess who can benefit Lucius rather

---

[35] Byrrhaena: 2. 3. 11–15; 2. 6. 1–5; Milo: 3. 12. 7–12, and cf. 7. 3. 1–7, where he
still calls Milo 'hospes mihi carissimus' and says that to murder him would have been
akin to parricide.
[36] Chaucer, *Troilus and Criseyde* 5. 1814–25. On *voluptas* in Apuleius, see Ebel (1970:
169–72); cf. also *Met.* 11. 24. 22 (not included in Ebel's discussion) where *voluptas* is
used of the joy Lucius feels at contemplating the image of Isis.

than lead him to disaster. We must remember also that both Fotis and Isis are associated with Venus (2. 17, 11. 2). What had been trivial and misguided in the case of Fotis is now used to enhance the awe inspired by the beauty of Isis; it is part of the change from sexual to spiritual *voluptas*. Later, in describing his initiation into the cult of Isis, Lucius warns the reader against the || penalties of *temeraria curiositas* (11. 23. 22), thus serving notice that he himself has moved beyond his chronic enslavement to curiosity, and at the same time light-heartedly turning against the reader the same sort of joke which used to take Lucius himself as its butt. Lucius gradually sloughs off his faith in external appearances as he begins to realize the importance of a man's inner self; Apuleius slyly suggests this change when Lucius, who had earlier made a fetish of human hair, discovers that the tonsured priests of Isis by sacrificing their physical beauty have become *terrena sidera* who worship the unearthly beauty of the goddess (11. 10). Lucius' own triple initiation into the cult will involve a similar sacrifice, first of the sexual *voluptas* for which he had come to strive so eagerly, and finally, of his own attractive head of hair (cf. 2. 2. 18–19) which he must shave off before becoming a priest of Osiris. In the very last sentence of the novel, Lucius reports that this symbolic sacrifice did not cause him any shame (as would have been true of his earlier self) but that he went about rejoicing and openly displaying his tonsured crown to all whom he saw.

The change which we have outlined in the narrator's perspective in book 11, pervasive though it is in altering his personality and elevating the tone of the narrative, can help only in part to account for the unexpected switch in *personae* in 11. 27, where the narrator is suddenly—and seemingly offhandedly—identified as *Madaurensis*, 'the man from Madaura' (Apuleius' own birthplace in North Africa) rather than 'from Corinth,' which is Lucius' home. Although some of the older commentators sought to emend this word[37] or dismissed it as a careless mistake on Apuleius' part,[38] a more recent tendency is to interpret it as a deliberate clue by the author that he has abandoned fiction for autobiography in at least some parts of book 11.[39] Such an assumption may appear unavoidable to many readers but is not

[37] For *Madaurensem* Goldbacher substituted *mane Doriensem* (recorded in Helm's critical apparatus).

[38] See Oudendorp (1786) and Hildebrand (1842, *ad loc.*).

[39] Typical comments are those of Schissel von Fleschenberg (1913a: 94); Morelli (1915: 94–111); Perry (1967: 242).

susceptible to final proof.[40] Moreover such a change of *personae*, if totally unprepared ‖ for, would seem to imply, as one critic has said, 'a certain attitude of disinterest toward the reader and the rules of the genre.'[41] Is there an alternative way of making some sense of the reference in its context?

In 11. 27 Lucius is warned by Isis that he has not yet completed all his required religious initiations; he then realizes that he has so far neglected consecration to Osiris, 'the highest father of all the gods.' He is subsequently visited in a dream by a certain Asinius Marcellus, a member of the college of *pastophores*, or priests of Osiris. Lucius is sure that the visitation has some special meaning for him, since Asinius' name, being close to the word *asinus*, seems to recall the beast into which Lucius was transformed. Sure enough, soon after awakening Lucius is visited by the priest in person, who informs him that he himself has had a dream matching Lucius' own. Some divinity (apparently Osiris, but there is a gap in the manuscript at this point) appeared to Asinius in a dream and informed him that a certain man would be sent to him the next day. In context, the man in question must be the narrator, i.e. Lucius, but it is not Lucius who is named:

nam sibi visus est quiete proxima, dum magno deo coronas exaptat . . . et de eius ore, quo singulorum fata dictat, audisse mitti sibi Madaurensem, sed admodum pauperem, cui statim sua sacra deberet ministrare; nam et illi [Madaurensi] studiorum gloriam et ipsi [Marcello] grande compendium sua comparari providentia.

The great god Osiris promises 'the poor man from Madaura' that he will win great glory for his studies, thanks to the *providentia* of the god. This is the first we have heard of Madaura in the novel, and if we did not already know that Apuleius came from there the point of the reference would be lost on us entirely; moreover this sudden intrusion of the author does not seem more than a momentary break in the stride of the narrative. True, the narrator is never named again in the closing chapters of the novel after the conclusion of the prophecy (which might seem to leave open the possibility that he has

[40] The supposed points of correspondence with known facts about the author are interesting, but not close enough to be really compelling. In 11. 28 the narrator says that he has used up most of his patrimony due to travels and the high prices in Rome, and mentions pleading causes in the Roman forum; Apuleius himself was once a student in Rome (*Florida* 17; p. 31 Helm), was initiated into religious mysteries in Greece (*Apologia* 55; p. 62 Helm), and used up his patrimony through 'travels, studies, and liberality' (*Apologia* 23; p. 27 Helm).   [41] Veyne (1965: 241–2).

by then been 'transformed' into Apuleius himself), but he has pointedly reminded us just previously that he was once transformed into
an ass, as if ‖ Apuleius wanted to emphasize paradoxically that the
dramatic convention is still being observed even here where it would
appear to be broken. Now note that, while Asinius and the narrator
both understand at once that the prophecy refers to Lucius, it is
Osiris, not either of the men, who calls Lucius 'the poor man from
Madaura.' Despite the apparent casualness of the reference, it comes
in a passage which gives it a special emphasis: a prophecy attributed
to the great Osiris himself, and relating to the narrator, is naturally
of great importance and interest to the reader. But Osiris has the
special prerogative of divinity: his prophecy is likely to see further
than his human listeners can comprehend, and may have a secret
meaning unknown to anyone in the story. The failure of Asinius
and Lucius to express bafflement at the (to them) unintelligible
Madaurensem is puzzling, and compounds the obscurity of the passage
for us; they behave, in fact, as though they did not hear the word at
all. For whatever reason, the author is refusing to guide us further
here, so that his readers, rather than his fictional characters, are forced
to assume the role of prophetic interpreters. In Osiris' prophecy the
emphasis is on the glory and honor to be received through Isis and
Osiris; we cannot know what connection with these divinities
Apuleius may have had in real life, but at the very least he seems to
be saying here, 'this honor in the eyes of the gods is one which I am
proud to assume for myself.' It may be objected, of course, that
Apuleius could have chosen a much simpler and clearer method of
associating himself with the favor of Osiris. For example, he could have
caused the dream of Asinius Marellus to refer to 'the man from
Madaura' as a third person (unrelated to Lucius) to whom the god
was also showing favor. As it is, by momentarily 'becoming' the
narrator he has taken the risk of confusing the reader rather than
edifying him. Yet the problem may be less than it seems, if we consider an earlier prophecy in the novel which helps put the vision of
Osiris in a better perspective.

   While staying at the house of Milo, Lucius describes to his host
how he was once told by Diophanes, a Chaldean prophet, that he would
be immortalized in literature: 'mihi denique proventum huius pere-
grinationis inquirenti multa respondit et oppido mira et satis varia;
nunc enim gloriam satis floridam, nunc historiam magnam et incredundam fabulam et libros me futurum' (2. 12. 12–16). Diophanes'

prophecy is clearly a tongue-in- ‖ cheek reference to the *Metamorph-oses* itself: the *libri* which will record Lucius' adventures are the eleven books which make up the novel as we have it. But having recorded this half-humorous prophecy, Apuleius at once implies a doubt that it will ever be fulfilled. Milo recalls an anecdote in which Lucius' Chaldean prophet was exposed as a mercenary fraud. It seems that on a voyage across the narrow strait of water between Euboea and Thessaly Diophanes suffered a disastrous shipwreck, and moreover was robbed by pirates. His fate vividly demonstrates his inability to proph-esy a successful voyage for himself, let alone for others; he could not overcome the fickleness of *saeva fortuna*. The irony of this scene is unusu-ally complex. On the one hand, of course, the Chaldean's prophecy is destined to come true: Lucius' adventures will be the subject of a book, namely the *Metamorphoses* itself. But the *gloriam satis floridam* which he will gain through such immortalization is not what he expects. At the start of book 3, when Lucius is anticipating arrest for the 'mur-der' of the wineskins, he notes with chagrin that Diophanes has tricked him; his stay in Hypata is destined to win him disgrace and ridicule rather than glory (3. 1. 11–12). Later, after he has been seized by the magistrates and is being led forward to be put on display at the mock trial in the Festival of Laughter, Lucius is amazed to note that the spectators are all doubled over with laughter at his plight: 'obli-quato tamen aspectu rem admirationis conspicio: nam inter tot milia populi circumsecus vadentis nemo prorsum, qui non risu dirumpere-tur, aderat' (3. 2. 9–12). This hilarious reaction of the crowd to the ridiculous situation in which Lucius finds himself typifies the 'glory' which he, a fictitious character, is to win as the hero of Apuleius' *Metamorphoses*. Diophanes, the quack prophet, had predicted that Lucius' adventures would be the material for an *incredundam fabulam*, 'a fantastic story,' but Lucius had hoped that he would be the valor-ous hero of such a story, not a comic character who is changed into an ass. Diophanes himself was unable to overcome the force of power-ful *fortuna*, and he and his prophecies are not to be taken very seri-ously, any more than is Lucius of Corinth, the unfortunate ass, who is himself buffeted about by fortune until his rescue by the gods.

The discrediting of Diophanes gives an added importance to the prophecy of Osiris in book 11. While Apuleius always dissociates himself from Lucius, the comic character, in Osiris' prophecy he ‖ momentarily identifies with (by the extreme method of seeming to *become*) Lucius, the recipient of the glory of Isis and Osiris. The prophecy of Diophanes, predicting the eternal glory of Apuleius' novel, is trivial and untrustworthy at best; the prophecy of Osiris, predicting the eternal glory bestowed by the gods, must be believed. For unlike the classical Roman poets,[42] Apuleius (at least in the *Metamorphoses*) is unable to take himself seriously enough to make an eloquent claim that his literary monument will win him immortality. His attitude toward literary fame, as suggested by the Diophanes scene, is self-effacing to a degree which, on the strength of his minor writings alone, we should hardly have guessed that Apuleius could attain. But in dealing with Isis and Osiris, Apuleius discards the irony with which he views his novel. To demonstrate the depth of his emotional commitment to these powerful deities, the author takes the unusual step of intruding personally into his narrative, in order to testify that the glory of acceptance by Isis and Osiris is what matters most to him. ‖

AFTERWORD 1997

This paper is an expanded version of some of the themes raised in my doctoral dissertation (Smith 1968). It called for a new look at the resonance and depth of narrative technique of Apuleius, who was certainly then, though less so now, one of the more neglected and underrated Latin writers. One of the paper's important contributions was to make a clear distinction between the narrator himself, with his imperfections and limited perspective, and the author, who uses his narrator as a comic foil while at the same time continually introducing surprises for and tricks on the reader. On pages 208 ff. I leave too vaguely motivated the presence of comic surprise in a novel of magic metamorphoses. In later papers I develop this more satisfyingly as part of a Gothic style and a religious view of the world in which uncertainty and unpredictability prevail; at its most profound, this view takes us far beyond the superficial practical jokes of a comedy (Smith 1993, 1994). Such an approach is developed meaningfully in Shumate (1996a). In the new atmosphere of greater respect for the depths of Apuleius' novel, it no longer seems heretical to see him as an isolated genius, a kind of lone wolf amongst the writers of later antiquity, or indeed to conclude that the *Golden Ass* looks forward to the spiritual agonizing of such different authors as Augustine and Kafka.

---

[42] Notably Horace, *Carm.* 3. 30 and Ovid, *Met.* 15. 871–2.

Too much is also made in this paper of Lucius as a kind of naive simpleton who seems unaware of the effect of his own words. This had its use at the time as a corrective to a few commentators such as Helm and Perry, who sometimes seemed to see Apuleius himself as an unskilled craftsman who had little interest in consistency. In transferring the naiveté to the narrator, my paper invited a new and modernized method of narrative technique in Apuleian criticism. However, the *auctor–actor* dichotomy (to use Winkler's phrase) can only be maintained just so far; and I now see Lucius the narrator himself as much more of a clever manipulator who makes a deliberate choice to advance or hold back information and wants to keep us as readers at arm's length.

I think that the analogies I made in the paper with Aristophanes, Plautus, Chaucer, and Sterne are all helpful ones which could have been fruitfully developed further. Those who have quoted the paper over the years have sometimes left a misleading impression of it by implying that the Plautus analogy was the main subject of my study. Plautus is helpful as a comparison, but he hardly takes us to the depths of complexity that we find in the *Golden Ass*. There is still much about Apuleius to explore.

10

Fabula graecanica: Apuleius and his Greek Sources

H. J. MASON

It would be curiously perverse to attempt to consider the *Golden Ass* without considering its sources. In the prologue, such phrases as 'sermone isto Milesio'[1] and 'fabula graecanica' are clearly meant to make the reader think about the work's relationship to various literary forms, and there are phrases elsewhere, notably *Met.* 10. 2 (237. 12) 'scito te tragoediam non fabulam legere', which have the same purpose. Besides, Apuleius was, as can be seen from the *Florida* and the philosophical works, a man widely read and not averse to reproducing others' ideas,[2] and, in matters of vocabulary at least, 'nihil scribens sine exemplo'.[3]

The prologue closes with the sentences 'fabulam graecanicam incipimus. lector intende: laetaberis'. Although we have been warned to think twice before taking any statement in the prologue at face value,[4] this seems unambiguous: the story about to be told is (in some sense) Greek, and the reader will derive pleasure from it. I find it difficult not to draw the conclusion that the Greekness of the story is one of the things which will cause pleasure.

The phrase *fabula graecanica* is not, however, entirely straightforward. *Fabula* clearly has a general meaning of 'tale' or 'story', perhaps with a little more of the sense of 'fiction' than those English words; but it also has a number of specific meanings, such as 'fable', 'myth' and 'play',[5] which are singularly appropriate for the interpretation of

---

[1] See Scobie (1975).
[2] Note the derivative nature of *Flor.* 15, marked by such phrases as 'sunt qui . . . aiant' (14), 'fama obtinet' (15), and Beaujeu's comment (1973: p. xi), 'habitué à faire sa pâture de connaissances prises chez les autres.'
[3] Oudendorp (1986) on *Met.* 4. 5 (see i. 246 of his edition).
[4] Wright (1973: 217–18).
[5] *Oxford Latin Dictionary*, s.v. *fabula* (fasc. 3, p. 665).

Apuleius. It would be typical of Apuleius' use of language for a word to bear more than one meaning at the same time,[6] and hence a pity to suggest a translation such as 'romance',[7] which, however suitable as a description of the *Golden Ass*, eliminates the possibility of more than one meaning.

Graecanicus is not simply a variant form for *graecus* chosen for the sake of the prose rhythm, but has a very precise meaning, which can be seen in Varro, *LL* 10. 70–1,[8] a discussion of the terminations of proper names; forms with Greek endings (e.g. *Hectora*) are *graeca*, those with Latin endings (e.g. *Hectorem*) are *graecanica*. *Graecanicus* means something like 'adapted' (into Latin) 'from Greek';[9] it is useful to compare *Met.* 10. 29 (260. 21 f.) 'Graecanicam saltaturi pyrricam', remembering that the *pyrrica*, of Greek origin, had become a favourite dance form in Rome.[10] The story is described as Greek, but adapted to Latin in some way. In terms of sources, we are perhaps reminded to consider Roman intermediaries for the transmission of Greek material.

What did Apuleius mean to tell his reader by the assertion that he was starting a *fabula graecanica*? The obvious answer has always been to say that he was alluding to a written Greek version of the story, especially since one is extant in the work called Λούκιος ἢ Ὄνος in our manuscripts of Lucian, which I shall call *Onos* for short. Beroaldus explained *fabula graecanica* with reference to the *Onos* in this way, 'quia ad exemplar Luciani graeci scriptoris condita est, ex quo asinum aureum paene transcribit'. Since the text of Photius became available, the relationship has been seen as more complex; in *Bibliotheke*, cod. ‖ 129, the Patriarch described a work which he called Λουκίου Πατρέως μεταμορφώσεων λόγοι διάφοροι and compared with the Lucianic *Onos*. Modern scholars have tended to support Photius' view that the *Onos* was an abbreviation of the *Metamorphoseis*[12] of 'Lucius', and to consider that it was 'Lucius' work which Apuleius adapted when writing the *Golden Ass*.[13] But the argument about the

---

[6] e.g. the use of *curiose* in *Met.* 2. 1 (24. 24) 'curiose singula considerabam', and elsewhere (Scobie 1969: 77).   [7] Scobie (1975: 76).

[8] Scobie (1975) follows Molt (1938: 29) in supplying a wrong reference (*L* 9. 3) and ascribing to Varro words ('illa nempe . . . traducta'), which in fact derive from Hildebrand (1842)'s commentary *ad loc*.   [9] Pepe (1963: 131–2).

[10] Suet. *Caes.* 39; *Nero* 12; HA *Hadrian.* 19; Dion. Hal. *Ant.* 7. 7. 2.

[11] Oudendorp (1823: 12).

[12] I review the history of the question in Mason (1976).

[13] I refer to the reconstructed work as *Metamorphoseis* and to Apuleius' novel as *Golden Ass*, to distinguish them as much as possible, although citations of Apuleius are in the usual form (*Met.* 1. 1 etc.).

meaning of *fabula graecanica* remains the same; Apuleius labelled his book as a *fabula graecanica* to allude to its derivation from the Greek *Metamorphoseis* of 'Lucius of Patrae'.[14]

I believe that this was not Apuleius' purpose; but before entering into discussion of his intent, we should first consider the Greek *Metamorphoseis* and Apuleius' relationship to them.

First, their author. 'Who', as Perry asked in 1968, 'was Lucius of Patrae?'[15] The narrator of the *Onos* is called Lucius and is from Patrae (*Onos* 55. 3); it would be implausible to view the narrator as also the author of that work. It *is* possible for an author to use his own name in first-person narrative in a work of imaginative fiction, as Lucian does in the *Vera historia* (2. 28), but to do so has its risks. An interview with a modern writer of fiction, Jorge Luis Borges, is instructive:[16]

QUESTION. In your story, 'The Aleph', you have a character named Borges. Since I presume that what happens to him is fiction and not truth, I wonder why you use your own name.

BORGES. Well, I thought of that kind of thing happening to myself. Besides, I'd been jilted by Beatriz Viterbo [a character in the story]—of course under another name—and so I used my own name.

DI GIOVANNI. Which you've done in several places.

BORGES. Yes, I always do it; of course I don't try to make myself into a laughing butt.

But Lucius of the *Onos* is clearly made into a laughing butt.[17] It is unlikely that an ancient audience could be counted on to make the distinction which Borges demands of his readers, between Borges the author and Borges the narrator. Augustine's reading of the *Golden Ass* (*Civ. Dei*. 18. 18) rests on his failure to make such a distinction.[18]

If we follow the 'orthodox' (Bürger) view of the *Onos*, as a fairly mechanical epitomizing of the *Metamorphoseis*,[19] it follows that the *Metamorphoseis* also had as narrator one Lucius from Patrae, and the same arguments will apply to the original as to the *Onos*.

Rohde held that the *Onos* epitomized the *Metamorphoseis* (which he viewed as a 'serious' work dealing with magic and metamorphosis in

---

[14] Vallette (Robertson and Vallette 1940–5: pp. viii–ix), 'A supposer même qu'il n'entende pas par là présenter son oeuvre comme une traduction . . .'.

[15] Perry (1968: 97–101).   [16] di Giovanni (1973: 58).

[17] Perry (1920: 14), 'it is safe to say that . . . no pagan author of a humorous book would deliberately describe himself as an ass and a fool.'   [18] Perry (1967: 212).

[19] Bürger (1887: 54).

a spirit of belief) in such a way as to satirize them and their author by making him, although described as ἱστοριῶν συγγραφεύς (*Onos* 55. 3), the victim of a set of ridiculous adventures.[20] But this argument runs against Photius' account of the process of abbreviation, that the shorter work employed αὐταῖς τε λέξεσι καὶ συντάξεσιν as the longer, and it is inherently unlikely that abbreviation alone could have the effect of changing the tone of the ass-story from serious belief to satire.[21] 'Lucius of Patrae' is a fictional character, just like 'Lucius of Corinth' in the *Golden Ass*.

Lucian, as was argued clearly by Wieland, could never have been the author of an epitome of another's work.[22] Perry was right in arguing that, if Lucian had any connection with the story, it was with the original *Metamorphoseis*.[23] His case is well presented, and has convinced many;[24] but it is not clear to me that the process of epitomizing and ‖ the use of a style deliberately imitative of that of popular story-telling is enough to explain the linguistic differences from Lucian's work,[25] nor am I certain (a far more subjective judgement) that the *Metamorphoseis*, as we can reconstruct them on the basis of the *Onos*, were indeed the kind of thing which Lucian wrote.[26]

If it was not Lucian, we simply don't know who the author might have been; the Dilthey–Cocchia hypothesis, that Apuleius himself wrote the Greek *Metamorphoseis*, was never adequately defended and rested on some highly dubious assumptions.[27] Van Thiel's proposal, one of the sons of Flavius Alexander of Hypata, is guesswork at best.[28]

What we may assume about the author is that he wrote some time after the settling of a Roman colony at Patrae in 14 BC; the description of the close ties of Lucius' family with the Roman governor (*Onos* 55. 4) suggests a situation that developed somewhat later, in the time of Plutarch, rather than the age of Augustus.[29] The fact that the author does not follow 'Attic' linguistic norms[30] is significant, suggesting that

---

[20] E. Rohde (1869).   [21] Bürger (1902: 12–16).
[22] Wieland (1789: 296–305).   [23] Perry (1920: 59–74, 1967: 211–35).
[24] Mazzarino (1950: 85); McLeod (1967: 47–51); Vallette (Robertson and Vallette 1940–5: p. xv); Walsh (1970: 146).   [25] Cobet (1873: 260).
[26] Anderson (1976) attempts to show that the Greek ass-story is Lucianic by comparison with other works; I am grateful to the author for allowing me to see proofs of the work before publication.   [27] See Landi (1922).
[28] Van Thiel (1971b: 40–2); see Mason (1972).
[29] See Bowersock (1969) and Jones (1971).
[30] Van Thiel (1971b: 211): 'ist er kein Attizist.'

we should not expect him to be one of the 'establishment' of the Second Sophistic.[31]

But in any case, interesting though the discussion of authorship is, its solution would add very little to our understanding of Apuleius, except perhaps in matters of chronology, just as discussions of the authorship of the Greek original of a play of Plautus or Terence tend to shed more light on Menander and his contemporaries than on the Roman playwrights.[32]

What was in the *Metamorphoseis?* Perry, more than anyone else, demonstrated that they contained only the story of the ass, not a series of metamorphosis-stories.[33] The case of Bürger and others, that the *Onos* was an epitome of the *Metamorphoseis* and that it was the *Metamorphoseis* which Apuleius adopted, rests ultimately on relatively few passages. Notable among these are *Onos* 24 (the cross-roads), 38 (the whip of the Galloi), 40–1 (the rabid ass) and 44 (the soldier speaks Latin to the gardener).[34] In each of these places, there are *two* reasons for supposing that material in the *Golden Ass* but not in the *Onos* should be ascribed to the *Metamorphoseis*. First, there is something wrong with the text of the *Onos*, even without comparison with the Latin version—for example, ἐκείνῃ τῇ ... μάστιγι in *Onos* 38, with no antecedent for ἐκείνῃ, or πρῶτα μὲν ... τῇ Ἰταλῶν φωνῇ in *Onos* 44, with no answering δέ clause. Second, in each case Apuleius' text can be shown to be following the Greek very closely in the passages around the difficulties in the *Onos*, so that we are justified in assuming that those passages of Apuleius which can be used to make sense of the *Onos* are derived from an equally close rendering of passages in the *Metamorphoseis* which the epitomizer dropped.[35] There are quite rigorous conditions; Junghanns calculated that passages which

---

[31] Lucian's *Lexiphanes* and above all Phrynichus indicate that Atticism of grammar and vocabulary was the 'establishment' position.

[32] Gomme and Sandbach (1973: 4–10).   [33] Perry (1920: 21–31, 1967: 215).

[34] Perry (1920: 9–11).

[35] Perry (1920: 9–10) discussing *Onos* 38 makes these two criteria explicit: 'The second reference to the whip in Apuleius is an obvious translation of . . . the *Onos*. It was not, therefore, added by Apuleius himself but taken from that one of the Greek versions upon which he based his story. The same is also true of the first reference to the whip since the second presupposes it. Inasmuch as the two references are not found in the *Onos*, Apuleius must have taken them from the *Metamorphoseis*. . . . Comparing the two logical and consistent references to the whip with the single meaningless allusions in the *Onos*, no one can doubt that the latter work is an abridgement of the former.'

meet them would produce a *Metamorphoseis* about five pages longer than the *Onos*.[36] Even if we accept into the *Metamorphoseis* passages which might meet these criteria but were not included by Junghanns (e.g., some mention of Charite's marriage, *Met.* 7. 14 = *Onos* 27. 1),[37] the *Metamorphoseis* are seen to be a work of the same general dimensions as the *Onos*, and essentially similar in tone.

Some scholars have been willing to ascribe to the *Metamorphoseis* considerably more of the *Golden Ass*, notably the *novelle*. Here neither of the two criteria mentioned above applies, and a decision to ascribe the passages to the Greek original is based ultimately on assumptions about that original (e.g., if stories like those of Socrates and Aristomenes and of Thelyphron were included, it would make Photius' account of Lucius of Patrae as one who believed in magic more plausible). Such assumptions are notoriously difficult to prove; the discussion of the 'Diophanes' incident in Apuleius (*Met.* 2. 12–14) illustrates ‖ the problem beautifully. Van Thiel ascribes the incident to the *Metamorphoseis* because of similarities with the account of the Galloi in *Onos* 35–41, but Junghanns used the same comparison to draw the opposite conclusion, that 'Diophanes' was an Apuleian innovation.[38]

It may be plausible to suggest, as did Lesky,[39] that phrases such as λόγος πολὺς ἐν τῷ συμποσίῳ τῶν ἀνδροφόνων (*Onos* 21. 2) point to possible inserted stories in the *Metamorphoseis*. But that does not prove that they were the same ones as in Apuleius. Where an incident is reported fully in both extant versions, Apuleius is clearly capable of, and interested in, giving the topic a quite different treatment from the Greek; a notable example is the presentation of Photis-Palaestra.[40] For incidents where we do not have a Greek text, it is impossible for us to tell if Apuleius is making major changes as he does with the Palaestra incidents, or keeping closer to the original as he does with the Syrian priests or the account of intercourse with a woman. It seems to me, under the circumstances, methodologically unsound to ascribe to the *Metamorphoseis* anything more than what we can prove with reasonable certainty; this produces a *Metamorphoseis* much closer in content and dimensions to the *Onos* than to the *Golden Ass*.

---

[36] Junghanns (1932: 118) (See also Walsh 1970: 19; Scobie 1975: 43).

[37] Junghanns (1932: 79 n. 119); van Thiel (1971b: 125); Bianco (1971: 103–5).

[38] Van Thiel (1971b: 69); Junghanns (1932: 93 n. 142, 128 n. 16). Junghanns is surely right in suggesting that the theme of false prophecy is an Apuleian innovation in both places.   [39] Lesky (1941: 55).

[40] Scobie (1969: 56–65).

This also means that the *Metamorphoseis* were similar in *tone* to the *Onos*; Photius' contrast between Lucius, who believes in metamorphosis, and Lucian, who pokes fun at Greek superstition, then becomes difficult to accept. The correct explanation of Photius' opposition is first, to assume that the character Lucius in the *Metamorphoseis* made a statement comparable to that made by his counterpart in Apuleius (*Met.* I. 20 : 18. 22), 'ego vero . . . nihil impossibile arbitror',[41] and second, to suggest that Photius' judgement about Lucian reflects his memory of other works than the *Onos*. We should not forget that Photius' report in codex 129 was on his reading of the *Metamorphoseis*; it is legitimate to ask if his statements about the *Onos*[42] indicate that he went back and consulted that work again or merely based his report on the memory of a recent reading.[43]

Whether the *Metamorphoseis* should be viewed as a satire on Greek religious or philosophical ideas[44] or as something more serious and believing, depends on one's interpretation of the *Onos*; like Werner, 'beim besten Willen', I find traces of satire in the *Onos* hard to find.[45]

In general, if we assume that the *Metamorphoseis* were basically similar to the *Onos*, what has Apuleius done with his source? Obviously, even if we deny that the *Metamorphoseis* were satirical, it is clear that Apuleius has altered the tone of the story.[46] In addition to the obvious changes, Cupid and Psyche, the ending, the inserted *novelle*, Junghanns and others have demonstrated how Apuleius' general narrative technique differed from his original,[47] and we have learned much along these lines about 'l'Apuleianità di Apuleio' from recent works.[48]

Van Thiel's *Synoptische Ausgabe* has made possible the consideration of Apuleius' technique at a line-by-line level. It is quite instructive. There are some obvious places where Apuleius seems to be simply translating,[49]

Onos 46. 1	Met. 10. 1 (236. 10 f.)
τῇ δὲ ὑστεραίᾳ τί μὲν ἔπαθεν ὁ κηπουρὸς ὁ ἐμὸς δεσπότης οὐκ οἶδα, ὁ δὲ στρατιώτης . . .	Die sequenti meus quidem dominus hortulanus quid egerit nescio, me tamen miles ille . . . ‖

---

[41] Perry (1920: 51).   [42] Bürger (1887: 8).
[43] I have not yet seen Hägg (1975), which should throw light on Photius' methods.
[44] Merkelbach (1962: 338), 'Es war ein satirischer Roman der die pythagoreische Seelenwanderungslehre parodierte.'
[45] Werner (1918: 229).   [46] Perry (1967: 250).
[47] Apart from Junghanns (1932), see Paratore (1942) and Scobie (1969: 55–82).
[48] Mazzarino (1950: ch. VIII, p. 134).   [49] Knaut (1868: 16–17).

Onos 17. 2

ἐπεὶ δὲ ἦν αὐτὸ μέσον τῆς ἡμέρας, κατελύομεν εἴς τινα ἔπαυλιν συνήθων ἐκείνοις ἀνθρώπων.

Met. 4. 1 (74. 9 ff.)

Diem ferme circa medium, cum iam flagrantia solis caleretur, in pago quodam apud notos ac familiares latronibus senes devertimus.

But in most places, there are characteristic additions, such as the phrase 'divinato et antecapto meo cogitatu' (Met. 4. 5 : 77. 24) substituted for the Greek ἴσως ἐμοὶ τὰ αὐτὰ νοήσας (Onos 19. 4), or the lively account of what the animals carried, in Met. 8. 15 (188. 16 f.), 'quidquid infirmo gradu fugam morabatur, nostris quoque pedibus ambulabat'.

Apuleius often drops material from the Greek to give the story his own particular flavour; a notable example is Onos 11. 3 = Met. 3. 19.[50]

Onos 11. 3

οἶμαι δὲ καὶ σὲ οὐκ ἀπείρως τῆσδε τῆς τέχνης ἔχειν· τοῦτο δὲ οὐ παρ' ἑτέρου μαθών, ἀλλὰ παρὰ τῆς ἐμαυτοῦ ψυχῆς λαβὼν οἶδα, ἐπεί με τὸν πάλαι ἀδαμάντινον, ὡς ἔλεγον αἱ γυναῖκες, ἐς μηδεμίαν γυναῖκα τὰ ὄμματα ταῦτα ἐρωτικῶς ποτε ἐκτείναντα συλλαβοῦσα τῇ τέχνῃ ταύτῃ αἰχμάλωτον ἔχεις ἐρωτικῷ πολέμῳ ψυχαγωγοῦσα.

Met. 3. 19 (66. 15 ff.)

Quamquam mihi nec ipsa tu videare rerum rudis vel expers. Scio istud et plane sentio, cum semper alioquin spretorem matronalium amplexuum sic tuis istis micantibus oculis et rubentibus bucculis et renidenti-bus crinibus et hiantibus osculis et fraglantibus papillis in servilem modum addictum atque mancipa-tum teneas volentem.

Here the passages are comparable in length (fifty words in the Onos, forty-six in the Latin), and the Greek is perfectly coherent and shows no sign of epitomizing. As is often the case when the two texts are compared,[51] there are details (οὐ παρ' ἑτέρου μαθών κτλ.) in the Greek which are not in the Latin. The baroque descriptive sentence which makes up the bulk of the Latin passage, the imagery of slav-ery rather than battle which draws on Latin literary models, the sub-tle change in the account of Lucius' attitudes to women, from 'tough as steel, as the women say, never turning an eye towards any woman in a sexy way', to 'shunning matronly embraces'—these are all clearly Apuleian features, and it would be foolish in the extreme to suggest that they represent anything that could have been lost in

[50] Sandy (1978) discusses this passage and shows its debt to the sermo amatorius.
[51] Bianco (1971: 157), 'frequenti sono i brani latini, al confronto, più sommari.' Cf. Teuffel (1889: 572), and Junghanns (1932: 79 n. 118 ad fin), 'ja er kürzt sogar.'

the process of epitomizing the Greek text. In fairly long passages where the two texts run parallel, Apuleius may sometimes abbreviate the Greek version, as at *Onos* 12 = *Met.* 3. 21, the transformation of 'Pamphile',[52] or he may add to it, as in Lucius' transformation, *Onos* 13. 3 = *Met.* 3. 24 (79. 4 ff.), where σπεύδων ἤδη ἀποδύσας χρίω ὅλον ἐμαυτόν becomes: 'Quam ego amplexus ac deosculatus prius utque mihi prosperis faveret volatibus deprecatus . . . avide manus immersi et haurito plusculo uncto corporis mei membra perfricui'. The two passages are each important for the themes of metamorphosis, magic and sex, which are critical for the relevant sections of both books. Apuleius' decision to be brief in one and long in the other surely depends on his own artistic concerns (notably an interest in Lucius' personality, vividly portrayed in the transformation episode) more than on what he found in his primary source.

In dealing with details, as with the major plot, Apuleius appears to range from close dependence on his source to almost complete alteration. Mere translation is rarely continued for more than a sentence or two. It is useful to compare the adaptation of the *Metamorphoseis* with the version of the Aristotelian *De mundo* attributed to Apuleius, ostensibly a translation, but with several characteristic additions.[53]

It is a mistake, then, to describe Apuleius' use of his primary source in the terms used ‖ by Beroaldus, 'ex quo asinum aureum paene transcribit', or to criticize him, as did Butler, for plagiarism:[54]

The total impression made by the *Golden Ass* is astounding, when we consider how little the work contains that is really original . . . Apuleius may have been a literary parasite and a charlatan, but he possessed something near akin to genius and his thefts may be forgiven him.

Apuleius' adaptation is, after all, part of a long tradition of Roman reworking of Greek themes. To criticize him for plagiarism is to miss the point of much of Roman literature and to misunderstand the nature of the creative process. Borges, whom I have already compared to Apuleius, has built his substantial reputation as a writer of fiction on the adaptation of others' material, notably in *The Universal History of Infamy* and *The Book of Imaginary Beings*; his discussion at a seminar at Columbia of the development of his short story 'The Duel' from a

---

[52] Bianco (1971: 143).

[53] Beaujeu (1973: 113), 'Son auteur . . . a conçu son travail comme une adaptation de son modèle . . . Dans tout l'ouvrage, on compte à peine une dizaine de phrases traduites mot à mot.'   [54] Butler (1910: i. 20).

tale he heard orally from two sources is an excellent example of how a writer of fiction actually works.[55]

How should we imagine Apuleius worked with his text? The practicalities of using a papyrus roll make it unlikely that he had it open in front of him on his desk, as it were, while he composed the *Golden Ass*. I suspect he read the Greek text several times, probably half-memorizing it in the process, and then wrote the *Golden Ass* without too much direct consultation of the original. Another possibility is that he had an assistant read to him a chapter or two of the Greek and then, with this fresh in his mind, wrote the relevant section of his own work. The nature of his changes to the original suggest to me that he did not work with the Greek text on a line-by-line basis.

Substantial and complex though Apuleius' debt to the Greek *Metamorphoseis* is, I do not believe that 'fabulam graecanicam incipimus' is intended to acknowledge that relationship. The phrase is clearly coupled with the following sentence, 'lector intende: laetaberis'; the reader is more likely to expect pleasure if he thinks of a wide range of 'Greek stories', rather than one specific tale.

Especially if that tale is not well known. There is, after all, to my knowledge, no reference to *either* version of the Greek ass-story other than Photius' account. It remains to be demonstrated that Greek light literature of this type was widely read in the Rome or Carthage of Apuleius' day; Lucian, for example, is first mentioned in Latin literature by Lactantius, *Inst.* 1. 9.[56] The illustrations of an ass having intercourse with women,[57] and the line of Juvenal (*Sat.* 6. 334) 'quo minus imposito clunem submittit asello', which refers to the same thing,[58] illustrate the familiar topic of the ass's sexuality, but there is no suggestion that the ass is an *Eselmensch*.

Should we expect that Apuleius would formally acknowledge his source, even if it was known to his audience? In general, ancient authors did not make such acknowledgements; one might note that Lucian in the *Vera historia* advertises his criticism of Ktesias and Homer but does not mention his immediate source, Antonius Diogenes (see Photius, *Cod.* 166). The author of the Latin *De mundo* presents the work as his own composition (*De mundo* 289) rather than a translation of an existing work and included a chapter quoting Favorinus that is

---

[55] Di Giovanni (1973: 15–65).
[56] *PIR*[2] L 370; Lucian is cited in his familiar role as one who *diis et hominibus non pepercit.*   [57] Bruneau (1965: 349–57); see also Griffiths (1975: 25).
[58] Schmid (1891: 314 n. 7).

apparently taken whole from Aulus Gellius.[59] Even if the author is not
Apuleius, he offers a fair example of ancient writers' attitudes to
acknowledging sources.

If we accept a broader interpretation of *fabula graecanica* than the
Greek *Eselsroman*, ‖ the following literary categories seem to be suitable for description in Latin as *fabulae*, Greek in origin, and likely to
give the reader pleasure:

1. the short story or *novella*;
2. the extended fictional narrative we usually call the Greek romance;
3. myth and legend, edging over into what we call folk-tale;
4. the (Aesopic) fable;
5. drama, including the range from classical tragedy to mime and
   farce.

There are undoubtedly other Greek influences on Apuleius, most
notably Plato, but they do not fit the term *fabula* or seem relevant in
this context.

The short story. Apuleius' phrase 'sermone isto Milesio' in the prologue,
picked up by 'Milesiae conditorem' (*Met.* 4. 32 : 100. 19) clearly
points to an important form of short-story literature, the Μιλησιακά
written by Aristides and translated into Latin by Sisenna in the last
century BC.[60] Apuleius' allusion will have meant something to his audience; but we, unfortunately, know so little about the *Milesiaka* that
Apuleius' mention of them is not very much help. The most important data we can gather tell us something about their subject matter
and tone. Plutarch (*Crass.* 52. 2) and the author of the Lucianic
Amores (1. 1) term them ἀκόλαστα διηγήματα. Ovid argued in his
defence (*Trist.* 2. 413–14) that Aristides *iunxit crimina secum* without
being exiled, and in another place (*Trist.* 2. 444) called Sisenna's work
turpis iocos. Fronto described Sisenna as 'elegant(em) in lasciviis' (*Ad
M. Caes.* 4. 3. 2, p. 57 van den Hout). The implication surely is that,
like Ovid's *Ars* and *Amores*, the *Milesiaka* treated themes of sexual
behaviour without any moral judgement, and it is for this reason that
the Widow of Ephesus tale in Petronius (111–12) is routinely cited
as the typical example of the *genre*. There are clearly some incidents,
such as the *lepidam de adulterio fabulam* (*Met.* 9. 4–8), which reflect
the tone of the Milesian tales as described in our sources and may well
have derived from Aristides and Sisenna. It is possible that the

---

[59] Beaujeu (1973: p. xi).   [60] Lucas (1907: 16–35); Cataudella (1957: 133–7).

explicit sexuality and general tone of Lucius' dalliance with Photis might have found parallels in the *Milesiaka*, but the incident lacks the ironic 'punch-line' effect of the Widow of Ephesus story, something to justify Ovid's term *iocus*.

The ending of the *Onos* (56. 1–7) does have the appropriate tone; but the attempt to see in Sisenna fr. 10, 'eum penitus utero suo recepit', the direct source of *Met*. 10. 22 (254. 3 f.) 'totum me prorsus, sed totum recepit' (*Onos* 51 εἴσω ὅλον παρεδέξατο), and hence to argue that the ass-story in detail was found in Aristides and Sisenna, lacks a solid foundation.[61] There is, after all, nothing in the Sisenna passage to suggest bestial intercourse, still less intercourse specifically with an ass,[62] and I am far from certain that 'utero recepit' in fact describes intercourse at all.[63] The sexual joke of *Onos* 56 might have had a place in the *Milesiaka*, but the ass-story as a whole, as we can see it in the *Onos*, is much more than this one incident. Would the ass-story have served as a useful comparison for Ovid's *Amores* or, for that matter, upset the moral sensibilities of Parthian officers?

The phrase 'Milesiae conditorem') (*Met*. 4. 32 : 100. 19) suggests that Apuleius viewed his whole tale, or at least Cupid and Psyche, as a *Milesia*; but, even less than the Greek versions of the ass-story, neither resembles *as a whole* what we can discover about the works of Aristides. But there is the possibility that 'Milesio sermone' (and hence 'Milesiae conditorem') refers rather to the structure and style of the work; it has been suggested that the picture in the Lucianic *Amores* of Aristides τοῖς Μιλησιακοῖς λόγοις ‖ ὑπερκηλούμενος means that he told the stories as a *Rahmenperson* in the first person, and that his work had a '1001 nights' format;[64] Graves' explanation[65] (rather than translation), 'a string of anecdotes in the popular Milesian style' expresses this view very well. If Apuleius used 'Milesia' in a purely structural sense, he was surely using it in a novel, and forced, way. Do ancient genre classifications normally reflect technical matters such as structure rather than tone and topic?[66]

---

[61] Reitzenstein (1912: 55); Mazzarino (1950: 77); Kerényi (1927: 205); against, e.g., Walsh (1970: 17 n. 1). [62] Werner (1918: 254).

[63] Unless *uterus* is used to mean vagina, there is an anatomical inaccuracy, and I cannot find examples of *uterus* used in that way; might *utero recipere* mean 'conceive'?

[64] Lavagnini (1923: 9 n. 3); Schissel von Fleschenberg (1913a: 4); Perry (1967: 92–5). [65] Graves (1950: 27).

[66] Menippean satire, for example, might seem to be characterized primarily by its use of *prosimetrum*, but there were topics and attitudes typical of the genre; see Walsh (1970: 19–23).

It would be a mistake to restrict the study of *novelle* as a source for Apuleius to the *Milesiaka*. Even in the general area of love-stories, there was clearly a tradition of more idealistic tales, represented by such collections as Parthenius' *Erotika Pathemata* and Plutarch's *Amatorius*.[67] Many have observed the similarity of Apuleius' version of Charite's death to the tale of the Gallic woman Kamma in Plutarch, *Amatorius* 20.[68] Stories of this type are often set in an historical or mythical context, and were not intended to be viewed as fiction (were the *Milesiaka?*); but they clearly can be described as *fabulae*. Apuleius appears to have drawn on the tradition for some incidents, but the *Golden Ass* as a whole does not fit the category very well.

Lucian's *Philopseudes* reminds us of another important category of anecdotal literature, the collections of *paradoxa*. The fact that his collection is described by one of the speakers as κενῶν καὶ ματαίων ψευσμάτων (40) may even be part of the tradition; I am reminded of the comment by Aristomenes' *comes* (*Met.* I. 20 : 18. 18 f.), 'nihil . . . hac fabula fabulosius, nihil isto mendacio absurdius'. The fully serious collections of *paradoxa*, such as Phlegon's *Mirabilia*, are sometimes mere lists of alleged oddities of nature, but the genre can rise to full-scale ghost-stories of the same character as the tales of witchcraft in the early part of the *Golden Ass*; the first and most elaborate section of Phlegon's work also has as its theme πολυπραγμοσύνη (I. 12) or *curiositas*. By the use of *ut mireris* in the prologue, Apuleius may have intended to direct the reader's attention to the paradoxographers and to suggest the spirit in which to approach his tale. It is also possible that he actually used stories of this type as a source for individual stories,[69] but there is no tale preserved in this tradition which is closely similar to any of Apuleius' tales, and the theme of transformation does not seem to have played a very large part in the genre of paradoxography.

Various types of Greek *novelle*, it would appear, can be seen behind Apuleius' *novelle*, but it is difficult to see any of them as a significant source for the story as a whole.

The Greek romance. The extended Greek romance, with its sentimental assumptions and theme of love, might seem at first glance an unlikely source for the ass-story, except perhaps in an ironic, parodic

[67] Cataudella (1957: 164–72).
[68] Anderson (1909); Cataudella (1957: 76); Erbse (1950); Rohde (1914: 590).
[69] Scobie (1969: 43–54, 1975: 71).

way, the adventures of the ass paralleling those of the romantic hero and heroine. But in fact, as was argued most persuasively by Paratore,[70] many features of the ass-story in the Apuleian version find a close parallel in the romantic novels, and it is hard to deny the possibility of some connection.

The chronology of the various Greek romances is far from certain, but it seems likely that Chariton precedes Apuleius. Even if Apuleius did not use Chariton's novel, it may be used as a typical (indeed restrained) example of the kind of novel Apuleius had accessible to him.

Whatever view one may take of the religious interpretation by Merkelbach and others of the Greek romances, they (especially Xenophon)[71] provide an obvious literary model for the intervention of a divine saviour which Apuleius substituted for the comic end of the *Metamorphoseis*. The *nefaria fortuna* of Apuleius (11. 15 : 277. 18), whose power Isis breaks, and who is much more important, and far more often invoked, than the || βάσκανος δαίμων of the *Onos*,[72] finds a very close parallel in the τύχη βάσκανος or τύχη φιλόνεικος δαίμων of Chariton (1. 14, 2. 8, 4. 1, etc.), addressed in the same rhetorical manner as in Apuleius.[73]

Iamblichus and Achilles Tatius, approximate contemporaries of Apuleius, show that the romantic novel in his day readily admitted the kind of loose structure, complete with digressions, that is so characteristic of the *Golden Ass*.

Turning to details, and concentrating on Chariton, it may not be going too far to seek an explanation for Apuleius' making Lucius a relative of Plutarch in Chariton's identification of his heroine with a daughter of the historical Hermocrates.[74] Aristomenes' somewhat rhetorical attempted suicide (*Met*. 1. 16) is in much the same style as many such suicides in the romances (Charit. 1. 6, 5. 10; Iamblichus 18).[75] The prophecy to Lucius (*Met*. 2. 12 : 35. 10 f.), 'historiam magnam et incredundam fabulam et libros me futurum', with its ironic reference to the story itself, recalls Callirhoe's complaint (Charit. 5, 5) διήγημα γέγονα. The two trial scenes in the *Golden Ass* (3. 1–11, 10. 7–12) are remarkably similar to the trials in the romances (e.g. Charit. 3. 4). One might note, for example, that the use of torture, described by Apuleius as *ritu Graeciensi* (*Met*. 3. 9 : 58. 11) and *more*

---

[70] Paratore (1942: 35, 55, 67, etc.).   [71] Fredouille (1975: 28).
[72] Ciaffi (1960: 165).   [73] Kerényi (1927: 180, 189).
[74] Heine (1962: 50).   [75] Ciaffi (1960: 127).

Graecorum (*Met.* 10. 10 : 244. 21), closely parallels that in the Chariton
passage, with the same instruments, and that Lucius' inability to speak
(*Met.* 3. 4 : 55. 2 ff.) is exactly comparable to Chaereas' silence in Charit.
3. 4. The bandits in the central books of Apuleius are similar to those
in the romances,[76] somewhat romanticized and assimilated to real soldiers. Such features as their formal assembly and debate on Charite's
fate (*Met.* 7. 5, 9) recall details in Chariton (1. 7, 10). It is also at least
worth pointing out that the name which Tlepolemus chooses for
the father of the bandit-*persona* 'Haemus' is *Theron* (*Met.* 7. 5–6), the
name of the chief bandit in Chariton (1. 7). The whole 'Charite-
complex' was compared by Paratore with the romantic novels.[77]
The 'false death' of a young man due to a hypnotic administered
by a doctor (*Met.* 10. 11–12) recalls the endless *Scheintöde* of Greek
romances but above all Xen. *Eph.* 3. 5. 11.[78] The list could go on; it is
clear that Apuleius must have used the sentimental Greek romances
as a major source, and an examination of Cupid and Psyche would
suggest a still greater indebtedness.[79] The fact that elements from ideal
romances are set in the comic framework of the ass-story should not
be taken to imply that they are being parodied or criticized; it is perhaps the most significant part of Apuleius' *contaminatio* technique that
he attempted to integrate into a single work both a comic-ironic and
an ideal-sentimental view of the world.[80]

Myth and folklore. The central story of a man turned into an ass by
magic, in spite of its widespread appearance in modern folklore, does
not find a direct source in the vast store of Greek mythology and legend. Folk-lore in the modern sense, where we can trace it in antiquity, also does not record the story. Metamorphosis in the Ovidian
sense is, after all, normally a one-way street, a Just So story explaining something like Echo. Unfortunates changed into animals stay that
way; those like Io that do recover human form may have retained
human senses but the idea is not exploited as it is in the ass-story. The
companions of Odysseus turned into pigs, *Od.* 10. 239–240, whose νοῦς
ἦν ἔμπεδος ὡς το πάρος περ, provide a closer parallel, and there are
reminiscences of Homer elsewhere.[81] But Ovid's version (*Met.* 14.

---

[76] Riefstahl (1938: 90); Werner (1918: 261).
[77] Paratore (1942: 67); cf. Riefstahl (1938: 83 n. 11).
[78] Hammer (1925: 16); Hammer stresses 'quae sine dubio in fabellae suae compositione fabulis Romanensibus Apuleius debet' (17).
[79] Paratore (1942: 355); 'nello stesso ambiente morale degli eroi del romanzo greco.'
[80] Perry (1967: 282).   [81] Helm (1961: 23); the allusions are mostly comic.

276–305) makes more of the theme than Homer; Homer's brief narrative is probably not a very direct source for Apuleius' (or the *Onos*') treatment of transformation.

Griffiths may well be right in postulating a basically Egyptian origin, stressing Egyptian ‖ traditions of theriomorphic gods and of the theme of transformation; although 'an Egyptian version of the story is not actually attested',[82] there is a greater likelihood of an Egyptian than a Greek origin in mythological terms. It is possible that 'papyrun Aegyptiam argutia Nilotici calami inscriptam' (*Met.* I. 1) refers to the Egyptian background to the idea of metamorphosis, although Graves again overtranslates,[83] 'if you are not put off by the Egyptian story-telling convention which allows humans to be changed into animals'.

Fable. There is, of course, a form of literature which *assumes* that animals think like humans, the Aesopic fable. Many of the anecdotes concerning the ass in Apuleius recall ass-stories in the *Aesopica*, and the ass is one of the favourite animals in the tradition; Apollonius described the Aesopic tales as dealing with βάτραχοι καὶ ὄνοι καὶ λῆροι γραυσὶν οἷοι μασᾶσθαι καὶ παιδίοις.[84] The parallels with the *Eselsroman* were first noted by Crusius and have been discussed by many others.[85] Among the many Aesopic asses that resemble Lucius are those in *Aes.* 179 (Perry) (ὄνος καὶ κηπουρός), 181 (ὄνος καὶ ἡμίονος), 182 (ὄνος βαστάζων ἄγαλμα), 183 (the theme of κατακρημνίζεσθαι), 187 (the ass pretends to be lame), 359 (ὄνος παίζων), 459 and 460. Nearly all of these occur also in the *Onos*, so that the introduction into the ass-story of Aesopic themes should be traced back to the *Metamorphoseis*. But Apuleius was very interested in the Aesopic fable, telling the tale of the Fox and the Crow with characteristic rhetorical embellishments and calling it, significantly, a *fabula* (*Soc. praef.* 4, p. 168 Beaujeu). He reworked the tale of ὄνου παρακύψις (*Onos* 45. 8) to add a reference to ὄνου σκιά, 'umbra asini' (*Met.* 9. 42 : 236. 7).

I think that it is possible that Apuleius also used the tradition of the *Vita Aesopi*, which is Isiac in its oldest version.[86] The account of a stolen *phiale* hidden in the baggage on the ass's back (*Met.* 9. 9–10; cf. *Onos* 41. 4–5) may reflect a reconsideration of a similar incident in the *Vita Aesopi* (127–8); for example, the search through the baggage takes place

---

[82] Griffiths (1975: 20–31: 26).   [83] Graves (1950: 25).
[84] Philostr. *VA* 5. 14 = Perry (1952: T 100, p. 238).
[85] Crusius (1889); Wendland (1911); van Thiel (1971b: i. 184–6); Scobie (1974, 1975: 31–3).   [86] Perry (1952: 2).

after returning to the city in both Apuleius and the *Vita*, while still on the road in the *Onos*. The ironic description of Socrates as 'carus Endymion . . . Catamitus meus' (*Met.* 1. 12 : 11. 12) finds a close parallel in the description of Aesop by his owner's wife as Ἀπόλλωνα ὄψει ἢ Ἐνδυμίωνα ἢ Γανυμήδην, *Vita Aes.* (G) 29. There are also some similarities between the elaborate and humorous account of the sale of the ass in *Met.* 8. 23–5 and the sale of Aesop in *Vita* 22–7, though here I would not press the comparison too far. There is thus some indication that Apuleius may have had access to a *Vita Aesopi* as well as to the tradition of Aesopica already present in the *Metamorphoseis*.

From the Aesopic tradition, the ass-story could derive such themes as the animal's stupidity, stubbornness, sexual characteristics and even curiosity.[87] The Aesopic fable is surely one of the elements Apuleius alluded to in the phrase *fabula graecanica*, and one with a Latin tradition already existing (Phaedrus).

Drama. As in the case of Petronius, it is possible that Apuleius also drew on the traditions of mime. The elaborate Paris-mime at Corinth (*Met.* 10. 30–2) indicates Apuleius' interest in one form of the genre. It is apparent that there was a mime, ultimately deriving from Sophron, with a man in the form of an ass having a speaking part.[88] A fragment of Sophron may also include a scene of intercourse with an ass.[89] It is a pity that we know so little about this ass-mime, as we know so little about the *Milesiaka*.

There are also some individual scenes in Apuleius which recall mimes. The poison-cup incident (*Met.* 10. 26) resembles the 'Oxyrhynchus mime',[90] and the transformation || of Actaeon (*Met.* 2. 4) was treated in a mime.[91] There is a real possibility that mimes were a major source for the ass-story and individual incidents. There was a Latin tradition of mime and farce, and the *Atellana* of Pomponius entitled *Asina* may have dealt with the ass-transformation story, so that *fabula graecanica* seems a justifiable term.[92]

Apuleius translated a passage allegedly from Menander's *Anechomenos* (Beaujeu, pp. 169–170), and was aware of anecdotal material about an author of New Comedy (*Fl.* 16, on the death of Philemon). The phrase 'lector intende: laetaberis' recalls Plautine and Terentian prologues.[93] Many have seen in the treatment of Greek New Comedy

---

[87] Scobie (1975: 30).   [88] Reich (1904, esp. 127); Scobie (1973: 28 n. 8).
[89] Cataudella (1966).   [90] Sudhaus (1906).   [91] Paratore (1942: 39).
[92] Frassinetti (1953: 141); Scobie (1975: 28).
[93] Scobie (1975: 72); Molt (1938: 29).

by Plautus and Terence the closest parallel to Apuleius' adaptation of the Greek *Metamorphoseis*.[94] It is to Menander that Macrobius compares the two Roman novelists, in a class of *fabulae* designed only for entertainment (*Somn. Scip.* 1. 2. 6–12). We might then be justified in looking for a source of Apuleius in Menander.

There is, however, very little. One might argue that Lucius has some of the characteristics of the 'young man' type in comedy, or that Milo owes something to the typical *philargyros*,[95] but the parallels do not extend to points of detail, and Scobie shows how little Photis, for example, owes to a stock comedy type, the *ancilla*.[96] The most notable similarity is that of the brother-and-sister tale in *Met.* 10. 23–28 to the plot of Menander's *Perikeiromene*,[97] also set in Corinth.[98] Apuleius' casual and humorous allusions to mythology, e.g. *Geryoneae caedis* (*Met.* 2. 32 : 52. 3) and *meum Bellerophontem* (*Met.* 7. 26 : 174. 10 f.) are in a tone very similar to that used by Menander, e.g. *Dysc.* 153 (Perseus), *Sam.* 495–6 (Tereus, Oedipus, Thyestes).[99] Some of the names which Apuleius introduces seem to come from New Comedy, notably *Demeas* (*Met.* 1. 21), which is found in *Samia, Misoumenos* and many Latin comedies, and possibly *Pamphile* (*Met.* 2. 5), which occurs in *Epitrepontes*. But all of this is minor; with the possible exception of *Perikeiromene*, there is little to suggest that New Comedy was especially important in Apuleius' mind when he wrote the *Golden Ass*.

Apuleius signals quite clearly in *Met.* 10. 2 (237. 12 f.), 'scito te tragoediam non fabulam legere', what genre is influencing the novella which that sentence introduces.[100] The tale is in the tradition of the Phaedra story, and it is easy to suggest that it goes back to Euripides' *Hippolytus*. Similarly,, the murderess in *Met.* 10. 22–9 seems to recall Medea,[101] and Trenkner sees other tales which recall Euripides, Charite's suicide (*Met.* 8. 13) recalling the *Helen*, the 'Pasiphae' incident (*Met.* 10. 19) the lost *Kressai*, and the poison-cup incident (*Met.* 10. 25) the *Ion*.[102] Casual allusions seem to refer to Euripidean versions of tales, e.g. Medea (*Met.* 1. 10 : 9. 15) and Protesilaus (*Met.* 4. 26 : 95. 16).[103] The difficulty in these cases is to decide if Apuleius was

---

[94] Mazzarino (1950: 144).   [95] Bianco (1971: 40).
[96] Scobie (1969: 56–7).   [97] Trenkner (1958: 93).
[98] Mason (1971) deals with other Corinthian literary allusions.
[99] Helm (1961: 24), 'Diese Verwendung der Mythologie zum Zwecke der Komik teilt der Roman mit Komödie und Satire.'   [100] Paratore (1942: 195 n. 74).
[101] Mason (1971: 163); Cocchia (1915: 329).
[102] Trenkner (1958: 48, 57, 61).   [103] Helm (1961: 406).

directly influenced by Euripides, or by later authors who picked up his themes. The Phaedra-Hippolytus story, for example, was handled by Seneca,[104] the Greek novelists (Xen. *Eph.* 2. 3, 3. 2)[105] and in mimes.[106] Obviously, such plays as Euripides' *Hippolytus* and *Medea* would be very familiar to Apuleius and his audience; but it is likely that some details of the stories, the idea of adapting legends to the very different world of prose fiction, and even some verbal reminiscences, were drawn from later versions.

Euripides' particular contributions to drama, his concern with individual emotions, his willingness substantially to change traditional legends for his own purposes, his concept of fate, and his attitude to plot-construction and the use of the *deus ex machina*, all are extremely important for the background of prose fiction.[107] But his influence on Apuleius is restricted to the *novelle* of love and intrigue. ‖

Apuleius' debt to Greek literature was substantial. Apart from the obvious primary source, the Greek *Metamorphoseis* of 'Lucius of Patrae', it is suggested that the basic plot may have been found in mime, that much of the tone and spirit of the work reflects the Greek romances, and that several details, most notably the *novelle*, derive from Greek short-story forms, comic (*Milesiae*), serious and paradoxical, as well as from the Aesopic fables and from drama. The word *graecanicus* should remind us that much of this Greek literature will have been known to Apuleius in Latin forms (Phaedrus, Plautus, Seneca, Sisenna) as well as in the original Greek. Hammer's judgement of Apuleius' use of sources seems fair:[108]

fabulator ille singulari memoria praeditus, si forte in scribendo e litteris graecis vel latinis vel ex parte similia argumenta ei occurrebant, sedulo ea iuxta praecipuum exemplar in usum suum conferebat—recens adscita cum propositis coniungendo novaque induendo veste. ‖

AFTERWORD 1997

I have dealt with this topic twice since the publication of this article (Mason 1994, 1998). Like many submissions to *ANRW*, Mason (1994) came out almost a decade after most of the research was

---

[104] Hammer (1925: 18–20).
[105] Paratore (1942: 215 n. 107); Trenkner (1958: 65).   [106] Hammer (1925: 11).
[107] Perry (1967: 76, 152, 178).   [108] Hammer (1925: 26).

undertaken; updating and correcting for publication, after so long an interval, a bibliographical review that went back to Poggio strongly reinforced for me the contention that the *Onos* and Lucius of Patrae are less important in understanding Apuleius than a wide variety of other Greek sources. In particular, I would oppose Gerald Sandy's conclusion (Sandy 1994: 1570) that there is little connection between Apuleius and the love romances: I now believe that Persius' line (1. 133) 'post prandia Calliroen do' does indeed refer to Chariton's novel *Chaireas and Callirhoe*, and would place more emphasis on possible links between this work and Apuleius.

In the wake of Winkler (1985) I am now more cautious than I was in taking the narrator's statements about his generic connections such as 'sermone isto Milesio' in the prologue, or 'scito te tragoediam, non fabulam legere' (10. 2) at their face value.

In Mason (1998) I take up and emphasize the suggestion with which I closed this piece, that 'graecanicus' points as much to Latin adaptations of Greek works, such as Plautus and Seneca, as it does to Greek originals.

From a narratological standpoint, the question of language ('vocis immutatio', as the narrator calls it in the prologue) now seems to me crucial. Consider the statement in 4. 32 on Apollo's oracle: in Latin Apuleius says that the Greek-speaking Lucius states that the monolingual Greek *anus* told the Greek-speaking captive girl that the Greek Apollo gave an oracle in Latin 'propter Milesiae conditorem'. Whoever the *conditor* is, the narrative involution is as complex as that of Antonius Diogenes, *Wonders beyond Thule* (cf. Sandy 1989: 776), and the situation recalls Petronius' *Satyrica*, in which a Greek from Massilia comments in Latin on both Greek and Latin topics; on this, and on the nature of Milesian tales, Jensson (1996) is of particular interest.

11
The Unmasked 'I': Apuleius, *Met.* 11. 27

R. T. VAN DER PAARDT

For as soon as I say something, I split off myself, i.e., I am writing, I am a potential of myself but not the other, in short: I am a fictional character.

(tr. from H. Mulisch, *Voer voor psychologen*)

Nam sibi visus est quiete proxima, dum magno deo coronas exaptat, * * * et de eius ore, quo singulorum fata dictat, audisse mitti sibi *Madaurensem, sed admodum pauperem,* cui statim sua sacra deberet ministrare; nam et illi studiorum gloriam et ipsi grande compendium sua comparari providentia.

(Helm 1970: 388)

I

Apuleius has his hero Lucius narrate, in book 11 of the *Metamorphoses,* how he was re-transformed from an ass into a man by eating roses during an Isis-procession in Cenchreae. In gratitude to the goddess, Lucius had himself initiated as a priest of Isis. She admonishes him to go to Rome where, after some time, he finds that his initiation has not been completed: he has not yet become acquainted with Osiris, and initiation in his cult is indispensable. He sees in a dream how a pastophor, notable by his limping gait, will perform this initiation. The next day he sees the figure from his dream in person. This man, whose name (as Lucius will learn afterwards) is Asinius Marcellus—a name immediately referring to Lucius' own adventures as an ass[1]—, recognizes Lucius, too. This episode is followed by the text quoted above.

---

[1] See Griffiths (1975) and Fredouille (1975, *ad loc.*), and especially Marangoni (1974–5: 333–7).

238   R. T. van der Paardt   [96

If we assume with Helm that between *exaptat* and *et* something ||
has been omitted,[2] e.g. <*conspexisse numen divinum*>, we might give
the following provisional translation of the passage: 'For he had had
a dream the night before: while he was arranging garlands for the
great god <he had seen the deity>; and from his mouth, with which
he determines every single man's fate, he had heard that a man from
Madauros[3] was being sent to him—but a very poor one—whom he
had to initiate in his cult immediately; for by his providence glory in
arts and sciences was established for that man and a large reward for
himself'.

I consider myself absolved from the duty of giving a detailed explanation of the remarkably 'free' use of the pronouns[4] and restrict
myself to the main problem: the italicized words in the text, especially
the qualifier *Madaurensem*. Since it is not very probable that Asinius
is speaking of an anonymous third party, Lucius has to be the one who
is labelled as such.

This comes as a great surprise to the linear reader of the novel: up
to now, for ten books, the narrator has been a Greek. It is true that
nowhere he mentioned his place of birth explicitly; passing remarks,
however, indicated Corinth.[5] Anyone who knows that the author of
the novel is from Madauros,[6] cannot but conclude that a confusion
or blending of author and narrator has taken place.

Three courses are open to explain this crux: Apuleius has made ||
an error; our manuscripts are corrupt and a conjecture is needed to
eliminate the inconsistency; the blending of the author and his *alter
ego* is intentional on Apuleius' part. All three courses have been pursued throughout the history of Apuleian scholarship. I will follow the
various philologists in their pursuits in the order indicated above.

---

[2] A lacuna is also assumed by Robertson (1971) and Griffiths (1975). An attractive
conjecture is Luetjohann's *exaptaret* (adopted by Médan 1925 and Fredouille 1975)—
a small correction ($t > r$), which eliminates the necessity to assume a lacuna.

[3] This is probably the correct name; see Griffiths (1975: 60 n. 1).

[4] See Fredouille (1975, *ad loc.*) and in general Callebat (1968: 256 f.).

[5] 1. 22 (26. 12) 'litteras ei a Corinthio Demea scriptas ad eum reddo'; 2. 12 (35. 1–2)
'Corinthi nunc apud nos Chaldaeus quidam'. See e.g. Veyne (1965: 244–5);
Marangoni (1977–8, esp. n. 4).

[6] For evidence see Butler and Owen (1914: p. vii n. 2); *RE* s.v. Apuleius (Schwabe);
Schanz and Hosius (1935: 101). The 'strongest' evidence, viz. *Met.* 11. 27, should not
be used. The remark by Butler and Owen (1914, *loc. cit.*), 'The point would be settled
by August. *Civ. Dei*, VIII. 14, where he is called *Madaurensis*', is too optimistic: the possibility remains that *Madaurensis* has been taken from *Met.* 11. 27. Everything considered, one can be fairly sure that Apuleius was born in Madauros.

II

Apuleius has shamefully forgotten himself here. For how can that man come from Madauros, who throughout the work has represented himself as Lucius the Greek, descended from the famous Plutarch? These things are clearly inconsistent. The end of the story is better narrated by Lucian, or whoever is the author of the Greek story about the Ass.

The above-mentioned words are found in Oudendorp's commentary *ad loc.* (p. 812): unlike the author of the *Onos*, who consistently kept up the fiction of the narrating 'I', Apuleius is supposed to have committed an evident *lapsus calami*. Such an opinion shows little confidence in the author's attentiveness. Scobie[7]—who is practically the only modern Apuleius-expert who wants to keep open the possibility of a blunder on Apuleius' part—advances the argument that more inconsistencies and inadvertencies have been signalized in the novel. Apart from the fact that many of these *res neglegenter compositae*[8] admit of quite different an explanation than that of carelessness on the part of the author, one has to admit that an error of this nature has no parallel elsewhere. Therefore it seems little probable that this explanation of *Madaurensis* puts us on the right track.

III

We can only believe that the nonsensical and foolish *Madaurensem* is corrupt. Perhaps Apuleius wrote *mane Doriensem* instead. The form *Doriensis* is found also at Justin 2.6.16; and that Lucius as a Corinthian is immediately referred to as *Doriensis* might perhaps find its explanation in the fact that the priest is able to recognise him at once as such from his speech. (Goldbacher 1872: 417, tr. Harrison) ‖

The first who tried to solve the *Madaurensis*-problem by means of a conjecture, was Goldbacher; his name is associated with the theory (now generally accepted) that the *Met.* by Apuleius reaches back to a novel of the same name by Lucius of Patrae which has not been preserved, and that the Greek ass-novel ascribed to Lucian (the *Onos*) is

---

[7] Scobie (1969: 81).
[8] See the paragraph with the same name in Helm (1910: p. xv f.); Perry (1926: 242 with nn. 9–11); Stockin (1954: *passim*); van Thiel (1971*b*: I. 19 n. 54, 55); Scobie (1973: 82 and n. 39).

an epitome of the novel by Lucius. Palaeographically, his proposal[9] is made acceptable by a reference to readings like *Mandorensem* and *Maudorensem* in a few, more recent mss. Contextually, Goldbacher (see the quotation above) tries to support his suggestion by assuming that the priest instantly would be able to recognize Lucius by his accent—a random guess, since the novel contains no other allusions to a possible accent of the narrator.

Monceaux[10] and Dee[11] followed Goldbacher in assuming that the absurdity is due to a textual corruption, but did not offer a conjecture. This was done by Robertson in a detailed article.[12] Although Robertson no longer mentions his suggestion in his Budé-text (edited many years later)—not even in the app. crit.—it seems useful to pay some attention to his considerations which led to emendation.

Robertson criticizes not only the questionable identification of author and protagonist but also—thus following in Dee's footsteps —the use of *sed*. The implication of the use of this adversative conjunction would be that *Madaurenses* generally are rich and that Lucius consequently would be a very unusual specimen of this *genus Madaurense*[13]—naturally, we know nothing of such a reputation. These two objections inspire Robertson to the following ‖ reading: 'audisse mitti sibi mandare se <religiosum> sed admodum pauperem', i.e. 'that he (Asinius Marcellus) had heard that he (Osiris) gave orders that to him (Osiris) a religious but very poor man was sent'.

At first sight this would appear to be too drastic a change; Robertson's complete *retractio* seems sensible. Herrmann[14] thinks that *religiosum* differs too much from *Madaurensem* to be probable. But this remark shows that Herrmann does not know Robertson's arguments firsthand: not *religiosum* but *mandare se* replaces *Madaurensem*. 'The change from "*mandare se*" to "*Madaurensem*" is very slight, especially if the *n* in "*mandare*" was represented by a stroke or a small letter above the *a*: nothing would be needed but the erasure of one letter (or stroke), the addition of *v* above the second *a*, and of *n* (or a stroke) above the first *e*, or of *n* between the two words, and the addition of one stroke to the last *e*—"*madărensē*" '.[15]

[9] Goldbacher (1872: 417).   [10] Monceaux (1889: 299).
[11] Dee (1891: 58).   [12] Robertson (1910).
[13] Robertson's opinion (1910: 224) that *Madaurenses* were possibly known to be poor, too, 'so that the sense would be: a Madauran—and poor *even for a Madauran*', seems less probable.   [14] Herrmann (1972: 589).
[15] Robertson (1910: 226).

Somewhat more complicated is the explanation of the disappearance of *religiosum* (possibly followed by *quidem*):[16] after the corruption into *Madaurensem* has taken place, the disappearance of *religiosum* can be explained by haplography (or *saut du même au même*; the endings, with *Nasalstrich*, show a resemblance). This last explanation is not completely convincing; moreover, there are syntactical objections against the conjecture as such. These objections do not so much concern the fact that *sibi* and *se* are to refer now to Osiris instead of Asinius Marcellus,[17] as the peculiar use of *mandare* with the *accusativus cum infinitivo* where Apuleius usually has the (paratactic) subjunctive.[18]

The objections raised by the afore-mentioned Léon Herrmann against *Madaurensem* should be seen in the light of his opinion on the authorship of the various ass-novels. In contrast with what ‖ has generally been viewed—from Goldbacher on—as the correct relation,[19] Herrmann thinks that 'Lucius of Patras' is the author of both the Greek and the Latin *Met.* and that the *Onos* is Lucian's adaptation of it. This theory deprives Apuleius of the authorship of the *Met.*; the reading *Madaurensem* in 11. 27 militates against this theory and therefore cannot be but corrupt in Herrmann's eyes. Herrmann proposes the reading[20] *mitti sibi <a deo fo>rensem, sed admodum pauperem*, which indeed makes the antithesis stand out clearly. Of course this reading is not strong palaeographically: the addition *<a deo>* is contextually unnecessary, and the qualification *forensis* for Lucius is no less unexpected than *Madaurensis*.[21]

The most recent attempt to repudiate *Madaurensem* is at the same time the most ingenious. It stems from J. C. Fredouille and is discussed in the introduction of his recent edition (1975: 15–20). Fredouille's objections against the reading are not new in themselves: first, the coherence of the novel is disturbed by *Madaurensem*; secondly, *sed* implies an antithesis which is not effectuated by *Madaurensem* vs. *pauperem*.

---

[16] Robertson (1910: 225 n. 2).

[17] Cf. *providentia sua*, which has to refer to Osiris rather than to Asinius Marcellus (in the case of *sua sacra* this is a disputable point); see further the literature mentioned in n. 4.   [18] See Callebat (1968: 358).

[19] For a recent survey of the problems, see Mason (1978: 1–7).

[20] Herrmann (1972: n. 14); another possibility mentioned is *<advenam> forensem*, 'mais le fait d'être un *advena* ne constituait pas, bien au contraire, une compensation à sa pauvreté'.

[21] Herrmann himself urges the defence that now it anticipates *quaesticulo forensi* (11. 28: 290. 3), which is equally surprising (see Griffiths 1975, *ad loc.*).

He proposes to read *Corinthiensem*,[22] which solves both the problem of coherence and that of antithesis: Corinthians were proverbially rich[23] and Lucius is an exception which proves the rule. The explanation of the corruption of *Corinthiensem* into *Madaurensem* seems obvious: the scribe, like St Augustine (*Civ. Dei* 18. 18), has confused the author with the narrator or has incorporated a predecessor's marginal note into the text. ‖

Although the reasoning seems plausible, the arguments against the reading in the mss. are not irrefutable. The inconsistency of *Madaurensem* cannot be denied but may be explicable (I will come back to this in a moment); moreover, the objection against *sed*, shared with Dee and Robertson, is not so strong as it seems. Callebat, in his study of Apuleius' idiom, points out that *sed* in Apuleius—as so often in late Latin—does not have an exclusively adversative function: '*Sed* marque souvent chez Apulée moins une opposition, qu'un enrichissement, corrigeant en l'amplifiant un premier énoncé'.[24] The examples mentioned are 4. 31 (99. 5) 'vindictam tuae parenti, sed plenam tribue' (said by Venus to Amor: 'take vengeance for your mother, and fully, too') and 5. 10 (111. 17) 'lares pauperes nostros, sed plane sobrios'. With Gwyn Griffiths one might translate the passage very well in the following way: '. . . he had heard that a man from Madauros was being sent to him, one who was quite poor'.

Now that *sed* has been saved, we are able to consider the remaining problem: why the insertion of the reference to the author behind the narrator?

IV

And so it is certain that Apuleius has finally referred to his own affairs at that point when Lucius is restored to human shape, in order that what we read in the last book of the *Metamorphoses* may be taken as true evidence for his own life. Therefore I deny that it happens casually that Lucius gives himself the sobriquet Madaurensis, since it is by that very word that he gives a clear indication that a transition is being effected to his own affairs; Oudendorp's criticism in accusing the writer of negligence is refuted by this.

---

[22] *Corinthiensis* (instead of the usual *Corinthius*) occurs in Apuleius *Met.* 10. 35: 266. 2.
[23] See Otto (1890: 92); Mason (1971, esp. 164).
[24] Callebat (1968: 91); cf. LHSz 2. 487: '*sed* dient oft in der Umgangssprache der blossen Hervorhebung = "und zwar"'.

Lucius is referred to as a poor man from Madauros (*Madaurensem, sed admodum pauperem*), and the consensus of opinion has rightly seen Apuleius here in the art of dropping the mask and identifying himself with the Lucius of the story.

The above-mentioned quotations from Hildebrand and Gwyn Griffiths[25] reflect the standard solution of the disputed *Madauren-* || *sem*. In my opinion this explanation is inadequate (I will return to this later) even if it is tied in with the theory that *Madaurensem* acts as a *sphragis*.[26] The specific character of our passage is that it contains no reference by the author to himself, nor by the narrator to himself (like in the end of the *Onos*[27]), but an indirect reference to the author behind the narrator.[28]

An interesting explanation of this was given by Bürger,[29] recently supported by Veyne:[30] given that the novel has been published anonymously, *Madaurensem* should be regarded as a signal by the author which could have been appreciated by intimates only. Bürger's thesis is closely bound up with another problem with which the literary historian is faced: the date of the novel. Bürger subscribed to the opinion which in the last century was defended by Rohde,[31] namely that the *Met.* dates from the author's youth (this supposedly appears from the youthful enthusiasm emerging from the book[32]).

Traditionally, a cogent argument has been urged against this: in AD 158 Apuleius was forced to defend himself against a charge of having taken possession of the wealthy widow Pudentilla (and especially her money) by magical practices. If his novel—so much imbued with magic—had already been written at the time, it certainly would have been involved in the accusation and, accordingly, been mentioned in the defense. Bürger thought that his theory of the anonymous publication would at the same time knock || the bottom out of this argument against an early date, since the prosecutors would not have

---

[25] Hildebrand (1842: Praef. xix, tr. Harrison); Griffiths (1975: introd. 5).
[26] Thus e.g. Lesky (1941: 44); Paratore (1942: 65); Walsh (1970: 184 with n. 4); Griffiths (1975, *loc. cit.*). Fundamental for the study of the phenomenon as such is Kranz (1961).   [27] See van Thiel (1971*b*: i. 30).
[28] Cf. Scobie (1973: 82): 'In Apuleius' case a fictitious narrator cites the name (indirectly) of a real author'.   [29] Bürger (1888).
[30] Veyne (1965: 249 and more assertively in a postscript, 251).
[31] Rohde (1885, esp. 85).
[32] Cf. Lindsay (1932: 14): 'The tale has a youthful effervescence which suits better the enthusiast convert of Rome than the wordly-wise and flowery orator of Carthage'.

associated the novel with the defendant. But this, again, is improbable because he was brought to trial by his own relatives-in-law.[33]

There is another objection against Bürger's theory, which can also be raised against the standard opinion as formulated above. Lacking in both views is an explanation of why the identification of protagonist and author occurs in this passage and in this almost casual way.

Among the few who have paid attention to the question why the 'mask of the "I" ' is dropped here of all places, was Rohde. He rightly signalized that some autobiographical elements occur earlier in the novel: 'wenn sein "ego" frisch von der Hochschule in Athen kommt, *sacris pluribus initiatus* heisst, so ist nicht zu verkennen, wie hier Apuleius an einem flüchtigen Durcheinanderschillern des Lucius und seines lateinisch redenden Doppelgängers sich ergötzen wollte'.[34] But why is this 'flüchtig Durcheinanderschillern' replaced by a complete identification in 11. 27? Because (Rohde says) only from this moment on is a real biography being written. To Apuleius, not to Lucius of Corinth, does the *gloria studiorum* apply; the *paupertas* concerns the author, not the protagonist. When, in close connection with our passage, mention is made of a heavy loss of the *patrimonium* (11. 28: 289. 12 f.), this does not fit at all with the rich Lucius—but it does fit in with his spiritual father, who in *Apol.* 23 mentions a similar loss.[35]

This interpretation of the passage as what I would like to call 'referential humor', explains only one aspect. The question remains ‖ why the author does not take the pen from his narrator's hand himself, like Multatuli in his *Max Havelaar* ('Yes, I Multatuli who have borne much, take up the pen'[36]).

What situation do we find at *Met.* 11. 27? A fictitious person, a character in a novel (his name underlines the fictionality) learns by way of a divine encounter or message that the protagonist is no one else but the author. *Ille*, i.e. the *Madaurensis*, is predicted *gloria studiorum*:

---

[33] Cf. Molt (1938: i. 8 n. 2): 'Sed non verisimile est quemquam ex iis, qui Apuleium perdere vellent accusatione magiae, non intellexisse illum "Madaurensem", scribentem de tot miris rebus et plane studiosum rerum magicarum, ipsum Apuleium esse'.

[34] Rohde (1885: 77); see also my remarks on *sacris pluribus initiatus* (van der Paardt 1971: 15: 63. 8). Scobie (1973: 83 n. 41) calls Rohde's explanation 'very weak', but does not say why.

[35] *Apol.* 23: 'profiteor mihi ac fratri meo relictum a patre $\overline{HS}$ $\overline{xx}$ paulo secus, idque a me longa peregrinatione et diutinis studiis et crebis liberalitatibus modice imminutum'. See Butler and Owen (1914, *ad loc.* and introd., p. xi n. 5); Rohde (1885: 79).

[36] See Sötemann (1973: i. 114).

this is a reference to the literary fame of Apuleius himself—on account of this book, of course.

This is not the only occasion of internal reference in the novel. In the story of Amor and Psyche, the narrator (an *anicula delira et temulenta*, although the primary narrator[37] is, of course, Lucius) quotes an oracle from Apollo (4. 32: 100. 18): 'Sed Apollo, quamquam Graecus et Ionicus, propter Milesiae conditorem sic Latina sorte respondit'. Who is this *Milesiae conditor* other than our *Madaurensis?* Gwyn Griffiths, in a note on *studiorum gloriam*, rightly points out that there is an even earlier allusion to the fame of the novel.[38] During his stay in Milo's house, Lucius tells his host that a certain Diophanes, a Chaldean soothsayer, has predicted Lucius that he 'gloriam satis floridam . . . historiam magnam et incredundam fabulam et libros . . . futurum' (2. 12: 35. 9–11), in other words, that he would become a fictional character. Gwyn Griffiths is of the opinion that 'the reading *facturum*, as opposed to *futurum*, seems to be demanded by the present allusion, since something much more is meant than being a subject treated in literature'. But *futurum* is certainly correct: Lucius is not the author, Apuleius is—an insight shared only by gods, Apollo and Osiris.[39] ||

There is still another way in which the fusion of narrator and author in this passage can be explained, namely by placing it within the framework of the novel's theme, the metamorphosis.

What does the author of an 'I'-novel do? He dons (as Bremer says of 'I'-poetry[40]) a mask, he becomes someone else: Apuleius of Madauros becomes Lucius of Corinth!

Come, let me in Milesian fashion string various stories together for you and delight your willing ear with pleasant whispering, if you do not scorn to look into the Egyptian papyrus, inscribed with the pointed reed of the Nile; you will marvel at the shapes and adventures of people who, changed into another likeness by a reversed process, regained their original shape. (*Met.* I. 1: 1. 1–6)

---

[37] For this notion see van der Paardt (1978: 82).

[38] See also Smith (1972: 532 f.).

[39] Smith (1972: 534) especially emphasizes the different character of the prophecies of Diophanes and Osiris: 'The prophecy of Diophanes, predicting the eternal glory of Apuleius' novel, is trivial and untrustworthy at best; the prophecy of Osiris, predicting the eternal glory bestowed by the gods, must be believed'.   [40] Bremer (1978).

This is Lucius speaking of his man-ass-man adventure in a so-called 'personal text'.[41] But through these words[42] can also be heard the extra-diegetical 'I',[43] Apuleius. Within the framework of fiction it is granted only to the great god, who determines the fate of all mortals, to perform the last, definitive metamorphosis: he changes the narrator into what he used to be, the author! ‖

[41] For the triad fenotext–personal text–narrator's text, see Bronzwaer *et al.* (1977: 233).

[42] The ambivalent character of the prologue has been pointed out by Rohde in particular; see also Hijmans and van der Paardt (1978: 109).

[43] For this term, which originates from the French literary theoretician Genette, see Bronzwaer *et al.* (1977: 232).

12

The World of the *Golden Ass*

FERGUS MILLAR

Those who study and teach the history of the Ancient World suffer from a great disadvantage, which we find difficult to admit even to ourselves: in a perfectly literal sense we do not know what we are talking about. Of course we can dispose of a vast range of accumulated knowledge *about* what we are talking about. We can compile lists of office-holders in the Roman Empire, without our evidence revealing how government worked or even whether it made any impact at all on the ordinary person; we can discuss the statuses of cities and look at the archaeological remains of some of them (or rather some parts of some of them) without having any notion of their social and economic functions, or of whether it made any real difference whether an inhabitant of the Roman provinces lived in a small city or a large village. We can study the remains of temples, the iconography of gods and goddesses, the nature of myth, ritual and sacrifice; but how and in what way did all this provide an important or intelligible context for a peasant in the fields? In the case of religion in particular our attention turns persistently to the exceptional rather than the ordinary, to those aspects which were novel, imported, mystical or the subject of philosophical speculation. Let me take a precise example from the *Metamorphoses* or *Golden Ass*, Apuleius' brilliant novel of the second century AD. The exotic aspects of ancient religion which the novel reveals have always attracted attention; the hero's vision of Isis, and his conversion to the worship of Isis and Osiris;[1] the band of Syrian priests making their fraudulent way through the Greek countryside;[2] the wicked baker's wife who has abandoned the gods and worships what she says is a single god—in other words, is

This paper represents the almost unaltered text of an Inaugural Lecture given at University College London on 2 Mar. 1981. I am very grateful to Michael Crawford and Nicholas Horsfall for information and discussions on various points.

[1] *Met.* See esp. Griffiths (1975).   [2] *Met.* 8. 24–9. 10. See Cumont (1909: ch. 5).

a Christian.[3] But if we really want to understand how the divine order related to ordinary life in antiquity we should start from an incident a few chapters later (9. 33–4). Strange portents occur in a farm house: a hen lays a live chicken, blood rises from the floor and wine standing in jars in the wine-store begins to boil. The farmer and his friends are reduced to bewilderment: what steps should they take . . . with how many sacrifices of what sort are they to appease the threats of the heavenly powers? They are *afraid*, just as the pagan world was afraid when too many people began to follow the example of the baker's wife, and abandoned sacrifice to the gods.

This story, as Apuleius tells it, has another important characteristic. Rather as in *Wuthering Heights*, the remarkable and fantastic goings-on in Apuleius' novel take place in a solidly realistic background, in this case a farm-house with chickens in the yard, wine-jars in store, sheepdogs and sheep. Indeed I am going to suggest that the realism of tone in the novel may extend beyond purely physical descriptions, to realistic images of social and economic relations, the framework of communal life in a Roman province and even, here and there, to the wider context of what it meant to be a subject of the Roman Empire.

I must make clear first how paradoxical this claim is. What we are concerned with is a novel of some 250 pages written in Latin in the second century AD by Apuleius, who came from the province of Africa. It is set, however, not in Africa but in central and northern Greece, in the Roman provinces of Achaea and Macedonia.[4] The basic narrative is not original to Apuleius, for it already existed in the form of a longish short story in Greek, of which one version survives.[5] A brief summary of this story will also give the main narra- ‖ tive thread of the *Golden Ass*, which uses all the main incidents. A young man of good family from Patras named Lucius tells the story in the first person. He had been travelling on business in Thessaly, a region whose

---

[3] *Met.* 9. 14. See esp. Barnes (1971: app. 21); Simon (1974: 299).

[4] It is quite probable, as argued by Bowersock (1965: 277), that Thessaly was transferred from Achaea to Macedonia at the moment of Nero's grant of freedom in 67. As he points out (pp. 285 f.), *ILS* 1067 does not imply that Thessaly is within the same province as Athens, Thespiae, and Plataea. But it is in any case clear from Ptolemy, *Geog.* 3. 12, 13–14 and 42 (Müller), that in Pius' reign Thessaly was part of Macedonia; cf. L. Robert (1948: 29–30).

[5] I refer to *Lucius or the Ass* preserved in the works of Lucian (most readily available in McLeod 1967: 47 f.), and venture no further on the question of the authorship of this or its relation to the *Metamorphoses* of (?) Lucius of Patras, briefly summarized by Photius, *Bibl.* cod. 129. For all these questions see van Thiel (1971).

women had a reputation for magical practices.[6] In Hypata he had an affair with a slave girl, who allowed him to observe her mistress using magic arts to turn herself into an owl. Lucius asked for the same potion, got the wrong one and was turned into an ass instead (keeping his human intellect and power of observation). When robbers raided the house they took him away with them; after various adventures he was rescued, put to work in a mill, sold at Beroea in Macedonia to some Syrian priests, then in turn to a baker and a market gardener, was requisitioned by a soldier and finally bought by a rich man from Thessalonica. There a lady fell in love with him, and insisted on his making love to her. The master found out and decided to include a scene of the ass making love to a condemned female prisoner in a public show which he was about to put on. Just in time before this public degradation, the ass had been able to apply the formula for release—eating some roses—and was changed back into human form. At this point the story, which is curiously dull in Greek, reaches a rather fine black-comedy ending. For Lucius, in human form, rushes back to the lady, only to find that she thinks him no longer adequately equipped, and has him ignominiously thrown out. He sets off home, grateful to have escaped from the consequences of his asinine curiosity.

There is no possible doubt that Apuleius based his novel on a version of this story; indeed he explicitly tells the reader that it derived from a Greek original.[7] However, he has transformed it in various ways. Firstly, he makes the hero, again called Lucius, come from Corinth, and has the story end there rather than in Thessalonica. Secondly, he replaces the black-comedy ending by the famous and brilliantly described scene of the release of Lucius by the goddess Isis, and his subsequent conversion. Thirdly, curiosity (*curiositas*), and its improper application to supernatural things, now becomes a serious theme running through the novel;[8] at the end the priest of Isis says to Lucius 'because you sank to servile pleasures, you have earned the ill reward of your unfortunate *curiositas*' (11. 15). Fourthly, in the Isis scene, and the subsequent conversion, Apuleius *may*—as is generally assumed—be importing into the novel a profound personal experience; and he may even at the end intend to blur the distinction between

---

[6] For other allusions see Bowersock (1965: 278).
[7] *Met.* I. I. See esp. Mazzarino (1950); Mason (1978); Tatum (1979).
[8] See esp. Lancel (1961: 25); Tatum (1979: 22 f., 76 f.) and esp. Wlosok (1969: 68).

himself as author, from the African city of Madauros, and Lucius the hero and narrator; for Lucius, who comes from Corinth, has been to Rome to study rhetoric in Latin and finishes up (rather tamely) at the end of the novel as a successful advocate in Rome.[9] Apuleius himself, born in the 120s, had studied in Carthage, then went to Athens to pursue the study of Greek literature and philosophy and at some stage also practised as an advocate in Rome. In a speech before the proconsul of Africa in 162–3, Apuleius boasted that he had written a whole variety of literary works in prose and verse, in both Greek and Latin.[10] In other words the author of the novel and its fictional narrator have crossed the boundary between the Greek- and Latin-speaking worlds in very similar ways but in opposite directions.

So in the novel Apuleius is portraying a young man from a provincial upper class society closely parallel to his own. He also of course knew Athens, and very likely Corinth.[11] || But when he describes in the novel the world of the small towns of central and northern Greece, I cannot say whether he is using personal knowledge or imposing his conceptions of what was typical. In any case we must remember the distance between the author and his theme: he is describing in Latin a society which spoke Greek; but, far more important, in narrating the adventures of the ass he is making a fictional journey which descends through all levels of contemporary society. It is therefore a highly self-conscious literary process which has given us some of the very rare representations of lower class life in the literature of the High Empire. The framework of the existing story is used quite deliberately for social observation: precisely at the point where Lucius as the ass finds himself at the lowest context which he reaches on the economic and social scale—among the wretched slaves working in a mill—he reflects on the opportunities for observation which fortune has granted to him (9. 13):

---

[9] For the 'conversion' see n. 1 and e.g. Nock (1933: ch. 9). For speculations on the autobiographical element see e.g. Hicter (1944: 95, 1945: 61). But note the salutary scepticism of Fredouille (1975), who also argues (15–17) that the sense in 11. 27. 9, 'Madaurensem, sed admodum pauperem', requires 'Corinthiensem'. On that view the deliberate personal allusion would disappear.

[10] *Flor.* 9. 27–9. There is no need to rehearse here the biographical evidence about him, which is collected in Schanz and Hosius (1922: 100 f.).

[11] For his possible knowledge of Corinth and Cenchreae see e.g. Veyne (1965: 241); Mason (1971: 160). For Cenchreae see now Scranton *et al.* (1978, esp. 71 on the possible site of the shrine of Isis (Paus. 2. 2, 3)). For a collection of evidence on Corinth, Wiseman (1979: 438).

Nor was there any comfort for the torments of my existence except that I was sustained by my innate curiosity, in that ignoring my presence they all acted and spoke freely as they wished. Quite rightly the divine author of ancient poetry among the Greeks, wishing to portray a man of the highest wisdom, sang of how he had reached the highest qualities by travelling around many cities and gaining the acquaintance of varied peoples; so I myself give grateful thanks to my ass's shape, in that concealed behind it and tested by various fortunes I was rendered if not very wise, at least more experienced.

It is thus that Apuleius, looking through the eyes of Lucius transformed into an ass, can give his unique description of the slaves toiling in the mill, dressed in a few rags, their half-naked bodies scarred with the marks of beatings, their foreheads branded, their heads half-shaved, their feet in fetters, all of them covered in a fine dust of flour (9. 12). It is undeniable that the novel expresses a rare and distinctive level of sympathy with the working lives of the poor.[12] But that is all; I am not suggesting that Apuleius was a proto-Engels, writing his *Condition of the Working Class in Greece*. If there is a parallel to any work of nineteenth-century literature it is of course to Anna Sewell's *Black Beauty*, which by a similar device offers a rather underestimated portrait of the different levels of Victorian society, from the point of view of bourgeois sentimentality.

The *Golden Ass* has rightly been called an anti-epic,[13] in which the hero or anti-hero endures a variety of misfortunes before a final liberation from trials. But beyond that there are three original and significant features of its literary character, which are essential to its uses for the historian. Firstly, it is set firmly and unmistakably in the immediate present. The original Greek short story is indeed also set in the Roman Empire. But Apuleius makes Lucius the relative of two real historical persons, Plutarch, who had died in the 120s, and his nephew, the philosopher Sextus of Chaeronea, whom Marcus Aurelius still went to hear when he was Emperor after 161.[14] Secondly, and more important, Apuleius fills out the story with a whole series of separate tales or narratives related by characters in it. One

---

[12] See the interesting if not entirely convincing essay by Fick (1978: 86).

[13] See Cooper (1980: 436).

[14] *Met.* 1. 2, 2. 2–3. For Plutarch and his family see Jones (1971: ch. 1). For Marcus still hearing Sextus of Chaeronea while Emperor, Philostratus, *Vit. Soph.* 2. 1; Dio 71. 1. 2. For terminology in the novel implying a setting in the mid-second century see also n. 19 below.

of these, the romance of Amor and Psyche, which is narrated to comfort a young lady captured by the robbers, is quite distinct from the others, for it is set in an imaginary time and place and occupies some fifty pages; since it has no obvious literary or thematic connection with the rest of the work, endless displays of ingenuity and erudition have gone into demonstrating that this non-apparent connection really is there.[15] But all the other, much shorter stories which Apuleius has added are set in the same time, place and social context as the main narrative; all offer at least parallels to, or foreshadowings of, episodes in the main ‖ story; and the majority are necessary for explaining its development.[16] It is the combined total of the main story and these narrated episodes, some 200 pages of text, which I have called the world of the *Golden Ass*.

But, thirdly, the reason why it is worth exploring this world is the one which I hinted at earlier: that Apuleius clothes his sequence of fantastic episodes in a mass of vivid, concrete and realistic detail, on physical objects, houses, social structure, economic relations, the political framework of the local communities, and the wider political framework of the Empire. Let me start with an example relating to the Emperor. Apuleius borrows from the Greek short story the episode in which the ass, being driven towards their mountain hideout by the robbers, decides to appeal for the Emperor's protection (3. 29). Speaking in Greek of course, he starts off on the words 'O Caesar', can manage a loud bray of 'O'—but is not equipped to pronounce the rest. Apuleius makes him choose a moment when the robbers are passing by a large village (*vicus*), which is especially full of people because a fair is being held there. Both the short story and the novel offer a very

[15] See e.g. Grimal (1963); Binder and Merkelbach (1968); Hoevels (1979: 1): 'Die zentrale Frage der Apuleiusforschung war und ist bis heute die nach Sinn der Amor- und Psyche-Einlage im Eselsroman (4. 28–6. 24)'.

[16] The narrated 'real-life' episodes are (1) 1. 5–19, Aristomenes' story, told by himself and set in Hypata; (2) 2. 13–14, the story of Diophanes the Chaldaean at Corinth, told by Lucius' host Milo; (3) 2. 21–30, Thelyphron's story, told by himself and set in Larissa; (4) 4. 9–21, the story of the robber Lamachus and others, told by one of his companions and set in Boeotia; (5) 7. 5–8, the exploits of the pretended robber Haemus, told by himself (in reality Tlepolemus) and set in Macedonia and Epirus; (6) 8. 1–14, the story of Charite and Tlepolemus, told by one of her slaves; exact setting unclear, but in the same region as the rest; (7) 9. 5–7, the *faber* and his wife; narrator not indicated; (8) 9. 17–21, the decurion Barbarus and his wife's lover, told by an old woman to the baker's wife; (9) 9. 35–8, the fate of the three sons of the *hortulanus'* rich patron, narrator not identified; (10) 10. 2–12, the story of the wicked *noverca*, overheard from conversations by the ass, and set somewhere in Thessaly; (11) 10. 23–8, the story of the condemned Corinthian woman; no specific narrator.

significant image or model of how the Emperor was conceived of as an ever-present protector. Apuleius adds a revealing presumption about the structure and functioning of social and economic life in the countryside.[17] So, I suggest, we can use the representations in Apuleius in at least three ways: as portrayals of areas of social life which ancient literature usually passes over; as adding colour to patterns which we know already from other, more formal evidence; and—most important—as offering *alternative* models of society to those which we normally accept.

If we combine the main narrative and the stories attached to it into a 'world of the *Golden Ass*', we can see that this world of small Greek towns and villages is not at all isolated from a wider context. Lucius himself has been to Rome, and returns there at the end; a Chaldaean soothsayer plies his trade in Corinth (2. 12–14); a young man has come from Miletus to see the Olympic games (2. 21); an Egyptian prophet displays his magical skills in Larissa (2. 28); a group of Syrian priests journeys from village to village (8. 24–9. 10). Travel between different regions of the Empire is simply presumed as an aspect of the wider context.

That presumption affects the wider political framework too. The ass is briefly owned by a soldier, who sells him when ordered to go off to Rome with a letter for the Emperor (10, 13); letters carried by messenger between governors and Emperor were in fact the essential mechanism which allowed a centralized, if passive, government to be carried on. The Emperor is invoked in oaths and prayers (9. 41, 11. 17—along with the Senate, Equites and Populus Romanus), and there is no mistaking the consciousness of the characters that they live in a world with a single ruler,[18] whose name might in principle be used to gain protection. But a real and active intervention by the Emperor will only come about in very special circumstances. This is perfectly shown in the false story told to the robbers by a rich young man who arrives at their hideout in disguise to rescue his fiancée. He has to persuade them both that he himself is a famous robber who would add strength to their band, and that he has had a convincing piece of bad luck, leading to the destruction of his own band. So he says that he is the renowned robber Haemus whose band had

[17] For comparative material see the important article by MacMullen (1970: 333).

[18] For the theme of the function of the Imperial cult in inducing consciousness of belonging to a single political framework see Hopkins (1978: ch. 5): 'Divine Emperors or the Symbolic Unity of the Roman Empire'.

ravaged Macedonia. But by ill-luck a high-ranking *procurator* of the Emperor (a *ducenarius*)[19] had || lost favour at court and been exiled to the island of Zacynthus—and it was when he, his faithful wife and their escort of soldiers were staying en route at an inn at Actium that the robbers had happened to attack it, and were driven off. They had withdrawn unscathed. But the *procurator*'s wife had afterwards gone back to the Emperor and successfully petitioned him both for the release of her husband and for the despatch of detachments (*vexillationes*) of legions to destroy the band of robbers.

As it happens, we have an inscription from just this period which records that in about 176 detachments (*vexillationes*) of legions from Moesia were sent south to the territory bordering on Macedonia and Thrace to 'dislodge' a band of Thracian brigands.[20] But far more important is the implication that, in unimportant areas like Macedonia and Epirus, only an accident could have stirred the imperial will to action to restore public order; and, more important still, that the mechanism for bringing this about would have been the petition or literally 'prayer' (*preces*) of an influential person, answered by the assent, or literally 'nod' (*nutus*) of the Emperor. Precisely this model of the operations of government was the central theme of *The Emperor in the Roman World*.

If it was only in special circumstances that the Emperor would make his distant presence felt, what of the governor of the province—or rather the two governors of the two provinces, for when Apuleius was writing, probably around 170, Thessaly was part of Macedonia, whose proconsul had his base in Thessalonica.[21] Both he and the proconsul of Achaea, with his seat at Corinth, will have had a few auxiliary units of soldiers.[22] But in the world described by Apuleius neither they

---

[19] *Met.* 7. 6: 'procuratorem principis ducenaria perfunctum'. This is only the second recorded usage of the term, the earliest being Suetonius, *Claudius* 24. Documentary uses begin in the reign of Marcus Aurelius with *AE* 1962, 183: 'ad ducenariae procurationis splendorem'. See Millar (1963: 197) and Pflaum (1971: 349). For the deployment of a fairly new technical term note also 'fisci advocatus' (7. 10), used ironically of one of the robbers; it had come into use in Hadrian's reign, see HA *v. Had.* 20. 6; for the earliest attested case, Eck (1978: 228a).

[20] *AE* 1956, 124, see Pflaum (1960–1: no. 181 *bis*) (M. Valerius Maximianus): 'praeposito vexillationibus et at (*sic*) detrahendum Briseorum latronum manum in confinio Macedon(iae) et Thrac(iae) ab Imperatore misso'. On the Brisei see Pflaum (1960: 489).

[21] For the division see n. 4 above. The proconsul of Macedonia appears in the last section of *Lucius or the Ass* (54–5).

[22] See Ritterling (1927: 28); Sherk (1957: 52) (not considering the evidence from Apuleius).

nor any other forces perform regular police functions in town or country.[23] Indeed, when the slave-girl describes to Lucius the serious dangers of going out at night in Hypata, she says explicitly 'nor can the *auxilia* of the governor, far away as they are, rid the city of such carnage'.[24] In the scenes set in Thessaly the Roman proconsul never appears in person. But he is mentioned at least in the scene where the ass's current master, a gardener, is riding home from market; a soldier appears, questions him in Latin, and on getting no answer beats him with his stick.[25] Then he starts again in Greek, saying that the ass must be requisitioned for transporting the baggage of the governor (*praeses*) from the next village (9. 39). The gardener had evidently not read the *Discourses* of Epictetus, published a few decades earlier; for there the advice is given that in exactly this situation one should give up one's ass promptly when a soldier demands it, and avoid a beating.[26] At any rate he knocks down the soldier and makes off. This soldier apparently belongs to a unit which is escorting the governor,[27] and the scene provides a small fictional || example of much the most important area of contact and conflict between state and subject in the Roman Empire; that is, the provision of animals, waggons, supplies and accommodation for passing messengers and officials, or troops on the move. The tensions thus created are reflected in long series of complaints on the one side and of pronouncements by governors and Emperors on the other.[28] It is surely significant that in our

[23] In this the novel contrasts clearly with the martyr-acts, where Roman soldiers perform an active police role; see Lopuszanski (1951: 5).

[24] *Met.* 2. 18: 'nec praesidis auxilia longinqua levare civitatem tanta clade possunt'.

[25] The soldier is described simply as a *miles*, but has a *vitis* with a thickened end (9. 40; 'inversa vite de vastiore nodulo cerebrum suum diffindere'), normally thought of as the mark of a centurion, see e.g. Webster (1979: 132). Exactly the same contradiction confronts us in the grave-relief of a *miles* from Corinth, see Šašel Kos (1978: 22), who also notes (23) that there are a number of such depictions of soldiers with a *vitis* from Achaea and Macedonia, and suggests (24) some connection with service in the *provinciae inermes*.

[26] Epictetus, *Diss.* 4. 1. 79, quoted by Rostovtzeff (1957: ch. 8. n. 37) (also referring to the story of the *hortulanus*, the only episode from Apuleius used by Rostovtzeff).

[27] It is puzzling that the soldier should be described as a 'miles e legione' (9. 39). Apuleius might in this case have been misled by the system in Africa, where the legion III Augusta provided the *beneficiarii* for the proconsul (Tacitus, *Hist.* 4. 48). On the other hand the soldier's superior officer is described (10. 13) as a *tribunus* (compare the *tribunus cohortis* with Caecilius Classicus as proconsul of Baetica, Pliny, *Ep.* 3. 9. 18). *Tribuni* of auxiliary units must have been in command of *cohortes milliariae*, and what seems to be the same superior officer appears in 10. 1 as 'praepositum suum, qui mille armatorum ducatum sustinebat'. For comparable usages see Smith (1979: 263).

[28] See now Mitchell (1976: 106).

documentary evidence from outside Egypt far more attention is given to this issue than to that of direct taxation in cash or kind.

In Apuleius' story the gardener is eventually arrested, and the soldier takes the ass and loads him with his baggage, his lance prominently on top to terrify the passers-by. Coming to a small town, the soldier stays not in an inn but in the house of a town councillor (*decurio*, 10. 1)—the right *not* to be forced to accept official travellers was an exceptional privilege.[29] When he sets off for Rome, the soldier sells the ass, which he has acquired for nothing, and pockets the proceeds. As is generally recognized now, nothing could be further from the truth than Rostovtzeff's idea that the army of the Imperial period somehow represented an oppressed peasantry.[30] On the contrary, the soldiers were a privileged official class whose presence was feared by ordinary people.

This soldier is represented as being loosely attached to the entourage of the governor as he travels through the province, presumably on his judicial circuit.[31] But no governor appears in person in the story until the final stage at Corinth, the capital (*caput*) of Achaea.[32] In the famous scene in *Acts* set in Corinth we see the proconsul Gallio on his tribunal when Paul is dragged before him and accused. In Apuleius the proconsul is in his house, when one of the victims of a poisoner, just before death, rushes to the house demanding his protection, and by loud shouts and raising a disturbance among the people, causes the doors to be opened and a hearing granted (10. 28). The proconsul hears the case and condemns the female poisoner to the beasts.

Several things are significant in this process. The governor in a provincial city functions under the pressure of crowds following every interesting turn of events. He too may be staying with a local notable, for there is no certain evidence that the Roman state normally

---

[29] For release from the obligation of *hospitium* (ἀνεπισταθμεία) see e.g. Sherk (1969: no. 57); *FIRA²* I, no. 56; 73; *Dig.* 50. 4. 18. 30, 28. 1. 6. 8; Millar (1977: 460–1) (athletes); Drew-Bear *et al.* (1977: 355) (senators).

[30] See Rostovtzeff (1957: ch. 11).

[31] For the proconsul's assize tour see Burton (1975: 92). It is attested that Beroea in Macedonia was an assize-centre, and the system probably existed in all proconsular provinces (97). Note that the appointment of *tutores* for the children of a man thought to be dead is alluded to in *Met.* 1. 6: 'liberis tuis tutores iuridici provincialis decreto dati'. No deductions should be drawn from the use of this term, which simply means the proconsul, as does δικαστής in *Lucius or the Ass*, 55.

[32] *Met.* 10. 18: 'quod caput est totius Achaiae provinciae'.

owned official residences for governors.[33] Before her execution the woman is locked up in the public prison of Corinth ('de publico carcere', 5. 34)—for it was these city prisons which governors normally used. The governor is dependent on the city in another way too; for the wild beast show in which the woman is to die is one put on by a rich local magnate to celebrate his assumption of the chief office in the city. Apuleius' description perfectly catches the overtones of local office-holding; 'Thiasus, for that was the name of my owner, a citizen of Corinth . . . had held the lower offices in succession, as his descent and dignity demanded, and had now been appointed to the quinquennial magistracy; and as, in order to live up to the glory of assuming the *fasces*, he had promised a gladiatorial show to last three days, he was in the process of making provision for his munificence (*munificentia*).'[34] One of the most curious features of the judicial system of the Empire was that local office-holders, putting on shows at their own expense, could *buy* condemned prisoners from the || state and have them eaten by wild beasts for the delectation of large crowds. It was regarded as a remarkable act of benevolence by Marcus Aurelius and Commodus that in 177 they reduced the price which the provincial office-holders had to pay.[35]

We cannot understand the government, such as it was, of the peaceful provinces of the Empire if we do not think of the close personal relations which the governor was bound to have with the provincial upper classes, and above all with those of the city in which he spent most of his time. Exactly for this reason, when the well-born young Lucius from Corinth arrives in Hypata, he is questioned by his host 'about our native city and its leading citizens (*primores*) and finally about the governor himself' (1. 26). But in most places the governor was not present (obviously enough); and nor—which is perhaps not so obvious—were any forces, officials or representatives sent by him. The cities ran themselves. Or rather—and this is one of the most

---

[33] The evidence on this puzzling question is very well collected and discussed by Egger (1966), without revealing what sort of 'residence', owned by whom, was used by proconsuls in the 'capitals' of their provinces.

[34] *Met.* 10. 18. For Corinth see n. 11 above. The office of *duovir quinquennalis* in the *colonia* is well attested on inscriptions, see e.g. *Corinth* 8. 2: *Latin Inscriptions*, p. 157. The assumption that Lucius' first language will have been Greek is fully reflected in the rapidly changing balance of Latin and Greek inscriptions in the second century see *Corinth* 8. 3: *The Inscriptions, 1926–1950*, pp. 18–19. [Dio], *Or*, 37. 26 (perhaps by Favorinus) records the Hellenization of the city.

[35] For the well-known *senatus consultum* of 177 see Oliver and Palmer (1955: 320). For this interpretation see Millar (1977: 195).

vivid impressions left by the novel—they were run by a network of local aristocratic families, whose doings, public and private, were the subject of intense observer participation—approbation, curiosity, indignation, incipient violence—on the part of the lower classes of the towns. The leading families in Apuleius form a social class immediately distinguishable on sight from the rest of the people. Lucius sees a woman arriving in the market place of Hypata escorted by slaves; her rich dress 'proclaimed her a lady (*matrona*)' (2. 2); and the ass at once recognizes the gentle birth (*matronatus*) of a young girl captured by the robbers (4. 23). The upper classes have substantial houses in the cities, with households of slaves with carefully differentiated functions (9. 2, 10. 13). They may own landed properties at a distance (10. 4), in one case run by a slave overseer with a staff of slave shepherds (7. 15, 8. 15), and in another by a slave overseer (*vilicus*) who keeps his accounts (*rationes*) in his house (8. 22); alternatively we find a free tenant bringing a leg of venison as a gift to his landlord (8. 31).

The novel, like the pages of Plutarch's *Moralia*, written rather more than half a century earlier,[36] shows how a network of relationships connected the local aristocrats of different Greek cities. Lucius, from Corinth, is portrayed as a relative of Plutarch, from Chaeronea; and the grand lady whom he meets in the market place of Hypata is a relative of his mother (2. 2–3). He brings with him to Hypata a letter of recommendation from Demeas in Corinth, vouching specifically for his good birth (1. 22–3). On another visit to the market place he meets a friend with whom he has studied in Athens, and who is now aedile, or market supervisor, in his home town (1. 24).

As Apuleius' description of the magnate from Corinth implies, power and influence in these small provincial towns had become largely hereditary. Hence a group of young men (*iuvenes*) of the best birth were free to terrorize the streets of Hypata by night.[37] Or a poor man could be driven off his lands by 'a rich and powerful young neighbour who misused the prestige of his ancestry, was powerful in local politics and could easily do anything in the town' (9. 35). On the other side rich people could actively avoid local office and responsibility. When a group of robbers reaches Thebes, they ask who are the richest men there, and are told of a wealthy money-changer (*nummularius*) who

---

[36] See Jones (1971: ch. 5, 'Plutarch's Society: *Domi nobiles*').

[37] 2. 18: 'vesana factio nobilissimorum iuvenum pacem publicam infestat'. Cf. *Dig.* 48. 19. 28. 3 (Callistratus) on the difficulty for the governor in repressing the disorderly conduct 'in quibusdam civitatibus' of those 'qui volgo se iuvenes appellant'.

dresses poorly and uses every means to conceal his wealth 'for fear of office and public obligations (*munera publica*)' (4. 9). That touches of course on one of the most familiar themes from the city life of Antiquity: the extraction of value from the rich not by taxation but by laying on them the obligation to assume expensive functions directly and in person.[38] Here we see the necessary || social framework for that process: the man does his best—but everybody in the town knows that his well-guarded house is filled with riches.[39]

The people of the towns might of course follow the doings of the rich with favour and approbation. The young lady captured by the robbers had been engaged to an aristocratic young man 'whom the whole city had adopted as its public son', and the engagement had been celebrated by a procession of the family and relatives to make sacrifices at the temples and public buildings.[40] When he heroically rescues her and returns home, 'the whole city poured out to see the longed for sight' (7. 13; cf. 8. 2). But favour for one person could quickly turn, in the context of a public ceremonial, into a demonstration against another. So, after the death of a leading citizen in Larissa 'by ancestral ritual, as he was one of the *optimates*, the public funeral procession was conducted through the forum'. But the dead man's father shouts out that he had been murdered by his wife, and the crowd begins to call for fire and stones (2. 27), just as in another scene the crowd determines to stone a witch to death (1. 10). Again, in a town in Thessaly, an old man goes from the funeral of his younger son to the forum, and accuses the elder son of the murder; a regular trial then follows. 'By his lamentations he inflamed with such pity and indignation the town council and also the people, that they all shouted that the delays of justice . . . should be set aside and that he should be

[38] The best analysis of this situation, as it existed in the Classical and early Hellenistic Greek city, is provided by Veyne (1976: ch. 2). The remark of Rostovtzeff (1957: ch. 8 n. 41) that there is no adequate treatment of the history of liturgies under the Empire, remains valid. For a useful recent collection of legal evidence see Langhammer (1973: 237 f.). But see now Neesen (1981: 203).

[39] *Met.* 4. 9: 'parva se<d> satis munita domuscula contentus, pannosus alioquin ac sordidus, aureos folles incubabat'. In a very general way the term 'aureos folles', reflecting the custom of storing money in bags, foreshadows the usage which becomes official in the early fourth century, when *follis* becomes a term for a unit of currency. See Jones (1974: 330); Crawford (1975: 586).

[40] *Met.* 4. 26. As regards the remarkable expression 'filius publicus', I owe to Miss H. C. van Bremen the perception that the inscriptions of the Greek cities often emphasize the private virtues of members of the leading families as expressed in their public life.

stoned to death, to provide a communal punishment for a communal wrong.' But the magistrates fear that violence will get out of
hand, and persuade the council and people that a proper trial should
be held. It is conducted in the council-chamber (*curia*) with the coun-
cillors as jury, and if the charge had been proved the town executioner
(*carnifex*) would have carried out the sentence. But it turns out that
it was his stepmother who had tried to kill the boy, and had only
succeeded in giving him an overdose—from which (needless to say)
he is just waking up. So the stepmother is sent into lifelong exile, and
her slave accomplice executed.[41]

These are just the sort of differential penalties for condemned persons of different social status which are well attested in the Roman
Empire.[42] But there is a puzzle here, for on the established view only
the governor of a province could carry out capital sentences or
impose penalties such as exile;[43] and of course a moment ago we saw
the proconsul of Achaea doing just that in Corinth. The same problem arises with the famous scene of the mock trial of Lucius in
Hypata (3. 2–9). Here, Lucius, before his transformation, comes back
late one night from a party, slays (as he thinks) three robbers, is tried
next day by the city council and thinks himself near to a death
sentence—when it is revealed that the three victims were really
inflated bladders blowing about in the wind. Once again the trial, or
mock-trial, takes place in the context of intense crowd participation,
so much so that the people successfully demand that it should be transferred from the forum to the theatre—which was of course a normal
meeting-place in Greek cities.[44]

So Apuleius' novel presents one story in which trial and sentence
is carried out by a city council and another in which the whole dramatic point would surely have been lost, if the original readers would
have known all along that Lucius' trial could not possibly have been ||
real—that is if they would have assumed that only the governor

[41] *Met.* 10. 6–12. For the sentences, 10. 12: 'et novercae quidem perpetuum indi-
citur exilium, servus vero patibulo suffigitur'. *Patibulum* seems to be used here as a
synonym for *crux*, cf. Mommsen (1899: 920–1) (not discussing this passage), and *RE*
s.v. *patibulum*.   [42] See Garnsey (1970: pt. II).
[43] For a statement of the principle see e.g. Sherwin-White (1963: 35 f., 75 f.). For a
survey of the evidence which may cast some doubt on the general assumption that local
courts did not and could not carry out capital sentences see Schürer (1979: 219 n. 80)
and Nörr, (1966: 30 f.); note *Syll.*[3] 799 (Cyzicus, AD 38), showing that the city author-
ities there could impose a sentence of exile from the city.
[44] For meetings in the theatre see Colin (1965*a*: 342 n. 3; cf. 1965*b*: ch. 3) (assuming that the procedure depends on the freedom of the cities of Thessaly).

could carry out capital sentence. There seem to me to be three possibilities. We can accept that not only the particular course of events
but the entire context will have seemed pure fantasy to second-
century readers. Or, we can assume that both Apuleius and they knew
that the cities of Thessaly were free cities, in which the writ of the proconsul did not run and which had their own capital jurisdiction. But,
the trouble is, were they free cities? I can find no clear proof that they
were.[45] For that matter it is not possible to state exactly what 'freedom' for Greek cities under the Empire meant, or whether it always
meant the same thing.[46] In other words, if we switch back to the real
world, we find it just as confusing and ambiguous as fiction. Nothing
is more illusory than the idea that the real world of the Roman
Empire presents us with a clearly defined and intelligible system of public law and administration.

That being so, I should like to try a quite different hypothesis,
namely that what the novel represents is Apuleius' assumptions as
to how local justice worked in the cities, irrespective of their formal
status, when the governor was not there. In the real world too, we
must remember, he usually was not; the more privileged communities were visited by the governor of a province once a year; many never
saw him at all. We can of course find some cases where a prisoner is
duly locked up by city officials to await trial by the governor when he
comes.[47] But I do suggest that, especially when popular indignation
was aroused, it is impossible to imagine that such self-restraint normally operated.

Whatever may have happened in reality, in the world of the novel
justice is done and public order maintained, if at all, by self-help. When
Lucius disappears, having been turned into an ass, it is reported to
the robbers that he is thought guilty of the robbery; his slave has been

---

[45] Julius Caesar certainly granted freedom to the Thessalians, Plut., *Caesar* 48;
Appian, BC II, 368. Thereafter the situation is obscure, and neither the existence of
Thessalian coins, nor Thessalian votes in the Amphictyonic league (Pausanias 10. 8.
3) nor the adoption of new eras in AD 10–11 and again in AD 41 necessarily imply grants
of freedom—so Bernhardt (1971: 202, 208). *ILS* 1067, showing P. Pactumeius
Clemens, *cos. suff.* 138, as 'legato divi Hadriani Athenis, Thespiis, Plaetaeis, item in
Thessalia', *might* imply the freedom of Thessaly; but the freedom of Plataea is *deduced*,
e.g. by Larsen, *ESAR* 4. 447, from its presence on this inscription.

[46] Cf. the complex variations discussed by Bernhardt (1980) (on freedom from
tribute).

[47] This pattern is clear in the case of the martyrs of Lyon, Eusebius, *HE* 5. 1, and
especially in the martyrdom of Pionius at Smyrna, Knopf *et al.* (1965: no. 10);
Musurillo (1972: no. 10).

examined by the magistrates of Hypata under torture, and a group of men has been sent to Corinth to seek him out for punishment (7. 2). When the robbers are finally located, a party sets out from Hypata, catches them and simply executes them (7. 13). A little later some shepherds arrest a man on suspicion of murder and keep him bound overnight in a hut, intending to take him next day to the magistrates for punishment (7. 26). Similarly, an armed group of local men on horseback arrests the Syrian priests for robbery and takes them back to a prison, apparently located in a mere village (9. 9–10; cf. 9. 4). Even the passing soldiers who arrest the gardener bring him to the local magistrates; he is put in the public prison to await a capital penalty (9. 42).

The world we are looking at is one wholly without policing by any Imperial forces, except in one very extreme case. Justice is highly localized. A man who realizes that he will be suspected of murder simply abandons his family, moves to Aetolia and contracts a new marriage (1. 19). When a group of slaves on an outlying estate hears of the death of their mistress and fears a change of owner, they load all their belongings on pack-animals, go on what seems to be a journey of about three days, and settle in a city where they can live without discovery and support themselves (7. 15–23). The cities are not represented as exercising any check on arrivals; when Lucius reaches Hypata he has to go into an inn to ask which town it is (1. 21). Nor do the towns themselves have any significant police forces. The nearest to that which we meet are the attendants of the market supervisor in Hypata (1. 24–5), and the attendants of the magistrates there who burst into the house where Lucius is, arrest him and take him to his mock trial; the prosecution is conducted by the prefect of the night watch,[48] who duly claims to have observed the murder while on street patrol. But Lucius had carried his sword to protect himself, and in the several scenes elsewhere in ‖ the novel which represent robbers mounting assaults on the town houses of the rich, no organized police force appears. If the attacks are beaten off, as they twice are,[49] it is by self-help from within the house, or from neighbours.

Like the potentially violent crowds which demanded justice in the cities, and the arrests of criminals by armed groups, this self-help is

---

[48] *Met.* 3. 2–3: 'nocturnae custodiae praefectus'. The term must translate νυκτοστράτηγος, attested on a number of inscriptions from Greek cities, see esp. Jones (1940: 212).

[49] *Met.* 4. 9–11, 19–21. The realistic and unheroic character of the robbers' tales of defeat is well brought out by McKay (1963: 147).

an important aspect of the society represented in the novel. But it is by no means the only area in which the novel presents alternative models of ancient society to those which we normally accept. For instance, one influential modern view represents the typical small town in the Roman provinces as not primarily an economic entity, but rather 'a social phenomenon, the result of the predilection of the wealthier classes for the amenities of urban life'.[50] That very important cultural factor is indeed perfectly illustrated in Apuleius: Lucius' rich female relative in Hypata asks him, 'How are you enjoying our native city? To my knowledge we far excel all other cities in temples, baths and other public works. . . . At any rate there is freedom for anyone at leisure, and for the stranger coming on business a crowd of people like that at Rome' (2. 19). It is beginning to be recognized, however, that the latter part of that claim is also important. The economic functions of towns in a pre-industrial society can be complex and important in aggregate, even if the units of production and exchange are themselves small.[51] It is therefore all the more worth emphasizing that the towns in Apuleius function, not indeed as centres of production, but as the focus for organized exchanges of goods and the hiring of labour. All of this is conducted for cash; whatever else this may be, it is certainly a fully monetized economy. Admittedly, when the rich accumulate a surplus, they literally just accumulate it in cash. Lucius' miserly host at Hypata does lend out money against deposits in gold and silver (1. 21); but the bulk of his money simply rests in a heavily locked store-room (*horreum*) in his house. Everyone in the town knows it is there, and the robbers duly break down the door with axes and take away the money in bags (1. 21, 3. 28). But, otherwise, the cities are the scenes of active exchanges for cash: in the market place of Hypata fish is available for sale, and hay for horses can be bought for cash (1. 24). A man who is by profession a vendor of cheese and related products, travelling throughout Thessaly, Aetolia and Boeotia, comes to Hypata, perhaps for the day of a special cheese-market, only to find that a large operator (*negotiator magnarius*) has bought up the entire supply (1. 5). The poorest free person whom we meet in Apuleius is the market-gardener who works a small patch of land without even a house; none the less he too drives the ass to the town each morning to sell his produce to the retailers (9. 32). The market places are also the scene

---

[50] Jones (1974: 1, on p. 31).
[51] See the valuable article by Hopkins (1978: 35); the rest of that volume also presents much relevant material and argument.

of regular auctions; the runaway slaves can immediately have their animals auctioned for cash (8. 23–5), and a traveller short of money can find an auctioneer advertising for someone to be paid in cash for watching a corpse at night (2. 21–3). If all else failed, one could earn a poor income in cash by portering (*saccaria*, 1. 7), or just beg for coins at the crossroads (1. 6). No doubt the inns, where you also paid in cash (1. 17), did not receive quite as many people as those of Rome. But what is clear is that the towns are represented as providing real concentrations of activity both by way of exchange and in the hire of labour. Crowd reactions, to good or bad news, or the handling of wrong-doers, surely also imply chronic under-employment, and hence the availability of labour for hire. Given the constant exchanges of cash it is not surprising that the towns have professional money-changers (*nummularii*); when a slave pays a doctor a large sum for a drug, the coins are sealed in a bag, to be checked next day by a money-changer (10. 9).

What is more striking in Apuleius is the level and nature of eco-nomic activity outside the towns, first in villages (called *pagus, cas-tellum* or *vicus*), and secondly in the countryside itself. Before I give some examples I should remind you of how the economic life of the peasantry was described in a very interesting recent article: 'The economy of the Roman empire, in spite of its sophistication in some respects, was predominantly a subsistence economy. . . . The bulk of the labour force in the Roman empire, perhaps 80–90 per cent, ‖ were primarily peasants who produced most of what they themselves consumed and consumed most of what they produced.'[52] The same passage admits, however, that the countryside was affected by the mon-etary economy, and all I can say in this context is that it is this aspect of rural economic life which the novel puts before us. In the story a village too may have an auctioneer; one of these sells off the ass to a baker from the next village, who is also buying a quantity of corn for cash (9. 10). The baker's neighbour is a fuller (9. 22), and both households conduct their trade in their immediate living quarters, the one with wooden troughs in which flour is sifted (9. 23), the other with wickerwork frames on which cloth is placed for whiten-ing with sulphur (9. 24). In the same village where the ass is sold there is a *faber*, apparently a free man, who works under an *officinator* or owner of a workshop. He works for cash, to buy food; his wife works

---

[52] Hopkins (1980: 104).

at wool-making (*lanificium*), also for cash, with which they buy oil for lighting (9. 5). When pressed for cash they sell a large jar which is standing in their house (9. 7).

That a household could be a multiple economic unit is also clear elsewhere. The rich young lady with whom the ass is rescued gives him into the care of her slave chief herdsman (*armentarius equiso*) who takes him out to a country property. There the ass is used by the man's wife to turn a mill which grinds corn for the neighbours, and earns a cash revenue; the barley meant for the ass's upkeep is also ground in the mill and sold to neighbouring tenants (7. 15). Released from the mill, the ass is given over to a slave-boy whose job is to gather wood in the hills; but once again it turns out that he sells the wood for cash, for use in a next-door household (7. 17–20). I will come back later to this process of gathering from the wild. It is enough to emphasize now that the world portrayed by Apuleius involves cash exchanges for produce right down to the lowest levels. We even find that the slave shepherds in flight ask a goatherd grazing his flock beside the track whether he has milk or cheese for sale (8. 19). The only trace of a subsistence economy in Apuleius is a seasonal one; over the winter the market-gardener, having nothing left to sell, lives on overgrown vegetables from his plot which have run to seed (9. 32). In other words all the food-producing operations are specialized, and the products are exchanged for cash. Villages and countryside have small, domestic-scale establishments for processing food or clothes. When we have read Apuleius we might carry away the image not of a subsistence economy, but of something more like Alan McFarlane's deliberately provocative description of thirteenth-century England: 'a capitalist-market economy without factories'.[53]

Direct production for household consumption does appear, but seems to be more characteristic of the *richer* households, which can achieve the necessary variety of production. It is in that context, and only there, that transfers of produce occur which are not for cash, i.e. are gifts. So a wealthy neighbour of the market-gardener promises him a gift 'from his estates' of corn, olive-oil and two jars of wine (9. 33). The same background is implied when Lucius' rich female relative in Hypata sends him as gifts (*xeniola*) a pig, five chickens and a jar of wine, for use at dinner (2. 11).

In a different context, the tenant (*colonus*) of a rich landlord brings him as a gift (*munus*), a leg of venison—the product, as is explicitly

---

[53] MacFarlane (1978: 196).

stated, of a hunting expedition (8. 31). With that we come to another side of the ancient economy, and one which is almost wholly neglected. The oft-repeated modern doctrine that agriculture was the fundamental economic activity of the ancient world is of course obviously true, but none the less gives a wholly inadequate impression of people's relations to the earth and its products. In the world of Apuleius at least, the people of the countryside are not only agriculturalists; they are also pastoralists whose flocks live in wild country, and for that matter they are hunters and gatherers. To be strict, gathering appears only in the story of the slave boy collecting wood in the hills; but any description of the economy of the ancient world which ignored the gathering of food and other products from the wild would be hopelessly inadequate.[54] Hunting, however, is a fundamental feature of the world in which Apuleius' characters live. Human habitation exists against the backdrop of a landscape in which there ‖ are bears (4. 13, 7. 24), wolves (7. 22, 8. 15), boar (8. 4), deer (8. 31) and wild goats (8. 4), not to speak of the unspecified 'wild beasts' which the rich man from Corinth has come to collect in Thessaly for his show (10. 18). In consequence the group of shepherds in flight are armed with throwing-spears, heavy hunting-spears, arrows and clubs (8. 16). When force has to be applied against neighbours, a rich household in the country can deploy swords and spears, and call out large and ferocious sheepdogs (9. 36–8). Then again, when the Syrian priests are staying in the house of the leading citizen (*vir primarius*) of a town, the ass is thought to have rabies. The slaves of the household instantly seize spears and axes, until the ass demonstrates by drinking water that he does not have rabies. This town house is also equipped with a stable of horses and a pack of hunting-dogs (9. 2).

Nearly all the features which I have tried to isolate in the world of the *Golden Ass* come together in the marvellous mock-heroic story told in the robbers' hideout, and added to the main narrative framework by Apuleius (4. 13–22). One group of robbers had gone south into Boeotia; at Plataea they found busy talk of the show which was to be put on by a local notable, Demochares: 'for he was a man of distinguished birth, great wealth and eminent liberality, and was preparing public entertainments (*voluptates*) with a splendour worthy of his fortune'. He had assembled gladiators, *venatores*, to fight against wild

---

[54] I know of no serious reflection on this fact except Frayn (1975).

beasts, and condemned criminals (*noxii*) to be eaten by the beasts. The beasts were bears, acquired in three ways: by his own hunting expeditions, by purchase and by gift from his friends. Unfortunately, in spite of heavy expenditure on upkeep, many of the bears died; their corpses were thrown out on the streets and were seized and eaten by the starving poor.

The robbers therefore skinned one of these deceased bears and put one of their leaders inside it. They took the supposed bear to Demochares and produced a forged letter saying that it was a gift from a friend of his in Thrace who had caught it while hunting. With that they went off, richly rewarded with coins from the store kept in the house—and, in a touch which is typical of the narrative, the people of the town rushed to see the bear and commented ('consonaque civium voce') on Demochares' good luck.

At night the robbers came back, and the one disguised as a bear got up from the courtyard, killed the slave janitor, opened the door with his key and let them in. In the house he showed them the store-room (*horreum*) filled with silver, which they carried off in coffins taken from a tomb outside the town. But before they could come back for a second load, the household woke up, and the supposed bear was confronted with slaves armed with clubs, spears and swords, supported by fierce hunting-dogs. The story ends with a fine mock-heroic narration of his death—reminding us, if we needed it, that what we are reading is just fiction.

None the less the novel does offer us a complex and significant portrait of a provincial society: the network of relationships among the provincial aristocracy; the political functions, displays and generosities of the rich, as acted out in front of their local communities; the crude accumulation of wealth side by side with extreme poverty; an economy which was both monetized on the one hand and gave a large place to hunting in the wild on the other; a world where brigandage was rife, but where society could close ranks to exert force where it was needed, and was fully armed to do so. The forces of the governor were few and far away—to come back to a question which I raised earlier, I suggest that we should not believe for a moment that in the real world the execution of justice on local murderers or robbers was dutifully left to the governor's discretion. The Emperor's distant existence was felt by all. But only very special circumstances would bring his forces into action. We should not be surprised, after reading Apuleius, to find that just about this time Thespiae in Boeotia sent a contingent to fight on campaign with Marcus Aurelius,[55] or that when a marauding group of barbarians from the Black Sea reached Boeotia they were attacked and slaughtered by a local force.[56] We might recall that Apuleius says that the armed group of shepherds in flight needed only a trumpet to resemble a real army (8. 16).[57]

Of course we must not forget that all this is not only fiction, but is a Greek short story transformed and expanded in Latin by a rich and well-born writer from Africa. When he ‖ went to Athens, it was not to study the lives of the poor in the Greek countryside, but to earn the title which his fellow-citizens in Madaurus were to give him, 'the Platonic philosopher'.[58] In writing his novel, with its exuberant descriptive detail and powerful erotic elements, he was not, in intention, reporting anything, but inventing a world in which to set the adventures of Lucius. But the invented world of fiction may yet represent—perhaps cannot help representing—important features of the real world.[59] For the historian, the *Golden Ass* depicts levels of social and economic life which the vast mass of surviving Classical literature simply ignores; it adds depth and perspective to patterns which we know from other evidence, for instance in portraying the roles played by the local aristocracies, as seen from below. But above all it offers us alternative models—of the operations of justice or the nature of economic life outside the towns—to those which we generally accept. The images gained from the novel can be used, in other words, to apply new questions and new hypotheses to the bewildering mass of data which survives from the real world of the Roman Empire. ‖

[55] Plassart (1932).　　　[56] Pausanias 10. 34. 5.
[57] For comparative evidence note Brunt (1975).
[58] *Ins. lat. d'Alg.* 2115 (Madauros), cf. *PIR*² A 958.
[59] For comparable attempts to use ancient fiction, see e.g. Veyne (1961); Scarcella (1977). Both the title and the approach adopted in this paper were suggested by Morris (1964), using Murasaki's *The Tale of Genji*.

13

Curiositas and the Platonism of Apuleius' *Golden Ass*

JOSEPH DeFILIPPO

Curiositas has long been recognized as an important theme in Apuleius' *Golden Ass*, for obvious philological and critical reasons. The word itself is found in a literary text only once in extant Latin prior to Apuleius,[1] whereas it occurs twelve times in the *Golden Ass* alone, not to mention twelve occurrences of the adjective *curiosus*.[2] Yet these words occur not only frequently, but also in ways which make clear that they represent a notion of great interpretive importance. It is *curiositas*, for instance, that precipitates both Lucius' and Psyche's stories. Lucius' *curiositas* is irremediably piqued at hearing of Pamphile's magical powers and leads to the disastrous attempt at metamorphosis on which all subsequent action depends:

At ego curiosus alioquin, ut primum artis magicae semper optatum nomen audivi, tantum a cautela Pamphiles afui, ut etiam ultro gestirem tali magisterio me volens ampla cum mercede tradere. . . . (2. 6. 1–4)

I am most grateful to Christina Dufner, Michael Frede and Howard Jackson for their comments on earlier drafts of this essay, and to an audience at Duke University for a number of challenging criticisms. This essay is descended from one that was written for J. Arthur Hanson's Princeton seminar on Apuleius in the spring of 1984; it is dedicated to his memory.

[1] Cicero, *Ad Atticum* 2. 12. 2. Labhardt (1960: 209) comments: '*Curiositas*, dans la lettre à Atticus, serait une création du moment, un de ces néologismes sans lendemain que l'on risque dans une conversation familière, pour l'oublier aussitôt.'

[2] *Curiositas*: 1. 12. 21; 3. 14. 1; 5. 6. 16, 19. 9; 6. 20. 15, 21. 13; 9. 12. 7, 13. 14, 15. 8; 11. 15. 6, 22. 30, 23. 22.

Curiosus: 1. 2. 19, 17. 7; 2. 4. 27, 6. 1; 29. 2; 4. 16. 13; 5. 23. 1, 28. 16; 7. 13. 12; 9. 30. 5, 42. 4; 10. 29. 18. (*Curiosulus*: 11. 31. 6.)

Throughout this essay I assume a certain singularity of reference for *curiosus* and *curiositas*. That is, if someone is said to be *curiosus*, I take this to mean that he or she has the quality of *curiositas*. I do not make the corresponding assumption about the adverb *curiose*, which often, as in Latin quite generally, merely means 'carefully.' Since it would be both laborious and unnecessary for present purposes to justify my opinion about *curiose*, I shall let it stand as an assumption.

But I, being otherwise *curiosus*, as soon as I heard the long hoped for name of the art of magic, so far was I from being cautious of Pamphile, that I wilfully longed to hand myself over to such a teacher along with an ample supply of money.

Similarly, in book 5 Cupid warns Psyche in vain against succumbing to *curiositas*, which in turn will initiate the action of her story: ‖

. . . sed identidem monuit ac saepe terruit, ne quando sororum pernicioso consilio suasa de forma mariti quaerat neve se sacrilega curiositate de tanto fortunarum suggestu pessum deiciat. . . . (5. 6. 14–17)

But he repeatedly warned and even frightened her lest, persuaded by the pernicious counsels of her sisters, she should try to see her husband's form, and because of her *sacrilega curiositas* deprive herself of the height of fortune.

Over the last thirty years a great deal of attention has been paid to the general history of *curiositas*,[3] as well as to its specific importance as a theme in the *Golden Ass*.[4] Likewise, some scholarly work on Apuleius has aimed at delineating the boundaries of his Platonism as it is manifested in the *Golden Ass*,[5] and a few scholars have noted a Platonic significance for Lucius' transformation into an ass.[6] Yet no one, I believe, has appreciated the important role played by the theme of *curiositas* in connection with Apuleius' Platonism.[7] In what follows I shall attempt to establish what I believe this role to be and how understanding it helps to reveal the fundamental meaning of Lucius' transformations. ‖

But first a point about methodology. There is by now an established scholarly tradition of examining Apuleius' Platonism, both in his rhetorical and philosophical works and in the *Golden Ass*. In considering the Platonism of the *Golden Ass* one of two approaches is normally taken. According to what may be called the 'Platonic elements' approach, one attempts to cull from the text of the *Golden*

---

[3] Mette (1956); Labhardt (1960); Joly (1961); Walsh (1988).

[4] Lancel (1961); MacKay (1965); Schlam (1968a); Sandy (1972); Penwill (1975).

[5] Thibau (1965); Schlam (1970); Walsh (1981).

[6] Schlam (1970: 480) connects Lucius' asininity with the idea of the transmigration of the soul as it is found in Plato's middle period dialogues. Thibau (1965: 122) sees in Apuleius' ass an allusion to *Phaedrus* 260bc, where Socrates employs the example of an orator who tries to persuade the ignorant that an ass is a horse.

[7] Walsh (1981: 24) and Tatum (1979: 43–7) come close, but fail to make the connection between *curiositas* and Apuleius' Platonism because they do not recognize the symbolic significance of Typhon in Plato's moral psychology, which is discussed in Sect. II of this essay.

Ass specific passages which recall directly ideas that are expressed in the writings of Plato himself.[8] Such passages do exist in the novel, of which the most obvious and most thoroughly treated is the story of Cupid and Psyche.[9] The drawback of this approach, however, is that it leaves one with a list of Platonic elements in the *Golden Ass*, but without a good sense of why Apuleius bothered to include them, other than to have Platonic elements interspersed throughout the text.[10]

The other common approach to the novel's Platonism involves going to a set of sources more immediate to Apuleius, both in time and in intellectual orientation, namely Plutarch and other Middle Platonists, among them Apuleius himself. Scholars who follow this approach sometimes suggest that Apuleius is hardly directly influenced by the writings of Plato.[11] He seems to be influenced primarily by Plutarch, || and his Platonist interests are defined by the concerns of Middle Platonism, prominent among which is a belief in the influence of *daemones* in the sublunary world. While Apuleius' interest in magic and demonology obviously pervades the *Golden Ass* and his other works, I believe that considering this interest alone is not sufficient to reveal the true Platonist underpinnings of the novel.

I intend to straddle the two aforementioned approaches. I will not argue that any particular passage in the *Golden Ass* is derived from

---

[8]   This is the basic approach taken by both Schlam (1970) and Thibau (1965), though the uses to which they put their observed parallels differ greatly.

[9]   I am convinced by Penwill's excellent interpretation of the Cupid and Psyche story from a Platonist perspective (1975: 50–9), which is discussed in n. 16 below. Winkler (1985: 147 n. 13) has recently praised Penwill's overall interpretation as the best of what he disapprovingly calls the 'moralizing' readings of the *Golden Ass*. I agree with Winkler that it is a mistake to read the novel as though it were a treatise. Still, the very terms in which Apuleius chooses to tell his story suggest numerous moralistic implications; it is not a mistake to try to understand what these implications are. At the end of this paper I shall discuss briefly to what extent I believe a 'serious' interpretation of the *Golden Ass* is justified by its Platonic associations.

[10]   Schlam (1970) notes a number of allusions to Plato himself while remaining sensitive to the syncretism and mystical overtones of second century Platonism. Yet even he does not offer a compelling explanation why Apuleius would bother to 'Platonize' his novel, other than that he happened to be a Platonist who was writing a novel. There is of course no *a priori* reason to suppose that Apuleius had an overarching Platonic theme in mind. I shall argue, however, that the role of *curiositas* in the *Golden Ass* suggests a Platonist interpretation that (i) should be fairly obvious to anyone who has read his Plato carefully, and (ii) seems to fit perfectly with what we know of Middle Platonism.

[11]   For example, Walsh (1981: 21): 'it may well be more useful to view Apuleius' novel through the Platonist spectacles of a Plutarch than to expose the correspondences with the dialogues of Plato himself. Clearly the approaches ought to be complementary, but Plutarch is the figure looming closer in the forefront of Apuleius' mind.'

or reminiscent of any particular passage in Plato. I will, however, examine some Platonic images and metaphors for the soul which help to explain why the theme of *curiositas* would be of interest to someone with Platonist concerns. I will further appeal to Plutarch, in particular to his treatise *De Iside et Osiride (DIO)*, to establish that it was part of Apuleius' intellectual climate to interpret Isiac religion Platonically, again in such a way that *curiositas* becomes a theme of interest and importance to a Platonist. I hope to demonstrate that the Platonism of Apuleius' novel informs one of its most central themes, and is not limited merely to the incorporation of Platonic elements into a narrative that is otherwise decidedly un-Platonic.[12]

My procedure in the rest of this essay will fall into four sections. In Section I, I discuss *curiositas* in the *Golden Ass*, primarily with respect to Lucius. I then turn in Section II to examine briefly some ideas and images in Plato's *Republic* and *Phaedrus*, which help to explain the Platonic origin of the theme of meddlesomeness and its association with Typhon. In Section III, I consider Plutarch's Platonist interpretation of Isiac religion. Finally, I return in Section IV to the *Golden Ass* and ‖ conclude briefly with some remarks on the proper place of a Platonist reading in the interpretation of the novel.

I

Lucius' *curiositas* is portrayed as an ingrained and habitual aspect of his character, both before and after his transformation into an ass.[13] After Fotis has offered herself to be punished for her role in the goatskin incident—and along the way revealed the extent of her mistress' magical powers—Lucius describes himself as, 'incited by [his] *familiaris*

---

[12] In this respect, this essay ought to be considered a partial response to Winkler (1985: 124–5), who gives as his 'ultimate assessment of the *Golden Ass* . . . that it is a philosophical comedy about religious knowledge' (124). He sees in Apuleius' 'hermeneutic playfulness' a kind of limited skepticism and suggests lines of research which may ultimately show connections between the *Golden Ass* and Academic skepticism. My overall argument shall suggest that the philosophical background that is most important for understanding the *Golden Ass* is the more dogmatic brand of Platonism of the first and second centuries AD, which relies greatly on interpreting and developing ideas found in such Platonic dialogues as the *Republic*, *Phaedrus*, *Timaeus* and *Laws*, often in response to Stoic, Epicurean or Peripatetic views. It will become clear, I think, that the *curiositas* theme presents such glaringly obvious connections with dogmatic Platonism that this is prima facie the most promising place to look.

[13] Lancel (1961: 26–7).

curiositas and longing to discover the hidden cause of the matter'
(3. 14. 1). Nor is this the only time he characterizes his *curiositas* as
familiaris. In book 9, after his first day of work in the baker's mill, he is
both horrified and excited at the sight of the slaves' hellish lot there:

At ego, quamquam eximie fatigatus et refectione virium vehementer
indiguus et prorsus fame perditus, tamen familiari curiositate attonitus et satis
anxius, postposito cibo, qui copiosus aderat, inoptabilis officinae disciplinam
cum delectatione quadam arbitrabar. (9. 12. 5–9)

But, although I was extremely weary and greatly needed to restore my
strength and had been utterly devastated with hunger, nevertheless I was
sufficiently anxious and excited by my *familiaris curiositas* that I observed with
a certain delight the condition of the mill, without even touching my food,
which was in plentiful supply.

Thus, in two very different circumstances—as man and ass, as
forgiving lover and overworked beast of burden—Lucius is capable of
precisely the same reaction. The use of the same adjective in both
contexts indicates the consistent and integrated role Lucius' *curiositas* plays in his orientation toward the world. The fact that *familiaris*
is the adjective so used has further significance, for it emphasizes the
intimacy of the connection between Lucius' character and the quality of *curiositas*. Lucius is habitually *curiosus*: he carries this quality
with him wherever he goes and under whatever guise—whether in
the skin of a man or of an ass.[14] ||

Indeed, the continuity between Lucius as ass and man which his
curiositas provides serves even as a source of comfort to him when his
luck takes a turn for the worse in the baker's mill. Reflecting on the
sad condition of his companion horses and mules, he realizes that the
harsh demands of the mill will soon take a similar toll on him, and
he becomes morosely despondent:

Nec ullam uspiam cruciabilis vitae solacium aderat, nisi quod ingenita mihi
curiositate recreabar, dum praesentiam mean parvi facientes libere, quae volunt, omnes et agunt et loquuntur. (9. 13. 13–16)

Nor was any consolation for my torturous life at hand, except that I was reborn
because of my *ingenita curiositas* so long as everyone freely did and said what
they wanted, caring not at all for my presence.

---

[14] Winkler (1985: 151) comments interestingly without making specific mention of
Lucius' *curiositas*: 'The folk metaphysics of transformation tales requires that the person before and the animal after have a common core of identity. The same thinking
ego is transferred to a new body, there to discover new physical sensations . . . but with
memory, language, *value and personality* intact' (emphasis added).

It is not just that Lucius derives satisfaction from his newly un-
trammeled access to the supposedly hidden actions and words of others.
The *curiositas* which was such a prominent feature of his character
as a man also provides a point of contact with that previous life, during which, as he has just said (9. 13. 11), he enjoyed his share of good
fortune. This point of contact is underscored by the adjective *ingenita*,
'inborn,' which both emphasizes again how essential *curiositas* is to
Lucius' character and calls us back to the original Lucius. There is even
a poignant note to this mention of his *curiositas*, for it provides his only
solace in the present circumstances and is thereby responsible for a
kind of rebirth: '*recreabar*' he says, when what he most desperately wants
under the circumstances is a real *recreation* as a man.[15]

Psyche's *curiositas* is also modified by significant adjectives. In her
case, though, it is not the ingrained and habitual nature of the
curiositas that is emphasized, but rather its impetuosity and sacrile- ‖
giousness.[16] Cupid, when he finally allows her to see her sisters in the
passage quoted earlier, makes a single proviso: that she not be persuaded to look at him lest 'because of *sacrilega curiositas*' she 'deprive
herself of the height of fortune' (5. 6. 15–17). This is the first mention
of Psyche's *curiositas* and at this point in the story it is still only
potential. The adjective *sacrilega* serves then to set the tone for her subsequent actions. The misfortunes she ultimately endures for disregard-
ing this warning are implicitly a kind of punishment for an act of

[15] The irony of Lucius' comments about his *ingenita curiositas* in 9. 13 has been strangely
lost on commentators. Walsh (1988: 77–8) and Schlam (1968a: 123) both note that
Lucius' *curiositas* is here a source of consolation to him without mentioning the strong
resonance that a word like *recreabar* is bound to have in this context. Winkler (1985:
167) writes of '*solacium* and *recreabar* as defining the point of the comment,' but even
he does not say *what* point *recreabar* is defining.

[16] Virtually everyone who has written on *curiositas* in Apuleius has noted that the
striking parallelism between the stories of Psyche and Lucius centers on the fact that
both endure their particular hardships because of *curiositas*: Mette (1956: 231);
Labhardt (1960: 215, 1961: 34); MacKay (1965: 477–8); Schlam (1968a: 122); Tatum
(1969: 509); Walsh (1970: 190–3); Sandy (1972: 180); Walsh (1988: 76).

Penwill (1975: 50–9) has argued convincingly against the orthodoxy that the parallels between the stories of Psyche and Lucius 'serve the function of turning the
[Cupid and Psyche] episode into a restatement of the novel's main theme' (50–1). His
argument turns on recognizing that the story of Cupid and Psyche is, if anything, an
anti-Platonist allegory. The *Voluptas* to which Psyche gives birth is mortal (5. 11.
20–3). It therefore represents not the pleasure which the soul derives from contemplation of the form of Beauty, but rather the base pleasure which serves to enslave the
soul to the body (cf. *Phaedrus* 250e). Penwill writes: 'He who would seek salvation must,
like Lucius in book 11, *break* the tie between Psyche and Cupid: only then can he come
to an understanding of the truth' (59).

impiety. Psyche similarly fails to obey the tower's instructions in book 6, when her mind is seized by *temeraria curiositas* and she opens the box containing Proserpina's *divina formonsitas* in hopes of procuring a little for herself.

In order to appreciate these patterns in the usage of *curiositas* we need first of all an accurate idea of what it is supposed to mean. It is just here, however, that we encounter a stumbling block, for the word has almost no prior history in Latin, nor does 'curiosity' carry the same connotations in English. To illustrate this latter point we may take two examples, from the first and last books of the *Golden Ass*, respectively.

Curiosus first occurs early in book 1, when Lucius implores Aristomenes to tell his story:

Immo vero, inquam, impertite sermonis non quidem curiosum, sed qui velim scire vel cuncta vel certe plurima. (1. 2. 19–20)

Please, I said, share your conversation with one who is not *curiosus*, but who wishes to know everything or at least most things. ‖

The strong irony of Lucius' claim that he is not *curiosus* makes it difficult to tell how seriously we are supposed to take him. But read straightforwardly, his words here imply a contrast between *curiositas* and the plain desire to know many things. The form of his entreaty to these strangers he has met on the road is: 'do x for me, because I am not y, but only z.' For this entreaty to make sense, the qualities of y-ness and z-ness must not only be different, but y-ness must be recognizable as the more worthy of reproach. Otherwise, Lucius' words provide no incentive to Aristomenes to 'share his conversation.' Thus, near the very beginning of the novel, we find a distinction between *curiositas* and the desire for knowledge which implies that *curiositas* is blameworthy in a way that mere curiosity is not.[17]

---

[17] These lines are not always read this way. Penwill (1975: 67) translates: 'Please share your story with one who is not *just* inquisitive, but desires to know either everything or at least most things' (emphasis added). If this translation is correct, then Lucius is saying in effect that he is *extremely* curious, and the contrast which I see in these lines is not really there. There are two objections to Penwill's translation.

(i) The connotations of *curiosus* and *curiositas* in the *Golden Ass* are always pejorative. Though some commentators have seen in Lucius' comparison of himself to Odysseus (9. 13) a hint at a good kind of *curiositas* (Schlam 1968a: 123; Walsh 1988: 78), it is a slender hint and is supported nowhere else in the work. It would therefore be ridiculous for Lucius to describe himself as *extremely* curious as an incentive to converse with him. This would amount to recommending himself as a busybody.

(ii) Latin grammar prefers the interpretation offered here. The *'quidem . . . sed . . .'* locution is used to express a contrast between a pair of opposed terms, often with a

A contrast between *curiositas* and curiosity is also implied by Lucius' words in book 11, when he explains to the *scrupulosus lector* why he cannot divulge the secrets of his initiation into the mysteries of Isis:

Dicerem, si dicere liceret, cognosceres, si liceret audire. sed parem noxam contraherent et aures et linguae illae temerariae curiositatis. (11. 23. 20–2)

I would tell if it were right to tell, and you would learn if it were right to hear. But [your] ears and [my] tongue would contract an equal punishment for that *temeraria curiositas*. ∥

The fact that Lucius and the *scrupulosus lector* would contract an equal punishment for *curiositas* suggests that they are both equally guilty of it. But this is difficult to understand if *curiositas* is mere curiosity, for in telling about the Isiac rites Lucius would not be satisfying his own desire to know, but rather ours, as readers of the novel. One could explain this discrepancy away, as does Griffiths, by saying that 'the teller also is involved in the guilt of curiosity since he is attempting to satisfy it in another.'[18] This explanation begs the question at hand, however, for it assumes that *curiositas* and 'curiosity' are near synonyms, an assumption which there is reason to question. But more importantly it also ignores what is surely Lucius' point here, namely, that *he* will not now succumb to the impulses of *curiositas* by impiously revealing the secrets of Isis, since *he* is no longer a *curiosus*.[19] The question now is, how does the quality of *curiositas* differ from curiosity understood as the plain desire for knowledge?

The answer to this question is to be derived, I believe, from Apuleius' Platonist tradition. So far as I can tell, there is undisputed

concessive sense to the *quidem* side of the opposition. (See Kühner and Stegmann 1976: 623–4.) Penwill's translation, by his own reckoning, fails to preserve such a contrast, for he believes that Lucius' indiscriminate desire to know everything just *is* his *curiositas* (67–8).

[18] Griffiths (1975: 294).

[19] There is then an implied contrast between Lucius and Psyche which supports Penwill's thesis (see n. 16 above). Psyche's *curiositas* was specifically said to be *temeraria* when she looked into the box that was supposed to contain Proserpina's beauty (6. 20. 15), an act that is reasonably described as prying into and therefore meddling with divine secrets (cf. Schlam 1968a: 123). Lucius' language here in book 11 takes on the tone of an announcement that he will not succumb to the kind of temptation that proved too much for Psyche. This contrast between Lucius and Psyche is in line with a distinction observed by Lancel (1961) between two kinds of *curiositas* in the *Golden Ass*, '*curiositas* des *mirabilia*' and '*curiositas* ubristique,' the latter of which he describes as 'un sentiment d'impatience qui conduit à des initiatives sacrilèges accomplies suivant des techniques contraignantes, magiques pour tout dire' (31).

scholarly agreement that *curiositas* is a coinage that attempts to capture in Latin the meaning of the Greek terms *periergia* and *polupragmosunē*,[20] which are themselves frequently treated as synonyms (e.g., Plutarch, *De curiositate* 516a, 519c). If there is even a rough equivalence between the Greek and Latin terms, then two things are clear. First, 'curiosity' will not be adequate as a universal translation for *curiositas*, which ought to mean something closer to 'meddlesomeness.' This point is supported by Latin etymology as well: the *curios-* root suggests being full of cares, i.e., *too many* or *inappropriate* cares.[21] This ‖ does not mean that *curiositas cannot* mean 'curiosity,' only that the Latin word has a different semantic range: curiosity is, in some of its manifestations, just one species of meddlesome behavior.[22] Secondly, since Apuleius is an avowed Platonist, and *polupragmosunē* is a prominent metaphor in Plato's moral psychology, a consideration of *polupragmosunē* in Plato should provide a promising first step to uncovering both the meaning of the Latin word as Apuleius uses it, and the Platonism of his novel.

II

In book 4 of the *Republic*, Socrates describes justice in terms of the avoidance of *polupragmosunē*:

Καὶ μὴν ὅτι γε τὸ τὰ αὑτοῦ πράττειν καὶ μὴ πολυπραγμονεῖν δικαιοσύνη ἐστί, καὶ τοῦτο ἄλλων τε πολλῶν ἀκηκόαμεν καὶ αὐτοὶ πολλάκις εἰρήκαμεν. (433a8–b1)

We have heard from many others and have often said ourselves that justice is doing one's own and not meddling.

---

[20] Mette (1956: 229); Labhardt (1960: 206); Lancel (1961: 26); Schlam (1968a: 121); Walsh (1988: 75–6).

[21] Unlike *curiositas*, *curiosus* has an extensive history in Latin prior to Apuleius, and is not always used pejoratively, as one can tell from a glance at the entries in the *Oxford Latin Dictionary*. The pejorative sense of *curiosus* seems to have come to the fore with the Stoic notion that intellectual curiosity should be directed toward realizing moral goodness (see Labhardt 1960: 210–14; Joly 1961: 35–8; Walsh 1988: 78–80). Christian writers after Apuleius, most notably Augustine, took up the notion of *sacrilega curiositas* with a vengeance (see especially Walsh 1988: 81–4).

[22] This realization makes it easy to explain what Lucius has in mind at 11. 23. 20–2. *Curiositas* denotes meddlesome and inappropriate behavior, which comprehends *both* prying into things one is not supposed to learn *and* divulging information to those who ought not to learn it.

This is, in philosophical parlance, an other-regarding conception of justice, since whether one is just depends solely on one's behavior *vis-à-vis* one's neighbors. This formulation is represented by Socrates as relatively common and therefore uncontroversial. He is not content with merely describing just behavior, however, and therefore goes on to apply this definition of justice to the psychic life of the individual.

Later in book 4, after the soul has been divided into rational, spirited and appetitive parts, Socrates is able to characterize justice as consisting in a certain relationship among these three parts of the soul: ‖

Τὸ δέ γε ἀληθές, τοιοῦτόν τι ἦν, ὡς ἔοικεν, ἡ δικαιοσύνη ἀλλ᾽ οὐ περὶ τὴν ἔξω πρᾶξιν τῶν αὑτοῦ, ἀλλὰ περὶ τὴν ἐντός, ὡς ἀληθῶς περὶ ἑαυτὸν καὶ τὰ ἑαυτοῦ, μὴ ἐάσαντα τἀλλότρια πράττειν ἕκαστον ἐν αὑτῷ μηδὲ πολυπραγμονεῖν πρὸς ἄλληλα τὰ ἐν τῇ ψυχῇ γένη. . . . (443c9–d3)

Justice truly was some such thing, so it seems, though not with regard to doing one's own externally, but rather internally, concerning what is truly one's self and one's own; that is, one does not allow the parts of the soul each to do another's work, or to meddle with one another.

Justice, and therefore *polupragmosunē*, has been given an entirely new reference. A man's justice is defined not by his behavior toward others, but by an ordering of the parts of his soul, according to which each one performs its and only its function. *Polupragmosunē* is now not merely the name for a certain kind of political behavior, but also, and primarily, for a condition of the soul, wherein at least one of the parts pre-empts the work of another part. This conception of justice, unlike the non-controversial principle from which it is derived, is no longer entirely other-regarding, for in order to see whether someone is just we must look to his soul and not only to the way he treats his fellow citizens. Nor, on the other hand, can we tell whether someone is *unjust* merely by observing his behavior, for injustice is properly a kind of *psychic* meddling, whereby the appetitive and spirited parts of the soul seize from the intellect its decision-making function.

In *Republic* 9 Socrates puts this analysis to work to decide once and for all between the lives of justice and injustice. Here he constructs an image (*eikōn*) of the soul, which corresponds to the tripartite division of book 4 in the following way:

Part of soul	Part of image
Rational	Man
Spirited	Lion
Appetitive	Multiform and many-headed beast

The three parts of the image are attached so as to grow together (588d7), and then another *eikōn* is placed around them, the image of a man,

ὥστε τῷ μὴ δυναμένῳ τὰ ἐντὸς ὁρᾶν, ἀλλὰ τὸ ἔξω μόνον ἔλυτρον ὁρῶντι, ἓν ζῷον φαίνεσθαι, ἄνθρωπον. (588d11 e1)

. . . so that to one who is unable to look within, but sees only the outer shell, it seems to be a single animal, a human being. ‖

Socrates uses this image in his final attack on the proponents of injustice.[23] Within the soul of the unjust man, the true *polupragmōn*, the lion and multiform beast are dominant. Socrates describes their domination in a manner that is both picturesque and rhetorically effective: they starve and weaken the man, and are able to drag him wherever they choose to go (588e3–589a4). The unjust man therefore presents the outward appearance of a human being, while inside, where it really counts, he is more a wild and uncivilized beast. Plato seems to intend a strong sense in which the unjust man really is less a man than a beast; he is literally subject to a mass of unruly and bestial appetites, which effectively subdue the only properly human part of his soul.

Similar imagery occurs again in *Phaedrus*, though this time with a twist that provides an intriguing connection to Plutarch's interpretation of the Isis myth. Early in the dialogue, after reaching their *locus amoenus* outside the city, Phaedrus mentions to Socrates that he thinks this is supposed to be the place from which Boreas snatched Oreithuia. Socrates points out that the spot is actually 'two or three stadia away,' upon which Phaedrus asks whether he thinks the myth is true. Socrates responds that such considerations are not worth his time, and explains:

σκοπῶ οὐ ταῦτα ἀλλ’ ἐμαυτόν, εἴτε τι θηρίον ὂν τυγχάνω Τυφῶνος πολυπλοκώτερον καὶ μᾶλλον ἐπιτεθυμμένον, εἴτε ἡμερώτερόν τε καὶ ἁπλούστερον ζῷον, θείας τινὸς καὶ ἀτύφου μοίρας φύσει μετέχον. (230a3–6)
I do not investigate these things, but look only to myself, to see whether I happen to be a beast more complex and inflamed with desires than Typhon, or whether I am a gentler and simpler animal, possessing in my nature a share of something divine and un-Typhonic.

Poluplokōteron here has much the same associations as the adjectives *poikilon* (588c7) and *pantodapon* (588d5), which were used to describe

---

[23] See Irwin (1977: 243–8) for a discussion of this image and its adequacy as an answer to the challenge of Glaucon and Adeimantus in *Republic* 2.

the beast of *Republic* 9; *epitethumenon* plays on Typhon's name while also referring to the appetitive part of the soul. The difference between the two images is that here Socrates compares his soul to Typhon rather than to the *Republic*'s polymorphous monstrosity. Yet even this is not a great difference. In Hesiod's *Theogony* (821 ff.) Typhon is portrayed as ‖ quite variegated both in appearance and in the sounds he makes.[24] He is clearly a principle of violence and disorder. Plato is able to fill out this vague impression with the specific content of his moral psychology: Typhon represents that *polupragmosunē* within the soul which defines injustice. Nor was the significance of Typhon in the writings of Plato lost on Plutarch. He makes full use of it in *DIO*, which bears directly on Apuleius' Platonism as it is manifested in the *Golden Ass*.

III

DIO provides a wealth of information about the forms of Egyptian myths and rituals which pertain to Isis and Osiris and their ongoing conflict with the evil Seth. But it is clear that Plutarch's primary concern is not to record information about Egyptian religion. The treatise is addressed to his friend Clea, an initiate of Isis, and is intended to demonstrate to her that the rites and mythology of Isiac religion have a significance that can be properly revealed only by the application of a critical and philosophical intelligence.

Indeed, while Plutarch clearly believes that religious knowledge in general is acquired by means of a philosophical approach, it is also clear that he thinks such an approach has particular value in the case of Isiac religion. He makes this plain near the beginning of the treatise, in chapter 2, when he characterizes Isis as 'exceptionally wise and a philosopher' (351e) and the true Isiac as one who, regarding the rites of Isis, 'investigates with reason and philosophizes concerning the truth in them' (3. 352c). This attitude toward the religion of Isis is a direct correlate of his belief that it reflects truths that are universally applicable and not just peculiar to Egypt (66. 377cd, 67. 377ef). Such an attitude among Greeks toward foreign religions can be traced back at least to Herodotus, but Plutarch differs substantially

---

[24] Following West (1966: 252), I take Typhoeus and Typhon to be the same figure. There seems to be no controversy in doing this.

from Herodotus in that he has a sharply defined ideology as to the nature of the truths that religious practices and beliefs seek to express. This ideology is his own version of Platonism, a fact he announces explicitly when he writes, in chapter 48, that,

τὰ ἐπιόντα δηλώσει τοῦ λόγου τὴν Αἰγυπτίων θεολογίαν μάλιστα ταύτῃ τῇ φιλοσοφίᾳ συνοικειοῦντος. (371a) ||

the rest of the treatise (*logos*) will elucidate the theology of the Egyptians by relating it especially to this [i.e., Platonic] philosophy.

Plutarch's Platonizing interpretation of the Isis myth starts from a dualistic view of the world, which he bases on his view of the *Timaeus* and book 10 of the *Laws*. The presence of evil in the created world is to be explained by the existence of both good and evil world souls. The evil soul is necessary because if god were the cause of everything, then there ought to be no evil, whereas if he were the cause of nothing, there would be no good (45. 369a; cf. *De def. or.* 414f). The world, however, is manifestly both good and evil. Plato's *Laws* lends authority to this view, for at 896d the Athenian Stranger seems to posit at least two souls, one good and one evil, to explain the presence of good and evil in the world.[25] Plutarch introduces to this polarity a third intermediate nature, which has a natural affinity and longing for the good soul, but which may also be acted upon by the bad one (48. 371f). This third principle he identifies as Isis, and characterizes in terms which indicate he believes her to be the receptacle (*hupodochē*) of the *Timaeus* (49a, 51a):

Ἡ γὰρ Ἶσίς ἐστι μὲν τὸ τῆς φύσεως θῆλυ καὶ δεκτικὸν ἁπάσης γενέσεως, καθὸ τιθήνη καὶ πανδεχὴς ὑπὸ τοῦ Πλάτωνος, ὑπὸ δὲ τῶν πολλῶν μυριώνυμος κέκληται διὰ τὸ πάσας ὑπὸ τοῦ λόγου τρεπομένη μορφὰς δέχεσθαι καὶ ἰδέας. (53. 372e)

For Isis is the female principle in nature and is receptive of all generation, and accordingly is called 'nurse' and 'all-receptive' by Plato, but 'myriad-named' by the many, because in being transformed by reason, she receives all the forms and ideas.

---

[25] I say 'seems to posit' because it is notoriously difficult to discern Plato's exact intention here, especially since the *Timaeus* has not explicitly prepared us for an evil world soul. Dillon (1977: 203) writes: 'Plato, as so often, leaves this disquieting development in philosophy hanging in the air, but what he let slip in this passage is enough for a man like Plutarch to build on.'

Cherniss (1971) has argued forcefully that Plato does not posit an evil world soul in *Laws* 10. For a recent discussion of some of these issues, see Mohr (1985*b*).

As the principle which is receptive of Forms, which are the proper objects of the intellect, Isis is associated with the good world-soul, ‖ Osiris, and assists him in the perpetual conflict with Typhon, who is identified as the evil world-soul.

Now, this interpretation is clearly an inaccurate representation of Plato. The receptacle of the *Timaeus* is supposed to serve as a neutral substrate for the generation of sensible entities. As such it is intermediate between Forms and sensibles, not between good and evil souls, and therefore could not be a kind of soul, as Isis is supposed to be.[26] But whatever the defects of Plutarch's views as an interpretation of Plato, they comprise, as we shall see, the backdrop for some interesting connections to the *Golden Ass*.

First consider the opposition between Osiris and Typhon. Plutarch identifies Osiris as *nous* in the soul, and characterizes the good order of the seasons and heavenly bodies, in near-neo-Platonic language, as an 'emanation (*aporrhoē*) and manifest image' (49. 371ab) of Osiris. Typhon, however, is a principle of destruction in nature, and

... τῆς ψυχῆς τὸ παθητικὸν καὶ τιτανικὸν καὶ ἄλογον καὶ ἔμπληκτον ... (49. 371b)

... is the part of the soul which is passionate, titanic, irrational and impulsive.

As in Plato, Typhon represents those elements which are responsible for disorder in the soul, psychic *polupragmosunē*. Nor would it be unlikely that Plutarch has in mind the *Phaedrus* passage discussed earlier, for he actually quotes it verbatim elsewhere (*Adv. Col.* 1119b). This Platonic characterization of Typhon in *DIO*, when combined with the role Plutarch has assigned him in Isiac religion, introduces some new and important associations.

Recall Plutarch's initial exhortation to Clea to pursue a rationalistic, one might even say 'gnostic,' approach to Isis. Typhon is there opposed to her as well, because he is 'puffed up (*tetuphomenos*) with ignorance and deceit (*anoia* and *apatē*)' (2. 351f). Plutarch then describes the genuine Isiac attendants as 'those who carry in their

---

[26] Michael Frede has pointed out to me that it was natural for later Platonists, relying on *Phaedrus* and *Laws*, to suppose that the receptacle *was* ensouled, due to its shifting motions. Plutarch's interpretation of the source of evil in *De animae procreatione in Timaeo* (1014e–1015f) bears this out, though he stops short of claiming that matter in itself is evil. He attributes evil rather to the matter's disorderly motions, to which god put a stop when he created the world (1015e).

souls, ‖ as in a box, the sacred *logos* about the gods which is pure of all superstition and meddlesomeness (*periergia*)' (3. 352b, following Griffiths translation). It would perhaps be a mistake to overemphasize this occurrence of *periergia*, but neither should it be dismissed. Plutarch wrote a treatise on *polupragmosunē*, for which he unselfconsciously uses *periergia* as a synonym (516a, 519c). When he says in *DIO* that the *logos* of Isis is free of *periergia*, he no doubt means that one can only acquire knowledge of her when free of the interfering and unhealthy impulses which riddle the soul of the *polupragmōn*.[27] The idea that intellectual progress takes place only in the absence of strong and cumbersome attachments to material desires is nowhere more prominent than in the writings of Plato's middle period. There is, therefore, a thoroughly Platonic cast to Plutarch's representation of the opposition between Isis and Typhon, which clearly acknowledges the power of psychic meddlesomeness to obstruct one's progress toward truth and the goddess.

Of equal importance for present purposes is Typhon's special, though not exclusive, association with the ass.[28] Plutarch relates that at Coptos there are festivals which involve abusing men of ruddy complexion and tossing an ass off a cliff, 'because Typhon was ruddy and asinine in form' (30. 362f). In Busiris and Lycopolis the *salpinx* is not played because of the similarity of its sound to the braying of an ass, and the ass is generally believed to be impure and 'daemonic' (*daemonikos*) because of its similarity to Typhon (362f).

This symbolism of the ass in Isiac religion helps first of all to ‖ explain Isis' words to Lucius in book 11 of the *Golden Ass*, when she appears in his dream and instructs him first to eat the roses her priest will be carrying in the following day's procession and then to 'shed the skin

---

[27] It is a recurrent theme in Plutarch's *De curiositate* that *polupragmosunē* is a state of the soul which hinders one's progress toward knowledge and virtue. In his programmatic remarks in chapter 1 Plutarch describes it as one of the 'diseased and harmful affections which provide winter and darkness to the soul' (515c). Later he points out that inappropriate interest in the affairs of others has the pernicious effect of drawing one away from the many fine pursuits of life (519f; cf. 522e).

[28] It is of course Seth, not Typhon, who was originally associated with the ass in Egyptian religion. But the identification of Typhon and Seth in Greek thought reaches back to Herodotus (2. 144, 3. 5), Aeschylus (*Supplices* 560) and Pherecydes of Syros (see Kranz 1934: 114; Griffiths 1960, 1970: 259, 389–90). It must have been quite natural long before the time of Plutarch to use the name Typhon even when relating Egyptian myths. It is interesting too that the original Greek version of the Typhon myth seems to have been derived from earlier Asian origins. West (1966: 379–80) lists features of the Typhonomachy in the *Theogony* that associate it with Near Eastern myths of succession.

of that vile (*detestabilis*) beast that has long been most hated to me'
(11. 6. 6–7, following Griffiths' translation).[29] It is worth noting,
too, that Plutarch also says the Egyptians generally believe the ass
to be 'daemonic,' for *daemonikos* is a particularly Greek epithet.[30]
Superficially, the daemonic quality of the ass is its association with
Typhon. According to Plutarch, Isis, Osiris and Typhon were all
three originally daemones, though Isis and Osiris have been elevated
to the ranks of the gods because of their goodness (27. 361de, 30. 362e).
Typhon, however, remains a daemon, hence the daemonic nature of
animals associated with him.

Yet this explains only *why* the ass is called 'daemonic,' and not at
all what Plutarch or anyone else takes this adjective to mean. It
would therefore be helpful to have an idea of what a daemon is conceived to be in Middle Platonist thought. Here we may take as an
example Apuleius' own characterization of the differences among
human beings, *daemones*, and gods in De deo Socratis:[31]

Sunt enim inter nos ac deos ut loco regionis ita ingenio mentis intersiti, habentes
communem cum superis immortalitatem, cum inferis passionem. nam
proinde ut nos pati possunt omnia animorum placamenta vel ‖ incitamenta. . . .
quae propterea passiva non absurde, ut arbitror, nominavi, quod sunt iisdem,
quibus nos, turbationibus mentis obnoxii. (*De deo Socratis* 13)

They are situated between us and the gods both in the location of their
domain and in the nature of their souls, having in common with their super-
iors immortality, and with their inferiors the passions. For they are able, just
as we are, to suffer everything that either soothes or incites the soul. . . . and
so I have called them, not absurdly I think, 'passive' because they are vulnerable to the same perturbations of the soul as we.

[29] Griffiths (1975: 162) lists evidence for the Sethian ass-association, among which
is the depiction of Seth as an ass-headed man in the Greek magical papyri
(Preisendanz 1974: pl. 2, illus. ll), which is reprinted in Tatum (1979: 44).

[30] Hani (1976: 228–9) points out that there is no Egyptian word that corresponds
to the meaning of *daemon* and *daemonikos* in Greek, though he endorses a loose parallelism between the animistic tendencies of Egyptian religion and the role of *daemones*
in Greek thought.

[31] According to Beaujeu (1973), Apuleius' description of the characteristics of daemones is drawn from a ' "chatéchisme" platonicienne' (228). It certainly owes much
to an image employed by Xenocrates and related by Plutarch (*De defectu oraculorum*
416cd = Heinze (1892: fr. 23 166–8), according to which the divine is like an equilat-
eral, the daemonic an isosceles and the human a scalene triangle.

Apuleius attributes the great variety of religious rites and practices to the fact that
different daemones delight in different things depending on the disposition of their
souls (*De deo Socratis* 14). This is close to Xenocrates' ascription of unlucky days and
festivals that involve unpleasantries (lamentations, beatings, foul language, etc.) to evil
daemones (ap. Plutarch, *DIO* 361b = fr. 25 Heinze; cf. Dillon 1977: 318–19).

According to this description of the nature of *daemones*, the point of the epithet 'daemonic' should be to emphasize susceptibility to the passions of the soul. Evil *daemones*, such as Typhon, are especially subject to and representative of those passions most tied to the body, and that most hinder the progress of the intellect. This idea seems to be behind the Pythagoreans' calling Typhon *daemonikos* (363a), and Plutarch's assertion in another treatise that 'the irrational and disordered and violent element in us is not from the gods (*theion*) but is rather *daemonic*' (*De esu carnium* 996c).

Now, it may seem strange that an unembodied soul such as a daemon should be representative of, or even subject to, affections normally associated with a composite nature. Two things help to explain this feature of Middle Platonist demonology. First, Plato himself portrayed all three parts of the soul existing in the afterlife, most explicitly in the *Phaedrus* myth of the charioteer (cf. *Phaedo* 81c8–d4).[32] It would therefore have been unproblematic for a Platonist to think of an unembodied soul as having 'physical' desires. Secondly, later Platonists actually conceived of *daemones* as material beings. Apparently reading *Symposium* 202e into *Timaeus* 39e–40a, the Pseudo-Platonic *Epinomis* posits a scale of living beings in the order earth, water, air, aether and fire (984b2–d2). The aetherial beings are *daemones*, and the aerial beings are very similar to them in nature, though they are called only the *aerion genos* (984d8–e1). These beings, unlike the gods, are subject to feelings of pleasure and pain (985a4–7), and it is natural to suppose that this passionate aspect of their nature is due at least in part to their materiality. Apuleius himself adopts the *Epinomis*' arguments in *De deo Socratis* (8–11) in order to establish the existence of *daemones* as ‖ beings whose proper domain is the region between the moon and the stars and whose matter is aether.[33]

This very selective consideration of Plato and Middle Platonist thought makes it possible now to appreciate better the intellectual background of Lucius' metamorphoses in the *Golden Ass*. It is generally acknowledged that Apuleius was influenced as a Platonist by Plutarch, and the two references in the *Golden Ass* to Lucius' ancestor of the same name (1. 2. 2, 2. 3. 3) almost compel one to think of the historical Plutarch.[34] Given his Platonizing interpretation of the conflict between Isis and Typhon, and the appearance of Typhon

[32] See Guthrie (1957).
[33] See Taràn (1975: 162) on the *Epinomis*' influence on Apuleius' demonology.
[34] Walsh (1981: 22).

in the writings of both Plato and Plutarch as a symbol of those excessive appetites which are responsible for psychic *polupragmosunē* and *periergia*, the connection between a Platonist reading of the *Golden Ass* and the theme of *curiositas* is close at hand.

IV

Lucius' metamorphosis into an ass symbolizes his transformation into a Typhon figure. This transformation is both caused by and emblematic of his *curiositas*, that quality of soul which is the cause of meddlesome behavior and which itself consists in the meddlesome hindrance of the rational faculty by one's appetites and desires. Accordingly, what one scholar has said about the ass as a symbol for Lucius' sexuality applies at least as well to his *curiositas*: 'The metamorphosis changes his appearance, but it serves to objectify rather than alter his nature.'[35] Read Platonically, the *eikōn* of *Republic* 9 has, with an Isiac twist, been turned inside out: Lucius becomes outwardly what he had previously been only inwardly, a meddlesome ass. It is the intervention of Isis—worldly principle of rationality and order (cf. 11. 5. 1 ff.)—that allows the man inside Lucius to come to the fore and rule over the whole person, just as in Platonic moral psychology only the just soul is ruled by the man within and not by a horde of bestial appetites.

Now consider this interpretation of Lucius' metamorphoses in the ‖ light of Mithras' words to him in book 11, after he has been turned back into a man:

Nec tibi natales ac ne dignitas quidem, vel ipsa, qua flores, usquam doctrina profuit, sed lubrico virentis aetatulae ad serviles delapsus voluptates curiositatis inprosperae sinistrum praemium reportasti. (11. 15. 3–7)

Neither your lineage nor your dignity nor the education in which you abound did you any good, but down the slope of verdant youth did you slip into slavish pleasures and gather the sinister reward of your unlucky *curiositas*.

It is obviously important for the Platonist reading I am suggesting that Mithras here attributes Lucius' bad luck to his *curiositas*. But also intriguing is the connection implied by his words between 'slavish pleasures' and *curiositas*. This connection is both significant and not entirely obvious. Of 27 occurrences in the novel (excluding the name of Psyche's

---

[35] Schlam (1970: 481). See too the remarks of Winkler quoted in n. 14 above.

baby) the word *voluptas* refers 26 times to pleasures of the senses.[36] It often denotes sexual pleasure, as in the phrase *voluptas veneria* (1. 8. 2, 4. 27. 22; cf. 2. 10. 1, 17, 10. 20. 10), and frequently refers to the pleasure of some spectacular or beautiful sight, as in Socrates' *voluptas gladitorii spectaculi* (1. 7. 13)[37] or Psyche's gazing on Cupid *summa cum voluptate* (5. 2. 9; cf. 4. 13. 6, 14. 2). It may refer to the pleasure which motivates greed, as in Myrmex's deliberation: *illuc cruciatus, hic voluptas* (9. 19. 9). And we know from book 2 that Lucius was susceptible to the lure of erotic pleasure, especially if it promised to ‖ satisfy his hair-fetish—to say nothing of his desire to dabble in magic. What, however, does pleasure-seeking in general have to do with *curiositas*?

The answer implicit in Apuleius' Platonist tradition is that *curiositas* is really the daemonic, Typhonic or asinine condition of being under the control of one's appetites and the pleasures which motivate them. It is when the appetites predominate in the soul that one meddles, just as the appetites themselves meddle when they usurp from the intellect its role as decision-maker for the whole person. Accordingly, Lucius felt impelled to try his hand at magic, despite the knowledge that it would be dangerous and even impious to do so. So too Psyche could not resist sneaking a look at Cupid or Proserpina's beauty, though in each case she had been warned of the consequences of her actions. Under the sway of *curiositas* both Lucius and Psyche let rational considerations be overcome by the power of their sensual desires and pleasures, of their desires to do or know things they aren't supposed to do or know and which are somehow bad for them. They resemble Plato's *eikōn* of the unjust soul, whose human part is dominated and weakened by its two bestial parts. And what more 'bestial' desire

---

[36] The one non-physical *voluptas* in the novel is in book 11, where Lucius describes the pleasure he derives from contemplating the statue of Isis: 'Paucis dehinc ibidem commoratus diebus inexplicabili voluptate simulacri divini perfruabar, inremunerabili quippe beneficio pigneratus' (11. 24. 21–3). See Penwill (1975: 52).

[37] It is worth noting that Aristomenes' narration of Socrates' story in Book 1 bristles with references to *curiositas*, pleasure and transformation. First, Socrates attributes his misfortune to a detour he made to enjoy a gladitorial spectacle: 'Me miserum, infit, qui dum voluptatem gladitorii spectaculi satis famigerabilis consector, in has aerumnas incidi' (1. 7. 10–12). Aristomenes then denounces Socrates for preferring the 'voluptatem veneriam et scortum scorteum' (1. 8. 3) to his family. Socrates is alarmed by Aristomenes' strong language and relates to him a virtual litany of bestial transformations effected by Meroe (1. 9. 1–10). Later, when Meroe and Panthia catch up with them, Meroe announces that she will punish Aristomenes for his *curiositas* (which she associates with talkativeness): 'Faxo eum sero, immo statim, immo vero iam nunc, ut et praecedentis dicacitatis et instantis curiositas paeniteat' (1. 12. 1921; cf. 1. 17. 7).

could there be than Lucius' long-standing wish to *become* a beast by means of magic?

One commentator has recently referred to *curiositas* in the *Golden Ass* as 'the key to the novel.'[38] Whether or not one should accord overwhelming authority to any single theme in this complex work, it seems without doubt that *curiositas* is *one* of the keys to the novel. If the case I have been making stands up, then this one key cannot be properly understood without considering Apuleius' Platonist tradition. But it would certainly be a mistake to focus narrowly on Apuleius' Platonism and impute an entirely moralistic intention to the novel as a whole. The curious and meddlesome young man who accidentally turns himself into an ass is, after all, the butt of a hilarious joke. Nor is Lucius the *curiosus* a demonstrably bad person; he has his own particular desires and is attracted by the pleasures which satisfy them. Sometimes they get the better of him and cause him to take unnecessary and dangerous risks. At least once, we know, he has a bit of bad luck, gets turned into an ass and can't turn himself back again. It seems to me that in this respect Lucius is actually typical of his fellow human beings, and that this is part of Apuleius' point. The Middle Platonist synthesis ‖ of Platonic philosophy and Isiac religion offered Apuleius a handy matrix of meaning-laden symbols and themes. He made skillful use of this matrix to tell the story of a regular guy whose desire to become a beast one day got the better of him, with results that were both comic and disastrous. ‖

AFTERWORD 1997

The recent Groningen commentary on book 9 of the *Golden Ass* (Hijmans *et al.* 1995) contains an appendix by Hijmans which offers a classification of *curiositas* and related terms in the novel. Since Hijmans takes issue with my article at a couple of points, it seems appropriate to respond to him here, though limitations of space prevent me from doing so in much detail.

Hijmans disputes my contention (n. 17) that *curiosus* and *curiositas* always have a pejorative connotation in the *Golden Ass*, and seeks to show that there is also a good kind of *curiositas*. He does this by (1) adducing occurrences that are not attached to explicitly negative

---

[38] Walsh (1988: 76).

characterizations, and (2) casting doubt on many of the clearly pejorative uses by claiming that the judgement of the narrators who express them cannot be trusted. With regard to (1), it is true that some occurrences of *curiosus–curiositas* in the *Golden Ass* do not have explicit moral valuations attached to them, and I should have acknowledged this directly in my original presentation. Hijmans seems to think, however, that the absence of an explicitly negative valuation means that the narrator intends a positive one, which I do not accept. The many pejorative uses which I (and others) document establish that *curiositas* denotes a negative personal characteristic. If, as Hijmans believes, it is sometimes positive, one expects it to be qualified at least once by a term of positive valuation, as it is so often qualified by such terms as *temeraria*, *sacrilega*, and *improspera*. This expectation goes unfulfilled. Thus, while I admit to perhaps overstating my case, I still stand by the substance of my thesis, which is that the trait of *curiositas* is morally blameworthy, and that no praiseworthy *curiositas* is in evidence in the *Golden Ass*. With regard to (2), I do not see that the narratological considerations emphasized by Hijmans make much difference. If untrustworthy narrators as well as trustworthy ones use *curiositas* pejoratively, that is simply more evidence for my thesis; on the other hand, if all the narrators are untrustworthy, it is difficult to see how anything will count as evidence for anything.

Hijmans claims that my interpretation of 11. 23. 20–2 'goes awry' because the *temeraria curiositas* referred to by Lucius is only the potential *curiositas* of the present circumstance: 'The passage, therefore, cannot be used to show that in all other instances *curiosus* and *curiositas* have a negative load in the *Met.*'. Hijmans has failed to grasp my point: I nowhere infer that 'all other instances' of these terms are negative because this one is; indeed, such an inference would be preposterously illogical. As my article makes clear, this passage shows that *curiositas* and 'curiosity' differ significantly in semantic range: *curiositas* includes the improper *divulging* of information, a meaning that makes perfect sense given its etymology and Platonist associations, and a meaning that 'curiosity' cannot have. I see no reason to abandon my contention that 'meddlesomeness' is a better basic translation, though—as I have never disputed—there will be specific contexts in which 'curiosity' is accurate.

14
Psyche, Aeneas, and an Ass: Apuleius, *Metamorphoses* 6. 10–6. 21

ELLEN FINKELPEARL

When Apuleius undertook in the second century AD to write about a descent to the Underworld, he was, depending on one's views on literary indebtedness, at either a great advantage or disadvantage.[1] There was no way to avoid Vergil's memorable description in *Aeneid* 6, so that from the perspective of a critic like Harold Bloom, Apuleius was destined for a great struggle for originality. Yet at the same time, the existence of a prior literary tradition gave him a background against which to build, react, diverge, or coincide, and gave his descriptions a certain authority—not to mention an epic flavor.[2] Literary allusion has recently been the subject of many studies, and every critic seems to have a somewhat different idea of what it is all about—partly because the topic is so broad, encompassing not only different authors, but also different types of indebtedness.[3] There is also a difference in approach, with some critics discussing specific instances of allusion and categorizing them, while others write more generally ‖ and abstractly: 'la parole e come acqua di rivo . . .' (Pasquali) or 'tradition can be defined simply as poetic "langue"' (Conte). All these

---

[1] I would like to thank Richard Tarrant, whose assiduous supervision of my dissertation (of which this is a much-revised portion) was invaluable, James Zetzel, who made helpful comments on an earlier version of this article, and the anonymous referee, whose bibliographic suggestions were especially useful.

[2] This, of course, is the way one has to look at Latin literature which is so deliberately imitative. Seneca's assertion that 'condicio optima est ultimi' (*Epist.* 79. 6) supports the notion that Latin writers did not see their position as a burden, though they did apparently feel the need to emulate and improve on their models (cf. the discussion of Gerald Sandy in 'Apuleius, Infidus Interpres,' a paper delivered at the International Conference on the Ancient Novel, 1989).

[3] For example, many recent studies of allusion in Apuleius focus on his debt to Greek sources (*Onos*, *Odyssey*, Euripides' *Hippolytus*—to use the talks delivered at ICAN as a representative sample), and therefore do not address the question of verbal echoes at all.

approaches are necessary and conflict often because critics are discussing different texts and attitudes toward art. As Conte points out, Bloom's theories of struggle apply best to his own topic, the Romantics, and reference as scholarship, for example, applies best to Alexandrians.

Allusion is elusive and subjective, not only in the sense that two readers often disagree on whether any allusion (or 'echo' or 'reference' . . .) is being made, but also in the sense that the effect is usually not clearly obvious. The question of intentionality is another area where critics tend to disagree, and again it seems more reasonable to consider some allusions very deliberate and others as a function of the author's memory and the tradition that language contains. In either case, a focus on the texts and their relationship to each other is preferable (as Conte stresses) to guessing the author's state of mind while composing. Yet in my discussion I find it necessary to assume that Apuleius was deliberate in his allusions and often wanted to achieve a certain effect—or, in other words, that he was an artist in control of his creation to the extent that artists are—which means, of course, that much that is unconscious and embedded in the literary language also comes into play.[4]

Because I am treating Apuleius' process as more or less deliberate, I prefer to use the word 'allusion.' There are, however, as many terms as there are critics. A cursory collection would include the following: echo, allusion, quotation, parallel, reference, imitation, borrowing, memory, intertextuality, reminiscence—not to mention Bloom's 'clinamen,' etc. Critics tend to choose and define their own terms; Conte prefers 'intertextuality,' a term which emphasizes the relation between texts rather than the author or his intent.[5] John Hollander, in discussing 'echo' makes the distinction, 'In contrast with literary allusion, echo is a metaphor of, and for, alluding, and does not depend on conscious intention.'[6] Richard Thomas, choosing the term 'reference' partly to express the idea of conscious intent, explains, 'Virgil is not so much "playing" with his models, but constantly intends that his reader be "sent back" to them . . . the word "allusion" has implications far too frivolous to suit this process.'[7] The case of Apuleius, however, differs somewhat from either Milton or Vergil, partly in that Apuleius is a more comic writer, and it seems

---

[4] We have at least the testimony of the Elder Seneca that Ovid wanted his borrowings from Vergil to be recognized (*Suas.* 3. 7).   [5] See Conte (1986: 27).
[6] Hollander (1981: 64).   [7] Thomas (1986: 172 n. 8).

reasonable to talk about Apuleius 'playing' with his models even while he is being serious. Allusion, to me, involves more of an inter-play or dialogue between model and imitator than 'reference' which sounds, superficially, like a simpler process.

When Apuleius uses Vergil to construct his underworld, he takes no single approach to Vergil's prior text, but in this one episode dis-plays almost as many types of allusion as have been defined. Some-times casual and straightforward, sometimes extremely subtle, even scholarly, the late-silver prose-writing || Apuleius is sometimes as Alexandrian as an Augustan poet. Throughout this one episode, Vergil is his background, and while Apuleius plays off him in various ways in succession, I believe that there is an overall effect achieved by the accumulation of echoes that is different from the sum of the parts, since it is not possible to find any single tone or consistent rela-tionship to Vergil among these diverse allusions.

Apuleius' *katabasis* occurs in the story of Cupid and Psyche and is one of four labors imposed by a jealous Venus on the beautiful Psyche. First she is forced to separate different kinds of grains into distinct piles, a task accomplished by friendly ants (6. 10). Then she must gather wool from a flock of ferocious golden sheep—here she is aided by a reed (6. 11. 4–6. 13. 2). Her third labor involves collecting Stygian water from a spring high on a slippery cliff, a labor accomplished by an eagle (6. 13. 3–6. 15. 6). Finally, she is to bring back from the realms below some of Proserpina's beauty in a pyxis, and is saved from suicide by the tower from which she is about to jump (6. 16–21). This fourth labor, the voyage to the underworld and its indebtedness to *Aeneid* 6 will most concern us here, though some of the earlier labors do involve echoes of *Aeneid* 6, especially of Aeneas' preliminary task of procuring the golden bough.

Apuleius intentionally places the descent to the underworld in book 6 like his predecessor. While Vergil's *nekuia* was centrally placed in imitation of that in the *Odyssey*, Lucan had more specifically located his consultation of the omniscient dead in the sixth book of his epic (also like Vergil, he puts the beginning of a major battle in book 7 and a review of past history in book 2).[8] The device of

[8] See von Albrecht, 'Der Dichter Lucan und die epische Tradition,' in Durry (1970: 282). See also Morford (1967: 66–8), who mentions the intentional central placement of the *nekuia* and the deliberate contrast with Vergil (and Homer). The inquirer is un-worthy, the guide more so, the account of Rome's glorious future (*Aen.* 6. 756–853)

imitating an earlier poet in the same position in one's own work, and thereby announcing the imitation, was a well-established convention by Apuleius' time. For example, Vergil, Propertius, and Statius all allude to the beginning of the third book of Callimachus' *Victoria Berenices* at the beginnings of their third books.[9] Propertius also may have intended his placement of the word *sacerdos* as the last word of 3. 1. 3 to be a polemical reference to Horace's use of it in the very same spot.[10] Apuleius, then, is participating in this convention by placing his many allusions to *Aeneid* 6 in *Metamorphoses* 6.

Some of Apuleius' allusions to Vergil seem to consist merely of a pseudo-quotation of the model, with no more ambitious end than to recall the earlier || author.[11] Apuleius may be partly invoking the 'auctoritas' of Vergil, as the one who 'knows' what the underworld is really like.[12] This is usually the least interesting type of allusion, because, as Conte says, '[The new text] simply inserts the only [*sic*—old?] text statically within itself. Thus no interpenetration occurs between the two texts.'[13] It is possible in some cases that these are unconscious allusions, brought on by the heavily Vergilian context, but I prefer to think of these allusions as reinforcements of the large-scale imitation, and signals that other more subtle and complex allusions are present. Because, ultimately, I believe that these allusions aim to connect Psyche—and, via Psyche, Lucius—with Aeneas, it is important that Apuleius establish a thick groundwork of Vergilian reminiscences.

When Psyche is told by the vatic tower to carry for Cerberus 'offas polentae mulso concretas' (6. 18. 3), this seems to recall the sops thrown to that dog by Vergil's Sibyl: 'melle soporatam et medicatis frugibus offam | obicit' (*Aen.* 6. 420–1), though Apuleius has considerably demystified Vergil's poetic *melle soporatam*.[14] Similarly, Charon, referred to as *squalido seni* (6. 18. 7) in a shorthand allusion to Vergil's four-line portrait (*Aen.* 6. 298–301), transports the dead 'ad ripam

---

has become a parade of demagogues and a prediction of doom. Feeney (1986), however, points out the ways in which Lucan 'recognized Vergil's equivocations, and seized upon them as his point of departure' (17).

[9] Thomas (1983, esp. 95–105). Also see Thomas (1986: 181), where reference by position is grouped under 'technical reference.'

[10] Nethercut (1970: 386) and Commager (1962: 16).

[11] They are examples of what Thomas (1986) terms 'casual reference . . . where an atmosphere but little more is evoked' (175).

[12] See Conte (1986: 58–9).   [13] Conte (1986: 60).

[14] Purser (1910); Grimal (1963: 126); Wright (1971: 280); Walsh (1970: 56–7). On *soporatam* in *Aeneid* 6, see Austin (1977: 152).

ulteriorem sutili cumba' (6. 18. 5).[15] This recalls two different places
in *Aeneid* 6: a description of the unburied dead, 'tendebantque manus
ripae ulterioris amore' (*Aen.* 6. 314) and, more aptly for this context,
Charon's boat so unsuitable for heavy Aeneas: 'gemuit sub pondere
cumba | sutilis' (*Aen.* 6. 413–14).[16] While Apuleius has created a
Vergilian pastiche in this latter case, it does not appear that he is doing
anything much more complex than simply recalling *Aeneid* 6. If anything, he has rather detracted from the resonance of the phrases—
there is no longer a pathetic sense that the *ripa ulterior* is distant and
unattainable, and the *cumba sutilis* does not groan under Psyche's or
a spirit's lesser weight. Caterina Lazzarini discusses several Apuleian
reminiscences which involve a substitution of more referential vocabulary for the poetic, and a diminution of figurative language. That is,
in some sense, the situation here.[17] While Apuleius uses poetic language often enough and certainly gives words new shades of meaning, he seems to prefer to clarify or interpret his poetic sources rather
than adopt their poeticisms.[18] ||

Several other echoes are introduced simply for the sake of recalling Vergil though not necessarily *Aeneid* 6.[19] At 6. 18 the tower,
whose very breaking into speech, *prorumpit in vocem*, seems to echo
a Vergilian formula, *rumpit vocem*,[20] explains the geography of the
entrance to the underworld (which it locates at Taenarus, one of Lucius'
ancestral towns of origin):

---

[15] Grimal (1963: 127), Wright (1971: 281).

[16] See Wright (1971: 280). That *cumba sutilis* is an allusion to *Aen.* 6. 413–14 is noticed
by Gatscha (1898: 146), Purser (1910: 111), Médan (1925: 263), Grimal (1963: 127).

[17] Lazzarini (1985, esp. 153–4).

[18] Though Apuleius is not known for his love of consistency, he sometimes revises
what is barely comprehensible or vague in his models. So, while Seneca's Phaedra
mysteriously suffers from *lassae genae* (*Phdr.* 364), Apuleius' *noverca* exhibits the more
normal symptom of love-sickness, *lassa genua* (10. 2. 6).

[19] While I see the use of Vergilian language from outside Apuleius' *katabasis* as a
way of strengthening the Vergilian tone without significantly distracting the reader from
the specific Vergilian context being recalled, Lazzarini (1985) sees Apuleius' language
more as a construction from diverse models. Emphasizing the generic quality of many
scenes, in conjunction with the borrowing and variation of language from various spheres
and sources, she downplays most specific allusions (Lazzarini 1985: 153–4). While
Apuleius undoubtedly creates a seamless patchwork, borrowing from many sources
at once, the descent of Psyche does seem to be pointedly referring back to Aeneas' descent,
in language as well as theme.

[20] Grimal (1963: 124). See Vergil, *Aeneid* 2. 129, 3. 246, 11. 377. The *in* of Apuleius'
phrase could reflect the growing use of prepositions in later Latin, and thus a feature
of current language, but may also be a matter of a search for liveliness and imme-
diacy as well as personal preference. See Callebat (1968: 227–9).

inibi spiraculum Ditis, et per portas hiantes monstratur iter invium, cui te limine transmeato simul commiseris, iam canale directo perges ad ipsam Orci regiam. (6. 18. 2)

This sounds partly like the dwelling place of Allecto at *Aeneid* 7. 568: 'hic specus horrendum et saevi spiracula Ditis | monstrantur.'[21] It is clear from his use of the phrase elsewhere that Apuleius intends to quote Vergil (or poets in general): at *De mundo* 17, he appends *ut poetae volunt* to the phrase *Ditis spiracula*, thus conveniently giving evidence of his imitation.[22]

It is likely that Apuleius also intended the phrase *iter invium* in the geographical description above to recall the *via invia* of *Aeneid* 3. 383, the sort of oxymoron to which Apuleius would be attracted.[23] While *Aeneid* 6 does offer the phrase *regna invia vivis* (154), clearly *via invia* is closer to the Apuleian phrase, *iter invium*, for, as Purser remarks, 'in both places *invium* implies not absolute impassableness, but that the way is difficult and trackless, a "pathless || road." '[24] Moreover, the passage in *Aeneid* 3 also refers to Aeneas' impending descent. Conceivably, Apuleius may have had both Vergilian passages in mind, having been led from the use of *invia* in *Aeneid* 6 to a use of the word in a combination more congenial to his style.[25] Apuleius often works this way—passing by a chain of connections from a quotation in the area he has been imitating to a similar one elsewhere in the same author which is more appropriate (cf. below on *lenis crepitans*).

It is possible that Apuleius is also making an oblique reference to Ovid, who borrowed and refashioned the phrase *via invia* in his rendition of Aeneas' descent at *Metamorphoses* 14. 113: 'invia virtuti

---

[21] Gatscha (1898: 146); Purser (1910: 109); Médan (1925: 263); Grimal (1963: 125); Wright (1971: 280). Note that Apuleius dispenses with the poetic plural of *spiracula Ditis*.

[22] 'Sive illa, ut poetae volunt, Ditis spiracula dicenda sunt, seu mortiferos anhelitus eos credi prior ratio est . . .'. Here, because of the explanatory phrase, Apuleius permits himself the poetic plural. The authorship of the *De mundo* is still a matter of debate, but Beaujeu (1973) believes it is genuine. In a twenty-page survey of scholarship and approaches, he finds that the arguments against Apuleian authorship are unconvincing and inconclusive and that the attribution to a fourth century Platonist creates more problems than it solves. (Beaujeu 1973: pp: ix–xxix.) Apuleius also adapts for a generally Vergilian flavor the phrase *illi obstipuere silentes* (*Aen.* 11. 120) to express Psyche's bewilderment at the immensity of the task of separating all the grain that Venus has poured out: 'immanitate praecepti consternata silens obstupescit,' 6. 10. 4 (Gatscha 1898: 146). Again, there seems to be little point in the allusion beyond giving the scene a more elevated tone.

[23] Purser (1910: 109).   [24] Purser (1910: 109).

[25] If Vergil introduced the word *invia* to poetry (see Austin 1977: 86), it was perhaps for this reason more striking and deserving of imitation.

nulla est via.' Here, as in Apuleius, Vergil's phrase from *Aen.* 3. 383
is transplanted into the context of an underworld scene that relies on
the *Aeneid*. It is not likely that Apuleius is borrowing only from Ovid
here, given the surrounding Vergilian context. Probably Ovid helped
to suggest the transplantation of the phrase. In any case, it is not
unusual for Apuleius to allude to two literary predecessors simultaneously, one of whom imitated the other, as a way of pointing out
the borrowing and of setting himself in the long tradition of literary
imitation.[26]

One place where Apuleius at first seems to be perversely depriving
a Vergilian echo of its point is at 6. 14. 1 where the clause, 'at illa studiose gradum celerans,' describes Psyche rushing up a mountain to
the Stygian streams. Vergil had written of Dido's old nurse, Barce, 'illa
gradum studio celerabat (?) anili' (*Aen.* 4. 641), the point being, of
course, that she moved only as fast as an aged woman can, *anili* adding
a paradoxical touch.[27] Apuleius' omission of that crucial word leaves
Psyche actually hurrying—certainly not Vergil's meaning. But
Apuleius seems to have been attracted to the *context* of Vergil's line;
the nurse is unknowingly hurrying to help Dido commit suicide, || just
as Psyche here hopes to end her miserable life by jumping from the
mountain that she is climbing.[28]

Other allusions to *Aeneid* 6 offer a slightly more complex relationship to their source, involving, among other types of allusion, correction,
parody, significant *variatio*, and literary criticism of the original. The
region of the underworld guarded by Cerberus is called by Apuleius

---

[26] One of the more prominent examples is Apuleius' simultaneous imitation of
Seneca's *Phaedra* and Vergil's Dido-episode in his story of the Phaedra-like stepmother
at *Met.* 10. 1–12. Elaine Fantham has pointed out how much the language and emotions of Seneca's heroines owe to Dido (Fantham 1975). Apuleius' double borrowing
is his way of making the same point.

[27] Gatscha (1898: 146); Purser (1910: 102); Grimal (1963: 118). There is a question
of whether Vergil wrote *celerabat* or *celebrabat*, on which see the commentaries of Pease
(1935: 500–1) and Austin (1955: 185), both of whom support *celerabat*. Apuleius'
imitation would at first glance offer further support for this reading, but it is possible
that his text or memory was faulty (as in the case of his inaccurate rendering of a line
of Pacuvius in *Florida* 10. 1 where he gives *candentem fervido* rather than *micantem candido*, influenced partly by *fervido* in the next line). Mynors in his *Aeneid* apparatus (1969)
mentions the Apuleian parallel, but prints *celebrabat*. To complicate matters further,
Apuleius' best MS (F) seems to read *cele*rans*, there being a gap where a *b* might have
been.

[28] Especially in isolated allusions, Apuleius' effect depends heavily on our intimate
knowledge of the context within which the original quotation occurred, and the ingenious way that context meshes with Apuleius'.

vacuam Ditis domum (6. 19. 3), a clear and straightforward echo of Vergil's *domos Ditis vacuas* (*Aen.* 6. 269).[29] Yet here Apuleius may be adopting Vergil's phrase to reinforce the sense of futility of the three-headed dog's barking threats:

tonantibus oblatrans faucibus mortuos, quibus iam nil mali potest facere, frustra territando ante ipsum limen et atra atria Proserpinae semper excubans servat vacuam Ditis domum. (6. 19. 3)

Vergil's phrase forms the climax to Apuleius' description of the dog who, though huge and monstrous, terrifies in vain and guards an empty house. While Vergil's 'domos Ditis vacuas et inania regna' (*Aen.* 6. 269) expresses the insubstantiality of all in the underworld, Apuleius adds a touch of the absurd in the notion that such realms are being guarded.

Apuleius may also derive from Vergil this idea of the ineffectuality of Cerberus' barking. At *Aen.* 6. 400–1, the Sibyl sarcastically brushes away Charon's allegations that she and Aeneas might have come to steal Cerberus (or Persephone) with the biting words: 'licet ingens ianitor antro | aeternum latrans exsanguis terreat umbras.' These words correspond conceptually with Apuleius' portrait of the huge dog, 'tonantibus oblatrans faucibus mortuos.'[30] So when Apuleius adapts the Vergilian phrase *vacuam Ditis domum* to reinforce the sense of futility in Cerberus' barking, he intensifies and comically overdoes an idea already in *Aeneid* 6 by incorporating a Vergilian phrase from another location.

It is possible that the picture of Cerberus as a whole owes something to *Aeneid* 6, though it is difficult to determine whether the similarities are simply generic—dogs do bark, Cerberus was big and had three heads, etc.[31] That both Cerberi are described as *immanis* (*Aen.* 6. 418; *Met.* 6. 19. 3), that Vergil's is *recubans* (*Aen.* 6. 418) and Apuleius' *excubans* (6. 19. 3) is not remarkable.[32] Yet it was seen above that Apuleius depends on Vergil to develop his own telescoped portrait of the big noisy dog that does not scare anything.

In another passage, this time from Psyche's third labor, a combination of two lines from *Aeneid* 6 may act as a clarification or

[29] Purser (1910: 113); Grimal (1963: 129); Wright (1971: 281). Apuleius again dispenses with the poetic plural.   [30] Médan (1925: 263) cites the parallel.
[31] Wright (1971: 281) mentions Apuleius' similarities to *Aen.* 6. 417–18.
[32] Perhaps Apuleius is here again stressing Cerberus' role as watchdog by changing *recubans* to *excubans*, but Tibullus 1. 3. 72 also uses *excubare* of Cerberus, so it would be hard to claim that this has to be a Vergilian echo.

'correction' of the || Vergilian context.[33] Venus describes the complic-
ated configuration of mountains and streams to which Psyche must
proceed to gather water, and she asks:

videsne . . . verticem, de quo fontis atri fuscae defluunt undae . . . [et] Stygias
inrigant paludes et rauca Cocyti fluenta nutriunt? (6. 13. 4)

The end of this sentence partly alludes to *Aen*. 6. 323, 'Cocyti stagna
alta vides Stygiamque paludem,' where, in addition to the obvious
verbal parallel, there is a similar pairing of the Cocytus and the
Styx.[34] The Sibyl's declarative *vides* has become an impatient question
in Venus' mouth: (*videsne?*). Yet, instead of referring to the *stagna*
of the Cocytus, Apuleius transports another neighboring line to the
scene, *Aen*. 6. 327: 'nec ripas datur horrendas et rauca fluenta |
transportare . . .'. Thus while Vergil makes both rivers sluggish
(*Cocyti stagna, Stygiam paludem*) and then, a few lines later, somewhat
inconsistently refers to the *rauca fluenta* that must be crossed,
Apuleius, bringing together the two descriptions, tidily makes the Styx
a quiet pool and the Cocytus a raging river.[35] In creating the clear-cut
contrast he was not necessarily correcting Vergil in any polemical way,
but making sense of the river system by combining descriptions from
two different locations.[36]

There remains the question of what relationship such 'correction'
implies between the corrector and the source. Thomas says of correction, 'This type [of reference] more than any other demonstrates the

---

[33] Thomas (1986: 185) defines 'correction' in this way: 'The poet provides unmis-
takable indications of his source, then proceeds to offer detail which contradicts or alters
that source.'

[34] Vergil's *Stygiam paludem* becomes *Stygias paludes* in Apuleius. (Ovid, *Met*. 1. 737,
however, has *Stygias paludes*.) It is strange that he here reverses his usual practice (above)
and makes plural what was singular. Wright (1971: 281) sees this perverse reversal as
evidence of continued imitation.

[35] Both Norden (1899) and Austin (1977: *ad loc*. 295) point out Vergil's inconsistency in creating a system of waterways, though neither points out the apparent
inconsistency in lines 323 and 327. Perhaps the *rauca fluenta* refer to the effect of the
turbidus gurges of line 296, but Apuleius' 'correction' makes it clear that *he* saw a problem here.

[36] It should be noted that Apuleius does not use the word *fluentum* in the
Metamorphoses except in book 6, another sign of Vergilian imitation. The word does,
however, appear several times in his other works. See Oldfather *et al*. (1934: 165). Another
possible allusion, though not close verbally, to this section of *Aeneid* 6 and the infernal
rivers occurs when the eagle warns Psyche away from the waters, stressing their power.
'Quodque vos deieratis per numina deorum deos per Stygis maiestatem solere' (6. 15.
4) may recall Vergil's comment on Cocytus and Styx: 'di cuius iurare timent et fallere
numen' (*Aen*. 6. 324).

scholarly aspect of the poet and reveals the polemical attitudes that lie close beneath the surface of much of the best poetry of Rome.'[37] This situation in Apuleius is precisely parallel to Vergil's correction of the order in which Homer made the Giants pile Pelion, Ossa, and Olympus, as discussed by Thomas. Here Vergil's alteration is based not on an appeal to another authority (as are many 'corrections'), but on logical reasoning as to where Olympus should have been placed. Yet the effect that Apuleius' rearrangement has on the reader (or this reader, anyway) is to || encourage a re-reading and reconsideration of Vergil's self-contradiction—doubtless there must be some point behind it. It would be perverse to see Apuleius, who has been so much criticized for his own internal contradictions and who makes his heroine climb an extremely tall mountain to gather infernal streams, as engaging in any serious sort of polemic over consistency. In addition, if he is showing off his scholarship, it is in a much more subtle manner than in the *Apology*. Rather, his conspicuous clarity does in a literary way what Austin or Norden have done in their commentaries; that is, through his careful reading, he makes us read Vergil more closely, showing us another way Vergil could have arranged his rivers, but did not. As above (on *melle soporatam* and *cumba sutilis*), Apuleius has prosaicized the mysterious and poetic in Vergil. He has adapted Vergil to his own style in a way which does not allow Vergil's peculiarities to compete with his own. In correcting such inconsistencies, he has also shown that his own (though of a different sort) are intentional rather than oversights.

Humor, irony, and parody are other possible effects of literary allusion. A simple and obvious example of Apuleius' adoption of a Vergilian phrase for purely humorous purposes occurs when an ant rallies its species to Psyche's aid:

miseremini terrae omniparentis agiles alumnae, miseremini et Amoris uxori puellae lepidae periclitanti prompta velocitate succurrite. (6. 10. 6)

The eloquent ant not only speaks in an elevated manner, pathetically repeating *miseremini*, but also alludes to Vergil's description of Tityos:

> nec non et Tityon, terrae omniparentis alumnum
> cernere erat, per tota novem cui iugera corpus
> porrigitur . . .
>
> (*Aen.* 6. 595–7)

---

[37] Thomas (1986: 185).

Both the ants and Tityos may be *terrae omniparentis alumni*, having homes and origins in the ground, yet clearly there is a certain irony in the smallest creatures being described by an epithet originally belonging to this nine-acre monster, in these agile, hurrying insects being compared with the stationary Tityos.[38] If Servius is right that a phrase from Vergil's ant-simile at *Aeneid* 4. 404, 'it nigrum campis agmen,' was used by Ennius of elephants, Apuleius is here being quite Vergilian in his adaptation of Vergilian material.

A stranger example of Apuleian humor is found when a reed that advises Psyche how to collect the wool of the ferocious golden sheep is indirectly compared to the Sibyl as well as to the golden bough. Like Aeneas, Psyche must perform various labors before she goes to the underworld, and while these labors are not strictly related to her descent as plucking the golden bough is necessary for his, there is a structural similarity which is reinforced by the following ‖ verbal echo. When the heroine is (characteristically) about to give up and drown herself, the reed is (literally) inspired:

sed inde de fluvio musicae suavis nutricula leni crepitu dulcis aurae divinitus inspirata sic vaticinatur harundo viridis. (6. 12. 1)

The phrase *leni crepitu* recalls two places in the *Aeneid*. At 3. 70 the wind Auster is referred to as *lenis crepitans*, a use which seems to influence this description of a 'sweet breeze.'[39] Yet even more relevant to the present context is Vergil's similar line in book 6, describing the wind in the golden bough:

> talis erat species auri frondentis opaca
> ilice, sic leni crepitabat brattea vento.
>
> (*Aen.* 6. 208–9)[40]

It is appropriate that a bough and a reed, two growing things (described with the words *virere* and *viridis* respectively), should be

---

[38] Ironic and incongruous re-application of a line or phrase, even parodying the original, is one of the more obvious ways to adapt one's source, particularly if it is well-known. Elsewhere in the *Metamorphoses* we find the outrageous, 'quo usque tandem cantherium patiemur istum?' (3. 27. 5; cf. Cicero, *Cat.* 1. 1. 1 and/or Sallust, *Cat.* 20. 9); or, 'heu medicorum ignarae mentes!' (10. 2. 7; cf. *Aen.* 4. 65). Such humor need not imply a mockery of its source.

[39] Grimal (1963: 115). Apuleius intensifies the friendliness of this wind already implicit in *lenis* by his addition of *dulcis (aurae)*.

[40] The verbal parallel is here not strictly as close to Apuleius as that at 3. 70, but the proximity of *leni* with *crepitabat* gives a similar sound. TLL 5¹ 1617. 75 f. offers no other examples of *lenis crepitus* or of *lenis* with *crepito*.

compared, and it is certainly no accident that the golden bough should be evoked in the context of the golden sheep. Apuleius also appears to be punning in his use of *aurae*; in Vergil, a word for gold follows *leni crepitabat*, and one might then look for a word for 'gold' following *leni crepitu* in Apuleius. In fact, a word very close in sound to *aurum, aura*, does appear. (The reader also has prominently in mind the gold wool of the sheep.) Wordplay on *aura* and *aurum* appears to be common in Latin and even appears in *Aeneid* 6 a few lines before this passage, at *Aen.* 6. 204: 'discolor unde auri per ramos aura refulsit.'[41] Apuleius seems to be making a very private reference to the Vergilian play on words and, in a sense, recreating it himself by alluding to and echoing the context of the golden bough and using the word *aura* within it. Apuleius uses *aura* rather than *ventus* (which Vergil uses) in order to create an intertextual pun.[42]

As Apuleius' sentence continues, however, the reed, in the phrase 'divinitus inspirata sic vaticinatur,' sounds more like the Sibyl (referred to as *vates* at *Aen.* 6. 211) than the bough. In its capacity as prophet and adviser for the hero in pursuit of gold, the reed certainly functions as Psyche's version of the Sibyl. Though there are no very striking verbal parallels, a reference to the bough is bound to remind us of Vergil's prophetess. Thus the humble reed becomes, through a complex set of maneuvers, an ingenious and absurd conflation of the ‖ golden bough and the Cumaean Sibyl. What at first appeared merely a delightful little offshoot of folktale—like the ants and tower that likewise come to Psyche's aid—turns out to have its literary connections as well. Throughout this episode Apuleius constantly intermingles folk-tale and epic with frequently comic results stemming from the close juxtaposition of such unlike elements.

For all the connections to Vergil here, Apuleius creates simultaneously perhaps even deeper resonances with Ovid. Referring to the *harundines* that reveal the secret of Midas' ears, Ovid says:

---

[41] See also Horace, *Od.* 1. 5. 9 and 11 (*aurea* and *aurae* end these two lines). At *Aen.* 6. 204, there is question about the meaning of *aura*, but the jingle is clear. See Austin (1977: 100), on *Aen.* 6. 204. See also Fordyce on *Aen.* 7. 491, where he discusses this sort of word-play with reference to *Aen.* 6. 204 (Fordyce 1977: 150).

[42] Ahl (1985) makes clear how widespread wordplay of this sort was among Latin poets, and how it was used to establish etymological connections between similar words. Ahl mentions this Vergilian passage on p. 304 without much comment. Apuleius' allusive pun is not of the etymological sort because it refers for its play to a work outside itself to which it is establishing a connection.

leni nam motus ab austro
obruta verba refert dominique coarguit aures.

(Ovid, *Met.* 11. 192–3)

Here Ovid plays with *auster* and *aures*, having exhausted the pun
auras–aures at the ends of lines 184 and 186. The context here is won-
derfully apt: talking reeds (as in Apuleius), the gold of Midas, and ass's
ears.[43] Ovid does not seem to have Vergil's Golden Bough in mind here,
but Apuleius' *leni crepitu dulcis aurae* does appear to allude to Ovid's
leni nam motus ab austro as well as Vergil's *leni crepitabat brattea vento*.
Unlike Apuleius' simultaneous use of Ovid and Vergil in his phrase
iter invium (above) where the double allusion pointed out the chain
of borrowings in the creation of new Underworlds, this two-fold allusion seems to compose a relatively unstructured heap of developing
resonances. On the one hand the Vergilian connection brings to
mind the Sibyl, prophecy, the golden bough; on the other hand, the
Ovidian echo is both more specific in juxtaposing another talking reed
(or reeds) and yet brings up the much broader context of gold, metamorphosis, and human asses (Midas-Lucius). Elsewhere, Apuleius
uses this type of broad-based allusion; most obviously, he introduces
allusions to Io's metamorphosis even when the immediate context does
not involve cows or shape-changes, apparently for the sake of the relationship between the Io story and the Lucius story.[44] In a novel that
involves so many inserted stories, literary allusions that relate to the
frame narrative may act as a sort of adhesive.

One of the more mysterious examples of Apuleius' allusion to
Aeneid 6 is his apparent modelling of an anonymous old dead man on
Vergil's Palinurus. Psyche is warned by the tower that as she travels
on her way in the underworld, she will meet various people who will
ask her aid, but that she must refuse them. She will first meet a lame
ass with a lame driver, and later on some women weaving, but as she
crosses the river, she will meet this strange man: ‖

---

[43] Winkler (1985: 300–5) discusses the title *Asinus aureus* and the possible connections with, or even origins in, the Midas tale which involves the three themes of gold,
asses, and transformation. What the word *aureus* signifies in the title—the ruddy color
of Isis' ass-enemy, Seth, a good tale, an oxymoron in juxtaposition with *asinus?*—is mysterious, but in the present passage, gold grows on the sheep.

[44] Apuleius seems to echo Ovid's Io story at several points in his *Metamorphoses*
7. 25 where an innocent man is accused of killing a boy who was actually eaten by a
bear.

nec setius tibi pigrum fluentum transmeanti quidam supernatans senex
mortuus putris adtollens manus orabit ut eum intra navigium trahas, nec tu
tamen inlicita adflectare pietate. (6. 18. 8)

Although there is not necessarily any reason to attribute these obs
tacles to a literary source rather than folk-tale (though the lame ass
looks suspicious and will be discussed below), the floating old man does
bear a resemblance to Aeneas' pilot as he appears in the underworld.[45]
He, too, begs Aeneas (*oro*, *Aen.* 6. 364, *orabit*, above) as he is about
to cross the infernal river to offer him a hand and pull him across.
'Da dextram misero et tecum me tolle per undas,' 370, is picked up
in Apuleius' 'putris adtollens manus,' though the owner of the hand
is transferred. The language of the Sibyl's rebuke to Palinurus, 'desine
fata deum flecti sperare precando' (376), also seems to have influenced both verbally and conceptually the tower's advice, 'nec tu
tamen inlicita adflectare pietate.' Finally, the mention of *pietas* in the
context of an echo of the *Aeneid* cannot help but evoke thoughts of
the man most famous for his *pietas*.[46] Psyche in many ways is the image
of Aeneas in this episode, and here she even (indirectly) receives his
epithet. The purpose of the echoes, then, is not so much to identify
the old man consciously with Palinurus (as there seems to be no
conceivable reason why Psyche should meet the epic figure) as to to
emphasize the literary origins of much of the episode in order to contribute further to the connections between Psyche and Aeneas.[47]

In fact, if one were to ask what overall function the large network
of allusions to *Aeneid* 6 serves in this scene apart from the individual
effects already discussed, the answer would have to be, in part, that
Apuleius wants us to see Psyche as a version of Aeneas, as a hero
in an epic making the obligatory trip to the underworld. The constant echoes of *Aeneid* 6 make us feel that she is visiting the same
places, seeing and doing the same things. While Apuleius distorts and

---

[45] Wright (1971: 281) suggests the resemblance. On the folk-tale elements, see his
article and Swahn (1955).

[46] Cf. among the numerous examples, the use of the epithet in the vicinity of the
talk with Palinurus, *pietate insignis* at *Aen.* 6. 403 and again *tantae pietatis imago* two
lines later.

[47] To this allusion in particular one might apply Charles Segal's general statement
about the effects of literary allusion (from his introduction to Conte 1986: 10): 'allusion calls attention to the autonomy of the literary system, to the art world created as
something apart from the "real" or the experiential world. . . . By its very nature allusion calls attention to the fictive frame as fiction and thereby also calls attention to the
art and artifice of literary representation.'

transforms many of Vergil's formulas, he has here also left many untouched, and there remains a sense of indebtedness rather than parody.[48] And if Psyche's descent and accompanying labors have something of the folk-tale and fairy tale about them, Psyche must be taken seriously as one version—perhaps a Milesian tale and folk version—of the epic hero daring the ultimate. ‖

To some extent, the characterization of Venus as a goddess very much like the Vergilian Juno also reinforces the connections between Aeneas and Psyche. Both are pursued relentlessly by a goddess, and while Aeneas' antagonist is Juno and Psyche's Venus, we have to keep reminding ourselves that this Venus is not Juno, contrary to what the language and characterization are telling us. Earlier in the tale, at 4. 30–1, Venus gives a long speech which is unavoidably reminiscent of Juno's at the beginning of the *Aeneid*. In an equally sarcastic tone, she complains that her altars have been neglected and—a nice twist —that the judgment of Paris did her no good since Psyche's beauty is preferred. Then, like Juno, she calls in a subordinate god to take revenge.[49] There is also a reminder of this close association in the heart of Psyche's trials, just as Venus is about to send the girl into the under-world. The words, 'nec tamen nutum deae saevientis vel tunc expi-are potuit' (6. 16. 1) recall in their own contorted way the narrative of the *Aeneid* just before Latinus gives up the reins of state: 'saevae nutu Iunonis eunt res' (*Aen.* 7. 592).[50] So again, cruel Venus is connected with cruel Juno and we are forced to see the parallels between Psyche's obstacles and labors and those of Aeneas.

Further, in light of the much-noted parallelism of Psyche's story with Lucius', it seems that we are to see her as making the descent in his place, perhaps symbolically for him. Psyche's adventures mirror those of Lucius; both fall through *curiositas*, wander painfully pursued by Fortuna, and are finally brought to a higher state through divine intervention.[51] There could be no serious descent to the underworld by an ass, but structurally an Odyssean novel of travel and travail

[48] Perhaps the best support for the claim that the relationship is not one of parody is that Psyche's adventures do not seem essentially comic.

[49] See Tatum (1979: 49–50), who points out the connection with Juno while others see only the reminiscences of Lucretius in the speech which begins, 'en rerum naturae prisca parens' (4. 30. 1).

[50] S. J. Harrison notes several other parallels with Juno in *Aeneid* 7, in a paper, 'Apuleius and the Epic,' delivered at ICAN 1989 (see now Harrison, 1998*b*).

[51] On the parallels, see Tatum (1979: 56–62); Schlam (1968*a*: 120–5, 1969*a*: 511–15). More recently, see Hooper (1985).

requires one. While Lucius does make his own mysterious descent at 11. 23, it occurs too late, and is a reward rather than a test.[52] The text requires a central *katabasis*, and it is Psyche, as Lucius' temporary surrogate, who must do it.

Yet there is even more evidence to reinforce the analogy, for, strangely, Lucius—or rather some alter-Lucius—does seem to be in the underworld at the moment Psyche descends. As mentioned above, one of the people she meets and must not help is a lame ass-driver:

iamque confecta bona parte mortiferae viae continaberis claudum asinum lignorum gerulum cum agasone simili, qui te rogabit, decidentis sarcinae fusticulos aliquos porrigas ei, sed tu nulla voce deprompta tacita praeterito. (6. 18. 4)

Surely it is worth paying special attention to any ass one meets in the novel, and here the order of presentation emphasizes the ass rather than the 'similar ‖ master.' At *Met.* 4. 4–5, the other ass carrying stolen goods for the robbers acted as Lucius' alter ego in anticipating his thoughts and refusing to continue, and consequently suffering what would have been Lucius' fate. So, here, the ass resembles Lucius, and may be seen as acting for him. We have already seen that Lucius is *claudus* (3. 27. 6): 'debilem claudumque reddam'; 4. 4. 2: 'iam claudus et titubans'. Moreover, only Lucius and one of his masters (the miller) are called *claudus* in all of Apuleius.[53] The ass as 'lignorum gerulum' is reminiscent of Lucius in the service of the evil boy who makes him carry wood down from the mountain. This boy, like the ass-driver in the underworld, was called *agaso* at 7. 18. 2 and 7. 25. 6, and these are the only other uses of the word in Apuleius.[54]

It is also intriguing that the priest of book 11, Asinius Marcellus (whose name is so appropriate, as Lucius points out at 11. 27. 7), is also lame, though the word *claudus* is not used. His lameness is the very mark by which Lucius is to recognize him:

Is ut agnitionem mihi scilicet certo aliquo sui signo subministraret, sinistri pedis talo paululum reflexo cunctabundo clementer incedebat vestigio. (11. 27. 5)

---

[52] I refer to the famous 'accessi confinium mortis . . .'.

[53] See *Index Apuleianus*, sub *claudus*. It appears at 3. 27. 6, 4. 4. 2, 6. 26. 1 of Lucius, and at 9. 27. 1 of his master. *Claudicare* is used of Lucius at 6. 30. 4.

[54] See *Index Apuleianus*. There is perhaps also a hint of an internal echo of 'fusticulos aliquos porrigas ei' in 'cum deberet egregius agaso manum porrigere . . .' (7. 18. 2).

It is, then, in essence a lame 'ass' who will show Lucius the final mysteries. The lameness has now almost become graceful (*clementer*). Perhaps we are seeing how the lame ass in all its forms has, after all, been a vehicle of enlightenment.[55]

It is surely, by now, unnecessary to justify an interpretation based partly on a re-reading of the novel (i.e., when reading the Psyche episode, one has not yet encountered the boy in book 7). Though the experience of a first reading differs significantly from subsequent readings, the *Metamorphoses* was written with the expectation of readers revising their opinions.[56] Here, I think, we have heard enough about Lucius' lameness so that, even on a first reading, this limping ass in the underworld should look significant. Yet it is not at all illegitimate to reconsider him with the benefit of fuller knowledge and a concordance. For this ass is clearly built upon Lucius' adventures, as the coincidence of vocabulary and detail makes clear, rather than mythology or folk-tale; the very divergence from the figure of the ass of Ocnus—the rope-eating ass one usually encounters ‖ in the underworld—suggests that Apuleius designed this animal and rider for his own story.[57]

I do not for a moment intend to say that we should interpret the presence of this oddly familiar pair to mean that Lucius literally was in the underworld as an obstacle to Psyche's mission. Yet a surrogate ass and rider are there to suggest Lucius' spiritual and symbolic descent, perhaps hinting obscurely at his future enlightened knowledge of that realm, but perhaps simply to make Lucius doubly part of the present epic voyage.

In conclusion, then, Apuleius' echoes of Vergil, while individually serving separate functions and achieving different effects, together bring us a folk-tale that is epic, a Psyche who is an Aeneas. Lucius, too, is indirectly elevated to epic stature, both through Psyche and through a mysterious ass in the underworld. Such literary allusion is far from arbitrary or ornamental. Rather, Apuleius' creative imitation helps traverse the distance between Aeneas and an ass. ‖

---

[55] An opposite and ironic reading is, of course, possible. Ahl (1985: 151–2) sees in the name Asinius Marcellus a 'subversive implication that Lucius could now be making an ass of himself in a rather different way.'

[56] For the necessity of re-reading the *Metamorphoses* to correct our first assumptions about the narrative, see Winkler (1979, 1985). For a discussion of the ways Vergil makes the reader suspend judgment and re-read, see Williams (1983: ch. 3: 'Retrospective Judgment Enforced,' 40–50).

[57] Purser (1910: 110) and Grimal (1963: 126), both reject Ocnus as a source.

ACKNOWLEDGEMENTS

All the essays in this collection (apart from the Introduction) have been previously published elsewhere, as listed below. The editor and Oxford University Press are very grateful to the publishers of the relevant journals and books for their permissions to reprint.

1. Reprinted from *Transactions of the American Philological Association*, 102 (1971), 631–84.
2. Reprinted from *Phoenix*, 27 (1973), 42–61.
3. Reprinted from *Classical Philology*, 72 (1977), 22–31.
4. Translation by Barbara Graziosi of 'Trimalchione in scena', *Maia*, 35 (1985), 213–27.
5. Translation by Martin Revermann of 'Umwelt, Sprachsituation und Stilschichten in Petrons Satyrica', in *Aufstieg und Niedergang der römischen Welt*, II. 32. 3 (1985), 1687–1705, incorporating the author's revisions.
6. Translation by Barbara Graziosi of 'Tracce di narrativa greca e romanzo latino: una rassegna', in *Semiotica della novella latina*, Materiali e contributi per la storia della narrativa greco-latina, 4 (Rome, 1986), 219–36.
7. Translation by Martin Revermann of 'Zur Einheit der *Metamorphosen* des Apuleius', *Philologus*, 113 (1969), 68–84.
8. Reprinted from *Transactions of the American Philological Association*, 100 (1969), 487–527.
9. Reprinted from *Transactions of the American Philological Association*, 103 (1972), 513–34.
10. Reprinted from B. L. Hijmans and R. T. van der Paardt (eds.), *Aspects of Apuleius'* Golden Ass (Groningen, 1978), 1–15.
11. Reprinted from *Mnemosyne*, 34 (1981), 96–106.
12. Reprinted from *Journal of Roman Studies*, 71 (1981), 63–75.
13. Reprinted from *American Journal of Philology*, 111 (1990), 471–2.
14. Reprinted from *Transactions of the American Philological Association*, 120 (1990), 333–48.

REFERENCES

ABBOTT, F. F. (1911), 'The Origin of the Realistic Romance among the Romans', *CPh* 6: 257–70.

ABRAMS, P., and WRIGLEY, E. A. (eds.) (1978), *Towns in Societies: Essays in Economic History and Historical Sociology* (Cambridge).

ADAMIETZ, J. (ed.) (1986), *Die römische Satire* (Darmstadt).

—— (1987), 'Zum literarischen Charakter von Petrons *Satyrica*', *RhM* 130: 329–46.

—— (1995), 'Circe in den *Satyrica* Petrons und das Wesen diese Werkes', *Hermes*, 123: 320–34.

ADAMS, J. N. (1984), 'Female Speech in Latin Comedy', *Antichthon*, 18: 43–77.

AHL, F. (1985), *Metaformations* (Ithaca, NY).

ALBRECHT, M. von (1983), *Meister römischer Prosa*, 2nd edn. (Heidelberg).

ALPERS, K. (1980), 'Innere Beziehungen und Kontraste als "hermeneutische Zeichen" in den *Metamorphosen* des Apuleius von Madauros', *WJA* 6: 197–207.

—— (1996), 'Zwischen Athen, Abdera und Samos. Fragmente eines unbekannten Romans aus der Zeit der Zweiten Sophistik', in Billerbeck and Schamp (1996: 19–55).

ALTER, R. (1964), *Rogue's Progress: Studies in the Picaresque Novel* (Cambridge, Mass.).

ANDERSON, G. (1976), *Studies in Lucian's Comic Fiction, Mnemosyne*, Suppl. 43.

—— (1982), *Eros sophistes: Ancient Novelists at Play*, American Classical Studies, 9 (Chico, Calif.).

—— (1984), *Ancient Fiction* (London).

ANDERSON, W. (1909), 'Zu Apuleius' Novelle vom Tode der Charite', *Philologus*, 68: 537–49.

ANDRÉ, J. (1965), *Apicius: De re cocquinaria* (Paris).

—— (ed.) (1978), *Recherches sur les artes à Rome: Troisième cycle* (Paris).

ARAGOSTI, A. (1979), 'L'episodio petroniano del *forum*: Assimilazione dei codici nel racconto', *MD* 3: 101–19.

—— COSCI, P., and COTROZZI, A. (1988), *Petronio: L'episodio di Quartilla* (Bologna).

ARROWSMITH, W. (1959, repr. New York, 1960), *Satyricon* (Ann Arbor).

—— (1966), 'Luxury and Death in the *Satyricon*', *Arion*, 5: 304–331.

—— (1968), 'Euripides' Theater of Ideas', in Segal (1968: 13–33).

ASTBURY, R. (1977), 'Petronius, *P. Oxy.* 3010, and Menippean Satire', *CPh* 72: 22–31.

AUERBACH, E. (1953, repr. 1957), *Mimesis: The Representation of Reality in Western Literature*, tr. W. Trask (Princeton).

AUSTIN, R. G. (1955), *P. Vergili Maronis Aeneidos liber quartus* (Oxford).

—— (1977), *P. Vergili Maronis Aeneidos liber sextus* (Oxford).

BACON, H. H. (1958), 'The Sibyl in the Bottle', *Virginia Quarterly Review*, 34: 262–76.

BAGNANI, G. (1954), *Arbiter of Elegance: A Study of the Life and Works of C. Petronius* (Toronto).

BAKHTIN, M. (1981), *The Dialogic Imagination: Four Essays*, tr. C. Emerson and M. Holquist (Austin, Tex.).

BALDWIN, B. (1973), 'Ira Priapi', *CPh* 68: 294–6.

BANDINI, M. (1986), 'Il modello della metamorfosi ovidiana nel romanzo di Apuleio', *Maia*, 38: 33–9.

BARCHIESI, A. (1986), 'Tracce di narrativa greca e romanzo latino: Una rassegna', in *Semiotica della novella latina* (1986: 219–36).

BARCHIESI, M. (1981), *I moderni alla ricerca di Enea* (Rome).

BARNES, T. D. (1971, 2nd edn. 1985), *Tertullian: A Historical and Literary Study* (Oxford).

BARTONKOVA, D. (1976), 'Prosimetrum, the Mixed Style, in Ancient Literature', *Eirene*, 14: 65–92.

BEAUJEU, J. (1973), *Apulée: Opuscules philosophiques et fragments* (Paris).

BECATTI, G. (1951), *Arte e gusto negli scrittori latini* (Florence).

BECK, R. (1973), 'Some Observations on the Narrative Technique of Petronius', *Phoenix*, 27: 42–61.

—— (1975), 'Encolpius at the *Cena*', *Phoenix*, 29: 271–83.

—— (1979), '*Eumolpus poeta, Eumolpus fabulator*', *Phoenix*, 33: 239–53.

—— (1992), review of Slater (1989), *Phoenix*, 46: 69–72.

—— (1996), 'Mystery Religions, Aretalogy and the Ancient Novel', in Schmeling (1996a: 131–50).

BENZ, L., STÄRK, E., and VOGT-SPIRA, G. (eds.) (1995), *Plautus und die Tradition des Stegreifspiels*, Festgabe E. Lefèvre (Tübingen).

BERNARDO, A., and LEVIN, S. (eds.) (1990), *The Classics in the Middle Ages* (Binghampton, NY).

BERNHARD, M. (1927), *Der Stil des Apuleius von Madaura* (Stuttgart).

BERNHARDT, R. (1971), *Imperium und Eleutheria. Die römische Politik gegenüber den freien Städten des griechischen Ostens*, diss. (Hamburg).

—— (1980), 'Die Immunitas der Freistädte', *Historia*, 29: 190–207.

BERRETH, J. (1931), *Studien zum Isisbuch in Apuleius' Metamorphosen*, diss. (Tübingen).

BESSONE, F. (1993), 'Discorsi dei liberti e parodia del *Simposio* platonico nella *Cena Trimalchionis*', *MD* 30: 63–86.

BETTINI, M. (1982), 'A proposito dei versi sotadei, greci e romani: Con alcuni capitoli di "analisi metrica lineare"', *MD* 9: 59–105.

BIANCO, G. (1971), *La fonte greca delle* Metamorfosi *di Apuleio* (Brescia).

BILLERBECK, M., and SCHAMP, J. (eds.) (1996), *Kainotomia. Die Erneuereung der griechischen Tradition* (Freiburg).

BINDER, G., and MERKELBACH, R. (eds.) (1968), *Amor und Psyche*, Wege der Forschung, 126 (Darmstadt).

BLUMENBERG, H. (1961), 'Augustins Anteil an der Geschichte des Begriffs der theoretischen Neugierde', *REAug* 7: 35–70.

—— (1962), '*Curiositas* und *Veritas*. Zur Ideengeschichte von Augustin, *Confessiones* X. 35', in Cross (1962: 294–302).

BLUMENTHAL, H. J. and MARKUS, R. A. (eds.) (1981), *Neoplatonism and Early Christian Thought* (London).

BLÜMNER, H. (1911), *Die römischen Privataltertümer* (Munich).

BOISSIER, G. (1861), *Étude sur la vie et les ouvrages de M. T. Varron* (Paris).

BOLDRINI, S. (1989), 'Il pasto della vedova: Cibo, vino, sesso, da Petronio a J. Amado', in Hofmann (1989: 121–32).

BOLISANI, E. (1936), *Varrone Menippeo* (Padua).

BOMPAIRE, J. (1958), *Lucien écrivain* (Paris).

BOOTH, W. C. (1961), *The Rhetoric of Fiction* (Chicago).

BORGERS, O. (1960–1), 'Le Roman picaresque: Réalisme et fiction', *Lettres romanes*, 14: 295–305; 15: 23–38, 135–48.

BOWERSOCK, G. W. (1965), 'Zur Geschichte des römischen Thessaliens', *RhM* 108: 277–89.

—— (1969), *Greek Sophists in the Roman Empire* (Oxford).

BOWIE, E. L., and HARRISON, S. J. (1993), 'The Romance of the Novel', *JRS* 83: 159–78.

BOYCE, B. C. (1991), *The Language of the Freedmen in Petronius'* Cena Trimalchionis, *Mnemosyne*, Suppl. 117.

BOYLE, A. J. (ed.) (1990), *The Imperial Muse, II: Flavian Epicists to Claudian* (Berwick, Victoria).

BRANHAM, R. B., and KINNEY, D. (1996), *Petronius: Satyrica* (London).

BRANDT, E., and EHLERS, W. (1958), *Apuleius: Metamorphosen* (Munich).

BREMER, J. M. (1978), *Het gemaskerde ik* (Amsterdam).

BROCK, M. D. (1911), *Studies in Fronto and his Age* (Cambridge).

BRONZWAER, W. J. M., FOKKEMA, D. W., and KUNNE-IBSCH, E. (eds.) (1977), *Tekstboek Algemene Literatuur-wetenschap* (Béarn).

—— 'Over het lezen van narratieve teksten', in Bronzwaer *et al.* (1977: 220–36).

BROTHERTON, B. (1934), 'The Introduction of Characters by Name in the *Metamorphoses* of Apuleius', *CPh* 29: 36–52.

BRUNEAU, P. (1965), 'Illustrations antiques du *Coq* et de l'*Âne* de Lucien', *BCH* 89: 349–57.

BRUNT, P. A. (1975), 'Did Imperial Rome Disarm her Subjects?', *Phoenix*, 29: 260–70.

BÜCHELER, F. (1862), *Petronii Arbitri satirarum reliquiae* (Berlin).

—— (1865), 'Über Varros Satiren', *RhM* 20: 427–8.

—— (1922), *Petronii Saturae et liber Priapeorum*, rev. W. Heraeus 6th edn. (Berlin).

BURCK, E. (1961), 'Zum Verständnis des Werkes', in Rode (1961).

—— (1966), *Vom Menschenbild in der römischen Literatur* (Heidelberg).

—— (1979*a*), 'Das *Bellum civile* Petrons', in Burck (1979*b*: 200–7).

—— (ed.) (1979*b*), *Das römische Epos* (Darmstadt).

BÜRGER, K. (1887), *De Lucio Patrensi*, diss. (Berlin).

—— (1888), 'Zu Apuleius', *Hermes*, 23: 489–98.

—— (1892), 'Der antike Roman vor Petronius', *Hermes*, 27: 345–58.

—— (1902), *Studien zur Geschichte des griechischen Romans I. Der Lukiosroman* (Blankenburg).

BURNABY, W. (1694), *The Satyr of Titus Petronius Arbiter* (London).

BURNETT, A. P. (1960), 'Euripides' *Helen*: A Comedy of Ideas', *CPh* 55: 151–63.

BURTON, G. P. (1975), 'Proconsuls, Assizes and the Administration of Justice under the Empire', *JRS* 65: 92–106.

BUTLER, H. E. (1910), *The Metamorphoses or Golden Ass of Apuleius of Madaura*, 2 vols. (Oxford).

—— and OWEN, A. S. (1914), *Apulei Apologia* (Oxford).

CAHEN, E. (1925), *Le* Satyricon *et ses origines* (Lyons).

CALLEBAT, L. (1968), *Sermo cotidianus dans les* Métamorphoses *d'Apulée* (Caen).

—— (1978) 'La Prose des *Metamorphoses*: Génèse et spécificité', in Hijmans and van der Paardt (1978: 167–87).

—— (1992), 'Le *Satyricon* de Pétrone et l'*Âne d'Or* d'Apulée sont-ils des romans?', *Euphrosyne*, 20: 149–64.

—— (ed.) (1995), *Latin vulgaire—latin tardif* (Hildesheim).

CALONGHI, F. (1915), 'Il prologo delle *Metamorfosi* di Apuleio', *RIFC* 43: 1–43, 209–36.

CAMERON, A. (1969), 'Petronius and Plato', *CQ* NS 19: 367–70.

—— (1970), 'Myth and Meaning in Petronius: Some Modern Comparisons', *Latomus*, 29: 397–425.

CAMPANILE, E. (1964), 'Interpretazioni Petroniane', *SSL* 4: 115–26.

CAMPBELL, R. (1969), *Seneca: Letters from a Stoic* (Harmondsworth).

CARATELLO, U. (1963), 'Apuleio morì nel 163–4', *GIF* 16: 97–110.

CARLETON, S. B. (1988), 'The Widow of Ephesus in Renaissance England', *CML* 9: 51–63.

CARVER, R. H. F. (1991), 'The Protean Ass: The *Metamorphoses* of Apuleius from Antiquity to the English Renaissance', Oxford University D. Phil. thesis.

CATAUDELLA, Q. (1957), *La novella greca* (Naples).

—— (1966), 'Mimo e romanzo', *RCCM* 8: 3–6.

CÈBE, J.-P. (1966), *La Caricature et la parodie dans le monde romain antique des origines à Juvénal* (Paris).

CERVELLERA, M. A. (1975), 'Petronio e Seneca tragico', *RCCM* 17: 107–15.

CHALK, H. H. O. (1960), 'Eros and the Lesbian Pastorals of Longus', *JHS* 80: 32–51.

CHERNISS, H. (1971), 'The Sources of Evil according to Plato', in Vlastos (1971).

CIAFFI, V. (1955), *Struttura del* Satyricon (Turin).

—— (1960), *Petronio in Apuleio* (Turin).

CITRONI, M. (1975), *M. Valerii Martialis Epigrammaton liber primus* (Florence).

CITRONI MARCHETTI, S. (1983), 'Forme della rappresentazione del costume nel moralismo romano', *AFLS* 4: 41–114.

COBET, C. G. (1873), *Variae lectiones*, 2nd edn. (Leiden).

COCCHIA, E. (1915), *Romanzo e realtà nella vita e nell'attività litteraria di Apuleio* (Catania).

COCCIA, M. (1973), *Le interpolazioni in Petronio* (Rome).

—— (1996), 'Konrad Müller e le interpolazione in Petronio', *RCCM* 38: 319–28.

COFFEY, M. (1976), *Roman Satire* (London).

COLIN, J. (1965a), 'Apulée en Thessalie: Fiction ou vérité?', *Latomus*, 24: 330–45.

—— (1965b), *Les Villes libres de l'Orient gréco-romain et l'envoi au supplice par acclamations populaires*, Collection Latomus, 82 (Brussels).

COLLIGNON, A. (1892), *Étude sur Pétrone* (Paris).

—— (1905), *Pétrone en France* (Paris).

COMMAGER, S. (1962), *The Odes of Horace* (Bloomington, Ind.).

CONNORS, C. (1998), *Petronius the Poet* (Cambridge).

CONTE, G. B. (1986), *The Rhetoric of Imitation*, tr. C. Segal (Ithaca, NY).

—— (1996), *The Hidden Author: An Interpretation of Petronius' Satyricon* (Berkeley).

COOPER, G. (1980), 'Sexual and Ethical Reversal in Apuleius: The *Metamorphoses* as Anti-Epic', in Deroux (1980: 436–66).

COSTANZA, S. (1937), *La fortuna di Apuleio nell'età di mezzo* (Palermo).

COURTNEY, E. (1962), 'Parody and Literary Allusion in Menippean Satire', *Philologus*, 106: 86–100.

—— (1991), *The Poems of Petronius*, American Classical Studies, 25 (Atlanta).

CRAWFORD, M. H. (1975), 'Finance, Coinage and Money from the Severans to Constantine', *ANRW* II. 2. 560–93.

CRIBIORE, R. (1996), 'Gli esercizi scolastici dell'Egitto greco-romano: cultura letteraria e cultura popolare nella scuola', in Pecere and Stramaglia (1996: 505–25).

CROSS, F. L. (ed.) (1962), *Studia patristica*, vi (Berlin).

CRUM, R. H. (1952), 'Petronius and the Emperors', *CW* 45: 161–7, 197–201.

CRUSIUS, O. (1889), 'Vorlagen der apuleianischen *Metamorphosen*', *Philologus*, 48: 108–28.

CUMONT, F. (1909), *Les Religions orientales dans le paganisme romain* (Paris).

—— (1911), *The Oriental Religions in Roman Paganism* (London).

D'ALTON, J. F. (1931), *Roman Literary Theory and Criticism* (New York).

DAREMBERG, C., SAGLIO, E., and POTTIER, E. (eds.) (1877–1919), *Dictionnaire des antiquités grecques et romains* (Paris).

D'ARMS, J. H. (1981), *Commerce and Social Standing in Ancient Rome* (Cambridge, Mass.).

DEE, C. H. (1891), *De ratione quae est inter Asinum Pseudo-Lucianeum Apuleique Met. libros*, diss. (Leiden).

DEFILIPPO, J. G. (1990), '*Curiositas* and the Platonism of Apuleius' *Golden Ass*', *AJPh* 111: 471–92.

DEGANI, E. (1962), 'Laecasin = λαικάζειν', *RCCM* 4: 362–5.

DE JONG, J. L. (1989), 'Renaissance Representations of Cupid and Psyche: Apuleius versus Fulgentius', in Hofmann (1989: 75–86).

DE JONG, K. H. E. (1900), *De Apuleio Isiacorum mysteriorum teste*, diss. (Leiden).

DE JONGE, B. J. (1941), *Ad Apulei Madaurensis Metamorphoseon librum secundum commentarius exegeticus*, diss. (Groningen).

DELLA CORTE, F. (1939), *La poesia di Varrone Reatino ricostituita* (Turin).

—— (1953), *Varronis Menippearum fragmenta* (Turin).

DEL MONTE, A. (1957), *Itinerario del romanzo picaresco spagnuolo* (Florence).

DEONNA, W., and RENARD, M. (1961), *Croyances et superstitions de table dans la Rome antique*, Collection Latomus, 46 (Brussels).

DEROUX, C. (ed.) (1980), *Studies in Latin Literature and Roman History II*, Collection Latomus, 168 (Brussels).

—— (ed.) (1992), *Studies in Latin Literature and Roman History VI*, Collection Latomus, 217 (Brussels).

DE SMET, I. A. R. (1996), *Menippean Satire and the Republic of Letters 1581–1655* (Geneva).

—— (1997), 'Innocence Lost, or the Implications of Reading and Writing (Neo-Latin) Prose Fiction', in de Smet and Ford (1997: 85–111).

—— and FORD, P. J. (eds.) (1997), *Eros and Priapus* (Geneva).

DIBELIUS, M. (1917), *Die Isisweihe bei Apuleius und verwandte Initiationsriten*, SB Heidelberg, 4; repr. in *Botschaft und Geschichte. Gesammelte Aufsätze*, ii (Tübingen, 1956).

DI GIOVANNI, N. T. (ed.) (1973), *Borges on Writing* (New York).

DIHLE, A. (1977), 'Der Beginn des Attizismus', *A&A* 23: 162–77.

DILLON, J. (1977), *The Middle Platonists* (London).

DONINI, P. (1979), 'Apuleio e il platonismo medio', in Pennacini *et al.* (1979: 103–12).

DOODY, M. A. (1996), *The True Story of the Novel* (London).

DORNSEIFF, F. (1938), 'Lukios' und Apuleius' *Metamorphosen*', *Hermes*, 73: 222–33.

DOWDEN, K. (1982), 'Apuleius and the Art of Narration', *CQ* NS 32: 419–35.
—— (1994), 'The Roman Audience of the Golden Ass', in Tatum (1994: 419–34).
DREW-BEAR, T., ECK, W., and HERRMANN, P. (1977), 'Sacrae litterae', *Chiron*, 7: 355–83.
DUCKWORTH, G. E. (1967), 'Five Centuries of Latin Hexameter Poetry: Silver Age and Late Empire', *TAPA* 98: 77–150.
DUDLEY, D. R. (1937), *A History of Cynicism* (London).
DURRY, M. (ed.) (1970), *Lucain*, Entretiens Hardt, 15 (Geneva).

EBEL, H. (1970), 'Apuleius and the Present Time', *Arethusa*, 3: 155–76.
ECK, W. (1978), 'Iulius', *RE* Suppl. 15: 123.
EFFE, B. (1976), 'Der misglückte Selbstmord des Aristomenes (Apuleius Met. I. 14–17). Zur Romanparodie im griechischen Eselsroman', *Hermes*, 104: 362–75.
EGGER, R. (1966), *Das Praetorium als Amtssitz und Quartier römischer Spitzenfunktionäre* (Vienna).
EHLERS, W. (1983), 'Anhang', in Müller and Ehlers (1983).
ELSNER, J. (1993), 'Seductions of Art: Encolpius and Eumolpus in a Neronian Picture Gallery', *PCPS* 39: 30–47.
ELSOM, H. (1989), 'Apuleius and the Movies', in Hofmann (1989: 141–50).
ELSTER, M. (1991), 'Römisches Strafrecht in den *Metamorphosen* des Apuleius', in Hofmann (1991: 135–54).
ERBSE, H. (1950), 'Griechisches und Apuleianisches bei Apuleius', *Eranos*, 48: 107–26.
—— (ed.) (1956), *Festschrift Bruno Snell* (Munich).
ERNOUT, A. (1967), *Pétrone: Le Satyricon* (Paris).
—— and MEILLET, A. (1951), *Dictionnaire étymologique de la langue latine*, 3rd edn. (Paris).

FANTHAM, E. (1975), 'Virgil's Dido and Seneca's Tragic Heroines', *G&R* 22: 1–10.
FEDELI, P. (1981), 'Petronio: Il viaggio, il labirinto', *MD* 6: 91–117.
—— and DIMUNDO, R. (1988), *I racconti del Satyricon* (Rome).
FEENEY, D. C. (1986), 'History and Revelation in Vergil's Underworld', *PCPS* 35: 1–24.
FEHLING, D. (1977), *Amor und Psyche*, *AAWM* 9 (Wiesbaden).
FELDBRUGGE, J. J. M. (1939), *Het Schertsende Karacter van Apuleius' Metamorphosen* (Utrecht).
FERNHOUT, J. M. H. (1949), *Ad Apulei Madaurensis Met. librum quintum commentarius exegeticus*, diss. (Groningen).
FESTUGIÈRE, A.-J. (1954), *Personal Religion among the Greeks* (Berkeley).
FICK, N. (1978), 'Les *Metamorphoses* d'Apulée et le monde du travail', in André (1978).
FICK-MICHEL, N. (1991), *Art et mystique dans les* Métamorphoses *d'Apulée* (Paris).

FINKELPEARL, E. (1990), 'Psyche, Aeneas and an Ass: Apuleius *Met.* 6. 10–6. 21', *TAPA* 120: 333–48.

—— (1998), *Metamorphosis of Language in Apuleius: A Study of Allusion in the Novel* (Ann Arbor).

FLAMAND, J.-M. (1989), 'Apulée de Madaure', in Goulet (1989: 298–317).

FÖRS, H. (1964), *Dionysos und die Stärke der Schwachen im Werk des Euripides*, Tübingen University diss. (Munich).

FORBES, C. A. (1943–4), 'Charite and Dido', *CW* 37: 39–40.

FORDYCE, C. J. (1977), *P. Vergili Maronis Aeneidos libri vii–viii* (Oxford).

FOWLER, D. P. (1989), 'First Thoughts on Closure: Problems and Prospects', *MD* 22: 75–122.

FRAENKEL, E. (1953), 'A Sham Sisenna', *Eranos*, 51: 151–6; repr. in Fraenkel (1964: ii. 391–6).

—— (1964), *Kleine Beiträge zur klassischen Philologie*, 2 vols. (Rome).

FRANGOULIDIS, S. A. (1991a), '*Charite dulcissima*: A Note on the Nameless Charite at Ap. *Met.* 7. 12', *Mnemosyne*, 44: 387–94.

—— (1991b), 'Vergil's Tale of the Trojan Horse in Apuleius' Robber-Tale of Thrasyleon', *PP* 46: 95–111.

—— (1992a), 'Epic Inversion in Apuleius' Tale of Tlepolemus/Haemus', *Mnemosyne*, 45: 60–74.

—— (1992b), 'Charite's Literary Models: Vergil's Dido and Homer's Odysseus', in Deroux (1992: 445–50).

—— (1992c), 'Homeric Allusions to the Cyclopeia in Apuleius' Description on the Robbers' Cave', *PP* 47: 50–8.

FRASSINETTI, P. (1953), *Fabula atellana* (Pavia).

FRAYN, J. M. (1975), 'Wild and Cultivated Plants: A Note on the Peasant economy of Roman Italy', *JRS* 65: 32–9; repr. as Frayn (1979, ch. 4).

—— (1979), *Subsistence Farming in Roman Italy* (Fontwell).

FREDOUILLE, J.-C. (1975), *Apulée: Metamorphoses livre xi* (Paris).

FRIEDLÄNDER, L. (1891), *Petronii Cena Trimalchionis*, 1st edn. (Leipzig).

—— (1906), *Petronii Cena Trimalchionis*, 2nd edn. (Leipzig).

FRYE, N. (1957), *The Anatomy of Criticism* (New York).

FUSILLO, M. (1996), 'Modern Critical Theories and the Ancient Novel', in Schmeling (1996a: 277–305).

GAGLIARDI, D. (1980), *Il comico in Petronio* (Palermo).

—— (1993), *Petronio e il romanzo moderno* (Florence).

GALAND, P. (1989), 'Le Conte de la Matrone d'Ephèse: Rhétorique de "guidage" et reception. Pétrone lu par La Fontaine et Saint-Evremond', in Hofmann (1989: 109–20).

GARNSEY, P. (1970), *Social Status and Legal Privilege in the Roman Empire* (Oxford).

GASELEE, S. (1910), 'The Bibliography of Petronius', *Transactions of the Bibliographical Society*, 10 (1910), 141–233.

—— (1915), *Apuleius: The Golden Ass* (Cambridge, Mass.).

GATSCHA, F. (1898), *Quaestionum Apuleianarum capita tria* (Vienna).

GEFFCKEN, J. (1911), 'Studien zur griechischen Satire', *NJA* 27: 469–83.

GENETTE, G. (1980), *Narrative Discourse*, tr. J. E. Lewin (Oxford).

GEORGE, P. A. (1966), 'Style and Character in the *Satyricon*', *Arion*, 5: 336–58.

—— (1974), 'Petronius and Lucan *De bello civili*', *CQ* NS 24: 119–33.

GERCKE, A., and NORDEN, E. (1910), *Einleitung in die Altertumswissenschaft*, i (Leipzig).

GERSCHNER, R. (1997), 'Encolpius Etymologus. Die etymologischer Verwendung griechischer Wörter als Stilmerkmal von Petrons urbaner Prosa', *WSt* 110: 145–50.

GIANOTTI, G. F. (1986), *'Romanzo' e ideologia: Studi sulle* Metamorfosi *di* Apuleio (Naples).

GIARDINA, G. C., and CUCCIOLI MELLONI, R. (1995), *Petronii Arbitri Satyricon* (Turin).

GIARRATANO, C. (1929), *Apulei Metamorphoseon libri* XI (Turin).

—— and FRASSINETTI, P. (1960), *Apulei Metamorphoseon libri* XI (Turin) .

GILL, C. (1973), 'The Sexual Episodes in the *Satyricon*', *CPh* 68: 172–85.

—— and WISEMAN, T. P. (eds.) (1993), *Lies and Fiction in the Ancient World* (Exeter).

GILLELAND, M. E. (1979), 'Linguistic Differentiation of Character Type and Sex in the Comedies of Plautus and Terence', University of Virginia Ph.D. thesis.

GOLDBACHER, A. (1872), 'Über Lucius von Patrae, den dem Lucius zugeschriebenen Λουκιος ἢ Ὄνος und des Apuleius Metamorphosen', *ZöG* 23: 323–41, 403–21.

GOMME, A. W., and SANDBACH, F. H. (1973), *Menander: A Commentary* (Oxford).

GOULET, R. (ed.) (1989), *Dictionnaire des philosophes anciens*, i (Paris).

GRABAR-PASSEK, M. E. (1956), *Metamorphoses*, Russian tr. (Moscow).

GRAVERINI, L. (1997), '*In historiae specimen* (Apul. Met. 8. 1. 4)', *Prometheus*, 23: 247–78.

—— (1998), 'Memorie virgiliane nelle *Metamorfosi* di Apuleio', *Maia*, 50: 123–45.

GRAVES, R. (1950), *The Transformations of Lucius, Otherwise Known as* The Golden Ass (Harmondsworth).

—— (1957), *Suetonius: The Twelve Caesars* (Harmondsworth).

—— (1990), *Apuleius: The Golden Ass*, rev. M. Grant (Harmondsworth).

GRIFFITHS, J. G. (1960), 'The Flight of the Gods before Typhon: An Unrecognized Myth', *Hermes*, 88: 374–6.

—— (1970), *Plutarch's De Iside et Osiride* (Cardiff).

—— (1978), *Apuleius of Madauros: The Isis-Book (Metamorphoses, Book XI)* (Leiden).

GRIMAL, P. (1963), *Apulée: Metamorphoseis (IV. 28–VI. 24). Le conte d'Amor et Psyche* (Paris).

—— (1971), 'Le Calame égyptien d'Apulée', *REA* 73: 343–55.

GRIMAL, P. (1977), *La Guerre civile de Pétrone* (Paris).

GRONDONA, M. (1980), *La religione e la superstizione nella* Cena Trimalchionis, Collection Latomus, 46 (Brussels).

GRYSAR, K. J. (1854), 'Der römische Mimus', *SAWW* 12: 237–337.

GUIDO, G. (1976), *Petronio: Bellum civile* (Florence).

GUTHRIE, W. K. C. (1957), 'Plato's Views on the Nature of the Soul', in Guthrie (1957: 3–19).

—— (ed.) (1957), *Recherches sur la tradition platonicienne*, Entretiens Hardt, 3 (Geneva).

HÄGG, T. (1971), *Narrative Technique in Ancient Greek Romances* (Stockholm).

—— (1975), *Photios als Vermittler antiker Literatur* (Uppsala).

—— (1983), *The Novel in Antiquity* (Oxford).

HAIGHT, E. H. (1927), *Apuleius and his Influence* (New York).

HAMMER, S. (1923), 'De narrationum Apulei *Metamorphoseon* libro decimo insertarum compositione et exemplaribus', *Eos*, 26: 6–26.

—— (1925), 'De Apulei arte narrandi novae observationes', *Eos*, 28: 51–77.

HANI, J. (1976), *La Religion égyptienne dans la pensée de Plutarque* (Paris).

HANSON, J. A. (1989), *Apuleius: Metamorphoses*, 2 vols. (Cambridge, Mass.).

HARRAUER, C., and RÖMER, F. (1985), 'Beobachtungen zum Metamorphosenprolog des Apuleius', *Mnemosyne*, 37: 353–72.

HARRISON, S. J. (1990a), 'The Speaking Book: The Prologue to Apuleius' *Metamorphoses*', *CQ* NS 40: 507–13.

—— (1990b), 'Some Odyssean Scenes in Apuleius' *Metamorphoses*', *MD* 25: 193–201.

—— (1996), 'Apuleius' *Metamorphoses*', in Schmeling (1996: 491–516).

—— (1998a), 'The Milesian Tales and the Roman Novel', in Hofmann and Zimmerman (1998: 61–73).

—— (1998b), 'From Epic to Novel: Apuleius as Reader of Vergil', *MD* 39: 53–73.

HASLAM, M. W. (1981), *Papyri Greek and Egyptian . . . in Honour of E. G. Turner* (London).

HAVET, L. (1882), 'Observations critiques sur les *Ménippées* de Varron', *RPh* 6: 54–60.

HEINE, R. (1962), *Untersuchungen zur Romanform des Apuleius von Madaura*, diss. (Göttingen).

HEINZE, R. (1892), *Xenocrates* (Leipzig).

—— (1899), 'Petron und der griechische Roman', *Hermes*, 34: 494–519; repr. in Heinze (1960: 417–39).

—— (1960), *Vom Geist des Römertums* (Stuttgart).

HELLER, E. (1961), *Thomas Mann: The Ironic German*, rev. edn. (New York).

HELLER, S. (1983), 'Apuleius, Platonic Dualism, and Eleven', *AJP* 104: 321–39.

HELM, R. (1906), *Lucian und Menipp* (Leipzig).

—— (1910), *Apulei Florida* (Leipzig). Contains important preface to all of Ap.

—— (1914), 'Das "Märchen" von Amor und Psyche', *NJb* 33: 170–209; repr. in Binder and Merkelbach (1968: 175–234).

—— (1928), review of Paratore (1928), *PhW* 48: 1512–15.

—— (1931*a*), *Apulei Metamorphoseon libri xi*, 3rd edn. (Leipzig).

—— (1931*b*), 'Menippus (10)', *RE* 15: 888–93.

—— (1943), 'Bericht über die Literatur der römischer Satiriker (ausser Horaz) von 1936–40', *Bursian*, 282: 5–11.

—— (1956, 1961, repr. 1965, 1970), *Apuleius: Metamorphosen oder Der goldene Esel. Lateinische und Deutsch*, rev. W. Krenkel (1961) (Berlin).

HENRICHS, A. (1972), *Die* Phoinikika *des Lollianos* (Bonn).

HENRIKSSON, K.-E. (1956), *Griechische Büchertitel in der römischen Literatur*, *Annales Acad. Scient. Fenn.*, 102/1 (Helsinki).

HERAEUS, W. (1899), *Die Sprache des Petronius und die Glossen*, Gymn. Progr. (Offenbach).

—— (1915), '*Προπεῖν*', *RhM* 70: 1–41.

—— (1937), *Kleine Schriften* (Heidelberg).

HERRMANN, L. (1972), 'Lucius de Patras et les trois romans de l'âne', *AC* 41: 573–99.

HESELTINE, M. (1969), *Petronius: Satyricon*, rev. B. H. Warmington (London).

HICTER, J. (1944–5), 'L'Autobiographie dans l'*Âne d'or* d'Apulée', *AC* 13: 95–111, 14: 61–8.

HIGHET, G. (1941), 'Petronius the Moralist', *TAPA* 72: 176–94.

HIJMANS, B. L., JR. (1978), 'Asinus numerosus', in Hijmans and van der Paardt (1978: 189–210).

—— (1987), 'Apuleius philosophus Platonicus', *ANRW* II. 36. 1: 395–475.

—— and VAN DER PAARDT, R. T. (eds.) (1978), *Aspects of Apuleius' Golden Ass* (Groningen).

—— *et al.* (1977), *Apuleius Madaurensis Metamorphoses Book IV. 1–27* (Groningen).

—— *et al.* (1981), *Apuleius Madaurensis Metamorphoses Books VI. 25–32 and VII* (Groningen).

—— *et al.* (1985), *Apuleius Madaurensis Metamorphoses Book VIII. 1–27* (Groningen).

—— *et. al.* (1995), *Apuleius Madaurensis Metamorphoses Book IX* (Groningen).

HILDEBRAND, G. F. (1842), *Apulei omnia opera* (Leipzig).

HODGART, M. (1969), *Satire* (New York).

HOEVELS, F. E. (1979), *Märchen und Magie in den* Metamorphosen *des Apuleius von Madaura* (Amsterdam).

HOFMANN, H. (1992), 'Apuleius in Groningen', *Euphrosyne*, 20: 453–61.

—— (ed.) (1988), *Groningen Colloquia on the Novel*, i (Groningen).

—— (ed.) (1989), *Groningen Colloquia on the Novel*, ii (Groningen).

—— (ed.) (1990), *Groningen Colloquia on the Novel*, iii (Groningen).

—— (ed.) (1991), *Groningen Colloquia on the Novel*, iv (Groningen).

HOFMANN, H. (ed.) (1993), *Groningen Colloquia on the Novel*, v (Groningen).
—— (ed.) (1995), *Groningen Colloquia on the Novel*, vi (Groningen).
—— (ed.) (1996), *Croningen Colloquia on the Ancient Novel*, vii (Groningen).
—— (ed.) (1998), *Latin Fiction* (London).
—— and ZIMMERMAN, M. (eds.) (1996), *Groningen Colloquia on the Novel*, vii (Groningen).
—— —— (eds.) (1997), *Groningen Colloquia on the Novel*, viii (Groningen).
—— —— (eds.) (1998), *Groningen Colloquia on the Novel*, ix (Groningen).
HOFMANN, J. B., and SZANTYR, A. (1965), *Lateinische Syntax und Stilistik* (Munich).
HOLLANDER, J. (1981), *The Figure of Echo: A Mode of Allusion in Milton and After* (Berkeley and Los Angeles).
HOLZBERG, N. (1984), 'Apuleius und der Verfasser des griechischen Eselromans', *WJA* 10: 161–78.
—— (1995), *The Ancient Novel* (London).
HOOPER, R. W. (1985), 'Structural Unity in the *Golden Ass*', *Latomus*, 44: 398–401.
HOPFNER, T. (1940–1), *Plutarch über Isis und Osiris. Text, Übersetzung, Kommentar*, 2 vols. (Prague).
HOPKINS, K. (1978), 'Economic Growth and Towns in Classical Antiquity', in Abrams and Wrigley (1978).
—— (1978*a*), *Conquerors and Slaves* (Cambridge).
—— (1978*b*), 'Econimic Growth and Towns in Classical Antiquity', in Abrams and Wrigley (1978).
—— (1980), 'Taxes and Trade in the Roman Empire (200 BC–AD 400)', *JRS* 70: 101–25.
HORSFALL, N. M. (1989), 'Petronius' *Cena* and *The Uses of Literacy*', *G&R* 36: 74–89, 194–209.
—— (1991–2), 'Generic Composition and Petronius' *Satyricon*', *Scripta classica israelica*, 11: 123–38.
HUBBARD, T. K. (1986), 'The Narrative Architecture of Petronius' *Satyricon*', *AC* 55: 190–212.
HUBER, G. (1990*a*), *Das Motiv der 'Witwe von Ephesus' in lateinischen Texten der Antike und des Mittelalters* (Mannheim).
—— (1990*b*), 'Walter Charleton's "Ephesian Matron". Ein Zeugnis der Petron-Rezeption im England der Restauration', in Hofmann (1990: 139–57).
HUMPHREYS, A. R. (1942), 'Fielding's Irony: Its Methods and Effects', *Review of English Studies*, 18: 183.
IMMISCH, O. (1921), 'Über eine volkstümliche Darstellungsform in der antiken Literatur', *NJb* 47: 409–21.
IRWIN, T. (1977), *Plato's Moral Theory* (Oxford).
JAMES, H. (1934), *The Art of the Novel: Critical Prefaces* (New York).
JAMES, P. (1987), *Unity in Diversity: A Study of Apuleius' Metamorphoses* (Hildesheim).

JENSSON, G. (1996), 'The Recollections of Encolpius: A Reading of the Satyrica as Greco-Roman Erotic Fiction', University of Toronto Ph.D. thesis.

JOCELYN, H. D. (1993), 'Sprache, Schriftlichkeit und Charakteriserung in der römischen Komödie (Plautus Pseudolus 41–73, 998–1014)', in Vogt-Spira (1993: 125–39).

JOLY, R. (1961), 'Curiositas', AC 30: 33–44.

JONES, A. H. M. (1940), The Greek City: From Alexander to Justinian (Oxford).

—— (1974), The Roman Economy (Oxford).

JONES, C. P. (1971), Plutarch and Rome (Oxford).

—— (1980), 'Apuleius' Metamorphoses and Lollianus' Phoenikika', Phoenix, 34: 243–54.

JONES, F. (1987), 'The Narrator and the Narrative of the Satyricon', Latomus, 46: 810–19.

JUNGHANNS, P. (1932), Die Erzählungstechnik von Apuleius' Metamorphosen und ihrer Vorlage, Philologus, Suppl. 24/1 (Leipzig).

—— (1939), review of Wittmann (1938), PhW 37–8: 1002–7.

KAHANE, A., and LAIRD, A. J. W. (eds.) (forthcoming), A Companion to the Prologue to Apuleius' Metamorphoses (Oxford).

KATZ, P. B. (1976), 'The Myth of Psyche: A Definition of the Nature of the Feminine', Arethusa, 9: 111–18.

KAYSER, C. L. (1860), review of Vahlen (1858), Heidelberger Jahrbuch der Literatur, 53: 246–8.

KENNEDY, G. A. (1978), 'Encolpius and Agamemnon in Petronius', AJP 99: 171–8.

—— (1991), Aristotle: On Rhetoric (New York).

KENNER, H. (1956), Dublin's Joyce (Bloomington, Ind.).

KENNEY, E. J. (1990a), Apuleius: Cupid and Psyche (Cambridge).

—— (1990b), 'Psyche and her Mysterious Husband', in Russell (1990: 175–98).

—— (1998), Apuleius: The Golden Ass. A New Translation (Harmondsworth).

KERÉNYI, K. (1927, repr. Darmstadt 1962), Die griechisch–orientalische Romanliteratur in religionsgeschichtlicher Beleuchtung (Tübingen).

KIRCHOFF, A. (1904), De Apulei Metamorphoseon compositione numerosa, diss. (Berlin).

KIREMIDJIAN, G. D. (1970), 'The Aesthetics of Parody', Journal of Aesthetics and Art Criticism, 28: 231–42.

KISSEL, W. (1978), 'Petrons Kritik an der Rhetorik (Sat. 1–5)', RhM 121: 311–28.

KLEBS, E. (1889), 'Zur Komposition von Petronius Satirae', Philologus, 47: 623–55.

KLODT, C. (ed.) (1996), Satura lanx. Festschrift W. Krenkel (Hildesheim).

KNAUT, C. F. E. (1868), De Luciano libelli qui inscribitur 'Lucius sive Asinus' auctore (Leipzig).

KNOCHE, U. (1971), Die römische Satire, 3rd edn. (Göttingen).

KNOPF, R., KRÜGER, G., and RUHBACH, G. (1965), *Ausgewählte Märtyrakten* (Tübingen).

KNOX, B. M. W. (1966), 'Second Thoughts on Greek Tragedy', *GRBS* 7: 213–32.

KOZIOL, H. (1872), *Der Stil des Apuleius* (Vienna).

KRABBE, J. K. (1989), *The Metamorphoses of Apuleius* (New York).

KRANZ, W. (1934), 'Vorsokratisches I', *Hermes*, 69: 114–19.

—— (1961), 'Sphragis. Ichform und Namensiegel als Eingangs- und Schlussmotiv antiker Dichtung', *RhM* 104: 3–46, 97–124.

KRENKEL, W. A. (1973), '*Varroniana* III', *WZRostock* 22: 165–71.

KROLL, W. (1924), *Studien zum Verständnis der römischen Literatur* (Stuttgart).

KRONHAUSEN, E., and KRONHAUSEN, P. (1964), *Pornography and the Law: The Psychology of Erotic Realism and Hard Core Pornography*, 2nd edn. (New York).

KÜHNER, R., and STEGMANN, C. (1976), *Ausführliche Grammatik der lateinischen Sprache*, 5th edn. (Hanover).

KUNICK, H. J. (1955), *Der lateinische Begriff patientia bei Laktanz*, diss. (Freiburg).

KUSSL, R. (1990), 'Die *Metamorphosen* des "Lucius von Patrai". Untersuchungen zu Photius *Bibl.* 129', *RhM* 133: 379–88.

LABHARDT, A. (1960), '*Curiositas*: Notes sur l'histoire d'un mot et d'une notion', *MH* 17: 206–24.

LAIRD, A. (1990), 'Person, Persona and Representation in Apuleius' *Metamorphoses*', *MD* 25: 129–64.

—— (1993), 'Fiction, Bewilderment and Story Worlds: The Implications of Claims to Truth in Apuleius', in Gill and Wiseman (1993: 147–74).

LANCEL, S. (1961), '*Curiositas* et préoccupations spirituelles chez Apulée', *RHR* 160: 25–46.

—— (1987), 'Y-a-t'il une Africitas?', *REL* 63: 161–82.

LANDI, C. (1922), 'Apuleio o Luciano?', *Atene e Roma*, NS 3: 44–59.

—— (1929), 'L'epilogo delle *Metamorfosi* di Apuleio', *Athenaeum*, 7: 3–22.

LANGHAMMER, W. (1973), *Die rechtliche und soziale Stellung der 'Magistratus Municipales' und der 'Decuriones' . . . 2.–4. Jahrhundert der römischen Kaiserzeit* (Wiesbaden).

LA PENNA, A. (1985), 'Una novella di Apuleio e l'Iliupersis virgiliana', *Maia*, 37: 145–8.

LATTE, K. (1960), *Römische Religionsgeschichte* (Munich).

LAVAGNINI, B. (1923), *Il significato e il valore del romanzo di Apuleio* (Pisa).

LAZZARINI, C. (1985), 'Il modello virgiliano nel lessico delle *Metamorfosi* di Apuleio', *SCO* 35: 131–60.

LEHNERT, G. (1915, 1919), 'Bericht über die Literatur zu Apuleius und zur *Historia Apollonii regis Tyrii* aus den Jahren 1897–1914', *Bursian*, 171: 147–76, 175: 1–75.

LEJAY, P. (ed.) (1911), *Œuvres d'Horace: Satires* (Paris).

LELIÈVRE, P. (1954), 'The Basis of Ancient Parody', *G&R* 1: 66–81.

LEO, F. (1903), *Die römische Literatur des Altertums* (Berlin).

—— (1905), 'Coniectanea', *Hermes*, 40: 605–13.

—— (1912), *Die griechische und lateinische Literatur* (Leipzig).

LERNER, M., and MUMS, E., Jr. (eds.) (1933), 'Literature', in *Encyclopedia of the Social Sciences*, ix (New York).

LESKY, A. (1941), 'Apuleius von Madaura und Lukios von Patrai', *Hermes*, 76: 43–74; repr. in *Gesammelte Schriften* (Bern, 1966), 549–78.

LEUMANN, M. (1977), *Lateinische Grammatik. Laut- und Formenlehre* (Munich).

LEVIN, H. (1946), 'Literature as an Institution', *Accent*, 6: 159–68; repr. in Schorer *et al.* (1948).

LÉVY, P., and WOLFF, E. (eds.) (1974), *Mélanges d'histoire des religions offerts à Henri-Charles Pueche* (Paris).

LEWIS, A. (ed.) (1927), *The Satiricon of Petronius Arbiter in the Translation Attributed to Oscar Wilde* (Chicago).

LINDSAY, J. (1932), *The Golden Ass of Apuleius* (New York).

LÖFSTEDT, E. (1911), *Philologischer Kommentar zur 'Peregrinatio aetheriae'* (Uppsala; repr. Darmstadt 1966).

LOMMATZSCH, E. (1919), 'Bericht über die Literatur der römischer Satiriker (ausser Horaz) von 1908–17', *Bursian*, 175: 98–105.

—— (1925), 'Bericht über die Literatur der römischer Satiriker (ausser Horaz) von 1918–24', *Bursian*, 204: 215–18.

—— (1932), 'Bericht über die Literatur der römischer Satiriker (ausser Horaz) von 1925–30', *Bursian*, 235: 142–8.

—— (1938), 'Bericht über die Literatur der römischer Satiriker (ausser Horaz) von 1930–36', *Bursian*, 260: 94–100.

LOPORCARO, M. (1992), 'Eroi screditati dal testo: Strutture della parodia nelle storie di briganti in Apuleio *Met.* IV. 9–21', *Maia*, 44: 65–78.

LOPUSZANSKI, G. (1951), 'La Police romaine et les chrétiens', *Ant. Class.* 20: 5–46.

LUCAS, H. (1903), 'Ein Märchen bei Petron', in *Festschrift O. Hirschfeld* (Berlin), 257–69.

—— (1907), 'Zu den *Milesiaka* des Aristides', *Philologus*, 66: 16–35.

LUDWIG, E. (1869), *De Petronii sermone plebeio*, diss. (Marburg).

McCARTHY, B. P. (1934), 'Lucian and Menippus', *YCS* 4: 3–55.

—— (1936), 'The Form of Varro's *Menippean Satires*', in Robinson (1936: 95–107).

MacFARLANE, A. (1978), *The Origins of English Individualism* (Oxford).

McGUSHIN, P. (1992), *Sallust: The Histories—Volume 1, Books I–II* (Oxford).

MacKAY, L. A. (1965), 'The Sin of the Golden Ass', *Arion*, 4: 474–80.

MacKAY, P. A. (1963), 'Klephtika: The Tradition of the Tales of Banditry in Apuleius', *G&R* 10: 147–52.

MacKENDRICK, P. (1950), '*The Great Gatsby* and Trimalchio', *CJ* 45: 307–14.

McLEOD, M. D. (1967), *Lucian*, viii, Loeb Classical Library (Cambridge. Mass.).

MacMullen, R. (1970), 'Market-Days in the Roman Empire', *Phoenix*, 24: 333–41.

Magi, F. (1971), 'L'*adventus* di Trimalchione e il fregio A della cancelleria', *Archeologia Classica*, 23: 88–92.

Maier, H., and Sckommodau, H. (eds.) (1963), *Wort und Text. Festschrift Fritz Schalk* (Frankfurt).

Maiuri, A. (1945), *La Cena di Trimalchione di Petronio Arbitro* (Naples).

Maltby, R. (1979), 'Linguistic Characterization of Old Men in Terence', *CPh* 74: 136–47.

—— (1985), 'The Distribution of Greek Loan-Words in Terence', *CQ* 35: 110–23.

Mantero, T. (1973), *Amore e Psiche: Struttura di una fiaba di magia* (Genoa).

Marangoni, C. (1974–5), 'Il nome Asinio Marcello e i misteri di Osiride (Apul. *Met.* xi. 27)', *Atti e memorie dell'Accademia Patavina di Scienze*, 87: 333–7.

—— (1977–8), 'Corinto simbolico isiaco nelle *Metamorfosi* di Apuleio', *Atti dell'Instituto Veneto*, 136: 221–2.

Marbach, A. (1931), *Wortbildung, Wortwahl und Wortbedeutung als Mittel der Charakterzeichung bei Petron*, diss. (Giessen).

Mariotti, S. (1956), 'Lo *spurcum additamentum* ad Apul. *Met.* x. 21', *SIFC* 27–8: 229–50.

Marmorale, E. V. (1937), *Petronio nel suo tempo* (Naples).

—— (1947, 2nd edn. 1961), *Petronii Arbitri Cena Trimalchionis* (Florence).

—— (1948), *La questione Petroniana* (Bari).

Marquardt, J. (1879), *Das Privatleben der Römer*, 7 vols. (Leipzig).

Marshall, P. K. (1983), 'Apuleius', in Reynolds (1983: 15–16).

Mason, H. J. (1971), 'Lucius at Corinth', *Phoenix*, 25: 160–5.

—— (1972), review of van Thiel (1971b: i), *Phoenix*, 26: 315.

—— (1976), 'Apuleius and *Lucius sive Asinus* since Rohde', abstract, in Reardon (1977: 146–8).

—— (1978), '*Fabula Graecanica*: Apuleius and his Greek Sources', in Hijmans and van der Paardt (1978: 1–15).

—— (1983), 'The Distinction of Lucius in Apuleius' *Metamorphoses*', *Phoenix*, 37: 135–43.

—— (1994), 'Greek and Latin Versions of the Ass-Story', *ANRW* ii. 34. 2: 1665–1707.

—— (1998), 'The *Metamorphoses* of Apuleius and its Greek Sources', in Hofmann (1998).

Mass, E. (1989), 'Tradition und Innovation im Romanschaffen Boccaccios', in Hofmann (1989: 87–107).

Mattiacci, S. (1993), 'La *lecti invocatio* di Aristomene: Pluralità di modelli e parodia in Apul. *Met.* 1. 16', *Maia*, 45: 257–67.

—— (1996), *Apuleio: Le novelle dell'adulterio* (Metamorfosi ix) (Florence).

Maxwell-Stuart, P. G. (1975), 'Further Notes on Strato's *Musa Puerilis*', *Hermes*, 103: 379–80.

MAZZARINO, A. (1950), *La Milesia e Apuleio* (Turin).

MÉDAN, P. (1925), *La Latinité d'Apulée dans les* Métamorphoses (Paris).

MENDELL, C. W. (1917), 'Petronius and the Greek Romance', *CPh* 12: 158–72.

MERKELBACH, R. (1958), 'Eros und Psyche', *Philologus*, 102: 103–16.

—— (1962), *Roman und Mysterium in der Antike* (Berlin).

—— (1973), 'Fragment eines satirischen Romans. Aufforderung zur Beichte', *ZPE* 11: 81–100.

—— (1995), *Isis Regina—Zeus Sarapis* (Stuttgart).

METTE, H. J. (1956), 'Curiositas', in Erbse (1956: 227–35).

—— (1962), 'Die περιεργία bei Menander', *Gymnasium*, 69: 398–406.

MEYER-LÜBKE, W. (1899, repr. Darmstadt 1972), *Grammatik der romanischen Sprachen*, iii (Leipzig).

—— (1935), *Romanisches etymologisches Wörterbuch*, 3rd edn. (Heidelberg).

MILLAR, F. G. B. (1963), review of Pflaum (1960), *JRS* 53: 194–200.

—— (1977), *The Emperor in the Roman World* (London).

—— (1981), 'The World of the *Golden Ass*', *JRS* 71: 63–75.

MILLER, S. (1967), *The Picaresque Novel* (Cleveland).

MITCHELL, S. (1976), 'Requisitioned Transport in the Roman Empire: A New Inscription from Pisidia', *JRS* 66: 106–31.

MOERING, F. (1915), *De Petronio mimorum imitatore*, diss. (Münster).

MOHR, R. D. (1985a), *The Platonic Cosmology* (Leiden).

—— (1985b), 'The Sources of Evil Problem and the Principle of Motion Doctrine in the *Phaedrus* and *Laws* 10', in Mohr (1985a: 158–70).

MOLT, M. (1938), *Ad Apulei Madaurensis Met. librum primum commentarius exegeticus*, diss. (Groningen).

MOMMSEN, T. (1899), *Römisches Strafrecht* (Leipzig).

MONCEAUX, P. (1889), *Apulée: Roman et magie* (Paris).

MORELLI, C. (1913), 'Apuleiana', *SIFC* 20: 145–88.

—— (1915), 'Apuleiana III: In che tempo furono scritte le *Metamorfosi*?', *SIFC* 21: 94–157.

MORESCHINI, C. (1965), 'La demonologia medioplatonica e le *Metamorfosi* di Apuleio', *Maia*, 17: 30–46.

—— (1978), *Apuleio e il Platonismo* (Florence).

—— (1990), 'Le *Metamorfosi* di Apuleio, la fabula milesia e il romanzo', *MD* 25: 115–28.

—— (1994), *Il mito di Amore e Psiche in Apuleio* (Naples).

MORFORD, M. P. O. (1967), *The Poet Lucan* (Oxford).

MORRIS, I. (1964), *The World of the Shining Prince* (London).

MOSCA, B. (1937), 'Satira filosofica e politica nelle *Menippee* di Varrone', *ASNP* 41–77.

MRAS, K. (1914), 'Varros Menippeische Satiren und die Philosophie', *NJb* 33: 390–420.

MÜLLER, C. W. (1976), 'Chariton von Aphrodisias und die Theorie des Romans in der Antike', *A&A* 22: 115–36.

MÜLLER, C. W. (1980), 'Die Witwe von Ephesus. Petrons Novelle und die *Milesiaka* des Aristides', *A&A* 26: 103–21.

MÜLLER, H. (1998), *Liebesbeziehungen in Orios Metamorphosen und ihr Einfluß auf den Roman des Apuleius* (Göttingen).

MÜLLER, K. (1961), *Petronii Arbitri Satyricon cum apparatu critico*, 1st edn. (Munich).

—— (1995), *Petronius Satyricon reliquiae*, 4th edn. of Müller (1961) (Stuttgart).

—— and EHLERS, W. (1965), *Petronius: Satyrica (Schelmenszenen)*, 2nd edn. of Müller (1961) (Munich).

—— —— (1978, repr. 1983), *Petronius: Satyrica (Schelmenszenen)*, 3rd edn. of Müller (1961) (Munich).

MÜNSTERMANN, H. (1995), *Apuleius: Metamorphosen. Literarischer Vorlagen* (Stuttgart).

MUSURILLO, H. A. (1972), *Acts of the Christian Martyrs* (Oxford).

MUTH, R. (1956), 'Petronius, 1. Bericht', *AA* 9: 1–22.

MYNORS, R. A. B. (1969), *P. Vergili Maronis opera* (Oxford).

NARDUCCI, E. (1984), 'Commercio e *status* sociale in Cicerone e in Petronio', review of D'Arms (1981), *Quaderno di storia* 19: 229–45.

NEESEN, L. (1981), 'Die Entwicklung der Leistungen und Ämter (*munera et honores*) im römischen Kaiserreich des zweiten bis vierten Jahrhundert', *Historia*, 30: 203–35.

NELSON, H. L. W. (1947), *Petronius en zjin 'vulgair' Latijn*, diss. (Alphen aan den Reijn).

NETHERCUT, W. R. (1966–7), 'Petronius, Epicurean and Moralist', *CB* 43: 53–5.

—— (1970), 'The Ironic Priest: Propertius' Roman Elegies III. 1–5: Imitations of Horace and Vergil', *AJP* 91: 386–407.

NILSSON, M. P. (1961), *Geschichte der griechischen Religion*, ii 2nd edn. (Munich).

NISBET, R. G. M. (1962), review of Müller (1961), *JRS* 52: 227–32; repr. in Nisbet (1995: 6–17).

—— (1995), *Collected Papers on Latin Literature* (Oxford).

—— (forthcoming), 'Colometry of the Prologue to Apuleius' *Metamorphoses*', in Kahane and Laird (forthcoming).

NIXON, P. (1916), *Plautus*, i (Cambridge, Mass.).

NOCK, A. D. (1933, repr. London 1963), *Conversion* (Oxford).

NÖRR, D. (1966), *Imperium und Polis in der hohen Prinzipatszeit* (Munich).

NOLTING-HAUFF, I. (1974), 'Märchenromane mit leidendem Helden', *Poetica*, 6: 417–55.

NORDEN, E. (1892), 'In Varronis *Saturas Menippeas* observationes selectae', *JA* Suppl. 18: 265–72.

—— (1899, 3rd edn. 1915), *Die antike Kunstprosa*, 2 vols. (Leipzig).

OLDFATHER, W. A., CANTER, H. V., and PERRY, B. E. (1934), *Index Apuleianus* (Middletown, Conn.).

OLIVER, J. H., and PALMER, R. E. A. (1955), 'Minutes of an Act of the Roman Senate', *Hesperia*, 24: 320–49.

OTIS, B. (1967), 'The Uniqueness of Latin Literature', *Arion*, 6: 185–206.

OTTO, A. (1890, repr. 1960 and Hildesheim, 1971), *Die Sprichwörter und sprichwörtlichen Redensarten der Römer* (Leipzig).

OUDENDORP, F. (1786), *Apulei opera omnia*, i. *Met.*, ed. D. Ruhnken (Leiden).

—— (1823), *Apulei opera omnia*, iii, ed. J. Bosscha (Leiden).

PACCHIENI, M. (1978), *La novella milesia in Petronio* (Lecce).

PANAYOTAKIS, C. (1995), *Theatrum Arbitri: Theatrical Elements in the* Satyrica *of Petronius*, Mnemosyne, Suppl. 146.

PAOLI, E. U. (1937), 'L'età del *Satyricon*', *SIFC* 14: 3–46.

PARATORE, E. (1928), *La novella in Apuleio* (Palermo).

—— (1933), *Il Satyricon di Petronio*, 2 vols. (Florence).

—— (1942), *La novella in Apuleio*, 2nd edn. (Palermo).

PARKER, A. (1967), *Literature and the Delinquent* (Edinburgh).

PARSONS, P. J. (1971), 'A Greek *Satyricon*?', *BICS* 18: 53–68.

—— (1974), 'Narrative about Iolaus', *P. Oxy.* 42: 34–41.

PEASE, A. S. (1935), *P. Vergili Maronis Aeneidos liber quartus* (Cambridge, Mass.).

PECERE, O. (1975), *Petronio: La novella della matrona di Efeso* (Padua).

—— (1984), 'Esemplari con subscriptiones e tradizione dei testi latini: L'Apuleio *Laur.* 68. 2', in Questa (1984: 111–37).

—— and STRAMAGLIA, A. (eds.) (1996), *La letteratura di consumo nel mondo greco-latino* (Cassino).

PELLEGRINO, C. (1975), *Petronii Arbitri: Satyricon* (Rome).

—— (1986), *T. Petronio Arbitro: Satyrica. Introduzione, testo critico, commento*, i: *I capitoli della retorica* (Rome).

PENNACINI, A. (1979), 'Techniche del racconto nelle *Metamorfosi*: Analisi del libri 1, 2, 3', in Pennacini *et al.* (1979: 21–102).

—— DONINI, P. L., ALIMENTI, T., and MONTEDURO ROCCAVINI, A. (1979), *Apuleio letterato, filosofo, mago* (Rome).

PENWILL, J. L. (1975), 'Slavish Pleasures and Profitless Curiosity: Fall and Redemption in Apuleius' *Metamorphoses*', *Ramus*, 4: 49–82.

—— (1990), '*Ambages Reciprocae*: Reviewing Apuleius' *Metamorphoses*', in Boyle (1990: 211–35).

PEPE, L. (1963), 'Lucio di Patrae o Aristide-Sisenna', *GIF* 16: 111–42.

PERROCHAT, P. (1939, 2nd edn. 1952, 3rd edn. 1962), *Le Festin de Trimalchion* (Paris).

PERRY, B. E. (1920), *The* Metamorphoses *Ascribed to Lucius of Patrae* (Princeton).

—— (1923), 'Some Aspects of the Literary Art of Apuleius in the *Metamorphoses*', *TAPA* 54: 196–227.

—— (1925), 'Petronius and the Comic Romance', *CPh* 20: 31–49.

—— (1926), 'An Interpretation of Apuleius' *Metamorphoses*', *TAPA* 57: 238–60.

—— (1929*a*), 'On Apuleius' *Met.* 1. 14–17', *CPh* 24: 394–400.

PERRY, B. E. (1929*b*), 'The Story of Thelyphron in Apuleius', *CPh* 24: 231–8.

—— (1949), review of de Jonge (1941), *CPh* 44: 38–42.

—— (1952), *Aesopica* (Urbana, Ill.).

—— (1967), *The Ancient Romances: A Literary-Historical Account of their Origins* (Berkeley and Los Angeles).

—— (1968), 'Who was Lucius of Patrae?', *CJ* 64: 97–101.

PERUTELLI, A. (1985), 'Le chiacchiere dei liberti: Dialogo e commedia in Petronio 41–46', *Maia*, 37: 103–19.

—— (1990), 'Il narratore nel *Satyricon*', *MD* 25: 9–26.

PETERSMANN, H. (1977), *Petrons urbane Prosa* (Vienna).

—— (1983), 'Die pragmatische Dimension in der Sprache des Chores bei den griechischen Tragikern', *A&A* 29: 95–106.

—— (1985), 'Umwelt, Sprachsituation und Stilschichten in Petrons *Satyrica*', *ANRW* II. 32. 3: 1687–1705.

—— (1986), 'Petrons *Satyrica*', in Adamietz (1986: 388–400).

—— (1995*a*), 'Religion, Superstition and Parody in Petronius' *Cena Trimalchionis*', in Hofmann (1995: 75–86).

—— (1995*b*), 'Soziale und lokale Aspekte in der Vulgärsprache Petrons', in Callebat (1995: 533–47).

—— (1995*c*), 'Zum mündlichen Charakteriserung des Fremden in der Komödie des Plautus', in Benz *et al.* (1995: 123–36).

—— (1996–7), 'Die Nachahmung des *sermo rusticus* auf der Bühne des Plautus und Terenz', *Acta antiqua Hungarica*, 37: 199–211.

PFISTER, M. (1940), review of Riefstahl (1938), *PhW* 60: 533–41.

PFLAUM, H.-G. (1960–1), *Les Carrières procuratoriennes équestres sous le haut-empire romain*, 3 vols. (Paris).

—— (1971), 'Une lettre de promotion de l'empereur Marc-Aurèle pour un procurateur ducénaire de Gaule Narbonnaise', *Bonner Jahrbücher*, 171: 349–66.

PIOT, H. (1914), *Un personnage de Lucien—Ménippe* (Rennes).

PLASSART, A. (1932), 'Une levée de volontaires Thespiens sous Marc-Aurèle', *Mélanges Gustave Glotz*, ii. 731–8 (Paris).

PÖSCHL, V. (1964), *Die Dichtkunst Virgils. Bild und Symbol in der* Aeneis (Darmstadt).

POPMA, A. (1589), *Fragmenta Marci Terenti Varronis Satyrarum Menippearum* (Franeker).

PORTOGALLI, B. M. (1963), 'Sulle fonti della concezione teologica e demono-logica di Apuleio', *SCO* 12: 227–41.

POWELL, J. U. (ed.) (1933), *New Chapters in the History of Greek Literature*, 3rd ser. (Oxford).

PREISENDANZ, K. (1931), *Papyri Graecae magicae*, ii (Leipzig).

—— (1974), *Papyri Graecae magicae*, ii, 2nd edn. (Stuttgart).

PRESTON, K. (1915), 'Some Sources of Comic Effect in Petronius', *CPh* 10: 260–9.

PRETE, S. (1988), 'La questione della lingua latina nel Quattrocento e l'importanza dell'opera di Apuleio', in Hofmann (1988: 123–40).

PRICE, M. (1965), *To the Palace of Wisdom* (Garden City, NY).

PURSER, L. C. (1910), *Apuleius: The Story of Cupid and Psyche* (London).

QUESTA, C. (ed.) (1984), *Atti del convegno 'il libro e il testo'* (Urbino).

RAITH, O. (1963), *Petronius, ein Epikureer* (Nuremberg).

RANKIN, H. D. (1970a), 'Notes on the Comparison of Petronius with Three Moderns', *A. Ant. Hung.* 18: 197–213.

—— (1970b), 'Some Comments on Petronius' Portrayal of Character', *Eranos*, 68: 123–47; repr. in Rankin (1971: 11–31).

—— (1971), *Petronius the Artist* (The Hague).

RATTENBURY, R. M. (1933), 'Romance: Traces of Lost Greek Novels', in Powell (1933: 211–57).

REARDON, B. (1969), 'The Greek Novel', *Phoenix*, 23: 291–309.

—— (1971), *Courants littéraires grecs des IIe et IIIe siècles après J.-C.* (Paris).

—— (ed.) (1977), *Erotica antiqua* (Bangor).

—— (ed.) (1989), *Collected Ancient Greek Novels* (Berkeley).

REEVE, M. D. (1984), 'Apotheosis . . . per saturam', *CPh* 79: 305–7.

—— (1983), 'Petronius', in Reynolds (1983: 295–300).

REICH, H. (1903), *Der Mimus* (Berlin).

—— (1904), 'Der Mann mit dem Eselkopf', *Shakespeare-Jahrbuch*, 40: 108–28.

REICHENKRON, G. (1965), *Historische lateinisch–altromanische Grammatik*, pt. I (Wiesbaden).

REITZENSTEIN, R. (1906), *Hellenistische Wundererzählungen* (Leipzig).

—— (1912), *Das Märchen von Amor und Psyche bei Apuleius* (Leipzig); repr. in Binder and Merkelbach (1968: 87–158).

—— (1927), *Die hellenistiche Mysterienreligionen* (Leipzig).

—— (1930), 'Noch einmal Eros und Psyche', *ARW* 28: 42–87.

RELIHAN, J. (1993), *Ancient Menippean Satire* (Baltimore).

RÉVAY, J. (1922), 'Horaz und Petron', *CPh* 17: 202–12.

REXROTH, K. (1969), 'Petronius, the *Satyricon*', in *Classics Revisited* (New York), 99–103.

REYNOLDS, L. D. (ed.) (1983), *Texts and Transmission: A Survey of the Latin Classics* (Oxford).

RIBBECK, O. (1859), 'Über Varronische Satiren', *RhM* 14: 102–30.

RICCOMAGNO, L. (1931), *Studio sulle 'Satire Menippee' di Marco Terenzio Varrone Reatino* (Alba).

RICHARDSON, T. WADE (1972), 'Interpolation in Petronius', Harvard University Ph.D. thesis.

—— (1993), *Reading and Variant in Petronius*, *Phoenix*, Suppl. 30.

RIEFSTAHL, H. (1938), *Der Roman des Apuleius. Ein Beitrag zur Romantheorie* (Frankfurt).

RIESE, A. (1865), *M. Terentii Varronis Saturarum Menippearum reliquiae* (Leipzig).

RINI, A. (1937), *Petronius in Italy* (New York).

RISCH, E. (1963), review of Stefenelli (1962), *Kratylos*, 8: 211–13.

RITTERLING, E. (1927), 'Military Forces in the Senatorial Provinces', *JRS* 17: 28–32.

ROBERT, C. (1901), 'Archeologische Nachlese', *Hermes*, 36: 364–8.

ROBERT, L. (1948), *Hellenica*, v (Paris).

ROBERTSON, D. S. (1910), 'Lucius of Madaura: A Difficulty in Apuleius', *CQ* 4: 221–7.

—— (1924), 'The Manuscripts of the *Metamorphoses* of Apuleius', *CQ* 18: 27–41, 85–99.

—— and VALETTE, P. (1940–5, repr. 1956, 1965, 1971), *Apulée: Les Métamorphoses*, 3 vols. (Paris).

ROBINSON, R. P. (ed.) (1936), *Philological Studies in Honour of W. Miller* (Columbia).

RODE, A. (1783), *Der Goldener Esel* (Dessau).

—— (1956), *Der Goldener Esel*, ed. M. Wachter (Rudolfstadt).

—— (1960), *Der Goldener Esel*, ed. H. Rüdiger (Zurich).

—— (1961), *Der Goldener Esel*, ed. E. Burck (Reinbek bei Hamburg).

ROEPER, T. (1862), *M. Terenti Varronis Eumenidum reliquiae* (Danzig).

ROHDE, E. (1869), *Über Lucians Schrift Λουκιος ἢ Ὄνος und ihr Verhältnis zu Lucius von Patrae und den* Metamorphosen *von Apuleius* (Leipzig).

—— (1876, 3rd edn. 1914, repr. 1960), *Der griechische Roman und seine Vorläufer* (Leipzig).

—— (1885), 'Zu Apuleius', *RhM* 40: 66–113; repr. in *Kleine Schriften* (Tübingen, 1901), ii. 43–102.

ROLLO, D. (1994), 'From Apuleius' Psyche to Chrétien's Eric and Enide', in Tatum (1994: 273–90).

ROSATI, G. (1983), 'Trimalchione in scena', *Maia*, 35: 213–27.

ROSE, K. F. C. (1962), 'The Date of the *Satyricon*', *CQ* NS 12: 166–8.

—— (1966), 'The Petronian Inquisition: An *auto-da-fé*', *Arion*, 5: 292–5.

—— (1971), *The Date and Author of the* Satyricon, *Mnemosyne*, Suppl. 16.

ROSENBLÜTH, M. (1909), *Beiträge zur Quellenkunde von Petrons Satiren* (Berlin).

ROSTOVTZEFF, M. (1957), *The Social and Economic History of the Roman Empire*, 2nd edn., rev. P. M. Fraser (Oxford).

RUDD, N. (1992), *Juvenal: The Satires* (Oxford).

RÜDIGER, H. (1960), (1963), '*Curiositas* und Magie. Apuleius und Lucius als litterarische Archetypen der Faust-Gestalt', in Maier and Sckommodau (1963: 57–82).

RUSSELL, D. A. (ed.) (1990), *Antonine Literature* (Oxford).

SAGE, E. T. (1915), 'Atticism in Petronius', *TAPA* 46: 47–57.

—— (1936), *Livy XI: Books XXXVIII–XXXIX* (Cambridge, Mass.).

—— (1969), *Petronius: The Satyricon* (New York).

SALONIUS, A. (1927), *Die Griechen und das Griechische in Petrons Cena Trimalchionis* (Helsinki).

SANDY, G. N. (1969), 'Satire in the *Satyricon*', *AJP* 90: 293–303.

—— (1972), 'Knowledge and Curiosity in Apuleius' *Metamorphoses*', *Latomus*, 31: 179–83.

—— (1972–3), 'Foreshadowing and Suspense in Apuleius' *Metamorphoses*', *CJ* 68: 232–5.

—— (1974), '*Scaenica Petroniana*', *TAPA* 104: 329–46.

—— (1978), 'Book XI: Ballast or Anchor?', in Hijmans and van der Paardt (1978: 123–40).

—— (1989), introd. to Antonius Diogenes, in Reardon (1989: 775–7).

—— (1994), 'Apuleius' *Metamorphoses* and the Greek Novel', *ANRW* II. 34. 2: 1511–74.

—— (1997), *The Greek World of Apuleius*, Mnemosyne, Suppl. 174.

ŠAŠEL KOS, M. (1978), 'A Latin Epitaph of a Roman Legionary from Corinth', *JRS* 18: 22–5.

SCARCELLA, A. M. (1977), 'Les Structures socio-économiques du roman de Xénophon d'Éphèse', *REG* 90: 249–62.

SCAZZOSO, P. (1951), *Le Metamorfosi di Apuleio* (Milan).

SCHANZ, M., and HOSIUS, C. (1922), *Geschichte der römischen Literatur*, iii (Munich).

—— —— (1935, repr. 1967), *Geschichte der römischen Literatur*, ii, 4th edn. (Munich).

SCHERBANTIN, A. (1951), *Satura Menippea. Die Geschichte eines Genos*, diss. (Graz).

SCHIESARO, A. (1988), 'La tragedia di Psiche: Note ad Apuleio *Met*. 4. 28–35', *Maia*, 40: 141–50.

SCHISSEL VON FLESCHENBERG, O. (1913a), *Die griechische Novelle* (Halle).

—— (1913b), *Entwicklungsgeschichte des griechischen Romanes im Altertum* (Halle).

SCHLAM, C. C. (1968a), 'The Curiosity of the Golden Ass', *CJ* 64: 120–5.

—— (1968b), 'The Narrative Structure of the *Metamorphoses* of Apuleius', Columbia University Ph.D. thesis.

—— (1970), 'Platonica in the *Metamorphoses* of Apuleius', *TAPA* 101: 477–87.

—— (1971), 'The Scholarship on Apuleius since 1938', *CW* 64: 285–309.

—— (1976), *Apuleius and the Monuments* (University Park, Penn.)

—— (1990), 'Apuleius and the Middle Ages', in Bernardo and Levin (1990: 363–9).

—— (1992), *The Metamorphoses of Apuleius: On Making an Ass of Oneself* (Chapel Hill).

—— (1993), 'Cupid and Psyche: Folktale and Literary Narrative', in Hofmann (1993: 63–73).

SCHMELING, G. L. (1968–9), 'Petronius: Satirist, Moralist, Epicurean, Artist', *CB* 45: 49–50, 64.

—— (1969), 'Petronian Scholarship since 1957', *CW* 62: 157–64, 352–3.

SCHMELING, G. L. (1971), 'The *Satyricon*: Forms in Search of a Genre', *CB* 47: 49–53.

—— (1992) 'The *Satyricon*: The Sense of an Ending', *RhM* 134: 352–77.

—— (1994), '*Quid attinet veritatem per interpretem quaerere?* Interpretes and the *Satyricon*', *Ramus*, 23: 144–68.

—— (ed.) (1996*a*), *The Novel in the Ancient World*, *Mnemosyne*, Suppl. 159.

—— (1996*b*), 'Historia Apollonii regis Tyrii', in Schmeling (1996*a*: 517–51).

—— (1996*c*), 'Genre and the *Satyricon*: Menippean Satire and the Novel', in Klodt (1996: 105–17).

—— and STUCKEY, J. (1977), *A Bibliography of Petronius*, *Mnemosyne*, Suppl. 39.

SCHMID, D. (1951), *Der Erbschleicher in der antiken Satire*, diss. (Tübingen).

SCHMID, W. (1891), 'Bemerkungen über Lucians Leben und Schriften', *Philologus*, 50: 297–319.

SCHNEIDER, C. (1954), *Geistesgeschichte des antiken Christentums*, i (Munich).

SCHNUR, H. C. (1957), 'Recent Petronian Scholarship', *CW* 50: 133–6, 141–3.

—— (1972–3), 'Petronius: Sense and Nonsense', *CW* 66: 13–20.

SCHOBER, E. (1902), *De Apulei clausularum compositione et arte quaestiones criticae*, diss. (Halle).

SCHORER, M., MILES, J., and McKENZIE, G. (eds.) (1948), *Criticism: The Foundations of Modern Literary Judgment* (New York).

SCHÜRER, E. (1979), *The History of the Jewish People in the Age of Jesus Christ (175 BC–AD 135)*, ed. G. Vermes, F. Millar, and M. Black, ii (Edinburgh).

SCHUSTER, M. (1930), 'Der Werwolf und die Hexen', *WS* 48: 149–78.

—— (1931), 'Sachliche und sprachliche Bemerkungen zu Petrons Märchen', *WS* 49: 83–9.

SCOBIE, A. (1969), *Aspects of the Ancient Romance and its Heritage* (Meisenheim am Glan).

—— (1973), *More Essays on the Ancient Romance and its Heritage* (Meisenheim am Glan).

—— (1974), 'Notes on Walter Anderson's *Märchen vom Eselmenschen*', *Fabula*, 15: 222–31.

—— (1975), *Apuleius Met. (Asinus aureus)*, i (Meisenheim am Glan).

—— (1978*a*), 'The Influence of Apuleius' *Metamorphoses* in Renaissance Italy and Spain', in Hijmans and van der Paardt (1978: 211–30).

—— (1978*b*), 'The Structure of Apuleius' *Metamorphoses*', in Hijmans and van der Paardt (1978: 43–61).

—— (1983), *Apuleius and Folklore* (London).

SCOTTI, M. T. (1982), 'Il proemio delle *Metamorfosi* tra Ovidio ed Apuleio', *GIFC* 34: 43–65.

SCRANTON, R., SHAW, J. W., and IBRAHIM, L. (1978), *Kenchreai: Eastern Port of Corinth*, i: *Topography and Architecture* (Leiden).

SEDGWICK, W. B. (1925, 2nd edn. 1950), *Petronius: Cena Trimalchionis* (Oxford).

SEGAL, E. (1968a), *Roman Laughter* (Cambridge, Mass.).

—— (ed.) (1968b), *Euripides: A Collection of Critical Essays* (Englewood Cliffs, NJ).

Semiotica della novella latina (1986), Materiali e contributi per la storia della narrativa, greco-latina, 4 (Rome).

SHERK, R. K. (1957), 'Roman Imperial Troops in Macedonia and Achaea', *AJP* 78: 52–62.

—— (1969), *Roman Documents from the Greek East: Senatus consulta and epistulae to the Age of Augustus* (Baltimore).

SHERO, L. R. (1923), 'The *Cena* in Roman Satire', *CPh* 18: 126–43.

SHERWIN-WHITE, A. N. (1963), *Roman Society and Roman Law in the New Testament* (Oxford).

—— (1966), *The Letters of Pliny: A Historical and Social Commentary* (Oxford).

SHUMATE, N. C. (1996a), *Crisis and Conversion in Apuleius' Metamorphoses* (Ann Arbor).

—— (1996b), ' "Darkness Visible": Apuleius Reads Virgil', in Hofmann (1996: 103–16).

SIMON, M. (1974), 'Apulée et le Christianisme', in Lévy and Wolff (1974: 299–305).

SITTL, C. (1890), *Die Gebärden der Griechen und Römer* (Leipzig).

SLATER, N. W. (1989), *Reading Petronius* (Baltimore).

—— (1998), 'Passion and Petrifaction: The Gaze in Apuleius', *CPh* 93: 18–48.

SMITH, M. S. (1975), *Petronii Arbitri Cena Trimalchionis* (Oxford).

—— (1985), 'Petronius: A Bibliography 1945–82', *ANRW* ii. 32. 3: 1628–65.

SMITH, R. E. (1979), 'Dux, praepositus', *ZPE* 36: 263–78.

SMITH, W. S. (1968), 'Lucius of Corinth and Apuleius of Madaura', Yale University Ph.D. thesis.

—— (1972), 'The Narrative Voice in Apuleius' *Metamorphoses*', *TAPA* 103: 513–34.

—— (1993), 'Interlocking of Theme and Meaning in the *Golden Ass*', in Hofmann (1993: 75–89).

—— (1994), 'Style and Character in the *Golden Ass*', *ANRW* ii. 34. 2: 1575–99.

SOCHATOFF, A. F. (1962), 'The Purpose of Petronius' *Bellum civile*: A Re-Examination', *TAPA* 93: 449–58.

SÖTEMANN, A. L. (1973), *De struktuur van Max Havelaar*, 2 vols. (Groningen).

SOMMER, F., and PFISTER, M. (1977), *Handbuch der lateinischen Laut- und Formenlehre*, i, 4th edn. (Heidelberg).

SOVERINI, P. (1985), 'Il problema delle teorie retoriche e poetiche di Petronio', *ANRW* ii. 32. 3: 1706–79.

STEFENELLI, A. (1962), *Die Volkssprache im Werk des Petron im Hinblick auf die romanischen Sprachen* (Vienna).

STENDHAL (HENRI BEYLE) (1953), *Le Rouge et le noir: Chronique du xixe siècle*, ed. H. Martineau (Paris).

STEPHENS, S. A., and WINKLER, J. J. (1995), *Ancient Greek Novels: The Fragments* (Princeton).

STERNE, LAURENCE (1940), *Tristram Shandy* (New York).

STOCKERT, W. (1982), 'Zur sprachlichen Charakterisierung der Personen in Plautus' *Aulularia*', *Gymnasium*, 89: 4–14.

STOCKIN, F. G. (1954), 'Sequence of Thought and Motivation in the *Metamorphoses* of Apuleius', University of Urbana Ph.D. thesis.

STUBBE, H. (1933), *Die Verseinlagen im Petron*, *Philologus*, Suppl. 25/2.

STUCKEY, J. H. (1972), 'Petronius the "Ancient": His Reputation and Influence in Seventeenth-Century England', *RSC* 20: 145–53.

SUDHAUS, S. (1906), 'Der Mimus von Oxyrhynchus', *Hermes*, 41: 247–77.

SÜSS, W. (1926), *De eo quem dicunt inesse Trimalchionis cenae sermone vulgari* (Dorpat).

SULLIVAN, J. P. (1965, rev. 1977a), *Petronius: The Satyricon and the Fragments* (Harmondsworth).

—— (1967), 'Petronius: Artist or Moralist?', *Arion*, 6: 71–88.

—— (1968a), *The* Satyricon *of Petronius: A Literary Study* (London).

—— (1968b), 'Petronius, Seneca and Lucan: A Neronian Literary Feud?', *TAPA* 99: 453–67.

—— (1971), 'Petronius and Modern Critics', *Bucknell Review*, 19: 107–74.

—— (1976), 'Interpolations in Petronius', *PCPS* NS 22: 90–122.

—— (1977b), 'Petron in der neueren Forschung', *Helikon*, 17: 137–54.

—— (1985a), *Literature and Politics in the Age of Nero* (Ithaca, NY).

—— (1985b), 'Petronius' *Satyricon* and its Neronian Context', *ANRW* II. 32. 3: 1666–86.

—— (tr.) (1989), Ps. Lucian, *Onos*, in Reardon (1989: 589–618).

SUMMERS, R. G. (1967), 'A Legal Commentary on the *Metamorphoses* of Apuleius', Princeton University Ph.D. thesis.

—— (1970), 'Roman Justice and Apuleius' *Metamorphoses*', *TAPA* 101: 511–31.

—— (1972), 'Apuleius' *Juridicus*', *Historia*, 21: 120–6.

—— (1973), 'A Note on the Date of the *Golden Ass*', *AJP* 94: 375–83.

SWAHN, J. O. (1955), *The Tale of Cupid and Psyche* (Lund).

SWANSON, D. C. (1963), *A Formal Analysis of Petronius' Vocabulary* (Minneapolis).

TARÀN, L. (1975), *Academica: Plato, Philip of Opus, and the Pseudo-Platonic Epinomis* (Philadelphia).

TATUM, J. (1969a), 'The Tales in Apuleius' *Metamorphoses*', *TAPA* 100: 487–527.

—— (1969b), 'Thematic Aspects of the Tales in Apuleius' *Metamorphoses*', Princeton University Ph.D. thesis.

—— (1979), *Apuleius and the* Golden Ass (Ithaca, NY).

—— (ed.) (1994), *The Search for the Ancient Novel* (Baltimore).

—— and VERNAZZA, G. (eds.) (1990), *The Ancient Novel* (Dartmouth, NH).

TEUFFEL, W. S. (1889), *Studien und Charakteristiken*, 2nd edn. (Leipzig).

TE VELDE, H. (1967), *Seth, God of Confusion*, Probleme der Ägyptologie, vi (Leiden).

THEILER, W. (1933), 'Porphyrios und Augustin', *SB Königsberg*, 10/1: 37–42.

—— (1966), *Forschungen zum Neuplatonismus* (Berlin).

THIBAU, R. (1965), 'Les *Métamorphoses* d'Apulée et la théorie platonicienne de l'éros', *Studia philosophica Gandensia*, 3: 89–144.

THOMAS, É. (1900), 'Pétrone et le roman grec', *RIB* 43: 157–64.

—— (1912), *Pétrone: L'envers de la société romaine* (Paris).

THOMAS, R. (1983), 'Callimachus, the *Victoria Berenices*, and Roman Poetry', *CQ* 33: 92–113.

—— (1986), 'Vergil's *Georgics* and the Art of Reference', *HSCP* 90: 171–98.

TOBIN, J. J. (1984), *Shakespeare's Favorite Novel: A Study of* The Golden Asse *as Prime Source* (Lanham, Ill.).

TRELOAR, A. (1969), 'Animae ebullitio', *Glotta*, 47: 264–5.

TREMOLI, P. (1960), *Le inscrizioni di Trimalchione* (Trieste).

TRENKNER, S. (1958), *The Greek Novella in the Classical Period* (Cambridge).

TSANTSANOGLOU, K. (1973), 'The Memoirs of a Lady from Samos', *ZPE* 12: 183–95.

TURCAN, R. (1963), 'Le Roman "initiatique": A propos d'un livre récent', *RHR* 163: 149–99.

—— (1996), *The Cults of the Roman Empire*, tr. A. Nevill (Oxford).

TURNER, E. G. (1973), *The Papyrologist at Work* (Durham, NC).

VÄÄNÄNEN, V. (1966), *Le Latin vulgaire des inscriptions pompéiennes*, 3rd edn. (Berlin).

VAHLEN, J. (1858), *In M. Terentii Varronis Saturarum Menippearum reliquias coniectanea* (Leipzig).

VALLETTE, P. (1924, repr. 1960, 1971), *Apulée: Apologie, Florides* (Paris).

VAN DER PAARDT, R. T. (1971), *Apuleius: Metamorphoses Book III* (Amsterdam).

—— (1978), 'Various Aspects of Narrative Technique in Apuleius' *Metamorphoses*', in Hijmans and van der Paardt (1978: 75–94).

—— (1981), 'The Unmasked "I": Apuleius *Met.* XI. 27', *Mnemosyne*, 34: 96–106.

—— (1989), 'Three Dutch Asses', in Hofmann (1989: 133–44).

VAN MAL-MAEDER, D. (1997), '*Lector intende: Laetaberis.* The Enigma of the Last Book of Apuleius' *Metamorphoses*', in Hofmann and Zimmerman (1997: 87–118).

VAN ROOY, C. A. (1965), *Studies in Classical Satire and Related Literary Theory* (Leiden).

VAN THIEL, H. (1971a), *Petron: Überlieferung und Rekonstruktion*, Mnemosyne, Suppl. 20.

—— (1971b), *Der Eselsroman*, 2 vols. (Munich).

VEYNE, P. (1961), 'Vie de Trimalchion', *Annales economies sociétés civilizations* 16: 213–47.

VEYNE, P. (1964), 'Le "Je" dans le *Satyricon*', *REL* 42: 301–24.

—— (1965), 'Apulée à Cenchrées', *RPh* 39: 241–51.

—— (1976), *Le Pain et le cirque: Sociologie historique d'un pluralisme politique* (Paris).

VLASTOS, G. (ed.) (1971), *Plato*, ii (Garden City, NY).

VOGT-SPIRA, G. (ed.) (1993), *Beiträge zur mündlichen Kultur der Römer* (Tübingen).

VON ALBRECHT, M. (1970), 'Der Dichter Lucan und die epische Tradition', in Durry (1970: 267–301).

VON GUERICKE, H. (1875), *De lingua vulgari relata apud Petronium et in inscriptis parietibus Pompeianis*, diss. (Königsberg).

VON KORN, M., and REITZER, S. (1986), *Concordantia Petronian* (Berlin).

WAGNER, M. L. (1933), 'Über die Unterlagen der romanischen Phraseologie im Anschluss an des Petronius' *Satyricon*', *Volkstum und Kultur der Romanen*, 6: 1–15.

WALDE, A., and HOFMANN, J. B. (1930–55), *Lateinisches etymologisches Wörterbuch*, 3rd edn. (Heidelberg).

WALSH, P. G. (1970, repr. with addenda Bristol, 1995), *The Roman Novel: The* Satyricon *of Petronius and the* Metamorphoses *of Apuleius* (Cambridge).

—— (1974*a*), 'Was Petronius a Moralist?', *G&R* 21: 181–90.

—— (1974*b*), review of van Thiel (1971*b*) and Bianco (1971), *CR* NS 24: 215–18.

—— (1978), 'Petronius and Apuleius', in Hijmans and van der Paardt (1978: 17–24).

—— (1981), 'Apuleius and Plutarch', in Blumenthal and Markus (1981: 20–32).

—— (1988), 'The Rights and Wrongs of Curiosity (Plutarch to Augustine)', *G&R* 35: 73–85.

—— (1994), *Apuleius: The Golden Ass* (Oxford).

—— (1996), *Petronius: The Satyricon* (Oxford).

WATSON, G. (1969), *The Study of Literature* (New York).

WATT, I. (1957), *The Rise of the Novel* (London).

WEBSTER, G. (1979), *The Roman Imperial Army of the First and Second Centuries AD*, 2nd edn. (London).

WEHRLI, F. (1965), 'Einheit und Vorgeschichte der griechischen–römischen Romanliteratur', *MH* 22: 133–54.

WEINREICH, O. (1962*a*), introductory essay to Heliodorus' *Aethiopica*, tr. R. Reymer (Reinbek bei Hamburg).

—— (1962*b*), *Römische satiren* (Zurich).

WELLEK, R., and WARREN, A. (1956), *Theory of Literature*, 3rd edn. (New York).

WENDLAND, P. (1911), *De fabellis antiquis* (Göttingen).

WERNER, H. (1918), 'Zum Lukian zugeschriebenen Λουκιος ἠ Ὄνος', *Hermes*, 53: 225–61.

West, M. L. (1966), *Hesiod: Theogony* (Oxford).

Whittaker, J. (1987), 'Platonic Philosophy in the Early Centuries of the Empire', *ANRW* ii. 36. 1: 81–123.

Wieland, C. M. (1789), 'Über den wahren Verfasser des *Lucius*', in *Lucians Sämtliche Werke*, iv (Leipzig).

Wilamowitz, U. von (1905), *Die griechische und lateinische Literatur und Sprache* (Berlin).

Wilcken, U. (1901), 'Eine neue Roman-Handschrift', *Archiv für Papyrusforschung*, 1: 227–72.

Wildenow, E. (1881), *De Menippo Cynico*, diss. (Halle).

Williams, G. (1983), *Technique and Ideas in the Aeneid* (New Haven).

Wilson, D. di A. (1994), 'Homage to Apuleius: Cervantes' Avenging Psyche', in Tatum (1994: 88–100).

Wimsatt, W. K. (1949), *The Verbal Icon: Studies in the Meaning of Poetry* (Lexington, Ky.)

Winkler, J. (1979), '*Auctor* and *Actor*: Apuleius and his Metamorphosis', *Pacific Coast Philology*, 14: 85–6.

—— (1980), 'Lollianus and the Desperadoes', *JHS* 100: 155–81.

—— (1985), *Auctor and Actor: A Narratological Reading of Apuleius' Golden Ass* (Berkeley and Los Angeles).

Wiseman, J. (1979), 'Corinth and Rome I: 228 BC–AD 267', *ANRW* ii. 7. 1: 438–548.

Wittmann, W. (1938), *Das Isisbuch des Apuleius. Untersuchungen zur Geistesgeschichte des zweiten Jahrhunderts* (Stuttgart).

Wlosok, A. (1960), 'Laktanz und die philosophische Gnosis', *Ab. Ak. Wiss. Heidelberg*, 2: 48–142.

—— (1969), 'Zur Einheit der *Metamorphosen* des Apuleius', *Philologus*, 113: 68–84.

Wolff, C. (1963), 'Aspects of the Later Plays of Euripides', Harvard University Ph.D. thesis.

Wright, C. S. (1973), 'No Art at All: A Note on the Prooemium of Apuleius' *Metamorphoses*', *CP* 68: 217–19.

Wright, J. R. G. (1971), 'Folk-Tale and Literary Technique in Cupid and Psyche', *CQ* ns 21: 273–84.

Yeats, W. B. (1959), *Collected Poems* (New York).

Zeitlin, F. I. (1971*a*), 'Petronius as Paradox: Anarchy and Artistic Integrity', *TAPA* 102: 631–84.

—— (1971*b*), '*Romanus Petronius*: A Study of the *Troiae halosis* and the *Bellum civile*', *Latomus*, 30: 56–82.

Zimmerman, M. (1996), 'Apuleius von Madaura', in H. Cancik and H. Schneider (eds.), *Der neue Pauly* (Stuttgart), i. 910–14.

—— (ed.) (1998), *Aspects of Apuleius' Golden Ass*, ii. *Cupid and Psyche* (Groningen).